MODERN
ARMENIA

MODERN
ARMENIA

People, Nation, State

Gerard J. Libaridian

Transaction Publishers
New Brunswick (U.S.A.) and London (U.K.)

Library of Congress Catalog Number: 2003054129
ISBN: 0-7658-0205-8
Printed in the United States of America

Library of Congress Cataloging-in-Publication Data

Libaridian, Gerard J.
    Modern Armenia : people, nation, state / Gerard J. Libaridian
        p. cm.
    Includes bibliographical references and index.
    ISBN 0-7658-0205-8 (cloth : alk. paper)
        1. Armenia—History—1901- 2. Armenia—History—1801-1900.
    3. Armenian massacres, 1915-1923. 4. Turkey—History—20th century.
    I. Title.

DS195.L52   2004
947.5608—dc21   2003054129

To Nora

Contents

Part V

Acknowledgments

Chapter 1 is a slightly adjusted version of an article first published in William O. McCagg, Jr. and Brian D. Silver, eds., *Soviet Asian Ethnic Frontiers* (Pergamon Press, 1979) under the title "Armenian and Armenians: A Divided Homeland and a Dispersed Nation."

Chapter 2, first published in *Armenian Review*, 3, 1983, is reproduced here with minor changes.

Chapter 3, first published in Richard G. Hovannisian, ed., *Image of the Armenian in History and Literature* (Undena, 1981), is reproduced with minor changes with the kind permission of the editor.

Chapter 4 was first presented as a paper at the Symposium on Armenian History, University of Michigan, 1978.

Chapter 5, first published in Ronald G. Suny, ed., *Transcaucasia: Nationalism and Social Change* (The University of Michigan Press, 1983 and 1996) as "Revolution and Liberation in the 1892 and 1907 Programs of the Dashnaktsutiune," is reproduced here with minor changes with the kind permission of the editor.

Chapter 6 was first presented as a paper at the Middle East Studies Association Annual Meeting, University of California at Los Angeles, 1975.

Chapter 7, first published in Gerard J. Libaridian, ed., *The Crime of Silence* (Zed Books, 1985), reproduced in this volume with changes.

Chapter 8, first published in Isodor Wallimann and Michael N. Dobkowski, eds., *Genocide and the Modern Age: Etiology and Case Studies of Mass Death* (Greenwood Press, 1987), is reproduced here with minor changes with the kind permission of the editors.

Chapter 9 was first published in *Studia Kurdica*, 1-5, 1988.

Chapter 10, originally presented as a paper at the First Turkish-Armenian Historians' Workshop, University of Chicago, March 2000, was first published in *Insight Turkey*, 4, 2000, and is being reproduced here with some changes.

Chapter 12 was originally presented as a paper at the Second Turk-ish-Armenian Historians' Workshop, University of Michigan, Ann Arbor, March 2002, and is being presented here with substantial changes.

Chapter 13 was first presented as a lecture at the Armenian Cultural Foundation, Arlington, Massachusetts, November 2002, and is being presented here with substantial changes.

A Note on Transliteration

Except for recognized authors of Western Armenian descent and traditionally accepted place names, Armenian names in this volume are transliterated based on Eastern Armenian phonetics.

Preface

Creating this volume has been a recurrent idea for more than a decade. The book combines a selection from previously published material, previously written but unpublished chapters, and the newly written last section.

The idea became compelling for two reasons. In the last few years I found myself repeatedly referring friends, colleagues, and students to articles on modern Armenian history published earlier in edited volumes and journals; it was infinitely more practical to bring together, complete, and offer in one place such materials that seemed to interest an audience.

With the first hesitant and tentative plan, I also realized that the collection represents, in fact, a whole in two ways. First, it became obvious that with some adjustments and additions, the collection would cover the most important events and issues in modern Armenian history. Also uniting the volume, it seemed, was the interpretive dimension of the various parts, predicated upon the continuous search to understand the paradoxes and contradictions, discontinuities, and silences that characterize that history.

Research that sustains sections on the earlier period was done for published as well as still unpublished work and dates back to the early 1970s. The section on the more recent period is based largely on my personal involvement in Diasporan organizations and the new Republic of Armenia. From 1991 to 1997 I had the privilege to work in the first administration of the new republic in a number of capacities. That fact might explain any biases some readers will find in my assessments.

I owe a debt of gratitude to many individuals who made this work possible at different stages of its preparation. Kami Libaridian, Taline Voskeritchian, Marine Nercessian, and, especially, Asbed Kotchikian provided invaluable technical and editorial assistance. I am most grateful to my wife Nora, my friends and publishers Irving L. Horowitz and Mary Curtis, and my editor, Michael Paley, without whose advice, aid, and encouragement this project would not have reached completion. Shortcomings, of course, remain my responsibility.

Introduction

This volume consists of a series of essays initially written over a period of time which explore a few fundamental questions related to modern Armenian history: How have Armenians perceived politics, within the nation and in international affairs, at different stages of their history since the nineteenth century? Who has spoken for Armenians at different times and with what basis of legitimacy, especially when and where statehood was lacking? How and to what extent was the traditional sense of nationhood transformed into a modern one? How did the worldviews of political parties change Armenians' participation in the making of their own history and interact with forces and events beyond their control? What is the relationship between the notions of people, nation, and state in modern Armenian history? And, most importantly, what has been the significance of the "Turkish" factor in determining the limits and possibilities of Armenian political imagination?

Without claiming to present a comprehensive history of the period under consideration—from mid-nineteenth century to the present—or to fill the gaps that still exist in the current literature, this volume will challenge a number of interpretations and perceptions on the way that history evolved. A history claiming to represent the life of a nation is as good as the questions that are asked by the historian. Reformulating a question will often bring out facts that were considered secondary, events that were forgotten, or processes that were considered insignificant. The purpose of this book is to ask a few good questions. Even if the answers are wrong, the book will still have served its purpose if they goad others to find the right ones.

The analyses presented in this volume lead to some observations.

During the past two centuries, when for the most part they lived in a homeland divided between two competing empires, the Ottoman and the Russian, Armenians changed their collective character. From being a traditional ethno-religious subject people, political

1

parties (the Hnchakians in 1887 and the Dashnaktsutiune in 1890, as socialistic revolutionary organizations, to be joined later in 1907 by non-revolutionary and liberal Ramkavars) tried to redefine Armenians as a modern nation. To become a modern nation was their way to resolve compelling social and economic problems and to partake in "progress" inspired by Western thought. The interaction between them and their foreign masters as well as with the West led them to the idea of a territorially-based nation, the ultimate attribute of modern nationalism. However reluctantly, Russia accepted the outcome. The Ottoman Empire eventually rejected it even in its most modest articulation.

The transformation brought to the surface three conflicts with cultural underpinnings. First, the urban Armenian population in Istanbul and other cities, largely outside the homeland, and the mainly rural, majority segment made up of peasants, craftsmen, and small merchants in the historic homeland. Second, facing different sets of problems, a "national" agenda at times pitted Ottoman and Russian Armenians against each other. Third, although in the nineteenth century the ideology, strategy, and organization for change came from Armenians living outside the historic homeland, when a state did arise in Eastern Armenia, whether independent or Soviet, by its mere existence it challenged the premises and institutional bases of the Diaspora, including those accepted by the political parties that had initially given rise to the process of change. That challenge has often been met through political opposition. It is obvious that the task of creating a modern nation has had reversals and is not complete.

The programs and actions of the parties engendered political conflicts within the Armenian polity and within and between the parties themselves as well. The internal dynamics of these parties and of their interaction with other institutions within the community clearly affected their strategic decisions. These dynamics also tested severely the notion of unity implied by and sought within the "nation," because Armenians were too small an entity to afford disunity and too vulnerable to manipulation by external forces when disunited. Political parties and groups—with the exception of the original Marxists—ritualistically appealed for an elusive unity. The problem was that the founding of parties and groups implied membership conferred on those who accepted the particulars of a party or group. In that sense, by definition, the act of founding or joining a party constituted an act that at least separated, and often divided, the nation.

A few questions become unavoidable. How does one unite separating, or which party represents the idea or program which the rest of the nation should unite? What is the mechanism for that contest, especially when what are at stake cannot be defined as mere tactical differences but constitute fundamentally different, even conflicting, visions of the future and strategies to achieve it? As they interacted with the real world armed with heroes and martyrs, programs and ideologies, parties also battled each other, whether for ideological purity or as a form of internalized aggression. The larger threats from the external world and a basic agreement that Armenians needed a better environment to live in did not reduce the passion with which segments of the Armenian population dealt with the questions as to how to achieve progress and how to react to their successes and, more commonly, failures.

The establishment of a state should have facilitated the answers, since a state provides at least a framework within which to seek answers to these questions. In the Second Republic (Soviet Armenia, 1920-1991), unity was achieved by the forceful domination of the Communist Party and the elimination of others. However imperfect, the First and Third Republics (1918-1920 and 1991 to the present, respectively) adopted democratic principles that could provide the citizens of the country a choice.

And yet, all three republics have failed to be accepted by all parties as the ultimate context that could accommodate clashing visions. The Diaspora, which feels itself very much part of the Armenian nation, has not even tried to create a mechanism that could speak in its name legitimately. And relations between Armenia and the Diaspora do not entail a dialogue that can tackle such matters. The memory of the Genocide and the battle for its recognition remain the only instances where the nation appears as one. Yet these are not instances that readily yield common visions and strategies to resolve the different sets of problems faced by citizens of the Republic of Armenia on the one hand, and the Diaspora on the other. Contemporary arguments between two of the Diaspora-based organizations— the Armenian Democratic Liberal Party and the Armenian Revolutionary Federation—and the first administration of the Third Republic on what is the nation seem no different than the arguments between the Istanbul-based community and the people living on the historic homeland. Clearly, the transformation into a modern nation is still a process that has suffered setbacks and occasionally regressed.

Clashes of visions are resolved through the abstracted concepts and ideologies that are easy to sustain in the Diaspora but not in Armenia, whose population faces real problems of day-to-day survival and war.

The transformation of a people into a modern nation involved changes in leadership. By the end of the nineteenth century, revolutionary political parties formed by intellectuals and largely middle class activists and champions of the "people" replaced the remnants of the old aristocracy, churchmen, merchants, and courtiers as the cast that spoke in the name of Armenians and Armenia. What made these parties revolutionary was not always clear. At different junctures it meant the use of arms to react to repressive acts by local officials, guerrilla warfare to resist Ottoman oppression, rebellion to disturb the status quo and invite the intervention of foreign powers that might compel the Ottoman sultan to implement reforms, or their programs that proposed to change the character of the Ottoman Empire or establish an Armenian state. The political parties themselves were not clear as to which of these was a tactical measure and which a strategic weapon. The Ottoman government—just as later Turkish governments and official historians—found in this confusion enough room to view Armenians as a threat to the empire and the state and justify repressive measures, from the massacres of 1894-1896 to the Genocide of 1915-1917, to the active denial of those events. European powers, in turn, used it to further their own interests.

Equally important was the fact that the political parties constituted a new institution in Armenian society, a new form of group identification and representation that would compete with others for the loyalty and support of the people. Institutional conflict with the existing ones was inevitable. In some sense, the change of leadership became part of the larger process of democratization of Armenian politics that had been taking place since the end of the medieval Armenian states. Kings, princes, and the Church were dominant elements in Armenia and Armenian society until the demise of the nobility. In fact, these rulers and institutions constituted the nation, as far as their self-perception and their decision-making process was concerned. The comprador merchant class that arose in the Ottoman, Persian, and later Russian empires in the eighteenth century had filled the vacuum created by the demise of the old aristocracy, while the Church continued to mediate between imperial administrations and their Armenian subjects. The political parties, especially the Dashnaktsutiune or ARF, shared with the Church and occasional pockets of wealthy and prominent Armenians the leadership of the nation. But more often than not they set the agenda.

The parties also brought a change in the way political issues were thought about. While other institutions and leaders had sought change, including the National Assembly in Istanbul, parties introduced articulated ideologies as frameworks within which problems and crises were perceived and dealt with. Ideologies were supposed to represent the most advanced form of politics; after all, they emanated from European science and its immutable laws; they were all encompassing. They explained the past, interpreted the present, guided actors in history in their interventions, and assured a certain outcome. In their coherence ideologies were also comforting: the strength and coherence of their logic empowered those who were politically in a weak position and wanted to be active participants in the making of their own history. The new, articulated worldviews were bound to bring the parties in direct conflict with established institutions and threaten the security of privileged classes. These battles with the National Assembly in Istanbul and the Catholicos in Etchmiadzin were on occasion as fierce as those against the imperial centers.

In addition, the first two political parties adopted socialism, considered the most progressive of Western ideologies. Theirs was not a war of classes—that would not come until the Bolsheviks in the first decade of the twentieth century—but a class-conscious struggle, a precursor to the wars of national liberation.

Conflict among Armenian classes was not new. In the Russian Empire it came in the second half of the nineteenth century when Russian reforms changed economic and social relations and a new class of wealthy merchants supported by a liberal intelligentsia challenged the informal leadership of the old guard associated directly with the imperial administration. Conflict was more open within the Ottoman Armenian population. It manifested in the form of antagonism between the majority, dispossessed classes in the historic Armenian provinces and the comfortable segments settled in Istanbul and in control of the National Assembly that also had to deal with the increasingly large number of poor migrant workers who had come to the capital to find work. Historiography tends to ignore or understate these differences. Armenian society, especially in the Diaspora, has no "peasantry" to speak of; and class analysis, however relevant in explaining some dimensions of community life, remains irrelevant to a Diaspora focused on cultural self-preservation, collective memory, and a denied history. Armenian historians fear that such conflicts might undermine the significance of the Turkish-Armenian conflict that culminated in the Genocide, despite the fact that peasants and the rural population of historic Armenia became the main targets and victims of the Genocide, the least likely to survive; and for Armenians the construction and preservation of the idea of a nation requires the projection of a sense of oneness. For official Turkish historians and fellow travelers it is easier to justify Ottoman and Young Turk policy toward Armenians when they can be equated to a wealthy community that decided to be disloyal and seditious for nationalistic reasons.

The multiple battles also compelled parties to either change or split, or both. Individual activists evolved, changed parties, or established new ones. The Genocide and Sovietization interrupted this historical process. Within a decade the Genocide had stunted the ability of parties established to liberate Western Armenia to engage in critical self-examination and growth. As the full impact of the Genocide gradually dawned on the survivors, its memory conferred upon these parties a new kind of legitimacy, an aura of sanctity, as relics that, even if at times inconvenient, could not be discarded lest the act be regarded as completing what the Genocide tried to achieve. Denied a place in Soviet Armenia, the parties in time changed to accommodate new circumstances in the Diaspora; even if they preserved their ideologies and programs as relics of the past, they changed their role and became part of community institutions. In the Diaspora they were challenged by the Armenian Secret Army for the Liberation of Armenia, founded in 1975, but survived the challenge. With Sovietization, the evolution of Armenian Marxists—turned Bolshevik then Communist—froze. Their heirs were challenged and defeated by the Armenian National Movement in 1990.

Legitimation was a problem for the new political organizations. The remnants of the old nobility had had the legitimacy only history could provide. New aristocracies in the Russian and Ottoman Empires had been legitimized by their wealth and their acceptance by the courts in St. Petersburg and Istanbul, although none had a national audience. After the demise of the medieval Armenian kingdoms, the Church had remained the only institution that could claim a "national" character for Armenians within and outside the historic territories. The Church, headed by the Catholicos of All Armenians in Etchmiadzin near Yerevan, had jurisdiction over most of the communities around the world. The Church functioned on the basis of by-laws approved by the Russian government, which also involved itself directly in the elections of Catholicoses, thus providing a form of state sponsorship and control. In the Ottoman Empire the *millet* system—a de-politicized community whose members belonged to a single religion or religious denomination—headed by a patriarch was an institution set up by the Imperial government. The Church had no problem of legitimacy.

Political parties could not claim to constitute the nation, as princes and kings had done in the old days, nor did they have tradition or wealth. They certainly were not embraced by the sultan or the tsar. The political parties achieved legitimation through a number of mechanisms. They claimed to embody the people, to represent its interests, and sacrifice themselves for its cause as evidence that they deserved its support. The parties relied on the transformative value of their discourse, the universality of their program, and their role as the creators of a nation liberated from its torpor. The parties glorified the peasant and rural population as the keepers of the nation and the subject of their struggle. The millet leadership, after raising hopes, had been timid in its attempts to bring about change and reached the limits of political involvement set by the Ottoman state.

Transforming an inchoate and subdued people into a nation required the adoption of a new set of values and a new agenda. Yet to communicate these values and agenda to the people required using a discourse the people understood, marshalling images and paradigms from the past. The parties borrowed from the Church an iconographic program with a proven record of success. Revolutionary preachers and activists turned their poverty into weapons in their struggle to win the support of the downtrodden. Field workers for the parties were known as "apostles"; guerrilla fighters, who had given up comfort to sacrifice their lives for the people, became "martyrs for the cause"; priests blessed the soldiers on the eve of major battles in the example of the Armenian army in 451 led by Vardan Mamikonian, their commander, before they engaged the Persian army in a losing battle to defend Christianity. The Dashnaktsutiune gravitated toward representing the birth of the party through three founding figures in the image of the Holy Trinity. The struggle engendered against the Ottoman state was labeled "Surb Gords," translated most closely as the "Holy Task."

The Armenian cultural renaissance had found recourse in and made ample use of history. It had detailed and enshrined memories of past glory and greatness under the dynasties. The more radical elements had preferred to dwell on the occasional traditional resistance to imperial centers of foreign rule by remnants of ancient nobility in Karabakh and Zeytun. The semi- or non-educated rural Armenian population perceived the discourse of the revolutionaries in that context. In popular imagination, the hope that Europe would intervene in favor of reforms, whether in the form of the provisions in the Treaties of San Stefano and Berlin or as a result of armed actions by the revolutionaries, simply followed the pattern set by the last rulers of the last Armenian state, the kingdom of Cilicia, later part of the Ottoman Empire. In the fourteenth century, Cilician kings and Church leaders relied on a policy of appealing for assistance from the Crusaders to save the kingdom. The search for a savior king became a pattern in the sixteenth through the eighteenth centuries in plans to liberate Eastern Armenia from Persian rule, a search that ended with Russia. The role assigned the Great Powers in the strategy of revolutionaries fit that pattern. The pattern would be repeated as ideology to justify Armenia's membership the USSR and legitimize Communist Party rule in Soviet Armenia and as Diasporan strategy to secure recognition of the Genocide. History served both to inspire and to limit the program of those who sought to transform the people into a nation and the nation into a state.

Few questioned the gap between the socialist worldview of the political parties on the one hand, and Church linguistic iconography and rituals and idealized history on the other. It is possible to argue, of course, that all three reflect, in a sense, eschatological approaches to the progress of time leading to salvation, whether of the soul, of the state, or of the people.

In Armenian political thinking, the pattern of seeking recourse through a third force was validated by history and conditioned by the unequal power relations in dealing with their masters, especially the Ottoman Empire and Turkey. In that respect, the Genocide has been the great equalizer in modern Armenian history. The elimination of Armenians in their historic homeland through the extermination of most and the exile of the remnants interrupted history and conditioned its perception; it made the internal dynamics, relations between Armenians and the Ottoman state and institutions, and decisions made by Armenians—in fact history itself—preceding the

Genocide irrelevant; it made Turkey "the eternal enemy" from which Armenians had to save themselves; it made recourse to external forces natural and the idea of a modern Armenian state conditional.

Beginning in 1988, the Karabakh Committee in Armenia, later the Armenian National Movement or ANM, secured the independence of Soviet Armenia and governed it until 1998. But the ANM sought to break the historical pattern of reliance on a "third force" as ideology or strategy. Without questioning the fact of the Genocide, the ANM resurrected history, placed the Genocide in a historical context, and re-imagined relations between Turkey and Armenia. There were others, such as the Dashnaktsutiune and the Communist Party, once revolutionaries and now guardians of the faith, who had dominated Soviet Armenia and the Diaspora and whose legitimacy and perception of history depended on the image of the "Terrible Turk." Conflicts, deep seated and expressed, and clashes in Armenia and in the Armenian world since then should be seen in that context.

Contemporary Armenian history is the story of the unfinished agenda of nation building and the renewed effort toward state building. There is no agreement on whether these are antagonistic, separate, or complimentary goals. The absence of a consensus underlies Armenian politics today.

This volume tries to answer the questions raised above through two kinds of presentations: overviews and themes. Chapters 1 through 10 focus on the period from the 1850s to the 1970s. Chapter 1 provides an overview of developments and a picture of the Armenian world as it stood in the 1970s. Chapter 2 describes the rise of the Ottoman or Western Armenian problem and the failure of the established Armenian community in Istanbul working within the millet system to bring about social and economic reforms. Chapter 3 details the changes on the individual psychological level and value systems to make revolution possible. Chapter 4 describes the rise and evolution of revolutionary parties that replaced traditional institutions in the leadership for the struggle for reforms and in the development of a national agenda. Chapters 5 and 6 present case studies of evolution within the program of a revolutionary party, the Dashnaktsutiune, and a revolutionary individual, Yervand Balian, respectively. Chapter 7 introduces the ideology of the Young Turks and the Ottoman regime responsible for the Genocide. Chapter 8 details negotiations between Turkish and Armenian leaders preceding the Genocide and offers a new interpretation of its causes. Chapter 9 discusses problems in the history and historiography of relations between Kurds and Armenians. Chapter 10 examines the politics of Genocide recognition and related historiography.

Chapters 11 through 13 cover the 1980s to the present. Chapter 11 constitutes an overview of the period, covering the administrations of Presidents Levon Ter-Petrossian and Robert Kocharian. Chapter 12 presents the substance of relations between Turkey and Armenia and Turks and Armenians since independence. Chapter 13 considers whether Armenian has a strategic significance in the contemporary world and the relevance of domestic politics and the resolution of the Nagorno Karabakh conflict for that significance. A number of issues relevant to this period have been covered in detail in previous works by this author and are therefore not detailed here. The history of Karabagh and the rise of the conflict in the region in 1988 are introduced through documents in *The Karabagh File* (Cambridge, 1988); the debate on independence and Turkish policy in Armenia as well as the role of the Diaspora in that debate are covered in *Armenia at the Crossroads. Democracy and Nationhood in the Post Soviet Era* (Cambridge, 1991) and *The Challenge of Statehood: Armenian Political Thinking Since Independence* (Cambridge, 1999) relates the conflicts between the first, ANM-led administration of independent Armenia (1991-1998) and political forces on foreign and Karabakh policies within and outside the country that led to a change of administration.

Part I

1

From People to Nation: An Overview from the 1850s to the 1970s

The present border dividing historic Armenia dates back essentially to a treaty of 1639 between the Ottoman and Safavid Empires, which for a century had been contending for the domination of Mesopotamia and Trans-Caucasus. That treaty brought much-needed relief to the Armenian population from the ravages of war, but it also subjugated them to foreign rule, unwelcome because both empires imposed a harsh system of taxation and an oppressive social structure that discriminated against the non-Muslims. Before long, Armenians in both empires started searching for means to alter the status quo. For East Armenians, the growing power of the "Christian King of the North," the tsar, offered a viable alternative.[1] Russian expansion to the Caucasus occurred when modern Western imperialism was becoming the most pervasive force in international relations, and when technologically backward states such as the Ottoman and Persian realms were being integrated into the world market system. What once were issues of local significance acquired implications for major power relations, and decisions made in Europe affected the lives of peoples in remote areas of the globe.

Modern Armenian political consciousness evolved as a reaction against the suffocating effects of medieval Ottoman and Persian imperialism in the process of disintegration and as a response to new but problematic opportunities for liberation offered by increasing Western and Russian interests in the area. Thus, when Russia, a more secular and dynamic state, annexed Persian Armenia in 1828, it transformed the region into a lively arena of inter-European conflict, which in turn made the politics of Western powers accessible to Armenians. It introduced new patterns in East Armenian life, and a faster pace of change.[2]

13

Yet, despite a growing divergence between the Armenian communities on opposite sides of the border by the middle of the nineteenth century, circumstances made it possible to transform the cultural renaissance of the 1840s and 1850s into the common political program of the last quarter of the century. First, both sectors drew on a two thousand-year-old common history to assert a distinctive national identity. Textbooks and poetry published in Constantinople and Moscow revived ancient personalities whose grandeur and heroism contrasted sharply with the prevailing servile mentality and status of most of the Armenian population. Second, by the 1860s a liberal intelligentsia among East as well as West Armenians won its battle for secularization of institutions and values. Their use of modern Armenian instead of the classical language was most consequential. Although a different dialect was accepted by East and West Armenians as the norm, it now became possible for them all to understand each other's writing without much effort.[3]

Thirdly, the relative lack of discrimination and oppression in Russian Armenia allowed Armenians to focus their attention on the Ottoman sector, where social and economic conditions had deteriorated considerably and where a clear danger to the physical survival of the Armenian people was seen. This was particularly true during and after the famine that followed the war of 1877-1878. Although the Russian government later decided that another Bulgaria could not be tolerated on its flanks, at the time it did not object to the Russian Armenians' advocacy of West Armenia's liberation, particularly if that meant further tsarist annexations.[4]

The road to a political program for a new Armenian nation was not straight. Circumstances directly related to Armenia's betweenland position—lack of opportunities and protection normally provided by a national government; lack of communication for the joint exploitation of the land's resources; absence of security of property, particularly in the Ottoman sector—produced two Armenian bourgeoisies. In the Ottoman Empire evolved a commercial class, beneficiary of the growing trade with the West; in Russia the bourgeoisie became increasingly industrial and financial. Both flourished in the capitals and in major administrative and commercial centers of the two empires, outside the Armenian heartland where the majority of Armenians lived and which had become backwaters of the Ottoman and Russian territories. By mere economic necessity, and lacking a social basis to exert any political power, affluent Armenians linked their fortunes to the regimes in their respective states. Hence, the two bourgeoisies did not seek, and could not have achieved, a common program solely on the basis of their ethnic background, notwithstanding contacts between the liberal intelligentsias supported by each. Their interest in the improvement of the lot of the common man in Armenia proper did not exceed a mild reformism; under no circumstance did they antagonize the governments that had afforded them economic prerogatives.

Thus, the East Armenian bourgeoisie, which had earlier strongly supported Russian advances into Ottoman territories as a means of freeing the West Armenians, did not protest in 1885 against the closing of hundreds of parochial Armenian schools in East Armenia ordered by the tsar's government. Furthermore, when Russo-Turkish relations improved in the 1890s, and Russia actively opposed the anti-Ottoman activities of Armenian revolutionaries, the latter were denied any assistance by this wealthy class. Similarly, the West Armenian bourgeoisie lost much of its enthusiasm for systematic reforms in the eastern provinces once Sultan Abdul-Hamid II revealed his reactionary attitudes toward social change. The Armenian National Assembly in Constantinople limited its activities in this last regard to formal representations to the Porte. Most well-to-do Ottoman Armenians were only too willing to accept the sultan's occasional paternalistic favors to chosen individuals as a proof that his rule was benevolent and his society harmonious.

In the 1880s it became clear that the reforms advocated by the traditional leadership would not be carried out. By then, the Armenian bourgeoisie and the once powerful Armenian Church associated with them had retrenched from their earlier active participation in the process of political awakening. The Ottoman constitutional movement and Armenian liberalism had failed. Consequently, revolutionary political parties emerged, organized primarily by elements from the lower classes and by the radicalized segments of the intelligentsia.[5]

The ideologies espoused by the new parties were the first in Armenian history to be rooted in the needs of the masses. They all proposed to struggle against the political despotism, economic stagnation, and social inequality of the Ottoman system. The 1892 platform of the most influential of these organizations, the ARF or Dashnaktsutiune (Hay Heghapokhakan Dashnaktsutiune, or Armenian Revolutionary Federation, founded in 1890), called, for example, for the establishment of a popular-democratic government based on free elections. This government would guarantee security of life and right to work; equality of all nationalities and religions before the law; freedom of speech, press, and assembly; distribution of land to the landless; taxation according to ability to pay; abolition of the military exemption fee and its replacement with general conscription; establishment of compulsory education and promotion of national intellectual progress; and reinforcement of communal principles as a means to greater production and exports.[6]

The political parties viewed specific demands as means to achieve the larger goal of a dynamic progressive society. The slightly older SDHP (Social Democratic Hnchakian Party, founded in 1887 and 1888) asserted, for example, that "Political freedom for the Armenian people will be considered as only one of the conditions necessary for the realization of a series of basic and radical reforms in its political, social and economic life...that will insure a solid basis and the true path for the moral, intellectual, and material progress of society."[7] The ARF too believed that "the liberation of the people from its untenable condition in order that they may enter the mainstream of human progress could only be achieved through revolution."[8]

One feature that distinguished the new organizations from prior advocates of reform was their use of weapons to force the Ottoman state and the signatory powers of the Treaty of Berlin to live up to their responsibilities. But on a larger scale this revolution entailed first and foremost a campaign against the slavish mentality of the Armenian masses. Propaganda was to be reinforced by living examples of valor and martyrdom in situations of armed resistance to oppression. In addition to their psychological impact, the revolutionary parties viewed the acquisition of arms by the Armenian populace as the best means of defense against widespread lawlessness overlooked by the Ottoman government, and occasional pogroms condoned by it.[9]

Mass participation in the liberation movement was low despite an apparently widespread sympathy with the revolutionary activities. Many Armenians continued to believe that any opposition to the existing order would constitute an act of insubordination against God's preordained scheme for the world. Others, in areas sparsely populated by Armenians, were apprehensive of the reaction of their neighbors and overlords. Moreover, the Church, fearful of losing the few prerogatives it had managed to retain, remained aloof from the movement, although a few clergymen were involved in clandestine operations. The revolutionary parties considered the Church a lethargic and regressive institution. The Church, in turn, would not cooperate with parties that called for a struggle against patriarchal institutions and advocated a secular society. It is true that in 1903 the ARF had come to the support of the Church when the Russian government decreed the confiscation of Armenian Church properties; and following massive opposition and large scale demonstrations against the decree the revolutionaries had been able to force its rescission. But all of that was forgotten during the days of the first Russian revolution when a general assembly of Eastern Armenians was convened at the Holy See of Etchmiadzin. There most of the delegates elected were members or sympathizers of the ARF; the party felt strong enough to propose the distribution of Church-owned agricultural lands to the peasants who had tilled them for generations. The Assembly was disbanded in two days by the Russian police, most probably at the instigation of high-ranking churchmen.[10]

Relations between the political parties and the Armenian bourgeoisie had a similarly ambivalent character. Notwithstanding their programmatic antagonism toward all exploiting classes, the revolutionaries, especially the ARF leaders, expected the wealthy at least to provide financial assistance since the struggle undertaken had a national character.[11] Their press often criticized the Armenian upper classes for the latter's cowardice and lack of interest in the fate of the common Armenian. The mutual distrust dissipated in the Caucasus during the Armeno-Tatar conflict of 1905 to 1907. Unable to rely on government forces to protect their interests and properties, merchants, financiers, and industrialists turned to the ARF. The ARF accepted the challenge. Its leaders argued, firstly, that Tatar aggression had been instigated by the reactionary Russian government as part of a larger anti-Armenian policy; hence, it was as necessary to defend Armenian-owned property as it was to protect helpless Armenian peasants. Secondly, they argued, given employment discrimination against Armenian workers in non-Armenian concerns, the assistance provided to the Armenian bourgeoisie was tantamount to the safe-keeping of employment opportunities for Armenian laborers.[12] Paradoxically, this alliance coincided with the ARF's most intense socialist-oriented propaganda and activities in the Caucasus. It also allowed the flow of arms and financial assistance to the struggle in Western Armenia on an unprecedented scale. Yet the ideological inconsistency provided the best opportunity thus far to the nascent Armenian Marxist group to criticize the now dominant ARF.[13]

From the beginning, though, the revolutionary parties concentrated their efforts among the artisans, peasants, and petty bourgeoisie of Western Armenia. And here there was no lack of support in provinces and districts where lawlessness and poverty had reached unbearable dimensions. Furthermore, in regions such as Sasun, Mush, and Zeytun, where vestiges of the medieval Armenian feudal system remained subject to constant harassment by regular army troops and by Kurdish chieftains, the response to the appeal of the revolutionaries was immediate and overwhelming. Long before any of the parties were founded, local leaders in these mountainous districts had organized self-defense units and individual fighters had taken up arms to protect their families and villages.

The revolutionary parties provided a direction to those elements and attempted to coordinate their activities with newly organized units and within the framework of an overall strategy. Guerrilla fighters came mostly from traditionally devout families, and lacked the sophistication of urban intellectuals in the parties; but they overcame the impediments of religion by supplanting the God of submission and patience preached by most clergymen with the God of justice and retribution, or simply by deifying local saints who could "understand their situation" better.

Moreover, revolutionary parties were readily supported in cities and towns where educational institutions founded during the cultural renaissance had been instrumental in raising the level of political consciousness among the young. In fact, in the cities of Van and Erzerum, young Armenians had attempted as early as 1872 and 1881, respectively, to establish secret organizations devoted to the "salvation" of Armenia. Finally the movement acquired a large number of adherents among provincial Armenians who had moved to Constantinople or emigrated to the Russian Empire, Europe, and the United States to escape misery.

The new parties sought to achieve political emancipation in different frameworks.[14] The SDHP advocated the establishment of an "independent" homeland. Although the ARF used the vague expression "free Armenia," its goal was administrative autonomy for Turkish Armenia and the basic concern was for the essence of freedom, rather than for particular forms of political organization.[15]

But regardless of what framework was considered desirable or possible at any given moment, there is no doubt that these Armenian revolutionaries thought of Armenia as a distinct geographic entity. Here lay one of their weaknesses. "Turkish Armenia" referred to the six eastern vilayets of the Ottoman Empire: Erzerum, Van, Bitlis, Diarbakir, Harput (Mamuret-ul-Aziz), and Sivas. According to Turkish sources, during the years immediately preceding World War I 666,000 Armenians lived in those provinces (comprising 17 percent of their total population), and a grand total of 1,295,000 Armenians lived in the Empire. The Armenian Patriarchate of Constantinople claimed there were 1,018,000 Armenians in Ottoman Armenia (comprising 38.9 percent of the region's total population), and that there were 2,100,000 in the whole empire.[16] Neither set of figures is scientifically reliable, although the latter count seems closer to reality. Thus Armenians constituted at best a plurality in their homeland. Occasional attempts by revolutionaries at cooperation with similarly oppressed non-Armenian elements, which would have neutralized the numerical impediment, were largely unsuccessful.[17] But statistical facts were irrelevant to most Armenians. They simply argued that the depopulation of the Armenian plateau of its native inhabitants was the result of a deliberate Ottoman policy of reducing the number of Armenians (during the widespread massacres of 1894 to 1896 alone a minimum of 200,000 were killed) and a consequence of the lack of security and economic development. Armenians identified themselves with Ottoman Armenia, by far the larger part of the divided homeland, not because of numbers but because of a "force of history." In common usage "Armenia" (i.e., Ottoman Armenia) and "Armenian People" had been interchangeable. Conquerors, however long they lasted, would remain alien to the land on which the Armenian people were born and had built a glorious past.

In popular perception it was the historic past that sustained a sense of identity with the land; and in the revolutionaries' thought this relationship was evolved into a dynamic "force" that would achieve liberation. The practical problems involved in creating an independent state (not to speak of those involved in reuniting Russian and Ottoman Armenia) did not prejudice the new liberators against a deep-seated belief that weaknesses and distinctions predicated by Armenia's between-land position could be overcome and that the nation would participate in history again. This belief was expressed most passionately at times of crisis, such as in 1903 when the tsar's government decreed the confiscation of Armenian Church property. Anticipating the worst from the confrontation between tsarist police and politicized Armenian masses, Kristapor Mikayelian, one of the founders of the ARF and its most revered leader, exclaimed:

> Now that, following the massacres in Turkish Armenia, we might be on the eve of pogroms in the Caucasus, it is time to adopt as our general motto the indomitable will to struggle and fuse as one. It is necessary to erase those borders on maps drawn by this or that chief bandit. It is necessary to obliterate those geographic colors, which are separating us, which usually are not eternal, and at times are short lived. No oppression, no persecution and no border can separate a people, if that people, inspired by a consciousness of common interests, manifests an unwavering determination to fight as well...[18]

The National Program Thwarted

From his hatred of sultan and tsar alike, Mikayelian had reached the ideal of national union—even though ideals must be pursued within given political realities if they are to remain relevant. Thereupon, during the first decades of this century, the Armenian revolutionary groups experienced disasters. First, the Ottoman Empire proved to be more durable than anticipated. It was sustained rather than destroyed by rivalries among the Great Powers. Second, the attempted tsarist governmental confiscation of Armenian Church properties in 1903 and the bloody Armeno-Tatar clashes in 1905 to 1907 in the Caucasus compelled the Armenian parties to take responsibility for reorganizing the East Armenians as well as those of the West, shattering illusions regarding tsarist sympathies for Armenians and their struggle.

The most important development of the period was the emergence of the Young Turk movement in the Ottoman Empire. The beleaguered Armenian parties at first found cause to renew their hopes for reforms in the empire and its Eastern provinces. They consulted, negotiated, and cooperated with prominent Young Turks, and in 1908, when the latter took control of the Ottoman government and reinstated the Ottoman Constitution, jubilant Armenians welcomed the dawn of a new era, Armenian guerrillas put down their arms, and the parties made the necessary ideological adjustments. In its 1907 program the ARF had already endorsed democratic federalism as the system most suitable and desirable for the complex needs of Ottoman society.[19] In 1909 the SDHP renounced separatism and opted for a centralized government that would nonetheless allow cultural autonomy for its ethnic groups. Each party aligned with the Turkish organization closest to its ideas.[20]

The era of Armeno-Turkish cooperation did not last long, however. On the one hand, the Armenian leaders became impatient with the procrastination of the Young Turk CUP (Ittihad ve Terakke or Committee of Union and Progress) in implementing promised reforms. On the other hand, the more liberal democratic elements in the CUP lost control and a new ruling clique gravitated toward extreme nationalism. Turkish or Pan-Turanian doctrines began to supplant religion as the Ottoman state ideology, and the Armenians began to be regarded as a source of irritation for whom there was no room in a Turkish nation defined in territorial and linguistic-religious terms. Moreover, the CUP began to entertain ideas of expansion toward the East, and these also made the Armenians seem a nuisance.

At the end of October 1914, the militant faction of the CUP led the Ottoman Empire into war. In April 1915, systematic massacres and deportations of the West Armenian population began. The overwhelming evidence from a variety of written and oral sources indicates that these pogroms were coordinated, followed a predetermined course, and could not have been realized without the knowledge and resources of the Turkish government. By the end of the war at least one million Armenians had been killed or had perished otherwise. Some of the survivors had fled across the Russian frontier, others had settled in new lands to the south establishing a new Armenian Diaspora.[21]

Meanwhile, on the opposite side of the border, the Russian revolutions, the disintegration of the Caucasus Front, and the civil war temporarily ended Russian rule over the peoples of the Caucasus. In May 1918, following a brief and unsuccessful attempt at federation, the three major groups—the Georgians, the Azerbaijanis, and the Armenians—all declared their separate territories independent.[22] The government of the Republic of Armenia, dominated by the ARF, was confronted with the enormous task of caring not only for the native population but also for the tens of thousands of refugees from Western Armenia. Consequently, the inclusion of Armenian-populated areas of the Caucasus in the boundaries of the Republic became a crucial factor in its relations with Georgia and Azerbaijan; and its long-range foreign policy was aimed at extending its jurisdiction over Western Armenia. In 1919 the ARF declared a united and independent Armenia its political ideal, and the government of Armenia officially advanced its claim to Western Armenia. To realize these goals, the Republic sent plenipotentiaries to the peace conference of the victorious Allies in Sévres, France, there joining a separate delegation of West Armenians. As a result, the treaty of Sévres (August 1920) between the Allies, Armenia, and a defeated Turkey recognized the Armenian Republic and most of its claims. A new era seemed to have dawned for the Armenians. After the horrors of the massacres, the remotest prewar dreams were to be realized.

Then came the final debacle. As the Allied projects for dissolving the Ottoman Empire came to light, revolutionaries established a new regime in Ankara. Turkish leaders, for whom the concept of an integral territorial nation had become as crucial as it had for Armenians, began a campaign against the Republic of Armenia. Western intervention in the Russian civil war lent to an alliance between the Russian Bolsheviks and Turkish nationalists.[23] The resulting military and diplomatic cooperation shattered the Armenian dream. In December 1920, less than five months after the signing of the Sévres Treaty, independent Armenia collapsed. In 1921 the West Armenian lands (denuded by then of most of their Armenian population) returned to Turkish sovereignty; in East Armenia the Republic was Sovietized.[24]

The Soviet Armenians: Between Old and New

East Armenia formally entered the Soviet Union in 1922, a year after the dissolution of the independent republic. It was then considered part of the Transcaucasian Soviet Federation (along with Georgia and Azerbaijan), a grouping that survived until the promulgation of the Stalin constitution in 1936. Armenia was the smallest of the constituent republics of the USSR (30,000 km^2). It has a population of 2.5 million, 88.6 percent of which is Armenian. It contains only 62 percent of the 3.5 million Armenians in the USSR, however. Another million (26.3 percent of the total) live nearby in Caucasus, sometimes concentrated in areas such as the autonomous Karabakh province of the Azerbaijan Republic, where 80 percent of the population is Armenian. The final 350,000 Armenians are scattered in the Soviet territories outside the Caucasus. In all, the Armenians constitute 1.5 percent of the Soviet population.[25]

The path of Sovietization was difficult for the Armenia.. early promises by Revolutionary Russia.[26] Soon after assuming power, Lenin issued a decree that has been held up as a model of Russian understanding of Armenian political and territorial aspirations. The decree of December 31, 1917 stated that the new Russia "defended the right of the Armenian people to free self-determination in Russian occupied 'Turkish Armenia,' including even total independence"; it stated further that the realization of this overall objective required the return of all uprooted Armenians to Turkish Armenia and stringent measures to guarantee their security.[27] No practical steps were taken to secure any of the stated goals, however. In addition, Soviet Russia actively sought the demise of the Republic of Armenia on the eastern part of the land; and, once that goal was achieved in December 1920, the Soviet government lost interest in "Turkish Armenia" and even disposed of territories formerly under the control of the Republic.

At that time Armenia was contesting several districts with its neighbors—with Azerbaijan, the Mountainous Karabakh district to the southeast, with its dense Armenian population,[28] and the Nakhichevan region enclosed between Armenia and the Iranian frontier; with Georgia, the district of Akhalkalak, overwhelmingly Armenian-populated even today; and with Turkey, the provinces of Kars and Ardahan, which had been part of the Russian Empire from 1878 until 1917, and the district of Igdir, which contains the consecrated symbol of historic Armenia, Mount Ararat. In 1921 its control of the Caucasus in the balance and its relations with Turkey at a critical point, the Soviet government ceded all these districts to their non-Armenian claimants. Then, when the first Bolshevik commissars arrived in Armenia, they proved so thoroughly revolutionist in the poverty and disease stricken land and they so enthusiastically persecuted everyone associated with the leadership of the ARF-led Republic, that on February 21 they provoked a popular uprising, against which Lenin had to dispatch Red Army reinforcements.[29]

Once the revolt had been put down, Lenin sent to Yerevan Alexander Miasnikian, a more circumspect and disciplined leader, and advised Caucasian communists to take into consideration specific local conditions and to follow "a gentler, more cautious, and more conciliatory policy toward the petty bourgeoisie, the intelligentsia, and particularly the peasantry... What is feasible and necessary in the Caucasus is a slower, more prudent, and more systematic course of transition to socialism than was warranted in the RSFSR..."[30]

Once settled, Miasnikian's government started implementing programs of modernization in education, hygiene, transportation, and economic reconstruction. The government also attracted a number of prominent Armenians from Europe and other parts of the USSR to enhance academic, scientific, and cultural development, and it inaugurated a period of material development in East Armenia that may not be disregarded.

Subsequently, of course, there was another turn for the worse. Stalin rose to power. He ignored Lenin's admonitions and started his notorious drive for collectivization of the Soviet Union's agriculture. In Armenia again there was massive resistance. Peasants slaughtered cattle and stock willfully, producing a famine that lasted until 1934. Soon thereafter, the great purges of 1936 to 1939 claimed the lives of hundreds of Armenian intellectuals and a new generation of communist Armenian leaders.[31] It is notable that the most prominent among the latter, the popular first secretary of the Communist Party in Armenia, Aghassi Khanjian, was a West Armenian refugee from Van. Khanjian was fourteen years old when the massacres of the West Armenians began; he was a natural ally of the Soviet regime, and yet, like so many others, he was accused of harboring nationalist sentiments, and shot. Then came the war, which was perhaps not Stalin's fault, but in which Armenia was involved because it belonged to the Soviet Union. Over 450,000 Armenians were called upon to fight in the USSR armed forces between 1941 and 1945.

Paradoxically, World War II also opened new prospects for change. An important aspect of the war effort was the Soviet regime's toleration of Armenian national identity and pride. No doubt this was calculated to create enthusiasm for the now-threatened Soviet fatherland. But in 1945 the regime went further. Stalin abrogated the treaty of friendship and neutrality with Turkey, which since 1925 had stifled Armenian national territorial aspirations, he called for a revision of the Montreux Convention, which regulated the Straits, and his minister of foreign affairs, Molotov, orally demanded the return of Kars and Ardahan. Whatever the Soviet motivations, these developments allowed both Armenians and the neighboring Soviet Georgians an extraordinary new opportunity to express national hopes.

In a memorandum forwarded to the leaders attending the Moscow Conference in December 1945, the catholicos in Etchmiadzin,

Gevork VI, expressed the hope that justice will finally be rendered
to the Armenian people by the "liberation of Turkish Armenia and
its annexation to Soviet Armenia."[32] The first secretary of the Communist Party of Armenia, Grigor Harutiunian, declared in the electoral campaign of 1946 that "the question of the return of the provinces conquered by Turkey is posed by the Armenian people itself
in Soviet Armenia as in Europe, America, the Near and Middle
East. These claims are being defended by the government of
Soviet Armenia...and are of vital importance for the Armenian
people as a whole."[33] The speech, interspersed by much applause,
also assured that there were no strategic considerations in the
Armenian demands. Leaders in Soviet Armenia recalled the enormous sacrifices offered by Armenians in the struggle against fas-
cism—as opposed to Turkey's procrastination. They had thus
earned the right to see their fatherland expanded. Armenians also
argued that Soviet Armenia had the moral and historical duty to provide a homeland for Diaspora Armenians and that the territory of the
Armenian SSR could not accommodate the large numbers expected
to heed the call for repatriation.

The role of "government of all Armenians" was Soviet Armenia's
only for a brief moment in its history of course. The Soviet demands
on Turkey were explicitly retracted in 1953, immediately after Stalin's
death. But meanwhile there had been a considerable repatriation of
Diaspora Armenians. Between 1946 and 1948 approximately
100,000, mainly from the Middle East, "returned" to Soviet Armenia;[34] and in the Diaspora enormous enthusiasm was generated by
the Soviet initiative.

So erratic has been the record of Sovietization in Armenia that
radically different evaluations can be justified. Sovietization was
acclaimed as the salvation of the Armenian people and decried as a
new form of slavery. For some it represented the best available defense against Pan-Turanian imperialism and Turkish expansionism
which in 1920 could have resulted in the decimation or uprooting of
the East Armenian population as well; and by providing for a form
of statehood with secure borders, it granted the Armenian people the
opportunity to develop economically and culturally. For others this
same Sovietization forced Armenia back into an orbit where an independent pursuit of national interests was impossible. It made
Armenia's fate subject to the vicissitudes of Russian policy toward
Turkey, the degree of autonomy it allowed was conditional upon

decisions made in Moscow; and, because of it, Armenian culture fell into the danger of being submerged by the dominant Russian one.

To make sense of such contrasting evaluations, one must seek out realistic measuring tapes, and one is certainly the process of industrialization that affected Armenia under Soviet rule. Beyond any question there has been great benefit in this respect. Whereas the average increase in production in the USSR has been 113-fold between 1913 and 1973 (117-fold in the RSFSR), Soviet Armenia's production multiplied 222 times. The war effort accelerated the pace of production especially in the machine and chemical industries. Between 1950 and 1975, the output in electricity increased 9 times; chemical and petroleum products, 164 times; machine and metallurgy, 57 times.[35] The rate of urbanization was equally dramatic. Compared to a 10 percent urban population in 1931, by the 1970s, 59 percent of Armenians lived in cities (all-Union average, 56 percent). Soviet Armenia had one of the highest rates of workers in the sciences and professions and skilled workers with higher education in the USSR.[36] However much one weighs this sort of data against the arbitrary planning and the crash methods of the centralized Soviet economy, one must admit that East Armenia was transformed by Soviet rule in a fashion entirely unparalleled in the other countries of the Middle East. Population statistics provide an equally sensitive barometer of the benefits and disadvantages of Sovietization in Armenia. The Armenian SSR posted a 41 percent increase in its population between the census years, 1959 and 1970. The average 3.72 percent annual increase constituted the fourth highest in the USSR, exceeded only by Tajikistan (4.18 percent), Uzbekistan, Turkmenistan, and Kirgizia. Furthermore, during the same period, of all the major ethnic groups in the USSR, the rate of increase in the use of the mother tongue as a first language was highest among Armenians (1.5 percent).

Despite this optimal record, apprehensions concerning the threat of assimilation plagued official and nonofficial Armenian circles.[37] To begin with the same empirical evidence, the high rate of increase in population was due primarily to immigration. As a result of inter-republic migrations, 146,000 new residents came to Soviet Armenia from other areas of the USSR during the inter-census years mentioned above.[38] In addition, between 1963 and 1970 approximately 16,000 resettled there from the Diaspora.[39] The large increase in the rate of those using Armenian in the ASSR as a first language must also be ascribed to this same phenomenon; and on the other hand one must note that of the fourteen non-Russian "union republic" nationalities, Armenians ranked lowest in their preference for marital endogamy within their own republic.[40] Also, the tremendous increase of the number of women at work in an expanding industrial economy led to a reduction in size of the Armenian family. Since 1928 the birthrate among Armenians had declined steadily from 56 to 22.1 per thousand in 1970.[41] A survey conducted by an enterprising journal in Yerevan revealed causes for this phenomenon similar to those prevalent in the West: marriage at later ages; and rising concerns for the availability of childcare centers, time to spend with children, housing, and the quality of life. The researchers were thankful that very few mentioned conjugal problems as a factor, and that traditional Armenian marital harmony was still valued.[42] But this did not reduce the disturbing implications of the phenomenon for the future of the Armenian people.

In this connection one may note also that the percentage of Armenians using their native tongue as a first language varies in different parts of the USSR. In Armenia it was 97.7; in Georgia, 85; Azerbaijan, 84. In the province of Rostov (RSFSR), however, it was 71.5, and in the city of Moscow, it was only 35.5. The use of Armenian seemed to decrease with the distance of one's residence from Armenia. The age of a community and its historical relationship to Armenia continued to play an important role as well. Thus, of Armenians in the Autonomous Republic of Nakhichevan (2.6 percent Armenian in population by the end of the Soviet era) and what was the autonomous province of Mountainous Karabakh (still 80 percent Armenian in population), 98.5 percent and 98 percent respectively considered Armenian their first language. Most communities outside the Republic lacked facilities for the preservation of the Armenian language and culture. Also, for reasons of cultural and political nationalism in some areas, Armenian educational and community institutions were subject to severe local pressures. (These pressures might explain the sizeable recent Armenian immigration from Georgia and Azerbaijan to Armenia.)

The USSR was the heir of the Russian Empire and Russian was the lingua franca of the Union, as it was during tsarist times. To a large extent this was natural, given demographic and geographic realities. Opportunities for recognition and promotion on the all-Union level required the use of Russian for most professions, while economic interdependence growing out of regional imbalances in natural and manpower resources mandated the universalization of values consecrated and institutionalized in Moscow.

Of those emigrating from the Armenian SSR to other parts of the Union, 37.2 percent went to the RSFSR.[43] It is not surprising that there were as many Armenians with a higher education living outside as there were inside the Armenian Republic, and that the absolute majority of Armenians not knowing or using their mother tongue lived in the major urban industrial centers of the USSR. Assimilation was a real danger to the Armenian people in the USSR, an unavoidable concomitant of industrialization.

The Soviet regime became more permissive in Armenia after the death of Stalin. An early measure in this respect came in 1956 when the government allowed the election of a catholicos of All Armenians to the vacant seat at Etchmiadzin in the Armenian SSR. Beginning in the 1960s, the new supreme spiritual leader, Vazgen II, enjoyed a wider margin of movement and easier access to his people than his predecessors were allowed at any time since 1921. In 1965, on the fiftieth anniversary of the Genocide of 1915, there were subdued official commemorations in Yerevan and a monument was erected to it near the city, after which the republican leaders institutionalized government participation in this most symbolic and emotional of Armenian ceremonies on each April 24. In the 1970s, the new first secretary of the Communist Party of Armenia, Karen Demirjian, led the official delegations and masses of marchers to the monument.

Since 1956 references to places, events, and people tied to the history of Western Armenia abounded in Soviet literature and the arts. Historians dwelled at length on the human and political consequences of the Genocide. Earlier the term "liberation" had been exclusively applied to the activities of Armenian Bolsheviks, the effects of the November Revolution on Armenia, and the process of Sovietization, while the ARF and the SDHP were branded as reactionary. Historians rehabilitated the Liberation Movement in Ottoman Armenia by recognizing its mass appeal, and studying it in the proper historical context, even though the parties leading that movement remained subject to severe criticism for a while. A study published in 1976 even included a detailed description of the activities of guerrilla leaders whose names were long known and cherished by the public through revolutionary ballads.[44] A well-known novelist, Khachik Dashtents, based a new work on a fictionalized version of the same theme.[45] The Soviet Armenian language was gradually cleared of common words transferred from the Russian. Academicians developed a vocabulary of scientific and technical terms derived from the wealth of the Armenian language.[46]

These largely symbolic concessions did not reflect Soviet policy toward Armenian territorial aspirations. As noted above, the post-Stalin era opened with Molotov's deliberate retraction in 1953 of the Stalinist demands on Turkey of 1945. In 1965 Prime Minister A. Kosygin went further; he suggested a new non-aggression pact to achieve "good relations" with Turkey. He also stated that the USSR had no territorial designs against that country.[47] Although Turkey turned down the offer, Soviet-Turkish relations improved. The two governments cooperated on industrial projects in Turkey, which in the 1970s became the largest recipient of Soviet economic aid to any Third World country. Further, an economic cooperation pact signed between the two countries in April 1978 was followed by the visit of an official delegation to Turkey led by Marshal N. V. Orgakov, chief of staff of Soviet Armed Forces.[48]

Unusual manifestations of Armenian nationalism were in part reactions against these overtures to the traditional antagonist. In 1965 the official commemoration of the fiftieth anniversary of the Genocide was interrupted by violent outbursts of young demonstrators in Yerevan. They demanded action "to recover their lands" rather than ceremonies to honor the victims.[49] Those jailed by the government for leading the demonstrations included future members of the Karabakh Committee. It is probable that the major reason for the removal that year of Y. N. Zarobian as first secretary of the Communist Party of Armenia was his inability to prevent and to deal effectively with these demonstrations.[50]

Subsequently, illegal activities were carried on secretly. In 1969, 1970, and 1973 to 1974 Soviet Armenian courts tried, convicted, and imprisoned a number of activists—grouped under a "National United Party" founded by Paruyr Hayrikian—for having advocated the idea of a united and independent Armenia and for having formed cells to achieve their goal.[51]

Historically related to the territorial claims against the Republic of Turkey was the issue of Mountainous Karabakh within the Azerbaijan SSR (AzSSR). This district remained under the jurisdiction of the AzSSR despite a decision in 1920 by the Soviet Azerbaijanis to return it to Soviet Armenia.[52] Armenians have consistently charged that the Azerbaijani authorities have pursued a policy of cultural oppression, economic discrimination, and ethnic disadvantages against the overwhelmingly Armenian population of the district.[53] This policy reached such proportions in 1969 that the Soviet Armenian republican leaders reportedly went to Moscow to register their complaint and request the incorporation of the district in the Armenian SSR. The request was denied.[54]

In 1975 many Armenians were ousted from the Communist Party in Karabakh or imprisoned on charges of nationalist agitation contrary to "the principles of Leninist friendship of peoples and proletarian internationalism."[55] Having silenced all local opposition to the status quo, authorities in Karabakh and Azerbaijan declared the issue resolved to the satisfaction of all concerned.[56] These declarations, printed in an official publication and including derogatory statements toward the Armenian SSR, prompted one of Soviet Armenia's best known novelists, S. Khanzatian, to dispatch a letter of protest and indignation to L. I. Brezhnev. Khanzatian, a member of the Communist Party since 1943, reminded Brezhnev that "nothing hinders the development and strengthening of the solidarity between proletarian classes more than injustice against a people." He reiterated the demand for the return of Karabakh in the name of the same principles that had been called upon to justify the current situation. A commentary that accompanied a copy of the letter to the Diasporan press asserted that the systematic policy of forcing Armenians to leave the region through social, economic, and other forms of oppression is tantamount to genocide according to one definition in the U.N. Convention on Genocide to which the USSR is a signatory. The unknown author further revealed that according to an unofficial survey, Armenians in Karabakh wanted nothing more than to see their land under the jurisdiction of the Armenian SSR.[57]

To achieve a modus vivendi between official policy and Armenians' expectations, the Soviet state relied largely on bureaucratic methods of oppression rather than the massive violence of the past. At times it even initiated conciliatory steps to avoid large-scale, active opposition to the government. For example, the draft submitted for final approval of the new Constitution of the Armenian SSR had deleted the provision in the previous lawthat recognized Armenian as the official language of the republic. Following demonstrations against a similar proposal in Tbilisi for the Georgian SSR, the government reinstated the language provision in the new version in both republics.[58]

The change from Stalinist practices could be ascribed to the Soviet government's expectation that the emerging technological society would induce historical amnesia; or, conceivably, it might stem from calculations that Armenian irredentism against Turkey could be used to legitimize future annexations from that country. The relative leniency might also have reflected the price Soviet leaders were willing to pay for the success of their overall policies.

But still the Soviet government had difficulty in determining when nationalism was harmless in extent or form. Hence it did not hesitate to press the full power of the state against such manifestations it considered threatening. There was a barrage of criticism aimed at Armenian chauvinism, nationalistic tendencies, and disregard for Marxist-Leninist principles in the interpretation of Armenian history. The guardians of the faith did not spare writers and artists who deviated from the norms of "socialist realism."[59] In addition to those already mentioned, the list of political prisoners included the film director Sergey Parajanov or Sargis Parajanian, whose talent had been recognized within and without the Soviet Union.[60] Others were subjected to varying forms of censorship and silence. The interesting fact regarding the new wave of repression against intellectuals was that the works of these victims have displayed more humanism than nationalism.

It was true, nonetheless, that national aspirations had not retreated since the Revolution; and territorial aspirations formulated at the beginning of the century survive among East Armenians, many of whom traced their roots to historic Armenia outside the boundaries of the Soviet Republic. Moreover, a half-century of oppression and abnegation within the new empire tended to strengthen that nationalist sentiment. As a consequence, there was a growing cooperation between activists in Armenia and other parts of the Union, especially Russia and Ukraine; and, at least for some, the national issue was eliminated from its program, the strict ideological opposition to be reintegrated within the larger sphere of problems faced by Soviet society. An Armenian samizdat proliferated in Yerevan and a committee was formed there to monitor the implementation of the Helsinki accords.[61] In addition, a number of Armenians became involved in dissident activities in the Soviet Diaspora.[62] Even the National United Party, once an adherent of an exclusive nationalism, eliminated from its program the strict ideological opposition to the Soviet State.[63]

Soviet Armenian nationalism embodied, then, an unwillingness to accept the injustices of the past as well as resentment of Soviet oppression. In its extreme form it probably detracted from the ability of its adherents to deal effectively with the challenges of a changing, modernizing society. It remained, nonetheless, less abstract and far less idealized than that among Diaspora Armenians.

Armenians in Turkey: A Silent Minority

By the 1970s, an estimated 60,000 Armenians remained in the Republic of Turkey; a majority of these were concentrated in Istanbul. This estimate did not include perhaps an equal number of partially assimilated Armenians in distant provinces who, at best, preserved a blurred sense of their origins through rituals and symbols, since the former Armenian provinces were thoroughly Islamicized and Turkified during and after the massacres. In central and western Anatolia there are a few recognizable communities of Armenians. Some of these have churches at their disposal; but only three— Iskenderun, Kayseri, and Diyarbakir—have parish priests (all of the Apostolic or Gregorian faith); and the general demographic tendency in these provincial communities has been to move to Istanbul. For most Turkish Armenians, reaching that ancient city remained the only hope against total loss of identity.[64]

The leader of the Turkish Armenians is the patriarch in Istanbul, even though the Armenians of that city belong to more than one religious denomination. Once all-powerful over the whole Armenian population of the Ottoman Empire, the patriarch is now little more than a local prelate. His duties still include the representation of the interests and needs of the Anatolian flock and, with leaders of smaller Catholic and Protestant communities, the maintenance of various Armenian religious, educational, and charitable institutions.

Outwardly, harmony reigns between the Armenians of Turkey and the Turks. Atatürk's revolution separated state and religion, and the constitution of the Turkish Republic explicitly prohibits religious and ethnic discrimination. The mushrooming Turkish middle class has been in fact highly secular and assumes a tolerant attitude towards religious minorities. Those who live in Istanbul are involved primarily in trade, industrial production, the liberal professions, and crafts—social areas where secular views are likely to prevail. Although reduced in scope and prestige, the Armenian press and cultural societies continue to provide a forum for cultural activities. Nonetheless, there was strong evidence through the 1970s of both official political and social discrimination against the country's Armenians, and of harassment of their institutions.

This particularly affected the opportunity of Armenians to send their children to community-owned schools. The Turkish Ministry of Education required that the identity card of Armenian children bear official recognition of their Armenian origin before they were allowed to attend Armenian schools. This is not only contrary to the Turkish constitution, but the office granting these identity cards ruled against the use of such notations. As a result, it was difficult to obtain the proper certification, and an increasingly large number of Armenian children have been forced to attend public schools where they are denied any instruction in Armenian language, culture, or religion. Comparable vicious circles regarding the issuance of permits necessary for the restoration or relocation of Armenian community buildings exist.[65] Furthermore, there have been arbitrary administrative actions affecting Armenian culture. For example, in the summer of 1977, the refurbished Apostolic Church of Kirikhan (Hatay Province) was closed without explanation by order of the interior minister, who had earlier expropriated property belonging to that community.[66] Often travelers in eastern Turkey have found ancient and medieval monuments of Armenian architecture in a process of decay, at the mercy of the natural elements and marauders, and occasionally subject to willful destruction.[67]

In his 1977 annual report the patriarch, Archbishop Shnork Galusdian, disclosed that through unlawful taxation, bureaucratic procrastination, and administrative roadblocks the government was in fact discriminating against Armenian educational and charitable institutions, making it increasingly difficult for Armenians to use and ultimately to sustain them. He suggested that authorities were denying Armenian citizens essential human rights—rights that were routinely granted to non-citizen residents of Turkey—otherwise guaranteed by the Turkish constitution as well as by Articles 37 through 44 of the Treaty of Lausanne. The report concluded:

> For the last 10 to 12 years, we have duly reported these restrictions, discriminations and restraints to the respective departments of our State. But we confirm painfully that neither a positive nor a negative reply has been received. This means, that the demands

are so well founded, legal and rational, that nothing can be said against them. Nevertheless, we have never ceased hoping, because in the final resort justice and law shall prevail.[68]

A former Belgian representative on the United Nations Commission on Human Rights was much less restrained in accusing the Turkish government of systematic discrimination against Armenians.[69]

All this must be supplemented by mention of the social pressures that discouraged the use of the Armenian language in public places in Turkey and persuaded Armenians who wished recognition and advancement in business and professional circles to adjust their family name endings to Turkish patterns.

Faced with these conditions, the Armenians of Turkey abstained consciously and massively from political life, constraining the patriarch to reaffirm from time to time the total allegiance of his flock to the Turkish fatherland and state. Armenians in Turkey manifested none of the concerns evident elsewhere for the political, territorial, or moral issues emanating from the massacres and deportation of their people during World War I. The fiftieth and sixtieth anniversaries of the Genocide, ostentatiously commemorated in the ASSR and the Diaspora, were ignored by Armenians in Turkey. They are subservient to any and all governments lest any criticism be interpreted as unfaithfulness.

The return to power in June 1977 of Bulent Ecevit's *Cumhuriyet Halk Partisi* or Republican People's Party raised hopes that the most obvious of the transgressions against the rights of Armenian citizens of Turkey would be eliminated. During the electoral campaign Ecevit had charged the neo-fascist National Action Party with terror against non-Turkish minorities such as Kurds and Armenians. When he took office as prime minister, Ecevit rescinded the order of the previous government to restrict the entry into Turkey of foreigners of Armenian extraction regardless of their citizenship.[70] More importantly, he and other ministers of his cabinet met with Patriarch Galustian to discuss the legal and bureaucratic difficulties encountered by the Armenian community. Ecevit promised to end bureaucratic abuses and to study cases of legalized discrimination. The meetings took place at the end of March 1978, on the eve of annual commemoration of the Genocide in the Diaspora. This could hardly have been accidental. Ecevit and his colleagues suggested to the patriarch that their promises hinged on the patriarch's willingness to convince Armenians in other parts of the world to end anti-Turkish demonstrations, although the patriarch had no administrative or legal authority outside Turkey.[71] Following the meetings the patriarch issued an appeal to the Diasporan press inviting Armenians to refrain from political activities related to "past events" and to remember the dead only as a religious and spiritual duty.[72]

The only positive development was the return of the Kirikhan Church to the local community. On the other hand, a ruling by the Ministry of Education in December 1971 decreed that private schools, such as those under the jurisdiction of the Armenian Patriarchate, could close only on days officially designated by the government and would have to remain open during the traditional Christmas and Easter holidays.[73] In January 1978, moreover, bombs exploded in the Armenian Cathedral of Istanbul, in the chancellery of the Patriarchate, and in one of two Armenian orphanages in the capital. A secret Turkish organization claimed responsibility for the acts that were reportedly undertaken in revenge for similar attacks by Armenian groups against Turkish government offices in Europe.[74]

Armenians in Turkey have been reduced to a cultural group that can ill afford to acknowledge its own history. Many found emigration to Europe or North America a better alternative.

The Diaspora: Dilemmas and Dangers of Landlessness

Land has been an essential component of the Armenian ethos. The defense of the motherland provided chroniclers the raw material from which heroes and villains were created. Love of land permeated ancient Armenian mythology as well as the ideologies of the modern era. Yet paradoxically a history of just that land can in no way adequately cover the history of the Armenians. Frequent domestic and foreign pressures have forced waves of Armenians to seek security and prosperity beyond the boundaries of a homeland that lacked peace and an indigenous government. By the eighteenth century, the communities in India, Russia, and Europe were playing a significant role in the transmission of secular and western ideas of the Enlightenment to the Armenian people. Expatriates in Madras, Venice, Constantinople, Moscow, and Tiflis drew the contours of the nineteenth-century cultural renaissance. They also played an important political role. Until the nineteenth century, merchants and clergymen in London, Moscow, and Paris contributed to the plans to reestablish an Armenian state and attempted to insure the help of powerful western monarchs for the realization of their endeavors. By the end of the century the ranks of older communities had been swelled and new ones had been developed by the emigration of thousands of West Armenians of humbler origins. When the revolutionary activities erupted in Ottoman Armenia, communities in Egypt, Europe, the United States, and Russia provided essential organizational, logistical, and financial support. During World War I, many from Europe and the United States joined the Allied forces hoping to minimize the extent and effects of the massacres and deportations, which were to transform the Diaspora quantitatively and qualitatively.[75]

By the 1970s, there were about 250,000 Armenians in Europe, 450,000 in North America (primarily in the United States), some 100,000 in South America, and about 100,000 in Africa and the Far East.[76] But Diaspora Armenians have long regarded communities in the Near and Middle East as the more important because of their compactness, proximity to the historic lands, cultural facilities, and ability to resist assimilation. Close to 200,000 lived in an ancient community in Iran. Another 200,000 were in Lebanon, 100,000 in Syria, and a final 100,000 were scattered in Egypt, Iraq, Kuwait, Jordan, Israel, Cyprus and Greece. Diaspora Armenians were to a considerable extent people or the offspring of people who survived the Genocide by fleeing to other former parts of the Ottoman Empire. They carried on the impassioned political heritage they brought with them.

Between the two world wars several factors tended to inhibit the emergence of Armenian political activism in the Middle Eastern Diaspora. The most obvious is that as refugees their immediate concern was economic survival. In addition, they were preoccupied with the enormous task of creating, with meager resources, a community infrastructure of schools, churches, and community organizations in an alien environment.

An equally important factor was a matter of administration. The newly mandated Arab states of the 1920s preserved, in some form or another, in the sphere of civil law and religious affairs the institutions they inherited from the Ottoman Empire. As a result the Church became the primary forum of social organization, as was the case in the Ottoman millet system. In 1921 the Catholicossate of Cilicia was evacuated from Turkey and established in Lebanon. Originally established when the medieval Armenian kingdom had its center in

Cilicia, this See had since 1375 lost much of its glamour. With the Soviets in control of the Catholicossate of Etchmiadzin and the Constantinople patriarch's power limited to Turkey itself, the catholicos of Cilicia settled in Antelias, a suburb of Beirut, and assumed jurisdiction over Apostolic Armenians in Lebanon, Syria, and Cyprus. By definition and by tradition, the Church has functioned as an agent of "conservation" under circumstances created by non-indigenous forces. Within the conditions of the Diaspora that tradition acquired a new impetus and significance.

Finally, the revolutionary ARF and SDHP parties that had struggled to raise the political consciousness of the Armenian people had suffered greatly during the disasters of West and East Armenia. For them, the technical task of reorganization in new countries proved much more pressing and consequently easier than digesting the events and experiences of the past decade. Even then they spent their energy dealing with the immediate problems that the communities faced. In this they were assisted by a reinvigorated third party, the ADL. The ADL was founded in the Ottoman Empire in 1908 and reorganized in 1921. Based on upper and middle class elements, it was committed to the free enterprise system and its mission was to offer Armenians an alternative to the revolutionary, socialistic parties.[77] For the ADL the Church was an integral and essential part of Armenian culture. Diaspora conditions favored such an outlook and the ADL soon replaced the SDHP as the prime competitor of the ARF, which remained the strongest party. Nonetheless, within the Diaspora the ADL strengthened the inclination toward acceptance of reduced political goals and lowered expectations.

Generally speaking, these interwar arrangements in the Middle Eastern Diaspora provided quasi-legal recognition of Armenianness and a form of extraterritorial self-management; at the same time they fostered conservatism and created obstacles to cultural and political integration of the refugees into their new environments. Attachment of the refugees to their old homes and a continuing, pietistic hope of return enhanced the feeling of Armenian separateness and temporariness in the Arab states. But after World War II there were marked changes in this process of adjustment.

First, the rise of Arab nationalism provided a sharper focus to the cultural and political identity of peoples in those states. Second, the emergence of statism in the developing societies of the Near East, especially in Syria and Egypt, changed the relationship between citi-

zen and state. The success of the new state policies required control
and planning in the economy and to some extent in social relations.
The impact of these changes on Armenians was manifold. For some
it has meant the loss of prominence in industry, trade, and various
professions, and often an end to prosperity. All have been confronted
with the need to formulate a more integrative concept of national
identity to replace the self-containment of the past; and a problem of
assimilation emerged. The new generations born in the new milieu
were far better integrated than their parents could be. Enjoying conditions far less trying, and an environment far more conducive to a
normal life than was the fate of the refugees, the Diaspora youth
tended to know the local languages and felt more secure in their
legal and social standing.

The same factors that provided a degree of permanency caused a
rise in the political consciousness of the youth and in their interests
in Armenian affairs. If the passing generation defined its
Armenianness within the context of a helpless victim, and remem-
bered longingly but passively the ancestral lands, the new generation tended to come forth as the vindicator and consummated a rediscovered idealism in its role of claimant. The dual phenomena of
integration and "activism" thrust a new life as well as new burdens
on the two institutions of leadership: the political parties and the
Church.

The process of adjustment by the political parties to new, unfavorable realities started before World War II. The quasi Marxist
SDHP—the oldest but weakest of the groups—laid aside their erstwhile dreams of territorial grandeur and independence to adopt a
Sovietized Eastern Armenia as the realization of their program. The
liberal ADL also gradually accepted the status quo in Soviet Armenia and professed satisfaction with the technological and cultural
progress taking place there, though this policy was adopted largely
on pragmatic considerations and could not have emanated from their
ideology.[78]

The two made a coalition with the small number of Soviet-ori-
ented Armenian communists in the Diaspora to support the USSR's
claims against Turkey at the end of World War II. Further, they believed that the Soviet Union would respond more readily to avowed
sympathizers than professed enemies and thus, subsequent to the
war, they refrained from any activities that could have jeopardized
Soviet goodwill toward Armenians and their claims.

Meanwhile the once socialist ARF, still soured by its experiences with the Soviet state, remained more sensitive to antinationalist elements in Soviet practice and ideology. Hence it continued to insist on a free and united Armenia independent of Soviet influence and Turkish domination.[79] During the hopeful years of 1945 to 1947, nonetheless, the ARF declared that in relation to territorial demands the political question of Armenia's regime was of secondary importance. Along with all other factions, the anti-Soviet organization announced its readiness "to assist the USSR if that country took upon itself the defense of the Armenian Case."[80] But then, during the Cold War, the ARF became aggressively anti-Soviet.

The year 1956 turned these differences between the political parties into a deep dissension. In that year the Soviet authorities allowed the election of a new catholicos to the vacant seat of the See of Etchmiadzin. Vasgen I proceeded to reassert his authority over other administrative centers of the Apostolic Church as spiritual leader of all Armenians. The same year the See of Cilicia began increasing the number of Diaspora communities under its jurisdiction. Conflict between the two centers developed inevitably. Even though the programs of the political parties demanded dynamic secularization of Armenian values, they could not avoid involvement in the conflict of these traditionalist ethnic and religious centers. The Cilician See came under ARF control. The cause of Etchmiadzin was taken up by the SDHP-ADL bloc. Passions came to the surface that are best described as symptomatic of parties in exile. During the 1958 civil war in Lebanon the Armenian community there split asunder. The parties raised Cold War banners, supported opposite sides, and conducted their own mini-war against each other.

Relations between the opposing factions improved after 1960. The political parties realized that neither the USSR nor the West was as attractive and trustworthy as earlier rhetoric had made them appear. It became clear that the polarization had placed the national leadership, both religious and political, in direct contradiction to their professed concerns for the general welfare of the Armenian people. Irrelevance in the eyes of a new, politically conscious generation was an important factor in forcing the factions to reevaluate their mutual hostility in terms of Armenian needs. The ARF started arguing that, considering the total alienation of West Armenian territories and the threat of assimilation in the Diaspora, Soviet Armenia was a positive reality. The ADL-SDHP bloc recognized, on the other hand,

that Soviet Armenia was far from embodying the political and territorial aspirations of the Armenian nation. In 1965 joint commemorations of the fiftieth anniversary of the Genocide inaugurated an
era of partisan rapprochement. A manifestation of the rising spirit of
cooperation was the attitude of Armenian organizations toward the
new civil war in Lebanon. During 1975 and 1976 the three Armenian groups agreed on a policy of "positive neutrality," combined
their efforts to minimize the inescapable loss of life and property
within the Armenian community, and even tried to mediate between
the fighting elements.

Since the two segments began to perceive a commonality of interests, links between the Diaspora and Soviet Armenia multiplied.
Soviet Armenian artists, performers, and writers toured the communities abroad. Diaspora Armenians visited Soviet Armenia by the
thousands yearly. Groups of teachers, students, and often individual
performers were invited to spend time in that country. Through these
contacts the two segments appreciated each of the problems and
concerns, but also realized that some of these problems were common. Furthermore, each contributed to their solution in its own way.
Soviet Armenia's cultural viability infused fresh blood into a culturally stagnating and disintegrating Diaspora, although to satisfy the
masses there and to support the claim that Soviet Armenia is a home
for all Armenians authorities in Moscow and Yerevan had to make
serious concessions to Armenian cultural nationalism.

The improvement in the political climate also produced a rapprochement between the two Catholicossates. As a gesture of goodwill the catholicos of All Armenians in Etchmiadzin sent an official
delegation to represent him at the election and anointment in May
1977 of a coadjutor catholicos to the See of Cilicia. Karekin II, later
to be elected catholicos of All Armenians in Etchmiadzin, had been
instrumental as a bishop in promoting a tacit agreement between the
two Sees on the most crucial issue dividing the Armenian national
Church: the elimination from the statute governing the See of Cilicia
those provisions that had allowed extension of its jurisdiction over
communities in the Diaspora formerly under Etchmiadzin.

Yet the most characteristic development in Diaspora politics was
the adoption of a united front by the SDHP, the ARF, and ADL regarding the territorial claims against Turkey. In a memorandum submitted to the United Nations in 1975, and in other related documents, the three demanded "the return of Turkish-held Armenian

territories to their rightful owner—the Armenian people."[81] The deliberate vagueness of the formula accommodated differences of opinion beyond the crucial idea itself, provided for any eventuality in future international developments, and yet stressed the fundamental rights of the Armenian people as a nation. The document failed, however, to specify the exact boundaries of historic Armenia, although reference to the Sèvres Treaty suggested that these encompass the six eastern provinces of the former Ottoman Empire.[82]

Primarily by peaceful means, Diaspora Armenians multiplied their efforts on behalf of these claims. They propagated documentation of the Genocide and its effects. They organized public demonstrations, erected memorial monuments, made anti-Turkish propaganda through various publications, and approached the diplomatic missions of various countries and international agencies regarding moral, financial, and above all territorial reparation by the Republic of Turkey.[83] Yet it was altogether clear that if acquisition of a national territory was the national goal, none of these activities provided more than momentary respite. The centuries-old partition of Armenia would not be ended by public opinion drives. No Turkish government would willingly relinquish any part of its territory. No Western power had any interest in placing the Armenian case on the agenda of nations as "unfinished business." The more the rivalry between the superpowers abated, the less the chance that the USSR would challenge the legitimacy of Turkey's frontiers. The frustration growing out of the impasse was largely responsible for the non-peaceful means adopted by some Armenian groups. Beginning in 1975, such groups claimed responsibility for the assassinations of Turkish ambassadors and attempts on others, for the bombings of Turkish government offices in Europe, and two explosions in Istanbul itself.[84]

The territorial nationalism in the Armenian Diaspora was at least partially a reaction against the increasing threat of assimilation. One study has shown that even in Lebanon, the state with the highest concentration of Armenians in the Middle East, there was a detectable erosion in the ethnic orientation of Armenians during the 1960s and 1970s;[85] and the ethnic orientation was proven to be highest among those involved in the activities of the political parties.[86] In the unsettled world of the Diaspora, nationalism—the vision (however vague) of a territorially integral Armenia—satisfied two basic needs. First, it established an immediate link with the past through the most material of the elements of the past: land. Second, it offered a mental framework within which Armenians continued to perceive themselves as Armenians in foreign lands.

While it is true that not all Armenians in the Diaspora share the vision of a united Armenia as a political program, territorial aspirations were sustained, nonetheless, by the deep sense of injustice that Armenians generally felt. Turkey continued to deny the events of the past that caused the formation of a Diaspora; its government refused to compensate in any way the losses suffered during World War I; and its diplomatic representatives used their influence with foreign governments to hinder activities by Armenians that might have resulted in an unfavorable world public opinion toward their country. Consistently adhered to by successive Turkish governments, this policy of active denial was more effective in perpetuating Diaspora nationalism than any program the political parties could devise.

But this nationalism was also increasingly divorced from the social realities in which Diaspora Armenians lived. Under these circumstances, those who still carried the burden of the past tended to transform political concepts into abstract, moralistic values; and while the latter could provide a positive frame of identification for a threatened ethnic group, it could hardly bring any changes to the political future of a dispersed nation and its divided homeland.

Notes

1.   For a comprehensive and detailed view of developments in Armenia between the fourteenth and eighteenth centuries, see Ds. P. Aghayan et al., eds., *Hay zhoghovrdi patmutiune* [History of the Armenian People] (Yerevan, 1967), vol. 4, L. S. Khachikian et al., eds., *Hay zhoghovurde feodalismi vayredjki zhamanakashrdianum, XIV-XVIII DD* [The Armenian People during the Period of the Decline of Feudalism, XIV-XVIII centuries] (1972); similarly, vol. 5 of the same eight-volume series published by the Institute of History, Academy of Sciences of the Armenian SSR, Ds. P. Aghayan et al., eds., *Hayastane 1801-1870 tvakannerin* [Armenia during the years 1801-1870] (1974), provides the most adequate history preceding the rise of modern political nationalism. See also H. Pastermajian, *Histoire de l'Arménie depuis les origines jusqu'au Traité de Lausanne* (Paris, 1949); A. K.Sanjian, *The Armenian Communities in Syria under Ottoman Dominion* (Cambridge, 1965). For an introduction to the modern era in Armenian history, see R. G. Hovannisian's *Armenia on the Road to Independence* (Berkeley and Los Angeles, 1967), pp.1-68. The period discussed in this section is covered in S. Atamian's *The Armenian Community* (New York, 1955), an informative but biased study; and A. Ter Minassian's valuable and concise "La Question Arménienne," *Esprit*, April 1967, pp. 620-656.
2.   For the process of Russian expansion into the Caucasus, see W.E.D. Allen and P. Muratoff, *Caucasian Battlefields: A History of the Wars on the Turco-Caucasian Border 1828-1921*(Cambridge, 1953). See also V. Gregorian, "The Impact of Rus-

sia on the Armenians and Armenia," in *Russia and Asia*, ed. W. S. Vucinich (Stanford, 1972), pp. 167-218.

3.   See J. Etmekjian, *The French Influence on the Western Armenian Renaissance, 1843-1915* (New York, 1964); and A. Abeghian, "The New Literature of the East Armenians," *The Armenian Review* 3 (1977): 256-264.

4.   For what came to be known as the Armenian Question, see W. Langer, *The Diplomacy of Imperialism, 1890-1920, vol. I* (New York and London, 1935), pp. 45-166, 195-211, and 321-354; A. O. Sarkissian, *History of the Armenian Question to 1885* (Urbana, 1938); A. Beylerian, "L'impérialisme et le mouvement national Arménien," *Relations Internationales* 3, (1975): 19-54; and G. H. Cloud, "The Armenian Question from the Congress of Berlin to the Massacres, 1878-1894" (M.A. thesis, Stanford University, 1923).

5.   Political attitudes among the Armenian bourgeoisie are discussed in V. Rshtuni, *Hay hasarakakan hosankneri patmutiunits* [Of the history of Armenian social trends] (Yerevan, 1956), pp. 1-374; D. Ananun, *Rusahayeri hasarakakan zargatsume* [The social development of Russian Armenians] vol. 1 (1800-1870) and vol. 2 (1870-1900) (Etchmiadzin, 1916, 1922); L. Megrian, "Tiflis during the Russian Revolution of 1905" (Ph.D. diss., University of California at Berkeley, 1975); M. G. Nersisian, *Hay zhoghovrdi azatagrakan paikare trkakan brnatirutian dem, 1850-1870* [The liberation struggle of the Armenian people against Turkish despotism] (Yerevan, 1955), pp. 266-273; H. G. Vardanian, *Arevmtahayeri azadagrutian hartse* [The question of liberation of Western Armenians] (Yerevan. 1967), pp. 266-273; and L. Etmekjian, "The Reaction and Contributions of the Armenians to the Ottoman Reform Movement" (M.A. thesis, University of Bridgeport, 1974). For developments leading to the formation of revolutionary parties see M. Varandian, *Haykakan sharzhman nakhapatmutiune* [Prehistory of the Armenian movement] 2 vols., (Geneva, 1912, 1913).

6.   *Hay Heghapokhakan Dashnaktsutian Dzragir* (henceforth HHD Dzragir) [Program of the Armenian Revolutionary Federation] (Vienna, n.d.), pp. 17-19; this program was devised during the first General Congress of the party in 1892. M. Varandian's *H.H Dashnaktsutian patmutiune* [History of the A(rmenian) R(evolutionary) Federation] 2 vols. (Paris, 1932 and Cairo, 1950) still provides the best overview of the ARF's history despite its romanticized approach and polemical style. For an introduction to the early history of the political organizations, see L. Nalbandian, *The Armenian Revolutionary Movement* (Berkeley and Los Angeles, (1967). See also J. M. Hagopian's "Hyphenated Nationalism: The Spirit of the Revolutionary Movement in Asia Minor, 1896-1910" (Phd. diss., Harvard University, 1943). Many of the following observations are drawn from this writer's doctoral dissertation in progress, "Ideological Developments within the Armenian Liberation Movement, 1885-1908" (University of California at Los Angeles).

7.   *Hnchak* (Organ of the Hnchakian Revolutionary Party, Geneva), November (actually December), 1871, p. 1 (my translation). The Hnchakians later adopted the "social democratic" label. For their history, see L. Nalbandian, "The Origins and Development of Socialism in Armenia: The Social Democratic Hnchakian Party 1887-1949" (M.A. thesis, Stanford University, 1949); A. Kitur, ed., *Patmutiune S.D. Hnchakian Kusaktsutian 1887-1962* [History of the S(ocial) D(emocratic) Hnchakian Party 1887-1962] 2 vols. (Beirut, 1962-1963). Unfortunately this latter work falls short of fulfilling promise of its title.

8.   *HHD Dzragir*, p. 16.

9.   Ibid., pp. 19-20; "Dzragir Hnchakian kusaktsutian" [Program of Hnchakian Party], *Hisnamiak Sotsial Demokrat Hnchakian Kusaktsutian 1887-1937* (Providence. 1938), pp. 38-39.

10. Varandian, *H.H. Dashnaktsutian patmutiune*, vol. 1, pp. 468-472.
11. This was clearly stated in the first manifesto of the ARF published in 1890; see *Divan H.H. Dashnaktsutian* [Archives of the ARF] S. Vratsian, ed., vol. I (Boston, 1934), p. 89.
12. M. Hovannisian, *Dashnaktsutiune ev nra hakarakordnere* [The (AR) Federation and its Adversaries] (Tiflis, 1906-7), pp. 54-83.
13. For the rise of Marxism among Armenians, see V. A. Avetisian, *Hay hasarakakan mtki zargatsman Marks-Leninian puli skzbnavorume* [The beginnings of the Marxist-Leninist phase of the development of Armenian social thought] (Yerevan, 1976). This study includes a critique of other Armenian parties from the point of view of Soviet Marxism.
14. *Hisnamiak*, p. 38.
15. *HHD Dzragir*, p. 17.
16. Hovannisian, *Armenia on the Road to Independence*, pp. 34-37.
17. See Varandian, *H.H. Dashnaktsutian patmutiune*, vol. I, pp. 254-264 and G. Sasuni, *Kurt azgayin sharzhume ev hay-krtakan haraberutiunnere* [The Kurdish national movement and Armeno-Kurdish relations] (Beirut, 1969), pp. 153-191.
18. *Droshak,* Organ of the ARF, Geneva July 1903, pp. 97-98.
19. *H. H. Dashnaktsutian Dzragir* [Program of the ARF], (Geneva 1907), pp. 18-19.
20. *Hnchak*, August-September 1910, p. 2. The resolution was passed during the Sixth General Congress of the Party held in Constantinople, November 1909.
21. For sources on the genocide of the Armenian people, see R. G. Hovannisian's *The Armenian Holocaust: A Bibliography Relating to the Deportations, Massacres, and Dispersion of the Armenian People, 1915-1923* (Cambridge, Mass., 1978). There has always been a tendency among some historians to bring the academic view on the Genocide of the Armenians into harmony with the official position held on the subject by the Ottoman and Turkish governments—to deny that a genocide ever took place, and to blame the victims for whatever tragedy befell them. This tendency has been particularly strong among Western historians since Turkey joined the NATO Alliance. The most recent example of this sort of scholarship is S. J. Shaw and E. K. Shaw's *History of the Ottoman Empire and Modern Turkey, Vol. II, Reform, Revolution, and Republic: The Rise of Modern Turkey, 1808-1975* (Cambridge, London, New York, Melbourne, 1977), esp. pp. 7, 124-127, 188-191, 200-205, 238-247, 262-267, 276-281, and 298-333. For a critical appraisal of the volume, see R. G. Hovannisian, "The Critic's View: Beyond Revisionism," *International Journal of Middle East Studies* 9, no. 3 (August 1978): 379-388. The same issue of this journal also offers a response by the authors of the volume to Hovannisian's criticisms in pp. 388-400.

Reasons for the disparity between views held on the subject by Turkish, Western, and Armenian historians are explored in this writer's "Objectivity and Historiography of the Armenian Genocide," *The Armenian Review* 31, no. 3 (Spring 1978): 86-93.
22. For the history of the Armenian and other Caucasian republics, see R. G. Hovannisian, *The Republic of Armenia, Vol. I, The First Year 1918-1919* (Berkeley, Los Angeles, London, 1971); J. B. Gidney, *A Mandate For Armenia* (Kent, Ohio, 1967); F. Kazemzadeh, *The Struggle for Transcaucasia* (New York, and Oxford 1951); and R. Pipes, *The Formation of the Soviet Union* (New York, 1968), pp. 7-21, 93-107.
23. See R. G. Hovannisian, "Armenia and the Caucasus in the Genesis of the Soviet-Turkish Entente," *The Armenian Review* 27, no. 1 (Spring 1974): 32-52.
24. Pipes, *The Formation of the Soviet Union*, pp. 193-241. See also A. Caprielian, "The Sovietization of Armenia: A Case History in Imperialism," *The Armenian*

Review 20, no. 3 (Autumn, 1967): 22-42; and S. Vratsian, *Hayastani Hanrapetutiune* [Republic of Armenia] (Beirut, 1958), pp. 445-507.

25.   Unless otherwise indicated, statistical information regarding Armenians in the Soviet Union and Soviet Armenia is derived from the latest All-Union Census in the USSR in 1970. As usual, one must approach any statistical information, particularly from the USSR, with caution.

26.   For a detailed study of the early decades of Soviet Armenia, see M. K. Matossian, *The Impact of Soviet Policies in Armenia* (Leiden, 1962).

27.   J. S. Kirakosian, *Hayastane midjazkayin divanagitutian ev Sovetakan artakin kaghakakanutian pastateghterum* [Armenia in the documents of international diplomacy and Soviet Union foreign policy] (Yerevan, 1972), pp. 418-419.

28.   The background of the conflict is discussed in R. G. Hovannisian, "The Armeno-Azerbaijani Conflict Over Mountainous Karabakh, 1918-1919," *The Armenian Review* 24, no. 2 (Summer 1971): 3-39.
        See also A.H. Arslanian, "Britain and the Question of Mountainous Karabakh," paper presented at the Eleventh Annual Meeting of MESA, Los Angeles, 1977.

29.   S. Vratsian, *Republic of Armenia*, pp. 524-568. In Soviet Armenian historiography the event is known as the "February adventure" and presented as the attempt of a power-hungry ARF to regain control of the government. See, for example, Ds. P. Aghayan et al., eds., *Hay zhoghovrdi patmutiune* 7 (Yerevan, 1967): 136-154.

30.   G. Lazian, *Hayastan ev Hay Date - vaveragrer* [Armenia and the Armenian Case Documents] (Cairo, 1946), p. 306. The same document is discussed in conjunction with the New Economic Policy in *Hay zhoghovrdi patmutiune*, vol. 7, p. 176.

31.   The great purges in Soviet Armenia between 1936 and 1939 are covered with much detail in A. Atan's "Sovetahay Kiank" [Soviet Armenian Life] monthly chronicle in *Hairenik Amsagir* (Boston, an ARF monthly review) throughout the same period. For an eyewitness account, see A. Haroot, "The Purges in Soviet Armenia," *The Armenian Review* 4, no. 3 (Autumn 1951): 133-139.

32.   Lazian, *Vaveragrer*, pp. 346-350. See also S. Torosian, "Soviet Policy in the Armenian Question," *The Armenian Review* II, no. 2 (Summer 1958): 27-39.

33.   Lazian, *Vaveragrer*, pp. 371-372 (personal translation).

34.   A.M. Hakobian et al., eds., *Hay zhoghovrdi patmutiune*, vol. 8 (Yerevan, 1970), p. 254.

35.   *Sovetakan Hayastan Amsagir* [Soviet Armenia Monthly] (Yerevan), no. 6 (1976), p. 4.

36.   For these and other comparisons see B. D. Silver, "Levels of Socioeconomic Development Among Soviet Nationalities," *American Political Science Review* 68 (1974): 1618-1637.

37.   See M. K. Matossian, "Communist Rule and the Changing Armenian Cultural Pattern," in E. Goldhagen, ed., *Ethnic Minorities in the Soviet Union* (New York, 1968), pp. 185-197.

38.   V. E. Khodjabekian, "HSSH bnakchutiune, erek, aysor ev vaghe" [The population of the A(rmenian) S(oviet) S(ocialist) R(epublic) yesterday, today and tomorrow], *Lraber* (Yerevan), no. 12 (1972), p. 53.

39.   Computed from related data in Khodjabekian, "HSSH bnakchutiune," and R. Ezekian, "Hamayn hayutian hayrenike" [The Fatherland of all Armenians], *Garun Amsagir* (Yerevan, monthly), no. 11 (1970), pp. 88-93.

40.   L.V. Chuiko, *Braki i razvodi* (Moscow, 1976), p. 76.

41.   Khodjabekian, "HSSH bnakchutiune," p. 48.

42.   L. Davtian, "Amusnanal: erb. erekhaner unenal: kani" [To Marry: When? To Bear Children: How Many?], *Garun Amsagir*, no.10 (1971), pp. 73-77.

43. Khodjabekian, "HSSH bnakchutiune," p. 53.
44. Ds. P. Aghayan, *Hay zhoghovrdi azatagrakan paykari patmutiunits* [Of the History of the Liberation Struggle of the Armenian People] (Yerevan, 1976), esp. pp. 93-296.
45. Kh. Dashtents, "Ranchbarner" [Peasants], *Sovetakan Grakanutiun* [Soviet literature] (Yerevan, monthly), no. 7 and 8 (1976), pp. 20-74 and 12-73.
46. For a detailed study of all this material, see V. N. Dadrian's "Nationalism in Soviet Armenia—A Case Study of Ethnocentrism," G. Simmonds, ed., *Nationalism in the USSR and Eastern Europe in the Era of Brezhnev and Kosysin* (Detroit, 1977), pp. 202-258.
47. *New York Times*, June 26,1965.
48. *Christian Science Monitor*, April 27, 1978.
49. Dadrian, "Nationalism in Soviet Armenia," p. 247. Less violent, nonetheless unusual demonstrations occurred in Moscow as well; see V. N. Dadrian's "The Events of April 24 in Moscow—How They Happened and under What Circumstances," *The Armenian Review* 20, no. 2 (Summer 1967): 9-26.
50. M. K. Matossian, "Armenia and the Armenians," Z. Katz, ed., *Handbook of Major Soviet Nationalities* (New York, 1975), p. 158.
51. Cited in *Azdak Shabatoriak*, no. 17 (1971), pp. 272-274; no. 26. (1974), pp. 419-421. For a statement by the leaders of this group containing the objectives and by-laws of the party, see "Le Parti National Unifié en Armenié soviétique," *Haiastan* (Paris, monthly), No. 391-392, April-May 1978, pp. 38-40. The renewed national fervor might have caused the removal of yet another first secretary of the Communist Party in Armenia, A. Kocninian. See "Soviet Armenian Chronicle," *The Armenian Review*, 27 no. 1 (Spring 1974): 102-103; no. 3 (Autumn 1974): 325; no. 5 (Winter 1974): 435-437.
52. *Pravda*, December 4, 1920.
53. *New York Times*, December 11, 1977.
54. *Azdak Shabatorlak*. no. 6 (1969), p. 95.
55. *New York Times*, December 11, 1977.
56. Sarada Mitra and Adel Haba, "We Saw the Brotherhood of Nations," *Problems of Peace and Socialism* 20, no. 6 (June 1977): esp. 18-19, 25.
57. Both documents were first published in *Zartonk* (Beirut daily, organ of the Armenian Democratic Liberal Party), October 15, 1977.
58. *Sovetakan Hayastan* (Yerevan daily), April 15, 1978; *Christian Science Monitor*, April 28, 1978. On the question of minority languages see also S. Grigorian, "A Note on Soviet Policies Toward the Armenian Language," *The Armenian Review* 25, no. 3 (Autumn 1972): 68-76. For two contrasting views on the impact of language reforms in 1958-59, see H. Lipset, "The Status of National Minority Languages in Soviet Education," *Soviet Studies* 19, no. 2 (October 1967): 181-189; and B. D. Silver, "The Status of National Minority Languages in Soviet Education: An Assessment of Recent Changes," *Soviet Studies* 26, no. I (January 1974): 28-40.
59. The most vehement criticisms have come so far from the first secretary and secretary of the Central Committee of the Communist Party in Armenia, K. Demirjian and K. Dallakian, in speeches delivered to the Central Committee on January 30, 1975 and October 19, 1975; see *Grakan Tert* [Literary newspaper] (Yerevan), February 7, 1975 and *Sovetakan Hayastan*, October 21 and 22, 1975.
60. See *Le Monde*, June 23, 1977; *Libération* (Paris), April 8, 1977; and *Haiastan*, no. 383, July 1977, pp. 9-15.
61. *Hayastan*, no. 381, May-June 1977, p. 19.
62. P. Reddaway, ed., *Uncensored Russia: The Human Rights Movement in the Soviet Union* (London, 1972), pp. 103, 151 *passim*; comp. P. Litvinov, *The Trial of the*

Four (New York, 1972), pp. 399-405; and G. Sanders, *Samizdat: Soviet Opposition* (New York, 1974), pp. 368, 372.

63. "Le Parti National Unifie," *Haiastan*, pp. 38-40.
64. Sermon delivered by Archbishop Shnork Galustian, patriarch of Armenians in Turkey, on October 24, 1976 in Paris; see *Asbarez* (Los Angeles, semi-weekly), December 9, 1976. See also R. P. Jordan's "The Proud Armenians," *National Geographic* 153, no. 6 (June 1978): 846-853; this article provides one of the rare instances in western literature where reference is made to the status of Armenians presently living in Turkey.
65. Ibid, pp. 178-182. See also "Statement on Conditions (1976) by the Chancellery of the Armenian Patriarchate in Turkey," *The Armenian Review* 30, no. 3 (Autumn 1977): 302-305.
66. The patriarch's telegram to Mr. Porkut Eozali, director of the Ministry of Interior, Turkey, in *Asbarez*, September 19, 1977.
67. *London Times*, April 20 and 25, 1963; see also H. Dasnabedian's introduction, esp. pp. xii-xiv, to *Monuments of Armenian Architecture* (Beirut, 1972), published by the Central Committee of the "Hamazkaine" Cultural Association.
68. The Patriarch's Annual Report, p. 182.
69. J. Wolf, "Les Minorités en Turquie," *Notre Temps* (Brussels), January 21,1977.
70. *Christian Science Monitor*, July 20, 1977.
71. *Marmara* (Istanbul), March 30 and April 1, 1978.
72. Ibid., April 10, 1978.
73. *Hurriyet*, December 14, 1977.
74. *Marmara*, January 7, 1978; *Asbarez*, January 27, 1978.
75. A major attempt at providing a general picture of Armenian communities outside the homeland throughout the centuries is A. Alpoyajian, *Patmutiune hay gaghtakanutian* [History of Armenian Emigration], 3 vols. (Cairo, 1941-1961). For an example of eighteenth-century Diaspora-Armenia relations, see A. Hamalian, *The Armenians: Intermediaries for the European Trading Companies*, University of Manitoba Anthropology Papers, no. 14 (Winnipeg, 1976). Some of the problems in covering the most recent period are discussed in R. Mirak, "Outside the Homeland: Writing the History of the Armenian Diaspora," *Recent Studies in Modern Armenian History* (Cambridge, Mass., 1972), pp. 119-125.
76. These figures are generally accepted approximations, as there are no reliable statistics on this subject.
77. For the 1908 program of the ADL, see A. Darbinian, *Hay azatagrakan sharzhman oreren* [Of the Days of the Armenian Liberation Movement] (Paris, 1947), pp. 198-204; and Lazian, *Vaveragrer*, pp. 323-328.
78. H. Yervand, *Ramkavar Azatakan Kusaktsutiun. Ir aysore ev vaghe* [Democratic Liberal Party—Its Today and Tomorrow] (Boston, 1927); "Davanank ev oughegids Ramkavar Azatakan Kusaktsutian" [Credo and Conduct of the Democratic Liberal Party], G. Aharonian and H. Vahuni, eds., *"Zartonk" Batsarik"* [Zartonk" Special] (Beirut, 1962), p. 37.
79. See A. Caprielian, "The Armenian Revolutionary Federation: The Politics of a Party in Exile" (Ph.D. dissertation, New York University, 1975). For a Soviet view of Diaspora politics, see L. A. Khurshudian, *Spurkahay kusaktsutiunnere zhamanakakits edabum* [The Parties in the Armenian Diaspora in Their Contemporary Phase] (Yerevan, 1964).
80. Lazian, *Vaveragrer*, p. 352.
81. The National Council for the Sixtieth Anniversary Commemoration of the Genocide, *Armenian Memorandum to the United Nations; April 24, 1975* (Beirut, 1975).

See also "Two Memoranda on the Subject of the Sixtieth Anniversary of the Turkish Massacres of the Armenians," *The Armenian Review* 28, no. 1 (Spring 1975): 74-81.

82.   Legal aspects of Armenian claims are discussed in Sh. Toriguian's *The Armenian Question and International Law* (Beirut, 1973).

83.   See K. Donabedian, "Armenians Abroad," *The Armenian Review* 28, no. I (Spring 1975): 85-99.

84.   *Le Monde*, June II, 1978.

85.   A. Der-Karabetian and L. Melikian, "Assimilation of Armenians in Lebanon," *The Armenian Review*, no. I (Spring 1974), pp. 65-72.

86.   A. Der-Karabetian, "A Study of Assimilation in the Pluralistic Society of Lebanon: The Case of the Armenians," paper presented at the Tenth Annual Meeting of The Middle East Studies Association, Los Angeles, 1976.

Part II

2

Nation and Fatherland in Nineteenth-Century Armenian Political Thought

Nationalism has been generally regarded as one of the central concepts in the understanding of nineteenth-century Armenian political thought. Taking root in the 1850s, it came to embody the concerns and goals of many segments of the Armenian people. Nationalism is also an abstract concept; while universalizing the Armenian experience, it might tend to overshadow the exact processesthat give meaning to the term at different times and in different places.

One of those processes among Armenians in the Ottoman Empire was the increasing antagonism between the Armenian privileged urban population and the dispossessed rural masses. The two segments of the population once shared a self-definition imposed by the Ottoman state—the millet. Within this context the term *nation* described, in a sociological sense, the elite of the millet, represented by the clergy and the economically successful elements. That leadership, even when selected in democratic fashion, was limited to urban elements which by and large had no fundamental interest in pursuing the cause of the oppressed and repressed in the rural areas.

Thus, as the millet mechanism failed to resolve the social and economic crisis of the Armenian provinces and a political consciousness evolved among the rural and small town Armenians, many became aware of the political implication of social and economic stratification. For the rural Armenian, fatherland came to replace nation as the central component of Armenian nationalism. By merging with *hayrenasirutiune* (love of fatherland or patriotism), Armenian nationalism entered a new, more dynamic phase dominated by issues relevant to craftsmen, peasants, and non-skilled workers. Through patriotism the lower classes asserted the primacy of their own concerns in the determination of national goals beginning in the 1860s.

This democratization led to the revolutionary phase of the Armenian liberation movement by the end of the 1880s and the adoption of socialism as the ideology of emancipation.

The nationalism associated with the interests of the dispossessed classes in the provinces acquired additional potency since the laboring Armenian classes were in the Armenian provinces, where most Armenians lived; and what was seen as rural outposts from the perspective of the Ottoman government and the Istanbul Armenian establishment constituted the historic fatherland of the Armenian people. By grounding nationalism in a historically well-defined territory, love of fatherland gave the emancipation movement a political legitimacy denied to those whose love was for the abstracted cultural-religious heritage of Armenians.

The View from the Top

In the context of the Ottoman Armenian people, the difference between *azgasirutiune* (love of nation) and hayrenasirutiune reflected not only a chronological progression in political thought but also divergent, if not conflicting, class concerns. This was most clearly articulated in the debates that took place in the capital of the empire, Istanbul. Here, a large Armenian colony, headed by the patriarch, was given the impossible task of representing all Armenians.

Any political advantage that proximity to the center of power could have offered Armenians in the capital was neutralized by the *amira* class's control over the Patriarchate through the seventeenth and eighteenth centuries. The amira class, composed largely of *sarrafs* ("money lenders"), high-level Armenian bureaucrats, and a few other influential families, dominated the Patriarchate.[1] Because of their tight control of the millet structure, the position of all Armenians was identified with that of the sarraf.[2]

The outlook of the amira class reflected the concerns of an elite that was successful in the economic sphere but lacked political security. Their financial and often physical well-being was dependent on the success of Ottoman officials whose careers or projects they financed. The amiras accepted the definition of Armenians as a religious community represented by a state-imposed church hierarchy. This acceptance or bias was construed as a non-political attitude and, consequently, not subject to any judgment by political standards. For those who championed the cause of the amira class, this non-politics was articulated in the belief that "there was no solution outside the Armenian [Apostolic] Church."³ The best-known publicist of the cause of the amiras reasoned:

> It has been discussed, and it is undeniable that our people do not have, politically speaking, a national [institution]...but we do have an alternative through which our people will survive. The governments ruling over us have been protectors of this [alternative] institution and nucleus of union; to preserve our ethnic identity we do not need a political one. This link is the unity of religion through which all Armenians are related regardless of their place of residence or of the state of which they are subjects.⁴

By defining the Armenian predicament as one of survival of an ethno-religious identity, it became possible to formulate a political agenda that denied the Armenian people a political future. Political leadership, reduced in form and content, was assigned willingly to the clergy not because there was no political institution, but because there was no need for one. Unity through the Church gave the concept of nation a transcendent dimension and relegated other categories such as class and caste into secondary and expandable categories.

The sanctioning of the Church as the only legitimate context within which a commonness could be articulated signaled more than a mere appreciation of an old and quite flexible institution that had managed to survive the destruction of Armenian dynasties. It reflected a general view of society within which existing hierarchies in the economic and social spheres supported each other in the task of using the nation as the necessary but otherwise missing social foundation of conservative institutions.

This view was shared even by the Mekhitarists, the Catholic Armenian order headquartered in Venice and Vienna, who were instrumental in bringing about an Armenian cultural renaissance. Erudite monks from the Mekhitarist centers introduced the Armenian reading public to a large number of European concepts. Inspired by romanticism, they attempted, above all, to give Armenian identity historical roots. Yet the Mekhitarist view of Armenian culture and history had a wholesomeness, a harmony that Armenian society lacked. The discrepancy was particularly evident among Armenians in the Ottoman Empire whence most Mekhitarists were recruited and where most of the congregations' efforts concentrated. The Mekhitarists were most conscious of the cultural backwardness of Armenians and strove to educate and enlighten them. But they were careful not to transform cultural views into political trends. The Europeanization of the Armenian self-image was not intended to be a prelude to the adoption of the Western pattern of a radical-conservative antagonism in the political spectrum. There was to be an evolution in Armenian society, but not necessarily a dialectical one.

The Mekhitarists promoted a history built around heroes and villains, a historythat celebrated isolated individuals and events as the embodiment of a glorious yet tragic past. In 1861 the Mekhitarists of Vienna reissued in booklet form an article first published in 1849 when Europe was in turmoil and when a few Armenian young men who studied in Europe at that time knew that turmoil meant revolution.[5] The major portion of the booklet eulogizes some of the great figures from both Western and Armenian ancient histories. After ascribing the greatness of past heroes to classic patriotism, the author warns against the "abuses of patriotism" then rampant in European capitals. The booklet ends with a special plea to Armenians not to sympathize with these abuses or their perpetrators. To insure against such a possibility, the author defines what patriotism should mean for Armenians of different classes. For those who have wealth and power, "true patriotism" involves helping the less fortunate, respecting the law by not being whimsical, donating funds for the construction of public institutions, and not forgetting that wealth does not release one from the duties and obligations of "good citizenship." Those without money or power, the author of the article asserted,

> must respect the above mentioned [rich] Armenians and honor them as interpreters and executors of the law, as the lieutenants of God. [The lower classes] must have faith in them and must not nurture doubts without good reason. If they note any shortcomings in the upper class, they should not consider them unjust and evil or demean their names in the presence of others. Rather, to the best of their ability, they should cover up for the others' shortcomings and should praise them publicly. Even if they cannot honor the person, they should honor their rank and position, so that the respect for the rule of law is not diminished and law and order are not eroded. Those with average or no means should not be jealous of the rich and should not attempt to imitate the rich in everything the rich do. They should also not expect that the rich give all of their wealth to other causes.[6]

Cultural awakening, then, should not occur at the expense of the preservation of social harmony and national subservience for the benefit of the upper classes and the Ottoman state. Yet the author glorified Armenian historical or mythical figures like Hayk, Aram, Tigran, and Vardan, who distinguished themselves by rejecting foreign rule and subjugation to the will of others. The author most likely believed that identification with the past was a sufficient source of pride to obviate the need for emulation. History was introduced to neutralize political aspirations rather than inspire them. In this manner, historical figures were abstracted from their historical reality and then offered to Armenian readers as sources of pride. Acts of heroism, self-sacrifice, and courage were introduced as manifestations of spiritual values rather than tactical means to resolve a political crisis.

Middle Class Liberalism

By the middle of the nineteenth century the Ottoman Empire was brought within the sphere of the European-dominated world market system. Trade between the Ottoman Empire and the West increased tremendously, although the import of manufactured goods exceeded by far the exports from traditional industries such as dried fruits and rugs. Armenians, along with other largely non-Muslim groups, made up the merchant class that carried out this trade.[7] Gradually, in addition to the comprador bourgeoisie, the new middle class included professionals such as doctors and lawyers; literati such as writers, teachers, and editors; and small manufacturers. These groups had little involvement with tax farming, the economic basis of the sarrafs.

This new middle class began a process of secularization and democratization of Armenian institutions, which performed the classical function of liberalization. Yet this middle class lacked the social legitimacy and integration within dominant institutions that the amiras had enjoyed. The economic interests of this class placed them outside the political structure as well as in opposition to it. Political power, which could have guaranteed if not promoted class interests, was not to be found in the Ottoman Empire. Aside from their timid attempts under the Ottoman *Tanzimat* ("reforms"), the middle class made no effort to create a political power base. The economic activity of the middle class did not even have any relationship with the Ottoman elite. Thus, this new middle class was deeply alienated from the established Ottoman structure. To make up for its alienation, the middle class developed greater reliance on the West. Merchants sought their individual economic security through the acquisition of citizenship of Western countries. They also sought to establish social legitimacy by sponsoring a cultural renaissance. Inspiration for such a renaissance came from Europe and demonstrated their inclination to act as cultural mediators.[8]

The cultural-ideological relationship between the European and Armenian societies, while based upon unequal economic and political standings, was nonetheless dynamic because of the challenge the West presented to Armenians as a historical entity. The Armenian awakening was predicated by the answers to some basic questions raised by that challenge: Why did such a difference emerge between Asian and European societies? What is the substance of that difference? These seemingly rhetorical questions were asked to legitimize the overriding goals of "progress" and "enlightenment," to be achieved through education, science, learning, industry, and trade. The corollary questions were: How can Armenians close the gap between the two societies? In what political framework can they hope to do so?

The concept of nation was instrumental from the beginning in defining the Western challenge and Armenian responses to it. Certainly, in the 1860s the concept had evolved into more than a gathering of coreligionists. It included civilizational achievements of the past, albeit still devoid of a political context. The past was there to inspire and remind Armenians that they were once able to deal with Europeans as equals, and therefore they could expect the same in the future. The existence of a glorious past gave Armenians the right to recover their dignity. In fact, as early as in 1846 the Istanbul newspaper *Hayastan* clearly indicated this direction of thought:

> Wake up, Armenian nation, from your death-inviting slumber of ignorance; remember your past glory, mourn your present state of wretchedness and heed the example of other enlightened nations: take care of your schools, cultivate the Armenian language, learn other useful languages and liberal sciences [professions]...only then can you reach the goal of happiness.[9]

Liberalism introduced a dynamic concept of nation as opposed to the conservative religious definition. Yet enlightenment, the ultimate in individual and social happiness, was perceived to be attainable within the status quo because it was essentially a matter of culture and civilization. One of the chief architects of the national awakening, Servichen, placed the process of change strictly within the confines of the millet structure. He stated in his 1863 opening address to the newly elected National Assembly:

> Our duty is not only to protect our religion bequeathed to us by our ancestors but also to use all means for the single purpose of developing the national spirit: a spirit which is the lone factor in enlivening the nation and which we will try to reconcile first with the spirit and the course of our times and second with national obligations toward our benevolent government by rejecting foreign intervention.[10]

Nahapet Rusinian (poet, publicist, and physician) even considered banning the word "political" from the Armenian language to ensure the proper interpretation of national goals.[11] The best nation, argued a writer following the Zeytun rebellion, is one that respects the authority of the state and the best defense of people's liberties is obedience to the laws of the land.[12] The cultural definition of a national awakening was shared by most liberals and enthusiasts of education. For instance, the students of the Nubar-Shahnazarian School in Istanbul espoused literature, the most expressive mode of culture, as the ultimate solution: What Armenia needed was "not heroes, but geniuses; it does not need soldiers of arms but soldiers of Light... We will produce Madame de Staels and Lamartines."[13]

In the context of this national awakening, education and literacy became overriding concerns. The National Constitution insisted on free education for all Armenian youth.[14] Societies were also established to educate *pandukhds* (migrant workers) in Istanbul. They, in turn, were expected to return to their villages and spread literacy there. Literacy was the solution to poverty. The *Baregordzakan* (Benevolent) Society of Istanbul took the more practical step of setting up a model farm in Cilicia through which they educated local farmers in scientific agriculture.

Most Istanbul Armenians were concerned though with the goal of bringing education, progress, and enlightenment to the capital. The liberal creed of Armenians there was overwhelmingly an urban one. During a debate on the unequal distribution of deputies in the Armenian Assembly, the respected liberal *Masis*, the newspaper founded and edited by the French educated Karapet Utujian, defended the preeminence of Istanbul:

> Istanbul must have priority since, firstly, it is the capital of the state; secondly, it is the center of the national [Armenian] administration. The Patriarch is there, the progressive and educated elements of the nation are there. In one word, the great strength of the nation is there.[15]

According to this view, urban dwellers were the only subjects who needed to be educated in order to give substance to the idea of enlightenment. The nation, as understood by Istanbul Armenians, could have prospered in and by itself in the capital. The strength of the nation, based upon the unity of goals such as progress and enlightenment, would be secured when each class accepted its own function in society. According to *Masis*, the upper class was responsible for the care of the poor; the middle class was to submit to and cooperate with the upper class; and the lower class was to accept thankfully what was given to them by the other classes.[16] Unity, the ultimate precondition for happiness, would be achieved when moral and financial virtues were spread.[17]

The "Hayastantsis"

For a long while the provincial Armenians shared the urban social vision based on communal harmony. Garegin Srvantstiants, a clergyman who devoted his whole career to the welfare of the rural Armenian population, was hopeful for the future. He believed that common good could be achieved by people caring for each other: the rich helping the poor, the healthy caring for the sick, the older assisting the younger, and the fortunate looking after the unfortunate. He founded his vision on a particularized version of "patriotism," however. In 1861 he declared patriotism "the real root of all good," and defined the "good" to be the welfare of the community. He thus pointed out common misconceptions that should be corrected:

> I feel more sorry for those who, although educated, hold the idiotic opinion that one's fatherland is where he was born... They say "Here is our fatherland, where we acquired wealth, where we have properties and inheritances. I must work for this place, I must labor for the education of my children and progress of the city. We owe it to ourselves that our children grow happy. Thank God we have our Churches and masses, beautiful sceneries, spots of entertainment, and the means to have a good time. And we feel secure. This is our fatherland, the comfort which we seek."[18]

The criticism of this Diasporan thinking and its culture also led to a further distinction between hayrenasirutiune and azgasirutiune. While the first advanced the people as the dominant and dynamic force, the latter focused on the concept of nation as an abstract and timeless entity. Quite early in his career Srvantstiants pointed out that culture, however enlightened, cannot supplant the love of the fatherland, i.e., a sense of history and of the individuals that assure its continuity. Thus, "true patriotism" required a change in focus:

> Our fatherland is where our history, our heroes and saints are. It is the people there that make our fatherland real with their sufferings. It is they who need and are worthy of assistance. Had it not been for the hayastantsi [inhabitant of Armenia], Armenia would have turned by now to a thing of the imagination.[19]

Mkrtich Khrimian was instrumental in developing a critical look at urban perceptions and values. Khrimian was a self-taught clergyman born in Van who identified himself with the interests of the provincial Armenians. He began as a teacher and ended his career as catholicos of All Armenians. As a young teacher he encouraged his students to look at the past, which for him began with the Bible, to legitimize change. The Bible allowed him to be critical of all existing political authority within an accepted framework. Through his student, Srvantstiants, he asserted: "God did not create the enlightened soul so that it is kept in the dark, and he did not condemn any nation to slavery. Let us become like Adam [in the Bible]."[20] Another of Khrimian's students proclaimed: "Only national history gives life to dead souls."[21] The student presented a long list of Armenian heroes from Hayk, the mythical founder of the nation, to Tigran, the best known of Armenian kings (95-75 B.C.); he expected this knowledge to have a liberating effect on all Armenians. Khrimian himself used history effectively to recreate the dilemma of the nation. In an imaginary conversation between a "glory-seeker" and a "patriot," Khrimian presented the quintessential Armenian political issue:

Glory-seeker: Was it not the patriotic Vardan[22] who got into something above his head and caused the death of thousands of young men? The Patriot: For the welfare of my people I am willing to sacrifice everything. If Armenia had not been covered with the blood of young men, the Armenian people would not have blossomed now.[23]

By elevating the welfare of the people above all other considerations, Khrimian began a shift in Armenian political thought from an abstract nationalism to a concrete populism, although he was not to be the one to articulate the populist program.

Much of the implied advice in these discussions was obviously directed at the Armenian leadership in Istanbul, an advice that was also not heeded. Gradually it became clear that conflicting interests rather than harmony dominated the Armenian community. By the sixties, the contrast between urban and rural life became a major theme in Armenian journalism. At the height of the debate on the ratification of the National Constitution in 1862, Khrimian's Van-based monthly journal published an imaginary dialogue between a city dweller and a peasant. While the article highlighted the importance each group had for the economy and general welfare of society, the primary purpose of the dialogue was to present the case for an equitable if not proportional share of seats for provincial Armenians in the National Assembly. To the scorn shown by the urban dweller, the peasant responded, "your laws are like traps in which the poor and the weak peasants are caught. You suck our bloods like spiders through bribery, restrictive measures, prohibitions, and other forms of injustice."[24] In his dialogue, the city was the home of money-seeking hypocrites who professed but did not live by the liberal creed; of a power-hungry clergy; of journalists who were more impressed by the parliamentary rhetoric of Gladstone than the utter poverty and wretchedness of most Armenians surrounding them; and of middle class parvenus who spoke loudly of philanthropy but spent most of their money on dresses believing, meanwhile, that they had saved the nation by having organized dances.[25]

During the debate on the National Constitution Bishop Khrimian had shared the view that "Constantinople must be the focus of Armenian political power since it is the seat of the Sultan." Nonetheless, Khrimian had invited Istanbul Armenians to make Western Armenia the focus of their attention.[26] In 1862 Srvantstiants was wondering whether any of Khrimian's messages had any value for the millet. In an article in which he discussed the government's torture practices, Srvantstiants asked:

> Does the government have the right to torture? Of course not. But who is objecting, who is knocking at the government's door? Where are the intermediaries, where are the modern leaders, the leaders of the nation? Thank God we have them, but they are being cautious.[27]

Khrimian made *pantukhts*, the migrant workers, and the provincial masses the focus of his attention. His efforts merely earned him the label *"hayastantsi vardabet"* or "the priest from Armenia." *Hayastan* (Armenia) was thus reduced to a locale like so many others.[28] While the label intimated a provincialism unbecoming urban intellectuals and bourgeoisie, the reduction of Armenia to a mere geographic entity enabled "the enlightened" to regard Istanbul as the proper location for the rebirth of the nation. For Mateos Mamurian, an editor and novelist from Izmir, who once chaired the National Executive Committee, nothing should have been expected from the millet leadership anyway, since its leaders were too busy fighting each other.[29]

Nonetheless, for the majority of Armenians in major urban centers the capital city continued to represent "the strength of the nation" while historical Armenia was an alien place. The literati of Istanbul devoted much time to discussing administrative details, resolving conflicts related to churches, charities, and schools. They called their efforts the *azgayin* or national business.

The program for progress and enlightenment proposed by the literati and the middle class of the capital acquired its legitimacy from contact with European cities and cultures as well as from the conviction that such a program had universal validity. It is not surprising, therefore, that the liberals applied their agenda for attaining enlightenment and progress to the provinces without consideration of the issues raised by the rural Armenians. The inherent values of the ideology and Istanbul Armenians' need for legitimacy became important factors in the belief of the urban liberals that their program provided a fundamental solution to the ills plaguing the rural population.

This belief was further encouraged by the spirit of the Tanzimat, which led many to believe the Porte was ready to support essential reforms. In fact, the Armenian National Assembly in Istanbul, in a daring and imaginative act, elected the "hayastantsi" Khrimian as patriarch. Khrimian began his brief tenure in Istanbul by encouraging provincial Armenians to submit reports on their social and economic problems to the Assembly. They followed his advice. Activist teachers and clergymen in the provinces helped communities prepare reports, which poured into Istanbul. Based on these reports, a final study indicated that, in addition to not having benefited in any way from the Tanzimat, provincial Armenians were heading toward economic ruin and suffering increasing social deprivation and dislocation, a process leading to the disintegration of Armenian collective life in the historic homeland as well as to total dehumanization. The report also made recommendations to end the obvious inequalities in taxation, justice, and religious intolerance, which, if enacted upon by the Porte, would alleviate the desperate situation. Furthermore, rather than denying the authority of the central government, the report asked the Porte to strengthen its position with regard to provincial governments to guarantee that local officials follow directives sent to them from a capital now interested in reforms.[30]

The Assembly was divided on the question of actually submitting the report to the Ottoman government. Some thought it would invite the Porte to question the loyalty of Armenian leaders, hence affect their privileged position in the capital. At the end, a milder version of the report was presented. Ultimately, it was discarded by the government and conveniently forgotten by the Assembly.[31]

Khrimian also sought, without success, a revision of the National Constitution in order to give provincial Armenians a larger share of representatives in the Assembly. The Constitution had ensured an absolute majority control by the Armenians of Istanbul. The patriarch realized that without proportional representation the cause of the provinces would be lost. He realized that the Istanbul bourgeoisie acted only in the interest of its own security and perception of Ottoman institutions. Moreover, he fought for the creation of a second *kaghakakan* ("civil" or "political") council, which would deal specifically with provincial issues. The existing council provided by the Constitution was composed of Istanbul Armenians who interpreted *kaghakakan* as civil, to mean largely non-religious matters, such as schools and orphanages.

Khrimian resigned in 1873. His support of provincial Armenians made him an enemy of many influential Armenians in Istanbul. His opponents accused him of arbitrary rule, hence of opposing the Constitution.[32] They also charged that Khrimian spent too much money on pantukhts, neglected the prestige of the Church, diminished the power of Istanbul in favor of the provinces, and supported the cause of the poor and oppressed at the expense of others. His critics disapproved of his closing the prison of the Patriarchate where opponents could be jailed by the order of the patriarch or the Assembly. They were dismayed at his refusal to use the state police to secure Armenian compliance to millet decisions. Finally, he spoke so much of the conditions and problems of the provinces, remarked an opponent, that he "endangered the nation."[33]

Khrimian's brief term became a test of Armenian liberalism for the middle class. The limitations of that liberalism were clearly exposed by its timid and reluctant approach to the question of reform. By acquiring the privilege of playing democracy in the capital, the Armenian intelligentsia and middle class assumed responsibility for absorbing the shocks of social discontent in the poverty-ridden rural areas of Western Armenia.

Thus the failure to achieve concrete reforms remained the more fundamental cause for Khrimian's resignation. The expectation that the millet system, however democratically designed, could be used to mediate a change in the structure of the Ottoman state was a subversion of the purpose for which the millet system had originally been established. The temporary enthusiasm of the Assembly in pursuing the cause Khrimian advocated had stretched to the limit of whatever ambiguity one could read into the role of the millet. The 1863 Constitution of the Armenian millet spoke eloquently of the rights and responsibilities between the Armenian collective and Armenian individuals; but it disregarded the more essential relationship between the Armenian individual and the Ottoman state while asserting that "in particular circumstances [the patriarch] is the medium of the execution of the orders of the Ottoman Government" with regard to the millet. The reverse, the right of the patriarch or the Assembly to represent the interests, and especially the complaints, of Armenians as a collective was not inherent in the document; it depended on the goodwill or political mood of the Porte.

A Bourgeois Nation

The urban enlightened continued the quest to reconcile its ideology of progress with the difficulties inherent in the situation. They believed a solution was on hand when European powers temporarily assumed the sponsorship of reform in the Ottoman Empire through the Treaty of Berlin in 1878. Confident that the Ottoman state could be coerced into implementing reforms in the Armenian provinces, the usually timid liberal Armenian community poised to lead the reforms; after all, no other segment of the people was better equipped to apply European concepts among Armenians.

While a number of writers expressed reservations with regard to the usefulness of Article 61 of that Treaty prescribing the reforms in the Armenian provinces, others wanted to see in it the ultimate opportunity for the realization of the liberal political program. The most important and effective spokesmen for that position were Patriarch Nerses Varjapetian and Bishop Maghakia Ormanian. Varjapetian had a vested interest in presenting the result of the Congress of Berlin (and at San Stefano before that) as a success: after all, he was responsible for the Armenian diplomatic initiatives. Ormanian was a highly educated, concerned, and ambitious clergyman. Soon after the Treaty was signed, the two put forth a vision, which constituted a close approximation to a bourgeois program for nation-building. In lectures and booklets they argued that the international concern for Armenia assured a rush toward the exploitation of its natural resources. Varjapetian was convinced that British capital would soon invade Western Armenia. The immediate task of the nation was to ensure that Armenian capital from coastal cities and Europe gained ownership and control of resources in Armenia and, by bringing progress and enlightenment, assure a better life for all. The nation was invited to send to Armenia its best industrialists and doctors, teachers and preachers, financiers and bankers. Capital and culture, until then viewed as Western commodities, were to be Armenianized to achieve what the diplomacy of begging had started.[34]

Ormanian emphasized the need for social harmony if the program was to succeed. Unity became the panacea for the problems of an inherently impotent institutional structure.[35] Ormanian argued that the Church was best equipped to bring about that unity.[36] He further argued that Armenianism should begin to break away from an abstract-intellectual context, and the promised reforms provided that opportunity. "If a person is inspired by the question of reforms," he stated in a lecture, "he would not consider it below him to labor [in Armenia], he would not consider it worthless to do commerce there or help the arts [crafts] flourish, or be a landlord and landowner there."[37] Ormanian developed his ideas further in a lecture in 1880 on the responsibilities of the youth. He urged provincial Armenian youth to learn reading and other technical skills. But it was important that Armenians do the teaching for, if the Europeans did it, they alone would benefit from it. Ormanian exhorted, "Those who know how to establish their interests in that land...the land will know how to reward its benefactor. Blessed are those who will be the first to undertake that task, since not only will they have given content to patriotism and be praised for it, but also because they will reap the profits of their endeavors and labors."[38]

Except for a few highly motivated teachers, history does not record an influx of capital or of men to the provinces neither Armenian nor British, not until the Armenian revolutionaries did later in the century. The waning of Western interest and increase in Ottoman oppression produced only a loss of appetite for issues related to the provinces among the liberals. The capital community finally made its peace with the Porte when the Patriarchate and the Assembly agreed not to meddle in affairs that were outside its sanctioned jurisdiction. Thus, the millet leadership could present *takrirs* ("petitions") regarding churches and monasteries, but not political matters.[39] The Assembly expressed its intention to remain within its prescribed limits by requesting that Ottoman censors cease the publication of the Istanbul-based newspaper *Meghu*. The editors of this maverick newspaper had dared to criticize the Assembly for its inaction regarding the situation of Armenians in the provinces.[40]

The Politicization of Culture

The ethnic identity of Armenians in the provinces was rooted in the historic land on which they lived. The residents of Van did not need to labor at cultural edifices or intellectual definitions to assert a link between themselves and history. Dead heroes and living legends served to integrate the physical environment of mountains, valleys, and rivers into the cultural environment that included ancient fortresses and medieval monasteries. The peasants' link to the land of Armenia was neither culturally inspired nor politically negotiable. Rather, it represented the most basic relationship between man and nature. The land was their source of livelihood, just as it had been for their ancestors throughout the centuries. This identity was not, therefore, in and by itself an acceptance or rejection of Ottoman rule, just as Armenians' attachment to the land was neither a threat to nor a confirmation of Ottoman territorial integrity.

The politics of rural people revolved around survival, which hinged on the basics of land, water, harvest, and taxation. The goal of the peasantry was to create an environment where the preservation of traditional norms was possible as well as desirable for each successive generation and where change was manageable. All else was judged within this context. Irrelevant national or international politics were reduced to legend. Legends included words uttered by kings and foreign potentates, words that were adjusted instantly into local terminology. These legends were measured against accepted local wisdom, which was ready to analyze and amplify the significance of events that had relevance to their own affairs. Whether there to oppress or to assist, the outsider had to adjust to the world of the peasant and, to some extent, become a part of it. Culture had meaning only if understood in the widest social sense. As such, it could not be removed or alienated from politics through bureaucratic or legal definitions.

The religious-ethnic definition of the Armenian, imposed by the Ottoman system and glorified in the capital, had not really pervaded the depths of consciousness of Armenians in the provinces. To be sure, the millet was still the structure through which civil matters were formally regulated; Armenians continued to adjust to and explain in this context the routine policies and daily practices of the ruling Ottomans. But in the provinces, especially in those areas with the least amount of formal cultural development, political-economic oppression meant cultural oppression. The corollary was also true. Cultural enlightenment was understood as political change; cultural pride was not dissociated from political self-respect. The middle class and clergy, on the other hand, continued to believe that culture, economy, and politics were distinct activities as alien from each other as their professions often were from the course of Ottoman policies and developments. The provincial Armenian, totally dependent on domestic laws, practices, and conditions, could not afford such delusions. The patriotism of the Armenian peasant and town dweller (who often lived not so distant from rural life), consisted of a simple attachment to a land invested with historical and spiritual significance. Patriotism was a natural part of their identity. The new, culture-laden *azgasirutiune* of Istanbul had been a distortion of the patriotism, *hayrenasirutiune*, of the provinces.[41]

This patriotism was injured before and after the Russo-Turkish War. Fires of suspicious origin destroyed the Armenian market sectors in a number of cities, including that of Van in 1876. Confiscation of Armenian land by Turks and Kurds became a common occurrence in the Diarbekir and Van provinces. But it was the war itself that most devastated the economy and fueled the patriotism of provincial Armenians. Ottoman armies passed through Armenian provinces as if the latter were being conquered anew. The armies destroyed crops, treated civilians cruelly, and made extraordinarily harsh demands for provisions, which turned a requisitions policy into officially organized looting. Western Armenians were filled less with the celebrated sympathies toward the Russian armies than with outrage against the Turkish soldiers. It was as if the Ottoman state sought to punish the Christian Armenians for the sins of Balkan peoples.

It was to these devastated people that a few urban liberals such as Mkrtich Portukalian and Martiros Sareyan came to speak of enlightenment, progress, and national pride following the Treaty of Berlin. Their words could be absorbed by the rural population only in the context of its own, yet unarticulated, political agenda.

Consequently, as soon as Western pressure decreased, the Porte adopted a policy of systematic repression under the Sultan Abdul Hamid II. The sultan lacked the commitment to social and political reforms that some of his predecessors had. He perceived his role primarily as the embattled ruler of a once-powerful empire now threatened by foreign encroachments. The millions of subjects of different religious and ethnic backgrounds whose welfare depended on his policies were significant only in relation to the higher and narrower goal of the survival of his state and the preservation of the status quo. He was open to modernization in those areas that strengthened the army and the power of the state. Thus the government was extremely sensitive to any signsthat might have signaled the rise of a political consciousness among Armenians. It therefore established strict censorship on all publications and scrutinized the activities and words of any element that might have given independent articulation to Armenian discontent.

Ultimately, the efforts of the government backfired. Its attempts to prevent the politicization of culture through the suppression of culture radicalized discontent. Names of historical figures such as former kings, once devoid of any emotional charge, acquired political significance when uttered against the laws of censorship. Ordinary people were transformed into heroes and martyrs for having used words such as *azatutiune* (freedom). For the new heroes, the act of imprisonment, exile, or torture by a hated government became more ingratiating than the original infraction of the law.

Eventually, these incidents acquired a historical significance. But in the eighties they were still isolated cases, which no one interpreted as the beginning of a revolution. Nonetheless, at that time it was clear that the situation in the Armenian provinces was rapidly deteriorating and the community was threatened on many fronts. In a long and bitter piece of correspondence to Mateos Mamurian in November 1883, Bishop Garegin Srvantstiants, who once dissuaded his compatriots from converting to Russian orthodoxy to secure protection, noted:

Although it is the compatriots in Akn who do not let me leave, the state of national affairs in Istanbul and confused situation on the roads also are considerations in my decision to stay here a while longer. Let conferences, plenipotentiaries, 16ers [sic, reference to those supporting Article 16 of the Treaty of San Stefano, 1878] and 61ers [article 61 of the Treaty of Berlin] give and take, let writers and editors beat their drums without coming to their senses, without recognizing the ones who are actually pulling the strings and watching them fight, and without realizing who is in fact benefiting from the noise we are making. We see the paths of the foreigners and follow them, although our purpose is to reach our fatherland. The path of the foreigner leads to the city of the foreigner; yet we get there, we get tied down there, and then we tell our nation that that is the path to the fatherland. Even more amazing are those who knew the foreigner well and used to point out its traps to the nation, warning us to run away; those same [individuals] are sitting today in the halls of congress [of the foreigner] as agents from within and from without. There is no need to write their names; the ones who were close to you, you know well; the ones at a distance you called them glory-seekers. How many have we seen of the devoted who turned devotees of profit and glory; self-denying and patriotic ones who, in the name of the Armenian Question, sought personal benefit and glory; those who secured their cuts from the funds collected for the starving only declare themselves benevolent; those who opened schools for the benefit of their relatives and, having robbed the nation through fundraising, closed down the schools, leaving to the nation only the blame for their own acts and the deficit of their spending. They planted a Catholicos in Sis and now are forcing the fruits of that action down the throat of the nation; they assign the glory of Zion to the Patriarch, but his debt to the nation; the prelates they have assigned to the largest sees, the nuncios and directives they forwarded have resulted in parishes and districts that remain unattended and in people subject to oppression; a number of Armenians are rotting in prison, others are trampled upon by bandits; these [Armenians] are denied protection since speaking on their behalf and sup-plication are being left unanswered by the *barekhnam* ["the one who takes good care," an adjective used for the Sultan]. Fallen materially and exhausted spiritu-ally, times such as this I do not believe Armenians have had to endure. The wheel of 61 turns in many directions and some of the children are running behind it, falling in ditch after ditch. The wheel is turning North. Finally the Catholicos too has decided to act [but] the commotion on that subject is meaningless. The murderous and roaming tribes from Russia are filling the Armenian province on this side; Armenians, cut off from the land and from the hope of land, are forced out...[42]

Beyond the hopelessness it conveys, the letter suggests a relation-ship between corruption in community institutions and inadequacy at the diplomatic level. Most importantly, it constitutes a summary of the criticism directed toward the liberal program of the Armenian middle class from the perspective of provincial Armenians and a few urban radicals.

By 1881 the right of Istanbul to lead Armenians was challenged radically. Arsen Tokhmakhian, a student who toured the provinces and published his thoughts, reasoned:

The Western intelligentsia is in Istanbul. They are fine people, writers and rhetoricians. But they are living in an imaginary world. They are solely concerned with the Patriarch-ate and the National Assembly. They declare each other great men and geniuses. But what have they done to deserve those adjectives?[43]

Khrimian and the provincial intelligentsia of the sixties and sev-enties were unable to shed their original belief in the goodwill and benevolence inspired by an unadulterated Christianity. Others were more willing to project the existing conflicts and divisiveness into the past and learn new lessons. Tokhmakhian argued that a cohe-sive, undifferentiated, and idealized history that failed to relate the desperate present to the distant and glorified past was an obstacle to a clear vision of the future:

Ancient Armenians have never lived, never ruled as one nation, as children of one fatherland. They were divided into many tribes, which eroded each others' strength in incessant struggles... The turning point at which one can speak of an all-national idea came when the *nakharar* [nobility] and dynastic houses were eradicated from within, leaving behind the sorry consequences that are still with us...[44]

Tokhmakhian too wanted to glorify Armenians, but he had a different group in mind:

What has kept our nation going is the working class, not religion. It is the nation that has kept religion, and suffered because of it; while the Church was unable to keep the old colonies, the peasant was able to preserve the nation... I beg you to turn your attention to and study all aspects of the life of the peasants who constitute the root of nationhood; [I beg you] to know him and the world in which he lives, which is called fatherland.[45]

It was obvious that by the early 1880s the Armenian millet, the Ottoman state, and the Western powers had failed to fulfill their promise of reform for the majority of Armenians living on their historic lands. While the search for alternative strategies began earnestly with the founding of the newspaper *Armenia* in Marseilles by Mkrtich Portukalian, a shift in political terminology had already taken place. Patriotism had come to signify a whole range of new problems. The role of nationalism itself, and therefore its historical significance, had moved toward a radical direction.

Notes

1.   H. M. Ghazarian, "Arevmtian hayastan" [Western Armenia], *Hay zhoghovrdi patmutiune* [History of the Armenian People], Ds. B. Aghayan, et al., eds., (Erevan, 1964) V, pp. 20-25; also, by the same author, *Arevmtahayeri sotsial-tntesakan katsutiune 1800-1870 tt* [The socio-economic condition of Western Armenians during 1800-1870] (Erevan, 1967), pp. 377-378; Sarkis Atamian, *The Armenian Community* (New York, 1955), pp. 29-30.

2.   Louise Nalbandian, *The Armenian Revolutionary Movement* (Berkeley and Los Angeles, 1967), pp. 43-45; Mikayel Varandian, *Haykakan sharzhman nakhapatmutiune* [Prehistory of the Armenian movement] (Geneva, 1913), II, pp. 73-94.

3.   Garnik Guzalian, *Hay kaghakakan mtki zargatsume ev H.H. Dashnaktsutiune* [The development of Armenian political thought and the A.R. Federation] (Paris, 1927), p. 42. In Eastern Armenia Sedrak Manandian expressed the same view: "How should we cover it up? We are all fanatic lusavorchakans (members of the Apostolic Church); we consider Armenianism and the creed of the Lusavorich as one, since that is our national peculiarity," quoted in Guzalian, p. 87. See also Mikayel Varandian, *Haykakan sharzhman nakhapatmutian* (Geneva, 1912), I, 287-291.

4.   H. Chamurjian-Teroyents in *Erevak* (Istanbul, 1861), no. 109.

5.   H., *Khosk vasn hayrenasirutian* [Discourse in favor of Patriotism] (Vienna, 1862).

6.   Ibid., p. 23-24. In other publications the Mekhitarists expressly criticized Balkan and Italian national movements as well, and generally speaking, democratic tenden-

cies in political movements. See also Ghazarian, "Arevmtahay hasarakakan hosanknere" [Western Armenian social currents], *Hay zhoghovrdi patmutune*, V, p. 428.

7. A. J. Sussnitzki, "Ethnic Division of Labor" in Charles Issawi, ed., *The Economic History of the Middle East, 1800-1914* (1967), pp. 114-125; Stanford J. Shaw and Ezel K. Shaw, *History of the Ottoman Empire and Modem Turkey* (London, New York, Melbourne, 1977), II, pp. 242, 244.

8. See, for example, James Etmekjian, *The French Influence on the Western Armenian Renaissance: 1843-1915* (New York, 1964); Nalbandian, pp. 32-34

9. *Hayastan* (Istanbul), July 27, 2846. See also V. Ghukasian, "Arevmtahay lusavorichnere ev hayastan terte" [The Western Armenian enlighteners and the Newspaper Hayastan], *Banber Erevani Hamalsarani*, 2 (1969):214-224. The concept of national development as a prerequisite for progress is also discussed by Guzalian p. 59.

10. Varandian, II, p. 6.

11. Ibid., p. 66.

12. Dj. Aramian, *Zeytuntsik ev lusavorchakan hayk* [The People of Zeytun and Apostolic Armenians] (Istanbul, 1867).

13. Varandian, II, p. 261.

14. Avedis Sanjian, *The Armenian Communities in Syria under Ottoman Dominion* (Cambridge, 1965), pp. 40-41.

15. *Masis*, July 5, 1861.

16. Ibid., December 31, 1859.

17. Ibid.

18. Garegin Srvantsiants, "Hayrenasirutiun ev hayrenik" [Patriotism and fatherland], *Ardsvi Vaspurakan*, 3(1861):92.

19. Ibid., pp. 93-94.

20. *Ardsvi Vaspurakan*, 1 (1862).

21. Ibid.

22. Vardan Mamikonian, a commander and later a saint, led a losing battle in 451 against still Zoroastrian Persians who wanted Armenia to give up Christianity.

23. Ibid., 10 (1862):289-308.

24. Ibid., pp. 289-308.

25. Much of satirist Hakob Paronian's writings depict not only the superficiality of the claims of westernization of an essentially "oriental" community in Istanbul, but also the use of that claim to ignore the appeals of Armenians in the provinces.

26. *Ardsvi Vaspurakan*, 1(1857):1-3.

27. Ibid., 3 (1862-63): 79.

28. Khrimian Hayrik complained that the Armenians of Istanbul knew more about Europe than about Armenia; see Sarukhan, *Haykakan khentirn ev azgayin sahmanadrutiune* [The Armenian Question and the National Constitution] (Tiflis, 1912), p. 61. An 1850 geography textbook has scant reference to elements of Armenia's geography in a general chapter on Asia; Agheksander Vardapet Baljian, *Ashkharhagrutiun ev hrahangs* (Vienna, 1850), pp. 123-134.

29. Rouben Berberian, "Hay masonnere ev 'ser' otiake polso mech" [Armenian masons and the "Love" Lodge in Istanbul], *Hairenik Monthly* 5 (1937): 80-81. The novelist Raffi thought the National Constitution was a weapon in the hands of the Ottoman government to distract Armenians from their real problems; see his *Erkeri zhoghovadsu* (Erevan, 1958), IX, p. 263.

30. Varandian, II, pp. 50-63. For a detailed presentation of this report, see Lilian Etmekjian, "The Armenian National Assembly of Turkey and Reform," *Armenian Review*, 1 (1976): 38-40.

31. L. Etmekjian, pp. 42-43.
32. The charges of anti-constitutional behavior were leveled against Khrimian when he based some of his actions on the "spirit rather than the letter of the Constitution." The patriarch's resignation speech included the response to the charge: "The pages of the Constitution are even gentler than the petals of a rose; if you handle them rudely, they will fall apart.... I want to embrace the Constitution, but I do not want to press it so hard as to strangle it."
33. Hayk Ajemian, *Hayots Hayrik* (Tiflis, 1929), p. 452.
34. Berberian, pp. 158-160.
35. The lecture was printed in booklet form under the title *Miutiun Hayutian* [Unity of Armenians] (Istanbul, 1879). The lecture was delivered in Scutar for the Krtasirats Miutiun, or Education Society.
36. Ibid., pp. 24-38.
37. Ibid., pp. 39-42.
38. The lecture was delivered in Istanbul on February 24 and published the same year as *Hay yeritasardutian* [To the Armenian Youth]; p. 39.
39. Rafik Hovannisian, *Arevmtahay azgayin-azatagrakan sharzhumnere ev karini "Pashtpan Hayreniats" kazmakerputiune* [Western Armenian Liberation Movements and the "Defenders of the Fatherland" organization of Karin (Erzerum)] (Erevan, 1965), p. 205. The instruction was given in 1880. Reporting that the Porte would no longer accept takrirs on provincial Armenians, Hakob Paronian wrote: I suggest that a letter be forwarded to Kurds to inform them that henceforth they should spare our property, our lives, and our honor and violate only our religion; see Paronian's *Amboghdjakan gordser* [Complete Works] (1962-1977), IV, pp. 447-448.
40. Berberian, p. 125.
41. This explains, at least in part, the unusually enthusiastic reception in the provinces accorded the adoption of a National Constitution in 1863. The Polsetsis knew what they were getting; the provincials did not make the necessary distinctions between millet and state to avoid disappointment; Rafik Hovannisian, p. 220; Ajemian, p. 556; Artak Darbinian, *Hay azatagrakan sharzhman oreren* [Of the days of the movement for Armenian liberation] (Paris, 1947), p. 118.
42. Srvantstiants to Mamurian, November 1, 1883; in *Divan hayots patmutian*, G. Aghanian, ed., (Tiflis, 1915), XIII, pp. 451-454.
43. Arsen Tokhmakhian, *Hayreniki pahandjnere ev hay gughatsin* [The needs of the fatherland and the Armenian peasant] (Tiflis, 1881), p. 7.
44. Arsen Tokhmakhian, *Masis lerneri haravayin storotner* [The southern slopes of the Masis mountains] (Tiflis, 1882), Book I, pp. 21-23.
45. Tokhmakhian, *Hayreniki pahandjnere...*, pp. 60-61.

3

The Changing Armenian Self-Image in the Ottoman Empire: *Rayahs* and Revolutionaries

To speak of the self-image of the Armenian under Ottoman rule during the last century of that empire is to consider two basic ingredients of modern Armenian history. First, Armenians did not have a uniform view of themselves. The content and characteristics of being Armenian varied according to class, geographic location, and level of education. Second, whereas some groups maintained the same self-image throughout many decades of change and political upheaval, others, threatened by social, economic, and spiritual degeneration, strove to change theirs.

Radical changes in the self-image of some Armenians accompanied changes in political ideology; in fact, the docile and meek Armenian, given the name *rayah*, or herd, had to define himself differently before he could take up arms against his oppressor and become a revolutionary. Moreover, to bring about such a change was the aim of systematic efforts by political writers and activists on the one hand, and the single acts of rebelliousness by individuals acting independently on the other.

Three Images

At the cost of simplifying social structures, it is possible to delineate three distinct self-images of the Armenian under Ottoman rule.

The first is the self-image of the Armenian in Zeytun, an Armenian district in the Taurus Mountains in Cilicia. He is the fierce fighter of the mountains, the embattled remnant of a kingdom that had long disappeared, but the autonomy of which was tolerated by Ottoman rulers before they discovered that for the empire to survive in the modern world there had to be centralization of authority and uniformity of rule. Despite the significance that outsiders attached to the rebellions in Zeytun throughout the nineteenth century, the Zeytuntsi regarded himself as the heir to a medieval principality whose affinity to the successors of the crusading European states was at least as strong as that which he felt toward contemporary Armenian society. Limited in number and in vision, the Zeytuntsi perceived of himself as the only worthwhile Armenian, and of Zeytun as the natural center of the Armenian world. The Armenian people had to come to Zeytun, spiritually speaking. Nineteenth-century rebellions against central authority and diplomatic demarches to European powers, the latter reminiscent of the policies followed by the last of the Cilician kings, were not acts of political imagination. Rather, they were steps undertaken for the preservation of the old order, the now threatened autonomy.

A second, dominant image of the Armenian is found in the prosperous, contented Armenian communities in Istanbul, the capital, in the coastal cities, and to some extent in other major cities, especially Izmir. Originally typified by the *sarraf*, or banker, this was later to be supplanted by the successful merchant and liberal intellectual or administrator and professional associated with the government.

Having rid themselves of the dangerous specter of involvement in the political affairs of the Ottoman state, the Istanbul Armenian cherished the label "faithful" millet or community, a euphemism for subservience to the Porte. Here the Armenian conceived of himself as a member of a protected community, directly or indirectly under the wings of the sultan, without whose benevolent attitude he certainly could not have achieved economic success. To sustain that image, the Istanbul Armenian had to loosen his ties with the rest of the Armenian people: the poor in his own city or those in the provinces. His interests were confined to the *azg* (nation), and the azg manifested itself through charitable, religious, and educational activities within the confines of the National Assembly. These ruled out the possibility of any involvement in politics as a community. Here in the context of the millet a good Armenian was involved in the elections of the neighborhood church board of trustees, supported the local school, and read newspapers that reported at length European fashions and parliamentary debates.

This was the self-image of a community that associated itself with European progress and enlightenment and followed the novelties of technology largely divorced from Ottoman urban culture. The cultural awakening, the fervor of adopting the Armenian Constitution, the idea of an Armenian parliament, all primarily beneficial to the Istanbul community, came to reinforce the belief that the "azg," the Armenian, was doing well, was progressing.

As long as the conflict within the azg was limited to debates between liberals and conservatives, the Armenian in Istanbul could feel contented in his status. Indeed, it must have been a rare privilege to be able to disagree with each other, to play democracy, and discuss fine points of parliamentary rules. The Armenian in this category congratulated himself for his ability to follow in the footsteps of Western Enlightenment, and for having done so without resorting to violence, through the sheer understanding of the game of politics. The Armenian in Istanbul was clever and diplomatic, he had patience, he was cautious. He had become economically secure, and this showed his intelligence. But if he avoided confrontation with the state it was not only because he had no need for it but also because he was refined in mind and manners. Again, culture and progress turned for him into tools, which would justify his disdain for the uncultured peasant, for the exclusion of that peasant from the concept of azg.

The third dominant self-image is that of the Armenian in the provinces. He is typified by the defenseless, poor, dispossessed Armenian—the rayah. He is oppressed by the political system: looted, killed, and raped by the Kurd; exploited by the Turkish or Kurdish landlord, tax collector, administrator, and the Armenian moneylender. He is even despised by his own poverty-ridden parish priest who derived his sense of superiority from his clerical garb. The rayah has no world or vision beyond his daily existence. His is a dehumanized existence, the promises of an afterlife notwithstanding. Even his vague knowledge of a more dignified national experience in the past sensed through his attachment to the land, extant monuments of grandeur, and tales transmitted from generation to generation was challenged by fearful preachers who reduced religion to an explanation of poverty and history to a justification for subservience.

The first self-image was drawn from the historical memory of the Zeytuntsis and was eventually destroyed or otherwise absorbed by changes in Ottoman policy and Armenian political ideology.

But the other two were essentially derived from the conditions imposed by the dominant power to perpetuate acquiescence and subservience. Another common trait between the second and third otherwise contradictory self-images is that both survived the test of time. Although for reasons other than their pervasive veracity, the "contented Armenian" and the "deprived Armenian" became images in the eyes of modern-day writers.

The Genocide of 1915 has been the great equalizer in Armenian history. Since the historical and political conflict between Armenians and Turks has now moved to the field of historiography, Turkish or pro-Turkish historians have universalized the image of the "contented Armenian." By so doing they have aimed at undercutting the legitimacy of Armenian revolutionary activities, implied a pervasively benevolent Ottoman rule, and even represented the Armenian as that wealthy class of the empire that exploited the Turkish masses. Armenian or pro-Armenian writers, on the other hand, have perpetuated the image of the "deprived Armenian," since the massacres were directed against Armenians regardless of economic or social status and Armenians had a most compact existence in the historic provinces where the Genocide was the most effective.

Beginning to Change with Words, Thoughts, and Acts

Historiography has failed to explain the rise of the revolutionary, the *fedayee*, or guerrilla fighter. As can be expected of statist historians, apologists for Ottoman rule have ascribed revolutionary activities to foreign agitators and constantly referred to fedayees as terrorists, rather than making an attempt to understand the historical phenomenon. Sympathizers, on the other hand, have either taken the rise of the movement for granted or attributed it to the exposure of the deprived to new ideological tenets.

These explanations for the change of the Armenian from rayah to revolutionary are not adequate. Objective, historical realities, however repressive politically, oppressive economically, and discriminative socially, are not of themselves sufficient for latent discontent to become a manifest movement of protest and revolution. This is true particularly when the self-image of the rayah contains its own explanation for oppression and constitutes its own expiation rooted in extra-territorial arrangements. The assumption that exposure to new ideas is sufficient to bring about a change in political behavior has yet to be proven.

A number of writers in the early 1880s had realized that it was necessary for the Armenian to liberate himself from the mold imposed by historical and political conditions, if the Armenian people were to arouse themselves from the stupor of a rayah existence.

It was Mkrtich Portukalian who distinctly pointed out and systematically criticized the many areas of individual and collective behavior, which, as a result of centuries of Ottoman domination, perpetuated the sullen acceptance of a degenerated existence. Portukalian had been one of the early liberal and devoted activists in Istanbul and later the provinces, particularly Van, where he had started a teacher's school before being exiled by the government. Having settled in Marseilles in 1885, he began the publication of the first pro-revolutionary newspaper *Armenia*. Portukalian never committed himself fully to an armed revolution and was unable to free himself totally from the constantly wavering Armenian liberalism. Yet he played a crucial role in legitimizing the concept of a revolution and, through his newspaper, in attracting younger devotees abroad and inspiring his many followers in Western Armenia or the Eastern provinces of the empire where most Armenians lived.

Throughout his editorials and signed articles, Portukalian strove toward the development of a new Armenian identity. He criticized Armenian "sins" and extolled Armenian "virtues" in *Vardapetaran Hayastani Azatutian* (Catechism for the Liberation of Armenia), a booklet written in the format of questions and answers and printed more than once.[1]

The sins listed in this pamphlet included the migration of Armenians from their ancestral lands to become laborers elsewhere, denigration of the Armenian name by engaging in fraudulent actions, profit-oriented "patriotism," and betrayal of other Armenians. He severely criticized the habitual use of proverbs and maxims, which perpetuate a lowly self-image among Armenians.

Having rid the language of its inbuilt dispiriting, denigrating advice, Portukalian offered his own alternative of what an Armenian should feel and think. The good Armenian is one whose sole religion is the liberation of Armenia from foreign rule and whose only prayer is: "Oh Merciful God, help me liberate Armenia."[2] Armenian virtues include giving one's possessions and blood to the cause of the liberation, doing one's best to convince all to go to Armenia, and assisting all those who are laboring for the liberation of Armenia.[3] Thus the "sincere" Armenian is the one who strives for and assists in the task of liberation. All others "are useless Armenians and useless human beings."[4]

By pointing out the unconscious elements that had permeated the Armenian psyche, Portukalian made it possible to deal with obstacles to the transformation of the Armenian. And by elevating the task of liberation of the homeland to the level of a religion—one that even for this devout man would temporarily replace and permanently change the accepted notion of deity—he provided Armenians with a frame of identification that was against and outside the mold imposed by the millet. He asserted: "Political and religious principles justify revolt against the government, in fact it is a holy duty... The souls of those who die in battle go to heaven: they become martyrs and their names are commemorated forever by the Holy Church."[5]

In addition to writing his own articles and publications, Portukalian opened the pages of his newspaper to others who described the effect of Ottoman rule on the Armenian personality and mentality. Thus, Avetis Nazarbek, a Russian-Armenian activist who later helped found the Social Democratic Hnchakian Party (SDHP), discussed the child-rearing and educational system in Armenian society. The article concluded: "The education at home and at school has destroyed within us our strength, our self-confidence, and the initiative to speak and act freely according to our beliefs." The title of the article was, characteristically, "Inch enk ev inch piti linenk" (What We Are and What We Shall Be).[6]

A few writers, including Portukalian, were equally critical of higher education, regarded by the liberal establishment as the panacea for the Armenian problem. Portukalian himself observed that Europeanization rather than dedication to liberation was the ultimate effect of higher education on Armenians.[7]

Even agriculture, the preoccupation of the majority of Armenians, came under criticism because of the implications it had within the existing social relations and the impact it had on the Armenian. A writer from Van pointed out that the Armenian's involvement in agriculture was regarded by the non-Armenian ruling groups as a symptom of cowardice and his continued attachment to the land as a sign of his continued acceptance of his lower status. In addition, economic relations and the laws of the land insured his continued economic oppression and placed him in a position where mere survival would be his sole concern.[8]

Once the vicious circle was identified in all its dimensions, the status of the rayah presented the subject with an existential conflict. To continue accepted behavior would only perpetuate the system, and, under the circumstances, tighten the chains of oppression—a certainty that he could no longer accept. On the one hand, the promise of reform within the Ottoman and millet systems, even though unfulfilled, had legitimized Armenian grievances and raised expectations of a better life. On the other hand, the largely rudimentary education supplied in the provinces by pioneers like Portukalian and Sareyan had provided the new generation with an alternative image of the Armenian that included organized Armenian armies under ancient and Armenian kings and the heroics of Vardan and his associates. The Armenian could now find a historical, personalized model from his own history for taking matters in his own hands. He could find legitimacy within an alternative self-image, one that included the possibility of breaking the vicious circle through one's own efforts.

That the conflict was lived on the most basic, individual level can be seen from a number of articles published in Armenia and, subsequently, elsewhere. One writer, working in Manchester, England asked the basic question in the title of his article, "What Makes You a Human Being?" The answer was a clear statement: "We need a revolution to be able to answer 'freedom'"[9] Yet another contributor from Van thought that the "issue was honor..." Man without honor was dead. "If we want to live we must defend our honor... There is nothing left but revolution."[10]

While revolution remained a vague concept for some years, the dynamics of change on the individual level soon became apparent. It was often the single, personalized act of rebellion of an individual that transformed the life of that individual as well as the life of the community sharing the experience. Many are the examples of young Armenians who, by "impulse," usually ascribed to adolescent rebelliousness, objected to some act or insult from a bureaucrat, tax collector, or local gendarme that was otherwise accepted as routine occurrences accepted as part of one's fate. That single act of non-acceptance, occasionally turned into retribution against the perpetrator, would automatically make him an outlaw, a marked man.

Under the new circumstances, the individual would perceive his new status as more befitting to his evolving new image. He would find in his single act the basis for a new self-definition, he would "become" that act of rebellion. His new identity, based on the rejection of what he perceived to be injustice, acquired its own dynamics since injustice was widespread and deeply ingrained in the system. As a "social bandit," he became the prototype of the fedayee. Fearing for his life, his family would give him moral and psychological support. The community would be polarized; many, while fearing wholesale retribution, would understand him. They might make him a hero, tell tales about him, and thus participate in the making of the new self-image.

More than the tactical implications of his battles and beyond the ideology, which was formulated on the intellectual level, the fedayee was participating in a revolution: his own. The act of becoming a guerrilla fighter was the assertion, rather reassertion, of Armenian virility. He would regain his and his people's virility not only by the conscious forces of the intellect that get to know the past, glorify its forgotten heroes, and establish a direct lineage between the soldiers of the past and the present, but also through the living of the heroic act, by letting oneself live the almost irrational impulse of self-sacrifice, the ultimate act of martyrdom in the form of death on the battlefield for the cause. That experience, lived mentally a thousand times, would give sufficient meaning and respect to his life, to give it away as a worthwhile offering.

What is occasionally referred to as the "political romanticism" of Armenian revolutionaries was, in fact, the process of dignifying life in order to value its loss, to convince others of the worthiness of his cause, and to inspire them. The political corollary of this process— to die willingly in order to make the lives of others worth living— was certainly present. But the process remained an individual one through which the fedayee cleansed himself, and through himself, the sins of the collective.

One of the most rigid rules for becoming a guerrilla fighter was abstention from relationships with women, platonic or otherwise. Although the rule was usually defended for tactical and security reasons, the reverence with which it was held and the strictness with which it was obeyed indicate that abstention had a deeper meaning. It is possible that the fedayee had to absolve himself as well as past generations of the sin of being unable to defend his women from rape and kidnapping by conquerors, and that he had no right to such relations until he had regained his honor and proven his manhood in his own eyes. It is also possible that abstention was meant to show unequivocal devotion to the cause.

It is hardly an accident that those devoted to the liberation movement called it the "Holy Task" (*Surb Gordz*), that the people were called the devoted "disciples" (*arakyalner*), and that the ritual during the induction of a fedayee or revolutionary group duplicated the rite of baptism. Similarly, on the eve of battle, fedayees took communion and heard speeches glorifying martyrdom much as Armenian soldiers had done in A.D. 451, on the eve of the Battle of Vardanank for the cause of Armenian religious and cultural freedom.

The activities, real or imagined, of the fighters gave rise to a new genre of literature: the revolutionary songs. Spreading fast, those songs extolled the heroism of individual soldiers and served to spread the gospel of new values. Interestingly enough, many of the themes in these songs echo the problems identified earlier by writers and activists.

One of the recurring themes is the changing relationship between the Armenian and agriculture. In one song a mother from the much-ravaged Mush district begs the guerrilla fighters to take with them her beloved and only son and pleads with him to

> Leave the field, the plow and the plow tail...
> Play a little with the rifle,
> So that we are no longer fair game for the Kurd.[11]

"A Voice Thundered" relates the story of those who "left the field and instead of shovels took up rifles."[12] Armenians from the highlands who had not lost their fighting spirit acquired added meaning in the new context. In "The Brave of Talvorik" a youth exclaims

> I am the strong fighter of Talvorik,
> Not cowardly like the city-dweller,
> Child of the mountain, son of the rocks
> I am the remnant of the ancient, brave Armenians.
>
> I am the strong son of Talvorik
> And do not bow to the Turk;
> The free youth of rocky mountains,
> I have never seen a plow nor a plow tail.[13]

In the "Song of the Soldier's Mother," the mother informs her son that on that particular morning she is giving him arms instead of his usual books and that he is expected to go to the battlefield instead of the classroom.[14] A young man chides his well-built friend for "Knowing how to love but not how to die."[15] The qualities of the new Armenian are described in a song devoted to Aghbiur Serob, one of the most admired among guerrilla leaders:

Let him come he who is courageous,
Let him come he who thinks nobly,
Let him come he who has honor,
Let him come he whose bullet does not stray,
Let him come he who loves Serob.[16]

Similar qualifications were required of Armenians who joined the early political groups organized in the 1880s and the later revolutionary parties. It should be pointed out that the formation of these groups was partly a response to appeals for "unity" and "organization" in the press. This should seem paradoxical since Armenians under Ottoman rule were "unified" and "organized." By definition, under the millet system, any act that created another basis for grouping Armenians was also an act of creating distinctions between those who were part of the new group and those who were not.

The difference was, of course, that the unity and organization of the millet served the Ottoman state by insuring the subservience of the Armenian majority through catering to the politically harmless needs of the dominant Armenian minority within the community. As elsewhere, the unity of all under the millet had stifled diversity in points of view and the expression of conflicts.

A Question of Identity

Thus, the calls for organization in the 1880s were, in fact, assertions that alternative forms of identification and solidarity were needed. The appeals for unity were an invitation to unite behind an idea other than the millet, on a basis other than the simple fact of being Armenian and Christian. In effect, the consequence of the proposed unity would be to disunite the Armenian community, since not all disapproved of the function and goals of the millet; it would bring together those whose needs and interests were ignored by the millet hierarchy.

The early political groups and the revolutionary parties later provided that alternative. Members had to be dedicated above all to the idea of liberation, cooperation with one another, and strict discipline. They were sworn to secrecy and accepted severe punishment for breaches of security. Membership in those groups in and by itself was seen as a privilege and acquired a mystical aura. Yet despite the necessity of secrecy surrounding their activities, members of the early groups felt a deep-seated compulsion to somehow manifest their new identity and share it with the community. Thus in the 1880s the

Sev Khach (Black Cross, a name adopted most probably to indicate its policy of placing a black cross mark in front of the name of any member who became a traitor by cooperating with the authorities, thus marking him for death) of Van paraded in the streets of the city. The *Pashtpan Hayreniats* (Defenders of the Fatherland), established in 1881 Erzerum, printed membership cards despite many warnings from sympathetic observers such as Khrimian of the dangers involved in having any written documents. The group was liquidated and its members imprisoned when these cards were discovered by the local gendarmerie.

Finally, a word must be said regarding the phenomenon of political assassinations, which in Armenian political literature is referred to as the *deror* (derived from the word "terror," with the positive connotation of justified execution). All Armenian revolutionary groups and parties functioning in Western Armenia accepted the principle of political assassination as part of their tactics. Some did so with reluctance, others with enthusiasm. The deror served many purposes. At times it was used as a form of warfare against the Ottoman state; Armenians could not wage conventional battles. Revolutionaries struck down government officials as a show of power. More often than not these officials were the more cruel and unscrupulous; their elimination would provide relief to the populace on the local level. Such actions were also expected to spread fear among remaining functionaries who were thereby warned that their behavior would not go unpunished.

Deror was also used against Armenian traitors cooperating with the police to the detriment of the patriots. Such incidents were not rare. The motivations of Armenians in this category—monetary gain, advancement in office, fear, association with the powerful, or simply being looked upon favorably by Turkish officials in time of wholesale retribution—were seen by revolutionaries as signs of the degradation of Armenian character under Ottoman rule, a degradation that was to be halted. Equally important, then, was the function of deror as an accessible means of warfare and as a "tool to transform the Armenian personality and create a popular movement."[17]

By engulfing the whole being, rational and irrational, conscious and subconscious, revolutionaries strove to redefine the Armenian. Being a good Armenian was no longer a birthright and could no longer be equated with being subservient. Certainly, there was as much "faith" involved in the pursuit of the "Holy Task" as there was in the pursuit of the more accepted goal of mere survival. Yet this faith was now directed toward the ideals of a better Armenian and creating a better Armenia as projected, ultimately, in the outlook and goals of the Armenian revolutionary parties.

The parties, first the SDHP (Social Democratic Hnchakian Party) and later the ARF (Armenian Revolutionary Federation), assigned the Armenian a new role. To become a man, he had to participate in history. To become a progressive man, he had to have partaken in the general evolution of mankind as well as contribute to the building of its future.

For weak, helpless, and powerless people, what better ally than the iron rules of history, such as the ultimate redemption of the downtrodden, as advocated by the dominant socialist thought of the time? While national history would liberate the Armenian from the mental servility of the past, universal history would set the goal of achieving the new status of the Free Man. Armenian history was revised. Instead of the rise and fall of dynasties, the revolutionary parties discussed the general laws of historical development as accepted by socialist, positivistic thought and used them to understand the past and project the future.

Above and beyond expressing the founders' personal convictions, the new outlook adopted by the SDHP and ARF gave the Armenian liberation movement an intellectual-ideological component in the struggle to be freed from the psychological and social constraints brought about by centuries of foreign domination.

Yet a worldview, however coherent and attractive philosophically, could have had no permanent impact without that other dimension of which history is made: a change in the self-perception of enough individuals who, no longer able and willing to accept the status quo, manifest that change by doing with their resources and lives something other than what existing institutions had determined and expected, other than what they were used to doing.

This must have been well understood by revolutionary field workers who, at times single-handedly, transformed slumbering and forgotten villages into pockets of resistance to oppression and forged reliable links in the larger movement of liberation by preaching the gospel of the new, self-respecting man.

Notes

1. Second edition (Marseilles, 1891). The booklet was published by the short-lived Armenian Patriotic Union, founded and directed by Portukalian, who also edited the booklet. The identity of the actual author or authors is not known with any degree of certainty.

2. Ibid., pp. 11-12, 19.

3. Ibid., pp. 9-10.

4. Ibid., p. 6.

5. Ibid., p. 23.

6. *Armenia*, weekly newspaper, II, 2 (August 28, 1886). The article is signed Lerents, one of Nazarbek's pseudonyms.

7. *Vardapetaran*, pp. 12-13.

8. Gorun, "Hayer ev kurder" [Armenians and Kurds], *Armenia*, II, 17 (October 16, 1886).

9. Varand-Zadeh, "Inchov es mard" [What Makes You a Human Being?], *Armenia*, 1, 62 (March 20, 1886).

10. Ned, "Heghapokhutiune" [Revolution], *Armenia*, IV, 73 (June 19, 1889).

11. *Vazgen yergaran* [Vazgen Songbook], compiled by Tigran Teroyan (Boston, 1901), pp. 389-390; Teroyan, a fieldworker killed in 1898, compiled this work before his death. Vazgen was his revolutionary pseudonym.

12. Ibid., pp. 150-151.

13. Ibid., p. 407.

14. Ibid., pp. 41-42.

15. *Pataniyin yergarane* [The Songbook of the Young] (Beirut, 1959), p. 37.

16. Ibid., p. 31.

17. "Terorismi dere turkahay heghapokhakan gordsuneutian mech" [The Role of Terrorism in the Activities of the Turkish-Armenian Revolution], *Azatutian avetaber* (Tiflis), 1, 4 (February 1884), editorial. This publication was sponsored by the *Hayrenaserneri Miutiun* (Union of Patriots), the members of which eventually became one of the core elements of the Dashnaktsutiun.

Part III

4

Theory and Praxis: A Perspective on the Armenian Liberation Movement, 1890-1908

Armenian revolutionary parties and groups that emerged between 1888 and 1908 are usually described as nationalistic or Marxist. The terminology implies that the first aimed at the creation of an independent Armenian state while the latter devoted itself exclusively to a class struggle that denied national aspirations. While for some audiences it facilitates the placement of groups on a recognizable political spectrum, such terminology ignores the class-conscious thinking of those considered nationalist and the national dimension in the strategies of those considered Marxist. But it ultimately fails to explain the policies and actions of the revolutionaries and the ideological evolution of revolutionary thought.

A Legacy from the Distant and Immediate Past

The revolutionary movement was not the first that tried to change the status of Armenia and Armenians following the collapse of the last Armenian dynasty in Armenia in the eleventh century, and its final partition between Safavid Persia and the Ottoman Empire in 1639. During the sixteenth and eighteenth centuries there were a number of attempts, sporadic and limited in scope, that are relevant to what was to come. These attempts were undertaken by individuals or institutions that belonged to or represented the privileged classes in Armenian society. Some aimed at the creation of a new state ruled by an Armenian dynasty, others would have been satisfied if their plans could result in a change of the imperial power that ruled over Armenia. Obviously, the political and economic systems of the future Armenian state could not be more progressive than those that characterized the realm of the usually elusive savior-king. Furthermore, for the most part during this period, would-be liberators had in mind a change in the status of Eastern Armenia under Persian Safavid rule, and not the Western and larger sector that had become part of the Ottoman realm. Finally, except for the efforts of the *meliks*, or princes of Karabakh in the early eighteenth century, the strategies of liberation consisted of inviting a foreign power—of course a Christian one—to intervene militarily against the Safavids to save the "nation." The strategies drew upon the legacy of the medieval Armenian kingdom of Cilicia on the northeastern corner of the Mediterranean Sea and the last in Armenian history, whose rulers tried vainly to save their kingdom by appealing to the Crusader states of Europe.[1]

No doubt some form of patriotism, sense of history, and idealism were part of the personal motivation of the many of the historical figures who took the initiatives to liberate the historical fatherland. Also, the significance of popular support for or enthusiasm towards their ventures cannot be excluded. Yet, altruistic feelings and compassion for the suffering of the majority tended to surface and find currency among the catholicosses, or supreme leaders of the Armenian Church, meliks, and merchants only when the mutually beneficial co-existence between them and their overlords threatened their privileges or dissipated. Otherwise, it would be hard to explain the compromises with which Armenian princes of the Church, the mountain, and the market were willing to live for prolonged periods of time, the sporadic character of their attempts, and the limited nature of the changes they sought.

The vision of an Armenian state in the image of the past became irrelevant by the middle of the nineteenth century due to three developments. By 1828 Russia had wrested Eastern Armenia and the Transcaucasus from the Safavids and discarded the idea of an Armenian state by administrative fiat. In two other characteristic moves, the tsar's government exiled Bishop Nerses Ashtaraketsi, one of the most ardent supporter of Russian advance into Eastern Armenia, who subsequently complained of Russian disregard for their promises; and it recognized the extensive rights and power of largely Muslim landlords, the *begs* and *aghalars*, over Armenian villages. Nonetheless, most subsequent efforts toward change of status concentrated on Ottoman Armenia.

The political, cultural, and economic penetration of European powers in the Ottoman Empire was no less consequential for Armenian history. Along with the reforms of the empire that brought industrialization and the capitalist order to Russia, by the 1870s both segments of the Armenian population were living in empires integrating European-dominated production and market systems that engendered goods as well as ideas. The character of Armenian commerce and capital changed as a result in two important ways. A new, modern merchant and industrial bourgeoisie replaced the *sarrafs*, or money-lenders, of Istanbul and the merchants who had become prominent in international trade in the eighteenth century and, as a result, in Armenian society.[2] One effect of this process was that cultural and intellectual influences permeated Armenian life in both sectors.[3]

Yet neither of the Armenian bourgeoisies was located in the historical Armenian territories that had become backwaters for the two empires. The new classes developed in the capitals where political power resided and in major cities with strategic significance for regional or international trade. Both groups depended on non-Armenians for the development and security of their wealth and none thought of moving their capital to the Armenian provinces for patriotic purposes. The bourgeois program for the nation in the second half of the nineteenth century, therefore, was either to invest in community development in distant but safe cities or, at best, to seek reforms for Armenians in the Eastern or Armenian provinces through appeals to the sultan, the adoption of a constitutional regime, or the intervention of Western powers. For the Russian Armenian bourgeoisie it was possible to take a step further and encourage Russian occupation of as many Armenian populated provinces in the Ottoman Empire as possible, although by and large this became impossible due to European, especially British, obstacles to Russian expansion. During the war of 1877-1878, Russia occupied parts of the eastern provinces. Following the defeat of the Ottomans, in February 1878 Russia imposed on Istanbul the Treaty of San Stefano, which included, at the urging of the Armenian patriarch of Istanbul, provisions for reforms in the Armenian provinces to be undertaken by the sultan. Article 16 stipulated the continued occupation of territories under Russian control until such time as the promised reforms were actually implemented. Yet the Treaty was revised under the pressure of Great Britain in the Treaty of Berlin of July 1878. According to Article 61 of that agreement, Russia was to withdraw from most of the Ottoman lands it had occupied immediately and the sultan would be accountable to the Great Powers in general for his vague promise that reforms would be implemented. For its support of the sultan against the Russia, Britain received control of the island of Cyprus.[4] The two treaties did not bring about reforms but they produced the questionable result of internationalizing the issue of reforms in the *vilayets*, or provinces—creating the Armenian Question as a sub-category of the Eastern Question—and creating opposing camps of Armenians. A first controversy set those for whom the international-ization of the problem was a dangerous step that would make the Armenian millet suspect in the eyes of the sultan against those who thought of it as a diplomatic success that would lead to the solution of the problem. After all, the latter group argued, the sultan could not renege on the Treaty signed with a victorious Russia. A second controversy erupted between those who thought the provision in the Treaty of Berlin had been a fatal retreat from the Treaty of San Stefano where the provision for reforms was specific versus those who thought of the revision as a minor change or even an improvement, since the new Treaty had all of Europe guaranteeing the reforms. The latter quarrel came to be known as the "the 16ers against the 61ers."

The symbols of the often asserted but still imaginary Armenian nation of the nineteenth century were Russian Armenian generals victimized by their own successes in the Russian army, Ottoman Armenian merchants fearful of their own programs, and intellectu-als suspicious of their own hopes. The thrust of the revolutionary movement would come not from the idealized abstract nation of the cultural renaissance but the equally vague yet far more threatened and threatening "people."

At first a designation for Armenians in the Armenian vilayets, the notion of "people" came increasingly to represent the most deprived and oppressed elements in Armenian society: peasants, craftsmen, small shopkeepers, and families left behind by migrant workers in Istanbul whose future was as hopeless as their present was oppres-sive. It was ostensibly for these people that reforms had been advo-cated and for whom the liberal bourgeoisie and intelligentsia gov-erning the nation had run out of options.[5]

The political parties and organization that emerged beginning in the 1880s came to articulate the needs of the "people" when all else failed. Their revolutionary character was not defined solely by their willingness to resort to an armed struggle—a practice quite well known to Zeytun, Sasun, and Karabakh Armenians—nor in their goal to achieve reforms otherwise supported by well-meaning liberals. Rather, that revolutionary character is to be found in their willingness to relate the crisis of the provinces to an oppressive social structure and regressive political-economic system; to understand that system in the context of the most progressive social thinking of the times and to worldwide phenomena; and in their determination to transform the people from a subject of history into agents of change, thus achieving a radical transformation of society by whatever means necessary, within whatever political framework possible.

People and Territory

The revolutionary movement started when political parties redefined liberation to give precedence of the liberation of the people over that of a territory and related the participation of the people in the fight for a new system of government in the future.

To change the present and build a better future, they altered their concept of the Armenian past. The Social Democratic Hnchakian Party (SDHP) founded in 1887-1988 was, in this sense, the first revolutionary group to emerge. For the SDHP, the history of the Armenian people was no exception to the universal, objective laws of class struggle that, in the view of its founders, governed changes in society. Hence the liberation of Armenians would be achieved with the establishment of a classless Armenian society, which would guarantee freedom from all forms of oppression.

The SDHP chose Ottoman Armenia as the first arena for its activities since Western Armenians were in dire need of liberation and communities there could lose their viability if not saved soon enough. But, the SDHP argued, Ottoman Armenia lacked the necessary preconditions to achieve liberation within the Ottoman Empire. Reforms in the empire had failed. Moreover, non-Armenian elements in historic Armenia, such as the Kurds, were still at a lower stage of social development, in their view. Their way of life was not only a bane for the more developed Armenians, but also a threat to future progress. Hence the SDHP platform called for the establishment of an independent Armenian state as an immediate goal—a state that would eventually encompass Russian and Persian Armenia as well.

The SDHP derived its strategy from the opportunities of the moment rather than their interpretation of historical change. Their struggle to establish an independent state in Ottoman Armenia was based on the following five premises: 1) The Armenian people will snap out of their lethargy and support the revolution once they are informed of its goals because they are oppressed, 2) Privileged Armenian classes will support the first phase of the revolution because of its focus on political change, 3) Europe would support the Armenian movement despite its imperialistic interests because it had given the world scientific socialism and the nation-state and because it had committed itself to resolving the Armenian Question in the Treaty of Berlin, 4) Russia would not oppose the goals of the movement despite its despotic regime because of its imperialistic interests, and 5) Ottoman rule would collapse in Western Armenia from the first revolutionary assault from within and pressure from without because it was weak militarily and "sick" at its foundations.

The party was so confident in the imminent success of its strategy that in addition to demonstrations and uprisings against the sultan, it undertook the organization of an educational campaign to initiate the Armenian people with the rudimentary laws of class struggle.[6]

Subsequent developments came to show that these premises were partially or totally false. After six years of agitation, the struggle was bogged down in the initial phase of the revolution. The massacres of 1894-96 convinced many of the SDHP that the party's program must be reexamined.

The critics within the party turned to the basic contradiction its two goals suggested: a struggle for national independence would unite all Armenians at the exclusion of non-Armenian elements regardless of class interests; a struggle for socialism would bring all oppressed classes against all exploiters regardless of nationality and religion. One segment of the party blamed the failure of the movement on socialism. Even as an idea, this group argued, socialism had antagonized the Armenian bourgeoisie and the Church, and made the movement suspicious in the eyes of European governments. The efforts had failed, they argued, because they lacked national unity and Western support. They left the DSHP and formed the *Verakazmial* (Reformed) Hnchakian party, which rejected socialism. A smaller group, later to be known as the Armenian Socialist Party, argued that if the SDHP had really understood socialism and taken it seriously they would have sought alliances with similarly oppressed classes of all nationalities of the Ottoman empire rather than elements and powers that were by definition against socialism and revolution. They rejected independence as a means of liberation and proposed to expand the revolutionary effort to all countries where Armenians lived, although Ottoman Armenia would continue to occupy a special place in the struggle.[7] The internal divisions destroyed, for all practical purposes, the effectiveness of the SDHP.

The crisis of 1896 was not as traumatic for the then less important revolutionary group, the *Hay Heghapokhakan Dashnaktsutiune* (Armenian Revolutionary Federation, known also as Dashnaktsutiune or Dashnaks, ARF). Founded in 1890, the ARF shared with the SDHP the vision of a socialist society, the dedication to Ottoman Armenians, and the belief in a relatively brief struggle. These common traits led to their initial agreement to integrate the two organizations. But the ARF also differed from the SDHP in two essential respects, which brought about the nullification of that agreement even before it was put to effect.

For the founders of the ARF, to understand history and to change it one should account for subjective as well as objective factors. The party program asserted, for example, that Armenian peasants were oppressed in the Ottoman Empire because they were peasants and because they were Armenian. While their being peasants in a semi-feudal society accounted for certain forms of the oppression and exploitation—including some by Armenian landlords and usurers—their being Armenian and Christian accounted for other forms of oppression and rationalized exploitation. This more elaborate relationship between political and economic factors led to the second difference with the SDHP. Liberation for the Armenian people would be sought through graduated reforms in the political and economic spheres simultaneously. These reforms, the "minimum demands," constituted the sole concern of the party. The "maximum demands" were not articulated clearly. Socialism was implied as the ultimate ideal to which the inexorable march of history was leading and in which all clear thinking revolutionaries and enlightened individuals believed by definition. An independent Armenia was only suggested by the vague notion of *"azat Hayastan"* or a "free Armenia."[8]

The program of the ARF was less ambitious and more flexible than that of the SDHP. More importantly, the two phases of the liberation struggle with its minimum and maximum demands avoided the SDHP contradiction. Yet the ARF too accepted the many premises of SDHP strategy. It also was forced to explain the failure of the movement in achieving minimal success by 1896 and to chart a new strategy. Party leaders blamed the failure on the slavish mentality of the masses, the greediness of the Armenian rich, the self-centeredness of churchmen, the materialism of European governments, and the cynicism of the tsar, all of which allowed the sultan to institutionalize his policy of depopulating the Armenian plateau through persecutions and massacres. The solutions were almost self-evident. The revolution and guerrilla warfare required more preparation and a wider popular basis, which could be secured by more propaganda, more examples of heroism and tactical successes; the course of European diplomacy could be altered in favor of the Armenian movement if an appeal was made to its more enlightened public and progressive opinion-makers, the socialists, whose worldview the party shared. But the most critical change came in the further narrowing of the immediate concern on the removal of the person of a bloody, cruel, and despotic sultan, now the main culprit. This was a target around which it would be possible to find cooperation with non-Armenian peoples and organizations, thus expanding the support for the party's goals beyond the meager resources of the Armenian people. The policy of cooperation with Young Turks, Kurdish tribes, and other ethnic groups within Armenia were successful only occasionally. But these contacts helped create a further gap between the idea of independence and the ARF and emphasized those aspects of its program that dealt with grievances common to other discontented elements in Ottoman society.[9]

These adjustments turned the ARF into a force more formidable than any of the previous organizations. Yet they failed to produce any substantial results. In 1904 an offensive by Ottoman armies on Sasun preempted a planned uprising in selected spots of Western Armenia, an uprising that was to activate all other factors favoring the introduction of reforms. Equally debilitating for the morale and more consequential for the ideology of revolution were events on the other side of the border. Until the turn of the century, Russian Armenians filled the role of suppliers and supporters to the struggle in Ottoman Armenia. But the tsar's 1903 edict ordering the expropriation of Armenian Church properties, the first Russian Revolution, and the Armeno-Tatar (Azeri) civil war of 1905-1907 brought to the surface the question of political and economic oppression of Eastern Armenians. The events presented a new challenge to the idea of an Armenian revolution pursued until then in the context of Ottoman Armenia. The ARF, practically the only organized Armenia political force in the Caucasus, considered its duty to lead that struggle as well. The organization of popular opposition to the tsar's edict, the defense of Armenians against Tatars, and engaging in socialistic activities introduced further modifications in the idea of national liberation. Western Armenian leaders in the party, including some of the most well-known guerrilla fighters, and others objected to the course taken by the leadership. The fierce arguments threatened the unity of the party.

The leaders in the party believed that their idea of revolution in Ottoman Armenia applied to Russian Armenia as well since in both sectors the struggle was against political despotism, national oppression, and economic exploitation and that the differences in levels of economic and political development required a different emphasis in activities rather than a different struggle in each. Throughout the years 1903 and 1907, under intense criticism from within and without and threatened by a split in the organization, party leaders clarified and modified their ideology to emphasize the common basis and concerns of the two struggles. The party qualified its definition of "people" now to include only workers and peasants. The new definition made manifest the class aspect of the revolution but also accounted for the particular composition of Armenian exploited classes on both sides of the border. It drew up a set of minimum economic and political demands for Russian Armenians as it had done for Ottoman Armenians. As a political framework within which those demands would be realized, the ARF adopted federalism for both Ottoman and Russian Armenians, thus clearly rejecting the idea of independence for the first and raising the question of internal autonomy for the latter. The ARF also revised its general principles to bring them closer to the widely accepted concept of a scientific socialism. Thus throughout its crisis the party sought to preserve the class aspect of the revolution in Western Armenia and guarantee a solution to the national problem in the Russian empire. The struggle for Armenian liberation was now defined by the idea of a people separated by political borders, but united in dedication to a common revolutionary ideal that characterized the new nation.

The ARF survived the crisis. While this "different but united" formula satisfied some of its critics from within, it led others to become the most formidable opponents of the ARF.

Western Armenians could appreciate the necessity of defending Russian Armenian properties and lives. But many were weary that the party's concern with "surplus value" would detract Eastern Armenian support from the more essential question of "surplus blood" in Ottoman Armenia. Most were satisfied by the party's renewed assertions of its commitment to the Western Armenian cause. They also pretended to agree with the leaders that a democratic Russia, toward which the party's Eastern Armenian activities were geared, would eliminate the tsar—now the most ardent supporter of the sultan and his policies.

The more substantial criticisms came from ARF members in the Russian sector. Dissension regarding the party's ideology and strategy had begun as early as 1899 but were crystallized and aired only beginning with the 1903 Church crisis.

The argument that anti-tsar activities would assist the Ottoman Armenian cause was presented by one segment of the party as early as in 1899. But they considered the tsar to be the main obstacle to the success of reform programs, not just one obstacle. Furthermore, since in Russia anti-tsar was equivalent to pro-socialist, for these ARF socialism became a serious analytical tool as well as a program. Of this group, a few, to be known as the *Andjatakans* (separatists) disagreed with the party on two points. Firstly, they argued that differences between the struggles in the two Armenias were essential and could not be papered over with clever arguments. If, given the nature of reforms needed in the Ottoman Empire, one could tolerate the inclusion of bourgeois and socialist elements in the party, the Russian Armenian case could not do so, they thought. Hence they called for the separation of the ARF into two segments with different leaderships. Secondly, they argued that the pursuit of reforms in Ottoman Armenia through cooperation with leaders of other nationalities was counterproductive since, for example, neither the Macedonians nor the Young Turks had any social consciousness. Cooperation should be developed with the masses and not representatives of feudal and military interests. The *Yeritasard Dashnaktsakans* (Young ARFers), as they called themselves once separated, otherwise continued to support the idea and program of ARF, as a reaction to the national oppression against both segments of the Armenian people.

Another group was far more critical of the party's strategy and tactics in Ottoman Armenia. For these critics guerrilla activities had provided an excuse for and given an impetus to the massacres. The movement had failed, firstly, because the ARF had sought support from governments whose economic interests coincided rather than contradicted the political interests of the Ottoman regime; and the party had relied on occasional outbursts against a large army rather then securing mass support for its goals among all exploited classes. The solution to the Ottoman Armenian problem should be sought in the nature of Ottoman Empire, this group thought. As a colony of Europe it would be eventually divided into spheres of influence. Western Armenia would fall within Russia's sphere, and a socialist Russia would secure the necessary progress there. In addition to self-defense the role of the parties in Ottoman Armenia should be to educate oppressed Turks and Kurds in the laws of economic development and class interests. Armenians should be the vanguard of a socialist revolution rather than advocates of any program that might lead to separatism. This group called for the dissolution of the ARF, taking the separation of the two struggles for granted. It considered itself part of Russian social democracy since in their view liberation from all discrimination, antagonism, and oppression was predicated upon the successful end of the class struggle. Yet they recognized the special predicament of the Armenian people. They continued to advocate federalism, national-cultural self-determination in future Russia, and regional party autonomy for Marxists within the larger Russian Socialist Democratic Workers' Party (RSDWP). Known as the "specifists," they founded the Social Democratic Workers Armenian Organization.[10]

The final step in the transformation of revolutionary ideology came with the "Marxist Armenians," many of whom had had their political christening in their adolescent years as members of the SDHP or ARF. They accused the specifists of being infected with Dashnakism. They saw no need for a federated Russia or a separate Armenian-based organization within Russia's social democratic organization. There was no sense, they argued, in artificially preserving entities, such as the nation, which were historical rather than absolute categories. Only a total and unqualified dedication to a class struggle would secure the liberation of Armenians and all others from all forms of oppression and only the future Russia ruled by proletarians could assist Western Armenians.[11]

Thus, while the idea of an Armenian revolution remained essentially the same, its strategy changed gradually as revolutionaries sought its success in the resolution of contradictions between the theory of that revolution and the praxis of revolution as accepted in the original premises.

Forced by events beyond their control and lacking alternatives on the battlefield, revolutionaries substituted achievement with the satisfaction that ideals provided: they transcended failure with the hope that rational ideologies inspire, and eventually some of them replaced the doubts emanating from liberalism and Western Europe with the confidence only Marxism and Communist Russia could offer.

It is a measure of the significance of ideologies for the revolutionaries that the modern liberation struggle in Armenian history came to an end with the battle between the antagonistic forces of the nationalists, i.e., the ARF and the "Marxist," later Bolsheviks, over Sovietization. But perhaps it is ultimately far more significant for the understanding of revolutionary practice that the battle was fought for a republic that neither side had envisioned, but which the first group established in 1918, the second overtook in 1920, and both lost in 1991.

Notes

1.   See Gerard J. Libaridian, "The Ideology of Armenian Liberation: Armenian Political Thought Before the Revolutionary Movement (1639-1885)" (Ph. D. dissertation, the University of California at Los Angeles, 1987). This work, in revised from, will be published shortly.

2.   See Arpi Hamalian, "The Armenians: Intermediaries for the European Trading Companies," *University of Manitoba Anthropology Papers*, no. 14 (Winnepeg, 1976).

3.   See, for example, James Etmekjian, *The French Influence on the Western Armenian Renaissance, 1843-1915* (New York, 1964).

4.   See, for example, M. S. Anderson, *The Eastern Question*, 1774-1923 (New York, 1966); William Langer, *European Alliances and Alignments, 1871-1890* (New York, 1939);and *The Diplomacy of Imperialism, 1890-1902*, 2 vols. (New York, 1935); and B. N. Simsir, *British Documents on Ottoman Armenians, 1856-1890*, 2 vols. (Anakara,1982-1983).

5.   See Mikayel Varandian, *Haykakan sharzhman nakhpatmutiune*. 2 vols. (Geneva, 1912 and 1913).

6.   See *Hnchak* [Bell], the official journal of the SDHP, beginning from 1888; Louise Nalbandian, *The Armenian Revolutionary Movement*. Berkeley, 1967; and "The Origins and Development of the Socialism in Armenia. The Social Democratic Hnchakian Party, 1887-1949" (M.A. thesis, Stanford University, 1949;) Anaide Ter-Minassian, *Nationalism and Socialism in the Armenian Revolutionary Movement, 1887-1912* (Cambridge, Mass, 1984); Hagopian, J. M. "Hyphenated Nationalism: The spirit of the Revolutionary Movement in Asia Minor, 1896-1910" (Ph.D. dissertation, Harvard University, 1943); Ruben Khan-Azat, "Hay heghapokhakani husherits" [From the memoirs of a Revolutionary], *Hairenik Amsagir* [Hairenkin Monthly], 5(June 1927), 5(July-October 1927), 6(November-December 1927), 6(January-April 1928).

7.   See chapter 6.

8.   *Hay Heghapokhakan Dashnaktsutian Dzragir* [Program of the Armenian Revolutionary Federation] (Vienna, 1892); Leo (Arakel Babakhanian), *Turkahay*

heghapokhutian gaghaparabutiune [The Ideology of the Turkish-Armenian Revolution] (Paris, 1934).

9.   See, among others, *Droshak* [Flag], the official journal of the ARF, beginning in 1990, Geneva; Mikayel Varandian, *H.H. Dashnaktsutian patmutiune.* 2 vols. (Paris, 1932 and Cairo, 1950); Ter-Minassian, *Nationalism and Socialism...*; and chapter 5.

10.   Anaide Ter-Minassian, "Aux origines du marxisme arménien: les specifistes," *Cahiers du monde russe et soviétique*, 1-2 (1978: 67-117).

11.   See Ronald Suny, *Transcaucasia: Nationalism and Social Change* (Ann Arbor, 1983 and 1996) and *Looking at Ararat: Armenia in Modern History* (Indianapolis and Bloomington, 1993).

5

Rethinking the Nation:
Revolution and Liberation in the 1892 and
1907 Programs of the Dashnaktsutiune

The Hay Heghapokhakan Dashnaktsutiune (Armenian Revolutionary Federation, ARF) was founded in 1890 in Tiflis. First established as the Federation of Armenian Revolutionaries, the organization aimed at coordinating the activities of various student and radical groups devoted to Western Armenian liberation. Some of its founding members soon concluded, however, that without the authority to provide leadership and initiate action, the central executive body entrusted with the task of coordination was not effective. By 1892 it had also become clear that the ARF had failed in its efforts to include within the federation the first and until then most important of these groups, the SDHP (Social Democratic Hnchakian Party), founded in Geneva in 1887.

An assembly of representatives and leaders met in 1892 and decided to transform the ARF into a party in its own right. This First General Congress adopted a vaguely socialistic worldview and a decentralized organizational structure. The new party also decided to pursue the goal of "political and economic freedom in Ottoman Armenia through rebellion."[1]

The program of the party remained essentially the same until 1907 when the Fourth General Congress reformulated its worldview along the lines of Russia's Social Revolutionaries; it redefined its goal as the establishment of federal structures in both the Ottoman and Russian empires within which the two sectors of Armenia would constitute autonomous units; it also called for collaboration with the progressive forces in the Ottoman Empire and Europe as a major strategic weapon.[2]

The 1892 program of the ARF, which set the direction of the Armenian revolutionary struggle during the fifteen years that followed, was preconditioned by the focusing of Armenian political thought on Western Armenia, the democratization of Armenian politics, the unwillingness of the Armenian bourgeoisie to lead a national struggle, the failure of Western Armenian liberals and provincial radicals to develop a comprehensive strategy and, finally, the disparity between the "scientific" socialism of the SDHP program and the objective realities in Western Armenia.

During the second half of the nineteenth century the agrarian and economic crises in Western Armenian dominated the Armenian agenda. Whether designed to alter the demographic structure of the Eastern vilayets in favor of Turks or to prevent the transformation of a cultural Armenian community into a political power, Ottoman policies added a new dimension to the crisis of economic survival, the survival of the Armenians as a people.

Organizations founded by the provincial people, such as the Pashtpan Hayreniats in Erzerum in 1881 and Armenakans in Van in 1885, were unable to transform genuine feelings of patriotism and devotion to the "people" into a viable movement with an adequate strategy. These groups remained local; they failed to become national organizations not only because the state's intelligence apparatus prevented expansion, but also because their founders were limited in their imagination of the nation and thinking in terms of change of tactics and articulation of grievances did not encompass a strategic framework. This was particularly true of the Armenakans, who came closest to being a native revolutionary party, but remained urban oriented in their framework. For the Armenakans, the peasantry was to benefit from revolutionary change but would not be a participant in it, since cultural enlightenment, found mainly among educated city people, was considered a prerequisite for revolutionary consciousness.[3]

The first Armenian political party was founded by Eastern Armenians, who shared a sense of common history with Western Armenians—though not necessarily a common culture—and provided humanitarian assistance to them. The founders of the newspaper *Hnchak* and of the party known by the same name were all born in the Russian Empire. Many were forced to flee Russia because of their involvement in anti-tsarist revolutionary activities. Avetis Nazarbek and Maro Vardanian were both members of Russian populist organizations. They were acquainted with clandestine operations, they had a conceptual framework that related the particular Armenian experience to larger, universal historical forces, and they had a commitment to the cause of the common people. Most importantly, the Russian Armenian radicals were firm believers in the role of the peasantry in bringing about social and political change. Having idealized the Russian peasantry and its communal institutions, the early revolutionaries in Russia thought the peasants had something to teach to advanced but corrupt societies in cities.

On the one hand, the involvement of Russian Armenian radicals in the Western Armenian political struggle implied a retreat from the universal principle they thought they had while participating in the movement of liberation of the Russian peasantry. That involvement, on the other hand, signaled the beginning of the conceptualized approach to the problem. The Eastern Armenians were schooled in the tradition of seeing the world through the abstraction of theories of historical development. They thus introduced into the ideology of the national movement interpretations and perceptions based on a vague sort of socialism. Consequently, the liberation struggle was led by a class of radicals who considered the nation a historical rather than an absolute category, and whose commitment was to historically-conditioned patriotism rather than to blind nationalism.[4]

The parties came to articulate the needs of the people and devoted themselves to their satisfaction. Their revolutionary character was not defined solely by their willingness to resort to an armed struggle—a practice quite well known to Armenians in Zeytun, Sasun, and Karabakh—nor in their goal to achieve reforms otherwise supported by well-meaning liberals. Rather, that revolutionary character is to be found in their willingness to relate the crisis of the provinces to an oppressive social structure and regressive political-economic system, and in their determination to transform the people from subjects of history into agents of change, thus to achieve a radical transformation of society by whatever means necessary, within whatever political framework possible (see preceding chapters).

The revolutionary movement began when the political parties redefined the idea of liberation to include the emancipation of people and not just that of a territory, and thus qualitative changes in the future structure of society acquired at least as much importance as formal changes from one monarch to another.

The 1892 program of the ARF must be understood in this context.

A Moderate Revolution?

According to the 1892 program of the ARF, the basic pattern in history has been the exploitation and political domination of political and economic elites over the working majority. Although the specific forms of social and economic relations had changed over the centuries, class antagonism had remained a constant. The specific forms of the establishment of such an elite in the Ottoman Empire had resulted in the transformation of ethnic-religious groups, such as the Armenians, into an exploited class. This explanation recognized that some Armenians were among the beneficiaries of and exploiters within the system, while non-Armenian elements, including Turks, were among those exploited. Furthermore, change could not come by reliance on the good will of the rulers. An armed struggle was necessary for that.

Yet, at the same time, the struggle could not be conducted within the framework of a rigid, catechistic ideology; nor should the masses be misled into believing in the imminent establishment of an Eden on earth through the detailed description of an ideal system. The program stated:

> The sad and cruel lessons of history have demonstrated clearly that to achieve victory it is not sufficient for the suffering segment of humanity to understand its own condition, or even to develop the willingness to see it changed; that it is also necessary to obtain real power. But since that power cannot be created overnight, and since that power is the consequence of existing conditions, and changes accordingly, it is obvious that any form of social organization, however ideal, cannot be instituted at once, and that such an institution becomes possible only through the reform of existing conditions.
>
> It is for this reason that we do not come forth as proponents of this or that Utopian ideology; it is our purpose that our program be essential. Our attention is focused on the present condition of our land. Our goal is to subject...to an objective critique the causes that have given rise to the present condition;...to identify the causes of that condition based on the positive laws of the social sciences; and at the same time to wage a relentless struggle against the factors that have conditioned these causes.[5]

The platform of the ARF called for the establishment of a popular-democratic government based on free elections in the Ottoman Empire. This government would guarantee security of life and the right to work; equality of all nationalities and religions before the law; freedom of speech, press, and assembly; distribution of land to the landless; taxation according to ability to pay; abolition of the military exemption fee and its replacement with equal conscription; establishment of compulsory education; promotion of national intellectual progress; and reinforcement of communal principles as a means of greater production and exports.[6]

The party believed that "the liberation of the people from its untenable condition in order that they may enter the mainstream of human progress could only be achieved through revolution."[7] The reforms sought by the ARF were to be achieved through rebellion against the Ottoman state. Such a rebellion would be led by "revolutionary fighters."

Yet, the armed struggle aside, the actual strategy of the ARF was based on the following five premises: (1) the Armenian people would snap out of its lethargy and support the revolution once they were informed of its goals, simply because Armenians were oppressed; (2) privileged Armenian classes would support the movement since, after all, the movement was a national one aimed at reforms; (3) European powers would support the Armenian movement and intervene on its behalf, since Europe had been the cradle of revolutions and had committed itself to the resolution of the Armenian Question at the Conference of Berlin; (4) Russia would not oppose the goals of the movement despite its despotic regime, because of its long standing enmity with the Ottoman Empire; and (5) the Ottoman system would collapse without much delay from the revolutionary assault from within and European pressure from without, since the system was weak at its foundations.

The Tests of Reality

Subsequent developments included the massacres of 1894-1896, and diplomatic laud by the Great Powers, which caused the collapse of the SDHP, highlighted problems with these premises. The ARF was forced to explain the failure of the movement to achieve minimal success by 1896 and chart a revised strategy that led to a further refinement of tactics (see previous chapter).

The Armeno-Tatar conflict of 1905-1907 was another episode that strengthened the national character of the ARF. Among the many problems it posed was the threat to the position and properties of the Armenian bourgeoisie in the Caucasus. Relations between the political parties and the bourgeoisie had an ambivalent character. Notwithstanding their programmatic antagonism toward all exploiting classes, revolutionaries, especially the ARF, expected the wealthy to provide at least financial assistance. Their press often criticized the

Armenian upper classes for the latter's cowardice and lack of interest in the fate of the common Armenian. The mutual distrust dissipated in the Caucasus between 1905 and 1907. Unable to rely on government forces to protect their interests and properties, Armenian merchants, industrialists, and financiers turned to the ARF, practically the only organized Armenian force in the Caucasus. The ARF accepted the challenge. Its leaders argued, firstly, that Tatar aggression had been instigated by the reactionary Russian government as part of a larger anti-Armenian policy; hence, it was equally necessary to defend Armenian-owned property as it was to protect defenseless Armenian peasants.

Secondly, they argued, given employment discrimination against Armenian workers in non-Armenian concerns, the assistance provided to the Armenian bourgeoisie was tantamount to the safekeeping of employment opportunities for Armenian laborers.[8]

Paradoxically, the 1905-1907 period is also marked by a heightened sense of the socialist aspect of the ARF ideology. Until 1903, the party had avoided verbal or military confrontations with the Russian government, despite the lack of Russian support for Armenian goals and the anti-tsarist activities of ARF founders preceding the formation of the party. The confiscation of Armenian property released anti-tsarist sentiments. Opposition to the tsar's government on political and economic grounds too began to evolve around 1900 among many Russian Armenian students, including members of the ARF. This was part of the larger Russian movement that culminated in the First Russian Revolution. The ARF leadership had opposed involvement in Russia's internal affairs vehemently, arguing that the party's efforts should concentrate on the Western Armenian struggle. The struggle against the "surplus blood" that was being extracted from Armenians under Ottoman rule had priority over the struggle against "surplus value" being extracted from Russian Armenians, argued Kristapor Mikayelian, founder and ideologue, but apparently the opportunity to practice beliefs held in reserve and to participate in a revolution that had an opportunity to succeed was more appealing to some segments of the youth.

The party finally acceded to the rising demands for socialistic action. During a regional conference held in Tbilisi in 1905, it formulated the "Caucasian Platform," a document that sanctioned the involvement of party cells within Russia in socialist activities.[9] The party changed its position because it was afraid of losing a good portion of its most dynamic and devoted youth. The ARF was also concerned that the Armenian working class would pursue its social and economic interests under the banner of non-Armenian parties; this would weaken the social basis of the party. Under the guidance of non-Armenian parties, the Eastern Armenians might also lose interest in the struggle of their Western Armenian brethren. The platform temporarily resolved a potentially disruptive crisis.

Most members remained in the ranks. The "left wing" of the ARF began publishing newspapers and pamphlets. They introduced European socialist and democratic principles, theories, institutions, authors, and parties. They organized unions among Armenian workers and generally participated in anti-tsarist activities.

As an unmistakable sign of its rediscovered sense of economic justice in the socialist sense, to prove the relevance of socialism in Armenian life, and to show the sincerity of its devotion to socialist principles, the ARF pressured the catholicos of Etchmiadzin to convene a general assembly of Russian Armenian representatives to allow for popular participation in the management of Church affairs. Most of the parish delegates elected to the 1906 meeting were members or sympathizers of the ARF. Among other proposals, the party asked for the distribution of Church-owned agricultural lands to the families of peasants who had tilled them for generations. The party had not yet decided whether non-Armenian peasants on Armenian lands should be entitled to the same benefits when the meeting was disbanded by the order of Russian police, probably at the instigation of clergymen.[10]

Nonetheless, the "Caucasian Platform" did not satisfy all. Some argued that the party was following a dual ideology and could, therefore, serve neither side well. They split away to join existing socialist organizations or to start new ones. Western Armenians also objected to the platform. They considered it a dangerous waste of meager party resources and a betrayal of the original goal of liberating Western Armenians.

Party leaders argued that the Western Armenian struggle had never received more financial and material support from the Caucasus than at the height of socialist propaganda. The critique from the left in search of ideological purity was not as easy to countenance.

The Fourth General Congress of the ARF in Vienna in 1907 was a critical one. Most Western Armenian delegates, among them guerilla leaders with heroic pasts, expected the Congress to declare the

"Caucasian Platform" illegal. Some Russian Armenian representatives, mainly students who considered class and nation mutually exclusive categories, proposed that the party act realistically and responsibly by creating two separate organizations along existing ideological lines. In Western Armenia the ARF would continue its historic mission to assure the survival and other civil rights within the Ottoman Empire. In the Caucasus, the ARF would become the socialist organization of the Armenian people and pursue its struggle on the basis of the "Caucasian Platform."

A leadership composed of Western and Eastern Armenian members and strongly committed to preserve the organizational unity within a nation that was already small was able to prevail. The Congress produced a new program that satisfied most of its adherents without necessarily convincing all of the wisdom of the newly discovered "different but united" formula for the continuing struggle for liberation.

The new program was based on the premise that in essence Armenians on both sides of the border were engaged in a single revolution, since in both sectors the struggle was against political despotism, national oppression, and economic exploitation. The differences in levels of economic and political development between the two empires required a different emphasis of activities rather than a different struggle or organization in each. The program further clarified the concept of "people" to include only workers and peasants. The new definition made manifest the class aspect of the revolution but also accounted for the particular composition of exploited Armenian classes on both sides of the border.

Furthermore, The Fourth Congress revised its general principles to bring them closer to the widely accepted concept of "scientific socialism," without relinquishing its appreciation of the subjective factors in history. Thus throughout its new program the party sought to preserve the class aspect of the revolution in Western Armenia and guarantee, at the same time, a solution to the national problem in the Russian Empire. The new program stated:

> Class struggle becomes even more complex in those countries where representatives of the ruling ethnic element, having control of state and public institutions, oppress the weaker nations and minority groups.
>
> Deprived of the possibility of active participation in public and political life, suffering in both their material and intellectual development, the weaker groups are forced to lag behind the path of progress.

There is then a slowing of the universal human development as well as of the social liberation of the workers. This delay is caused by obstacles, on the one hand to the development of class struggle within the oppressed nations and, on the other hand, to class harmony between the exploited classes of the oppressing and oppressed classes.

While struggling against the bourgeoisie within their ethnic group, the working class of the oppressed but intellectually developed people is vigilant in guarding the course of national development which has created a unique popular psychology.

The struggle against ethnic oppression is even more sustained and assured of victory since national development is no longer led exclusively from the upper classes of the nation. The idea of national development permeates masses of the people, it is internalized by them and becomes the avenue of their progress. Popular masses that move from a state of lethargy to the arena of conscious life manifest a hidden potential for growth in the intellectual and social arenas.

Socialism strives toward the elimination of all barriers and all discrimination among nations, and toward the creation of a single, harmonious, all-inclusive humanity that would replace today's divided and antagonistic contradictory world; but socialism does not require the total assimilation of national entities which, through the inherited peculiarities of their history will enrich the future socialist humanity.[11]

The program also included a set of minimum economic and political demands for Russian Armenians as it had done fifteen years earlier for Ottoman Armenians. As a political framework within which those demands would be realized, the party adopted federalism for both sectors of Armenia, thus explicitly rejecting the idea of independence.

The struggle for Armenian liberation was now defined by the idea of a people separated by political boundaries but united through the dedication of both to common revolutionary ideals. The theoretical bond was to be further strengthened by the belief that a democratic Russia, toward which Russian Armenians would strive, would be more inclined to support reforms in Western Armenia. Also, the cooperation among various national groups in the Russian Empire during the 1905 revolution strengthened the strategy in Western Armenia of seeking reforms with the cooperation of Young Turks and other dissatisfied elements. Finally, the new program opened the way for the participation of ARF fighters and intellectuals in the constitutional movement of Iran from 1908 onward.

The diversity of factors with which the ARF had to come to terms produced a curious blend of nationalism and socialism. It can be regarded as the prototype of national liberation movements that evolved in other parts of the world following the First World War. Yet events, often beyond the control of the party or the Armenian people during and after the First World War, overtook formulas and theories, thwarting the national program and preempting the socialist ideal.

Notes

1. *Hay Heghapokhakan Dashnaktsutian Dzragir* [Program of the Armenian Revolutionary Federation] (henceforth *Dzragir, 1892*) (Vienna, n.d.), p. 17.
2. *H.H. Dashnaktsutian Dzragir* [Program of the Armenian Revolutionary Federation] (henceforth *Dzragir, 1907*) (Vienna, 1907).
3. An introductory study of these organizations in the English language can be found in L. Nalbandian, *The Armenian Revolutionary Movement* (Berkeley and Los Angeles, 1967). See also chapter 4.
4. The development of Marxism in the Caucasus and especially among Eastern Armenians is discussed by Anaide Ter Minassian in Ronald Suny, *Transcaucasia, Nationalism, and Social Change* (The University of Michigan Press, Ann Arbor, 1989 and 1996). See also Ter Minassian's "Aux origines du marxisme arménien: les specifistes," *Cahiers du Monde russe et soviétique*, 1 -2 (1978), pp. 67-117. The attraction to Marxism among Eastern Armenian intellectuals is partially explained by their propensity to theorize.
5. *Dzragir, 1892*, pp.5-6.
6. Ibid., pp. 17 - 19.
7. Ibid., p. 16.
8. M. Hovannisian, *Dashnaktsutiune ev nra hakarakordnere* [The Dashnaktsutiune and its Adversaries] (Tiflis, 1906/1907), pp. 54-83.
9. For the text of the "Caucasian Platform" see *Niuter H.H. Dashnaktsutian patmutian hamar* [Documents for the History of the Dashnaktsutiune], vol. II, H. Dasnabedian, editor (Beirut, 1973), pp. 231-236.
10. M. Varandian Hovannisian, *H.H. Dashnaktsutian patmutiune* [History of the Dashnaktsutiune], vol. I (Boston, 1934), pp. 468-472.
11. *Dzragir, 1907*, pp. 14-15.

6

A Case Study of Evolution:
The Socialist Review *Handes*

The rise of minor parties, whether successful or not, is an important chapter in the story of the establishment of Armenian political thought. Equally important are the changes that more enduring parties underwent in the sphere of ideas, paralleled by mutations in party membership.

This chapter is a case study of an unknown and short-lived political review, *Handes* (Arena), published from August to December 1900 in Geneva as the organ of a proposed Armenian Socialist Party (ASP). A presentation of the doctrine of the ASP as formulated in *Handes* and the party program of 1901 will be followed by an analysis of the development of that doctrine, and the political career of Yervand Balian, founder, editor, and ideologue of the new journal.

A Little Known Party

The first *Handes* editorial stated that the goal of the new monthly was "to represent and speak for the Armenian landless peasant, craftsman, and worker, since the essence and direction of their economic life had induced the need for new studies and course of action." The publication of a new forum for ideas had become a necessity then in order to define and defend the distinct interests of the economically exploited Armenians, otherwise neglected or misrepresented in the press. The legal Armenian newspapers in the Ottoman and Russian empires, argued the editorial, expressed the ideology of the bourgeois class and could hardly be expected to serve the oppressed. On the other hand, the *Hnchak* and *Droshak*, organs of the SDHP (Social Democratic Hnchakian Party) and the ARF (Armenian Revolutionary Federation) parties respectively, pursued the asserted goal of national independence. The *Handes* recognized the legitimacy of the struggle for national liberation but suggested that the cause of economic liberation could not be entrusted to these "insurrectional" parties, despite the latters' claim to the contrary. The distorted notions of socialism found in the programs of the revolutionary organizations had done even more harm than good to the workers; by confusing and often equating the national and class struggles, their misinformed leadership had denied the workers and landless peasants the opportunity to develop an autonomous class-consciousness. Hoping for a clear division of labor in the political arena, the ASP indicated that "each Party represents a moment in history, and should not try to be everything to everybody."

The assignment the ASP undertook for itself on behalf of the economically oppressed was derived from an ideological perspective most clearly formulated in the second part of the party program. This perspective can best be described as a summarized reproduction of the Marxist interpretation of history, closely following Kautsky's arguments in the Erfurt Program. Particular emphasis was placed on the role of capitalism in the development of industrialization and contemporary political and economic institutions. To say that such a doctrine lacked originality would be an understatement, undoubtedly. It is definitely more interesting and ultimately more important to consider the insight derived from the application of those adopted principles to Armenian society.

The new doctrine provided a theoretical framework within which class struggle was the matrix of political analysis, thus attributing an incidental role to the national liberation struggle. Consequently, the national unity and cohesiveness sought by the revolutionary parties was to be replaced by class antagonism, and the formation of an Armenian workers' organization to pursue goals consonant with their economic interests.

The adoption of Marxism, a system of thought developed in Western Europe, implied of course a belief on the part of the ASP in the universal validity of the precepts of that system. However, given the separate existence of the majority of the Armenian people under two distinct empires and the dispersion of the remainder over many parts of the world, the actual practice of class struggle would vary according to the stratification within each community and the level of socioeconomic and political development of the country where a given community resided.

Thus, the ASP determined that the estimated 20,000 Armenians, mostly industrial workers, living in the United States were in a position to immediately organize labor unions and, joining the Armenian Socialist Labor Party, engage in the struggle to win political power for the working class. Next in line was the Caucasus, which had begun feeling the impact of capitalism earlier than the Ottoman Empire and was in the throes of full-scale industrialization.

In the Caucasus, Armenians constituted a sizable segment of the rising urban proletariat. But here too, the ranks of the bourgeoisie were filled with Armenians who owned much of the capital invested in commerce and industry. At that time, the pursuit of economic interests in the Caucasus entailed antagonism within the nation and presupposed class-consciousness strong enough to transcend ethnic interests and loyalties. Moreover, within the particular circumstances of the Russian Empire, the education of the workers, their organization as unions, and preparation for the ultimate revolution had to be paralleled with a struggle for political liberties.

Similar analysis was extended to the cases of Bulgaria, Egypt, and Persia, where a considerable number of Armenians lived. Regardless of their present degree of economic development, the ASP thought industrialization was unavoidable, and foresaw increasing socialist activity as growing numbers of Armenians became subjected to exploitation in factories.

Undoubtedly, the implications of a class ideology were the gravest for the fate of Armenians in the Ottoman Empire, for whose benefit the national liberation war was being waged. First, Armenian communities abroad would no longer serve that struggle, in which they had been assigned a crucial supportive role by the revolutionary parties. Also, the SDHP and ARF avoided open class antagonism, considering cooperation between all segments of the Armenian nation a necessity for the liberation struggle, the legitimacy of which had been recognized by the *Handes* on many occasions. Thus, the ASP proceeded with great care in its analysis by first demonstrating that contrary to the general consensus, socialism was quite relevant for the Ottoman Empire and the fate of Armenians there. The 1901 program stated that the people in this semi-feudal state were already being victimized directly and indirectly by western European capitalism. First, increasing Ottoman financial dependence on Western Europe was causing huge increases in domestic taxes, with serious implications for the social and economic life of all citizens, including Armenians. In addition, taxes were being demanded in cash, forcing many small farmers into debt and ultimately bankruptcy. Secondly, machine produced goods being imported from Europe were destroying the traditional manufacturing system prevalent in the country and an economic sector particularly dominated by Armenians. Finally, through mining and communications concessions to European concerns, industrial development was making direct inroads into Western Armenia. Consequently Armenians, along with other nationalities in the Ottoman Empire, were being drawn into the capitalist world.

The significance of the program for the rural areas in the Ottoman Empire was twofold. Most farmers who lost their lands became share-croppers or tenant farmers, thus constituting the potentially revolutionary *maraba* class. Others migrated from the village. In the towns, many small shop owners and skilled craftsmen lost their markets and businesses. In addition to the migrant farmers, these provided the raw materials for what would have been an urban proletariat, had industrial centers developed in the empire. Instead, some moved to such countries as the United States, which could absorb them as factory workers. However, in the Ottoman Empire there still remained a majority made up of the dispossessed. Their political education and organization for the protection of elementary rights were to be the concern of the ASP. More importantly, the inevitable development of industrial manufacturing would bring about the formation of an actual urban proletariat in the empire. The process of industrialization required nevertheless the coming to power of a bourgeois class. It seemed more probable to the ASP that the domination of a bourgeois class in this case would be achieved through a more pervasive control of the Ottoman economy by European capital, guaranteed by a European administration. The second possibility was the establishment of an independent Armenia and that seemed somehow more attractive. Either way, the *Handes* welcomed the prospects of industrialization. It stated, characteristically:

> Railroad concessions have already been made by the Ottoman government to Europe... Our lands and natural resources will be used. Each segment of the Armenian population must realize its class interests and organize accordingly. The wealthy Armenian must secure Armenian control of these means of production. This will guarantee political rights and bring out the Armenian proletariat, which we will then defend.

Socialism, then, provided useful analytical tools to understand developments crucial to Western Armenians and guide them through the complex struggle of the future. If the bearing socialism had upon Armenians in the Ottoman Empire was limited to these two points, it is difficult to understand the ASP's claim of having attained a higher truth. First, as mentioned earlier, there was no denial of the legitimacy of the liberation struggle itself, and the ASP even preferred an Armenian bourgeois domination over any other; secondly, both the SDHP and ARF party programs displayed more awareness of the economic aspects of Ottoman oppression than the *Handes* was willing to credit them with. Finally, the SDHP program insisted that once independence of Armenia was achieved, the party would engage in socialist activities not unlike those projected by the ASP. There is, however, an essential difference between the ASP and the revolutionary parties. In the case of the latter, the concept of class analysis was used to interpret the historical evolution of Ottoman administration. For them, such analysis had no pertinence to a society, which instead of factory workers had peasants and small farmers needing protection from nomadic attacks and greedy usurers; instead of corporations had small shopkeepers searching for some security in a changing world; and instead of clearly developed classes had a nation longing for basic human rights if not survival. For the ASP however, class struggle, when placed within the larger Marxist framework, led to a critique of the assumptions and direction of the liberation struggle as it was being waged.

The *Handes* asserted that "The national liberation organizations constituted a reflexive reaction to a simplistic interpretation of class antagonism as ethnic oppression." It insisted that oppression along class lines sustained the Ottoman regime, against which the revolutionaries were fighting. Throughout the *Handes* and ASP Program, a direct correlation was seen between the rise of a capitalist bourgeois state and the securing democratic and political rights, which incidentally constituted the basis of the SDHP and ARF platforms. In other words, the lack of such rights in the Ottoman Empire could be ascribed to the absence of appropriate socio-economic conditions. Consequently, if the revolutionary parties were to become something more than a "reflexive reaction," they had to understand the laws of history—perceive social realities behind appearances and in cooperation with all oppressed elements in the empire, i.e., attack the root rather than the symptom of the problem.

In the analysis of the ASP, socialism was transformed within Armenian political thought from a mere ideal, to be reached in the future, into a living doctrine. Rather than remaining a universal value that encompassed any and all concern for all forms of human suffering, socialism, ostensibly Marxist and scientific, became an instrument for the understanding and interpretation of forces affecting society most deeply, projecting into the future and charting the most appropriate course of action.

The systematic application of Marxist analytical tools to Armenian society was first attempted in the *Handes* and represented an important step in the development of Armenian political thought. To understand this process of ideological evolution, it is necessary to be cognizant of the human dimension behind the abstract thoughts and their relationship to historical circumstances.

A Little Known Revolutionary

The little that is known of the individuals behind the *Handes* attests to the dominant figure of Yervand Balian, who as editor of the journal, author of major articles and the ASP program, and the driving force of the proposed party, for all practical purposes constituted a one man operation. Therefore, it is possible to see the *Handes* doctrine as the reflection of his political views without doing injustice to his associates or to history.

Born in the Crimea in 1869, Yervand Balian started his political activities as the leader of one of many student groups organized in the Nersisian School in Tbilisi and Gevorkian Seminary of Etchmiadzin. Student politics in the 1880s was permeated by an idealistic dedication to the cause of the "people," within both the Russian Narodnik and Western Armenian contexts of the word. Balian's circle kept a steady correspondence with university activists in Moscow. At the same time, the teenage seminarians followed events in Western Armenia by reading Mkrtich Portugalian's *Armenia*, a feat for which they were almost imprisoned. Soon the *Hnchak* replaced the irresolute *Armenia* as the favorite of the youth. The radical approach of the SDHP must have been more attractive, since eventually Balian joined the party. In 1891 he was in Baku as a field worker, organizing the first SDHP branch in the Balakhani district of the city. He is said to have involved his converts in the workers' movement, possibly an early indication that for Balian the party's ultimate goal of socialism had as much relevance for the present as the immediate one.

It was probably in 1895 that Balian went to Geneva to study social sciences at the University. On two occasions during his long career as a student he became a member of the SDHP hierarchy. Once, in 1896, he was called upon to serve on the Central Committee with Avetis Nazarbek, one of the founders of the party. His duties included membership in the editorial board of the *Hnchak*; he was also assigned responsibilities for corresponding with branches of the party in Russia, Persia, and the United States. However, soon he resigned. The second association with the Central Committee came in 1899 upon the invitation of Russian-Armenian SDHP. The latter had taken the initiative to reorganize the Central Committee after it had reached total paralysis with the resignation of the Nazarbek and his wife Maro and following the bloody strife with the *Verakazmial* (reformed) Hnchakian wing after the split in the party. The choice of Balian was due to his "expertise in Marxism." The new leadership had hardly started republication of the *Hnchak* when Balian resigned for the second time, ostensibly to continue his studies.

There might be some truth in the assertion made by the ARF writer Abraham Gulkhandarian that "Balian, who could have become one of our more competent public leaders, was left isolated because of his abrasive behavior." Nevertheless, personality conflicts, not uncommon among revolutionaries, cannot explain the decision of an otherwise respected person to break away from a party with which he had been associated for over a decade. The reasons must be sought elsewhere.

The years between 1896-1899, when Balian was involved closely with party affairs, were the most difficult for the revolutionary parties. It proved fatal to the SDHP, which was until then the strongest Armenian political organization. There was the dismal failure of the revolutionaries to force effective European intervention on behalf of Western Armenians. There also were the harsh realities of the 1894-96 massacres. An atmosphere of disenchantment, frustration, and powerlessness pervaded all concerned. Reevaluation became the order of the day.

Under such trying circumstances, personality conflicts within the SDHP acquired new meaning. There were charges of party mismanagement and mishandling of funds. Some had found a scapegoat in the leaders, mainly the Nazarbeks. The process of reexamination extended, however, to the ideological sphere as well, and struck at the dichotomy that characterized the party program. One challenge, from the same anti-Nazarbek faction, was directed against the socialism of the program as irrelevant, diversionary, and imposed by Eastern Armenians. The solution to the above two objections was found in the split of this faction from the party as the Reformed Hnchakians. The second, less celebrated, criticism against the program came from the opposite perspective. It reassessed the basic premises upon which the liberation struggle was based. The critique developed along the following lines: for the SDHP, the reforms or independence had been placed within socialism as a personal religion and an ultimate political goal. However, the relationship between struggle in the name of the nation and socialism on behalf of the workers was more chronological than inherently logical, whence the dichotomy within the SDHP program. This did not disturb the old leadership under the Nazarbeks, who were quite content with the major changes they had introduced in Armenian political life earlier in their careers by organizing armed rebellion and adding the word socialism to the Armenian vocabulary. Even their limited concept of socialism had been relegated to the background in the name of immediate concerns. Along the way however, the SDHP had failed to develop an accurate perception of social realities, which determine the content and direction of political movements. Because it lacked historical perspective then, the organization had become a "reflexive reaction," unable to learn from its experience, understand its failures, and cope with the impasse reached in 1896-99. The failure of the SDHP or the revolutionary movement did not consist then in its adoption of socialism as an idea, but rather in its refusal to fully comprehend the implication of that socialism, even in the primitive form as it was found in the SDHP program. It was not difficult, however, for an expert in Marxism such as Balian to realize the potential of socialism, cleanse its ideological impurities, and resolve the SDHP dichotomy. In the age of positivism, one could rely on a scientific approach to the interpretation of history to supply the cures of society's ills, and find a way to be on the right side in the future. Man's actions had to be accommodated to the precepts of a higher truth contained in ideology. The crucial decision consisted in the adoption of socialism as a total system of thought, whence a course of political action could be derived.

Yervand Balian made that decision when the first issue of the rejuvenated *Hnchak* appeared in September 1899. The editorial made an appeal "to the dedicated Armenian youth to join the SDHP struggle for a general uprising in Western Armenia, in the name of the broadest, socialist revolutionary principles." Balian could not entertain any more hopes that the party could take socialism seriously.

His resignation immediately followed that issue of the *Hnchak*. Eight months later appeared the *Handes*. Later, when writing the introduction to the ASP program, he referred to these circumstances:

> There were also Hnchakians preoccupied not so much with patriotism and national independence as with socialism. And today, this small number of Hnchakians, who are free of any self serving goals, having had integrity of thought and total dedication to public life, consciously and correctly left the Hnchak to become fighters of the genuine Armenian Social Democratic Party and the *Handes*.

Admittedly, a journal oriented towards intellectuals and representing an ideology awaiting its object could not, and apparently did not, amass a large following. Other than a group organized in 1904 in Bulgaria, there is no evidence of workers flocking to the ASP banner. The fact is that the *Handes* itself had folded by the time the Party Program was published. Subsequent attempts to revive it did not succeed.

Even in the absence of hardships common to newly organizing parties, there were major problems that would have been difficult to overcome for the ASP. First, the ASP had intermarried a dogmatic and often crude Marxism and lacked an empirical model suitable to a semi-feudal and complex society such as the Ottoman Empire. Furthermore, the discovery and dissemination of ostensibly scientific truth would have been hardly enough to raise class consciousness, particularly among emigrants These tended to view themselves as economic refugees who someday would return home; they were not that interested in acting out the dictates of history. Finally, there was in the case of the ASP, an ideological contradiction, expressed most clearly in the type of organization it attempted to be. After all, it was difficult to justify the founding of an Armenian Socialist Party and Armenian labor unions in different parts of the world, united as Armenians and separate from local workers organizations, when the only absolute accepted was class consciousness.

In 1903 a new party was organized in the Caucasus, the only area where the ASP could have potentially found acceptance and application. This was the Social Democratic Workers Armenian Organization, otherwise known as the Specifists. One source mentions Balian as being a field worker for it. Whether true or not, he could very well have been since the only significant difference between Balian and the Specifists was the latter's limitation of activities to the Caucasus with no claims for a worldwide organization.

It is difficult to evaluate the direct impact Balian or the *Handes* might have had on the subsequent ideological development had it had the means to continue its existence. Many insights and analyses first presented by Balian were repeated or developed later by a variety of groups. This could possibly have occurred independently.

The fact remains that the *Handes* did represent a transitional stage in the development of Armenian political thought. In a stateless people, it was a serious attempt to define the relationship between nation and class. The integration of the two was an important issue for the political parties and engaged both Eastern and Western Armenians.

A detail within the larger picture, the case of the ASP testifies to the formation of an intelligentsia in search of a suitable framework that would help them understand and define complex issues that could not so neatly fit into general categories of nationalism and socialism. One of the important characteristics of this period is the belief that history had a rational development. Yervand Balian epitomized a segment of the Armenian leadership that hoped that power of logic could substitute for naked power and the strength of ideology could succeed where heroism failed, not unlike the moral victory declared after the military defeat by Vardan Mamikonian at Avarayr in 451. The search for that ideology, enhanced by a dialectic relationship with more perceptible political events, caused Armenian political thought to evolve.

Had the ASP and Balian been an exception, they could have been easily dismissed. But the phenomenon illustrated here can be demonstrated to be valid for the duration of the critical period between 1878 and 1920. Unless this phenomenon is understood, the development of Armenian political thought and its intricate relationship to history cannot be explained.

Part IV

7

The Ideology of the Young Turk Movement

The ideology of the Young Turks, more specifically the Ittihad ve Terakke Jemiyeti (Committee of Union and Progress or CUP), has presented a special interest to historians. One obvious reason is that the leaders bear primary and ultimate responsibility for the planning and execution of the tragedy that befell the Armenians during the First World War. As such, it is useful to understand the concerns, principles, and values that motivated them. Their ideology becomes all the more interesting when one looks at the repetition of the crime of genocide in the twentieth century and its increasing practice as an accepted if not altogether condoned tool used by governments to resolve conflicts. The larger context within which this first genocide of the twentieth century occurred presents a further challenge. This was the period when Western states, far ahead on the path to modernization and of organizing themselves as nation-states, presented serious challenges to what is termed today the third world, creating new conflicts and giving new articulation to old ones.

One of the major changes affecting political and social relations was the structure of states. The legitimization of power on the basis of ethnic, cultural, and religious identity of the population acquired a dynamic significance for old empires and new states. For the Young Turks, who engineered and supervised the transitional stage, the creation of a new Turkish nation-state out of the old Ottoman Empire passed through the prism of the homogenization of the population.

The Ottoman Empire in the nineteenth century had the dubious distinction of being at once oppressed by many, often conflicting, Western imperial designs, and oppressor of its subject peoples, which included non-Turks such as Arabs and Kurds, and non-Muslim Armenians and Greeks. The two phenomena were further related. Elements in the Ottoman Empire opposing the sultan's regime borrowed their models of reform and revolution from the West. Western governments, meanwhile, often couched their aggressive policies toward Turkey under the cloak of humanitarian help to subject Ottoman peoples. The problem of withstanding Western technological and military challenge was thus intricately tied to the demand for reforms from within. In other words, the survival of the state could not be guaranteed without some fundamental change in its character and/or a redefinition of the role—symbolic and real—of the Turkish element within government.

Ottoman and Turkish reformers faced this dilemma throughout the nineteenth and twentieth centuries. Reforms satisfactory to all ethnic and religious elements, ostensibly supported by European powers, had to be based on the principle of equality, which threatened the principle of the dominance of Turks: reforms essential for the survival of a budding middle and industrial class and especially a disintegrating peasantry would have undermined an oligarchy that changed some of its color but excluded, characteristically, the masses of the Turkish and non-Turkish population from participating in the definition of the interests of the state or the nation.

This dilemma explains also a fundamental characteristic of reform in the context of Ottoman and Turkish society: it was always ordained from above. Yet the ultimate but consistent rejection of reforms, political, social, and economic, by successive Turkish oligarchies was rationalized by the need to resist foreign intervention. Often articulated in legal terms, the constant state of national emergency has become an integral part of the political process in Turkey since Ottoman times. The imposition of military or quasi-military rule under a variety of names has been facilitated by equating internal dissent, meaning demands for reform, with the interests of those who threaten the welfare of the fatherland. The crude equalization of the interests of a ruling oligarchy along with its exclusive vision of society with its abstracted concept of power and the survival of the state has eventually developed into a pattern. Turkish oligarchies, Ottoman Young Turk or modern Turkish, have contributed to a false consciousness among the Turkish people that sharing the ethnic identity of the ruler is tantamount to sharing in power. Once the pattern of such an equation has evolved, it is not too difficult to suspect that in some cases foreign threats and crises were manufactured to facilitate the suppression of reform movements.

Whatever the variations on the theme, oligarchies need legitimation that will account for power relations and articulate their principles through a terminology that sanctions the rulers' concerns. Each generation, consequently, found a new ideology to articulate its hopes and fears as well as to repress them. Each generation responded in its own way to the challenge of preserving the state while accommodating change. The questions have always been whether change accommodates more than an oligarchy, and if so at what cost.

For the reforming sultans of the 1830s and 1850s the West was not as yet the multifaceted challenge it was soon to become. Theirs was the sort of vision characteristic of benevolent yet secure rulers. Even the Young Ottoman generation of the 1870s took for granted the imperial character of the state: it continued to assume the coexistence of a variety of peoples under the predominance of the Turkish ethnic group. The Young Ottomans were ostracized and exiled by Sultan Abdul-Hamid II and had no real opportunity to test their principles. They also represented the last opportunity to develop a political framework capable of accommodating a variety of real, human, individual, and collective needs. For that sultan, as for many a subsequent Turkish government, serious reforms meant modernization of the military and related branches of the government that ensured efficiency and centralization.

In essence, the Young Turks inherited and led to its logical conclusion this endemic vision of change and survival. Their brief tenure of office (1908-1918) and the wars, which characterized that tenure, accentuated the characteristic dilemma of oligarchies in Turkey: the inability to reform by sharing power, while reform appears to be necessary for survival. The Young Turks accentuated those policies of the Ottoman government that obviated the need for reforms by silencing the call for change.

As a transitional government, the Young Turks began their career by sharing values with the Young Ottomans: willingness to liberalize the regime and accommodate non-Turkish and, initially, non-Muslim elements. Increasingly, however, they felt more comfortable with and shared Sultan Abdul-Hamid II's Pan-Islamic/Pan-Turkic formula to supplant the earlier Western and internal support for their liberal reformist program that was encouraged by, among others, Armenians. By 1919, they fully appreciated the vision that Mustafa Kemal was articulating for his people: a Turkish nation-state, where everyone was some type of a Turk by definition just because he/she lived within boundaries now recognized as Turkey's. In fact, it was their extermination of Armenians that made it possible for Mustafa Kemal to articulate fully such a vision of a modern Turkey.

This eclecticism explains the seemingly paradoxical charge leveled against the Young Turks, that of not having an ideology. Caught between what was and what was to be, the Young Turks were overly sensitive to the need to ensure a sense of the empire under an oligarchy that could both preserve the legitimacy that historical continuity provided and resolve rationally the challenge that a more fragmented world presented to them. They could then identify with the social and political conservatism of the sultan they deposed in 1909 and with the secularizing program of Mustafa Kemal that was to come. Thus, despite the political and historiographic controversies between the Young Turks and the sultan or the Young Turks and the Kemalists, there is a community of interests reflected in recent political positions and controversies appreciated by statist Turkish scholars.

The Young Turk vision that evolved between their assumption of power in 1908 and the execution of the plan of extermination of Armenians revolved around a flexible formula: at a minimum, it would guarantee a Turkified core for a nation-state; at most it would result in a Pan-Turanic or Pan-Turkic Empire that would be a worthy inheritor of the Ottoman Empire, albeit erected on a different principle of legitimation. The minimum program would accommodate defeat in the war, the maximum program looked forward to victory. The exclusive nationalism underlying the first and the racism extolled in the second were the two sides of the same coin. In both cases there was no room for the Armenians, those constant reminders of the need for reform, who, as surrogate Westerners, were targets more easily destroyed.

For Young Turks, ideology was as expendable as were the Armenian people, when faced with the more immediate need to survive in power. An integral component of that outlook was the claim of survival playing a crucial function in the realization of a manifest destiny.

By 1914 the Young Turks had a fully articulated ideology to the extent that exclusivism and abstraction of the state could be considered such. They also put to practice that ideology by gradually eliminating from government all those who might disagree with them.

Both in the capital and in the provinces, the CUP took control of the administration. They created a mechanism by which policies could be made and implemented without the few individuals responsible for the policies being held responsible for their actions. Momentous decisions could thus be taken, often with tragic consequences for the state and its subjects, without the chain of command or process of decision-making being altogether clear or subject to accountability. The decision of the Ottoman Empire to enter the war, and this on the side of Germany, the disastrous Caucasian campaign by Enver Pasha, and the extermination of Armenians could be accomplished with impunity. The triumvirate of Talat, Enver, and Jemal could get away with it because, on the one hand, they encouraged an atmosphere within which political discourse was limited to the terms "patriotism" and "duty." They, of course, reserved the exclusive right to define what each of those terms meant. The doctrine of responsibility of the state toward its subjects was replaced by the demand for total obedience in the name of the fatherland, a virtue extolled by intellectuals like Ziya Gokalp. In addition, the intellectuals in the party were able to adopt a sort of social Darwinism that, while claiming to participate in the modern, progressive world, allowed them to feel comfortable with their racism and state-sponsored violence.

Parallel to the manipulation of the ideological sphere, the CUP developed an effective way of government while avoiding the responsibility of governing. It created a dual structure of government: the official administrative structure and CUP operations at critical junctures of that administration. There were in place during World War I two chains of command, the second being the more critical and being subject to the Cemiyet, or party leadership: even then the CUP refused to function as a political party. It remained a secret society, whose deliberations were not subject to public scrutiny. Thus, in its 1910 and 1911 secret congresses in Salonika, the CUP seems to have decided on the Turkification of Anatolia, leaving the use of military means for the appropriate moment. This it did while pursuing a policy of cooperation with Armenians.

It was possible then, both ideologically and politically, to undertake a policy of homogenization of the population in 1914-15. The two principles underlying this process corresponded to the two major factors determining Ottoman-Turkish history: Western imperialism, which dismembered the outlying, largely non-Turkish provinces, and Turkification of non-Turkish elements within core provinces. The first decreased the number of non-Turks by secession, the second by extermination.

The actualization of what the CUP considered its manifest destiny in Turkish history has had a curious evaluation by those they deposed, the conservative Ottomans, and those who deposed them, the Kemalists. As a solution to the Armenian problem, it seems to have been successful. As such it has been appreciated, implicitly and explicitly, by all who considered Turkish supremacy, whether within an empire or nation-state, the ultimate principle to uphold. Nonetheless, the ideology of secularization seems to have led Kemal Atatürk to criticize the massacres and deportations of Armenians at least on one occasion. The criticism was on the basis that such an action showed discrimination on the basis of religious difference, something that the new nation-state should not tolerate.

It is important to note that the CUP also took action against the Jewish community in Tel Aviv and Kurds in Anatolia. In the case of the Jews, the rational was that the community might help the British in the war. That action was rescinded following the intercession of the American Ambassador in Istanbul. A partial deportation of Kurds, but not massacres, also took place in southeastern Turkey. The CUP ideology, based on an insatiable thirst for power, increasing nationalism, self-definition conditioned partially by hatred of an enemy or enemies, and visions of grandeur, recognized no boundaries.

Appendix: Document

Excerpts from the proceedings of the courts martial held in Istanbul from April to July 1919, against the leaders of the CUP (from Takvim-i Vekai, *the official journal of the Ottoman state) by the new government of the Ottoman Empire. From the conclusion and verdict of the First Session of the Courts Martial (*Takvim-I Vekai, *No. 3571):*

The criminal committee, the so-called Union and Progress, had represented itself as a political party, and under this guise, had published its by-laws: however, beyond the political organization, it evidently had other secret organizations and institutions. The leaders did not refrain, in practice, from working in that manner.

Dr. Nazim Bey, Atif Bey, Dr. Behaeddin Shakir Bey and some of the other most influential members had organized the Teshkilati Mahsusa, a commission which included also Kemal Bey, a member of the Central Committee, who had organized the Commission of Supply (Iase Komisionu) with his colleagues.

It is superfluous to reiterate what has repeatedly been said in the indictment about the activities and affairs placed in practice by the above-mentioned commissions of the party.

As is evident from the details of its correspondence, the party of Union and Progress had evolved and approved secret plans and special goals and had recourse to the imposition of tyrannical measures of every kind in order to have its programmes accepted without exception. The party even applied capital punishment in the case of Halil Bey, of Galata and others...

Under the pretext of carrying out the Law of Deportation, it organized all kinds of crimes that were uniformly perpetrated throughout most of the Ottoman territory. During these events, the deportation areas were under the jurisdiction (or supervision) of the representatives and responsible secretaries of the Union and Progress Party.

The chief leaders of the Union and Progress Party organized the Teshkilati Mahsusa commission in the above-mentioned areas. They confessed that they had accepted the chairmanship and active leadership of the Teshkilati Mahsusa. It is established, and evident that Dr. Behaeddin Shakir Bey, who supervised them (the gang leaders), organized the responsible delegates and inspectors of the Union and Progress Party with the same purpose.

It is evident that the Committee pre-planned and organized all the crimes which were committed.

So, the Committee ruled against Ottoman subjects, individuals, communities and peoples, without exception, in order to attain its goal, and it took all measures necessary to remove, permanently, all resistance from within the ranks of government officials.

In a series of events in our country beginning in 1908, and particularly during the Balkan War of 1912, the Committee revealed irrational aspirations, and entrusted the War Office to Enver Bey, who is now a fugitive, in order to carry out the decisions and realize the goals of the Committee. Enver had twice urged Ahmet Izzet Pasha, former Prime Minister (and Enver's predecessor as Minister of War), to resign from the War Office. On those occasions, they had terrorized Izzet Pasha.

During the deportations, they issued orders to the Governors of provinces to commit crimes. When some members of the government in the provinces refused to serve their criminal purposes, they had them dismissed immediately, particularly Jemal Bey, Mutesarif of Yozgat; Reshid Pasha, Governor-General of Kastamuni; and, Mazhar Bey, Governor-General of Ankara.

In his answers to the questions, Tahsin Bey, Governor-General of Erzerum, made detailed statements that established the above facts.

The Committee took in hand the direction of the government of the provinces by means of similar measures and threats and imposed its will on all of them. The Committee not only intervened in the affairs of the government, but also gave its most influential members offices in the Council of Ministers and accepted the presence of those ministers in the General Assembly (of the Party). Without any legal authority or jurisdiction, they held meetings and councils, and made decisions concerning the affairs of state.

Since its advent the Committee injected a coldness into the relations between the various elements of the population living in the country by using many unprecedented measures and threats. The Committee organized and enforced boycotts and deportations of Muslim and non-Muslim elements in the Anatolian provinces, where they lived together.

The above explanations provide evidence that the Committee certainly took the most extreme measures in order to realize its special programmes and was successful in usurping the power of the government.

As the Minister of Finance Javid Bey said openly in his statements reported in the minutes of the 5th section of the Chambre des Deputes on the 24th and 26th October 1334 (i.e. 1918) this group of action of Union and Progress has shown in its decisions concerning the destiny of the nation and of the country, an audacity and an over-confidence such that they did not think it fit to submit to the Council of Ministers the decision concerning the declaration of war, whilst even sovereigns do not take such decisions of their own initiative. Everybody having understood that this way of acting could not give good results, the acts of the Committee that the opposition itself had respected seemed blameworthy to level-headed people.

On the other hand, the fact that the state of siege which had been abolished necessarily at the time of the change of regime has been maintained almost without interruption, that the Sublime Porte has been attacked by a clique led by the senior members of the Committee of Union and Progress, that the War Minister Nazim Pasha and his aide de camp were killed and that a Union and Progress Cabinet was formed and that the Cabinet of Kiamil Pasha was overthrown:

that at the time of the two cabinets which followed, the able and honest and experienced civil servants were dismissed and replaced by persons affiliated to the Committee has had for result: to give rise to justified general complaints against the arbitrary and tyrannical administration, to the point of making people regret the despotic regime, to dissatisfy more particularly the non-Muslim populations and above all to bring the Armenians (who realized that their belief that freedom would insure security and justice was not founded) to seek a favorable opportunity for the realization of their national aims, which they envisaged before.

Questions of nationalities created between the different nationalities and even the Muslims have provoked cool feelings and divisions, interfering in so doing with Ottoman unity...

Considering that these facts have been established by investigations and inquiries and by the above-named bills of indictment; that there is no possibility to refute the five points set out and examined by our Court Martial or to maintain that they do not exist we have acquired the conviction in our conscience that the personal crimes above mentioned assigned to the Committee of Union and Progress have been committed in such a way as to cast a slur on its name...

Consequently it has been decided after deliberation, that in the light of the phases of this trial, the above-mentioned assertions of the Counsel have no value for the defense.

The Five points mentioned above are as follows:

1. The crime of the massacres of Trabzon, of Yozgad and of Boghazlyan which, it was established during the trials which took place at the Court Martial, was organized and executed by some chiefs of Union and Progress.

    In admitting even, as it was alleged during the defense, that there are among these some who came to know of these crimes only after their perpetration, they have not prevented their recurring, no more than they have done anything to punish those who committed them.

2. According to the declarations he made to the Chamber of Deputies and which are recorded in the minutes, Said Halim Pasha, Grand Vizir and President of the Committee Union and Progress, had at the beginning of the mobilization invited to his house the members of the Central Committee and had explained to them, giving useful arguments, that the participation of the country in the war would be very dangerous, and that neutrality would constitute the best attitude to assume in the conflict but that he had failed to make them adopt his opinion and consequently the State had entered the war.

Moreover, Riza Bey, one of the responsible delegates of the Union and Progress, has admitted during his trial, that without waiting for the declaration of war, he began the hostilities by means of persons belonging to organized bands at Trabzon, whom he sent into the interior of Russia.

Finally, Javid Bey, then Finance Minister, Churuk-Sulu Mahmoud Pasha, Minister of Public Works, Oskan Effendi, Post and Telegraph Minister, and Suleiman Elbostani Effendi, Trade Minister, gave their resignation, for the reason that the war had been declared without the previous decision of the Council of Ministers. These facts establish that the war had not been declared by decision of the Ministers responsible, but deliberately by the Union and Progress who wanted it so.

3. As it appears from the declarations of His Highness Ahmed lzzet Pasha, former Grand Vizir, his resignation from the War Ministry was provoked by the interference of the Party in the Government's affairs.

4. As it results from the report read in 1332 (1916) amidst the Congress of Union and Progress and unanimously approved by its members, and from the information that the Prefecture of the town has supplied in answer to the communications sent by this Tribunal, Kemal Bey, Delegate from Constantinople, who had been put in charge by the Central Bureau of the Union and Progress of the provisioning, and whose nomination was ratified later on by the General Council of the Union, has first instituted a Council of Trade and after several societies and associations which have monopolized commercial transactions and have by these means seized the whole fortune of the population. The public wealth being concentrated so exclusively in the hands of a limited number of persons and the above-mentioned societies, the result was that owing to an inadequate nutrition, many Ottomans were crippled or died and that the forces at the disposal of the State for its defense had been reduced.

The reading of the same documents has established also that the Union and Progress has provoked at the same time the meddling of its Constantinople Bureau in the functions of the Government.

5. The fact that the former Sheikhul Islam Musa Kiazim Effendi, answering an interpellation at the Senate regarding the transfer of the tribunal from the Sheri to the Ministry of Justice said: "Do not ask for my opinion, it is the Party which demands this transfer. It must be done so," and that he confirmed these declarations during the trial, constitute an obvious proof of the interference of the Party in the State's affairs...

The Court Martial, taking into consideration the above-named crimes declares, unanimously, the culpability as principal factors of these crimes of the fugitives Talat Pasha, former Grand Vizir; Enver Effendi, former War Minister, struck off the register of the Imperial Army; Jemal Effendi, former Navy Minister, struck off too from the Imperial Army;

and Dr. Nazim Eflendi, former Minister of Education, members of the General Council of the Union and Progress, representing the moral person of this party: as well as for that of the fugitives Javid Bey, former Finance Minister; and Mustafa Sheref Bey, former Trade & Agriculture Minister, members of the said Council known as having participated in the crimes in question...

The acts of Talat, Enver, Jemal and Dr. Nazim falling under Article 45 of the Civil and Penal Codes, 1st paragraph, those of Javid, Mustafa Sheref and Musa Kiazim of the same Article, paragraph 2, and Article 35 last paragraph, and these articles stipulating that "individuals who commit collectively a crime or each individual, being part of a certain number of persons, who in the case of a crime consisting of several offenses commits one or several of the latter with a view to accomplishing the offense are called co-authors and punished as the principal author," and "the person who is convicted of having by force modified or suppressed the constitutional Charter, the form of the Government or rule of the heredity of the Imperial Throne" is put to death. The accomplices of the execution of a crime are in the case of absence of a special disposition of the law, condemned to the following punishments: the accomplices will be condemned to hard labor for at least ten years if the main offense is punishable by death or by hard labor for life, the Court Martial pronounces, in accordance with the said stipulations of the Law the death penalty against Talat, Enver, Jemal and Dr. Nazim...

8

The Ultimate Repression:
The Genocide of the Armenians, 1915-1917

Exterminations of families, tribes, and ethnic or religious groups have been known to occur since the dawn of history. The particular heinousness of mass death, however, has brought the gradual recognition of such acts as legally defined crimes against humanity. Planned and systematic genocides have even acquired a wider scope, while technology has increased their efficiency. Given the technological advances in military and biological hardware, the degrees to which many groups depend on governmental policies for their survival, the abrupt changes that traditional societies undergo when facing the challenge of modernization, and the increase in tensions between nations due to the diminishing resources available for distribution, one can expect governments to have recourse to radical solutions such as genocide to solve real or imaginary problems. Genocide thus may become merely another manifestation of what differentiates a state from other institutions: its monopoly of the right to kill enemies of society and to ask its citizens to kill enemies of the state or to be killed doing it.

A corollary to the above hypothesis is that certain groups that seek change in a system, particularly a traditional one, are more likely to be victims of genocide. This is especially true when the ideology of the state characterizes a potential victim as both an enemy of society (of the internal order) and of the state.[1]

The Genocide of the Armenian people during World War I is the earliest case of a fully documented modern day extermination of a nation. Planned and carried out by the Ittihad ve Terakke Jemiyeti (Committee of Union and Progress or CUP) government of the Ottoman Empire, this first genocide of the twentieth century may also be a paradigm for "political" genocide since then. Twentieth-century genocides may have become radical means used by governments to resolve political problems. This chapter will briefly present the facts and impact of the Armenian Genocide, discuss the generally accepted explanations for the deportations and massacres as the final solution to a thorny problem, introduce some little known evidence on the relations between Armenian and Turkish leaders preceding the Genocide, and suggest that the CUP government perceived Armenians not only as an unwelcome ethnic group but also as a social group that threatened the traditional authoritarian order of Ottoman society.

The events between 1915 and 1917, the worst years of the Genocide, are quite clear and documented in gruesome detail.[2] In early 1913, the Young Turk government was taken over by its militaristic and chauvinistic wing led by Enver, Talat, and Jemal Pashas.[3] This triumvirate led the country into World War I on the side of Germany. Sometime in early 1915 that same government developed and put into effect a plan for the extermination of its Armenian population. Most Armenians lived in the rural and small-town environment of historic Western Armenia, a part of the Ottoman Empire since the sixteenth century.[4]

The plan was carried out in phases. In April 1915, the religious, political, educational, and intellectual leadership of the Armenian people, close to 1,000 individuals, most educated in the Western tradition, were taken into custody throughout the empire and killed within a few days. Then Armenian draftees of the Ottoman army, estimated at 200,000, were liquidated through mass burials, burnings, executions, and sheer exhaustion in labor battalions. Finally, the remainder of the population, now composed largely of elderly people, women, and children, was given orders for deportation in all parts of the empire (except the capital and a few cities with European presences).[5] While a few cities and districts resisted the orders, most followed them, with the faint hope that they might be given a chance to come back.[6]

The fate of the deportees was usually death. Caravans of women and children, ostensibly being led to southern parts of the empire, became death marches. Within six months of the deportations half of the deportees were killed, buried alive, or thrown into the sea or the rivers. Few reached relatively safe cities, such as Aleppo, Syria. Most survivors ended up in the deserts of Northern Mesopotamia, where starvation, dehydration, and outright murder awaited them. Subsequent sweeps of cities ensured the elimination of the Armenian people from the western and largest portion of their historic homeland.

The extermination was accomplished under the supervision of a secretive organization that functioned as part of the government, the *Teshkilat-i Mahsusa* or Special Organization, run by the highest government and CUP officials, manned by convicts released from jail, and acting under the immediate supervision of select members of the CUP.[7] The release of the vilest, unbridled animal passions served well the government's purpose of ensuring extermination in the most humiliating, de-humanizing fashion. The torture of thousands of women and children became a source of satisfaction for those who sought and found official sanction from government officials as well as some Muslim clergymen, since the murder of Armenians was characterized, like the war against the Entente, as a *jihad* or holy war. Human imagination labored to devise new ways of mutilating, burning, and killing. The suicide of a large number of women and children attests to the particular brutality of the methods used.

The carnage took place in full view of the military and diplomatic representatives of governments allied with the Ottoman state, such as Germany, and neutral ones, such as the United States (until 1917). In addition, Western missionaries, journalists, travelers, and even sympathetic officers of the Ottoman army described the death marches and atrocities in daily letters and accounts. Reports of the extermination and its methods forwarded to Washington, Berlin, and other capitals by eyewitnesses confirm the stories told by thousands of survivors in subsequent memoirs and oral history interviews.[8]

The methods used to bring about the extermination of the Armenians are very significant since they attest to the participation of a segment of the general population. The acquiescence of Turkish, Kurdish, and, to a limited extent, Arab civilians was made easier by the promise of loot, of appropriation of children and women, and of an afterlife in heaven. A governmental decree making it illegal to assist refugees or orphans might ultimately have been responsible, however, for the absence of wholesale assistance from Turks to their former neighbors and friends. The penalty for such assistance was death by hanging in front of one's own house and the burning of that house.[9] This did not stop some, nonetheless, from resisting orders. A number of Turkish governors and sub-governors were removed from office for their unwillingness to follow orders. Many Turks and Kurds, especially in the Dersim region, risked their lives to save straggling Armenians, and Arabs throughout the empire's southern provinces accepted and helped the survivors.[10]

It is not clear whether it was the absence of technologically viable means to exterminate swiftly or the desire to keep the appearance of "deportations" that led the government to achieve extermination through such methods. The Ottoman government had a record of massacres, some against Armenians. Of these, the 1894-1896 and 1909 are the best known.[11] But this was the first time such a wholesale operation was conducted, ending in the uprooting of a whole nation.

The impact of the Genocide was devastating. Of the 2 to 3 million Western Armenians, 1 million or so perished during 1915-1917. Up to 150,000 of those who had accepted Islam or had been kept, stolen, or protected by Turks and Kurds survived in Western Armenia without, however, any possibility of preserving a sense of national identity. Close to 400,000 survived by fleeing to Russian Armenia and the Caucasus (where many more died as a consequence of disease and starvation) or Iran; perhaps 400,000 survived by reaching the southern or Arab provinces of the Ottoman Empire.[12]

In addition to the death of some 50 to 70 percent of Armenians living under Ottoman Turkish rule, Armenians lost the right to live as a community in the lands of their ancestors; they lost their personal property and belongings. They left behind the schools, churches, community centers, ancient fortresses, and medieval cathedrals, witnesses to a long history. Survivors were forced to begin a new life truncated, deprived of a link with their past, subject to upheavals in the new lands where they suddenly found themselves as foreigners. The remnants of the largely peasant and rural population were now a wretched group of squatters on the outskirts of cities poorly equipped to handle an increase in population.

The Genocide constituted a radical break with the past for Western Armenians. The normal transmission of ethical and cultural values was cut off. The traditional ways of explaining tragedies could not accommodate the final solution. Orphans grew to remember and tell the stories of childhood years; they did not know what to think of their Turkish neighbors and found it difficult to imagine that they had once lived together in relative peace.

Enemies by Definition

The victims of twentieth-century premeditated genocide—the Jews, the Gypsies, the Armenians—were murdered in order to fulfill the state's design for a new order. War was used in both cases (an opportunity anticipated and planned for by Germany but simply seized by Turkey after World War I began) to transform the nation to correspond to the ruling elite's formula by eliminating groups conceived of as alien, enemies by definition.[13]

So argues Helen Fein in *Accounting for Genocide*. This provides a basic and adequate explanation for the dynamics of the Armenian Genocide. Whatever political, sociological, and other explanations one may end up accepting as part of the causal process, only such an encompassing, exclusive characteristic of the human mind can account for the radical nature of the "solution," for the act of genocide. It is when man plays God and wants to recreate the world in his own image—however perverted the man or the image—that the other can be reduced to a nuisance, to an enemy that by definition must be destroyed regardless of his or her actions and policies.

Explanations of the Armenian Genocide have generally agreed with Fein's conclusion. The "formula" historians have ascribed to the CUP elite may vary; some stress a Pan-Islamist vision at work, others a Pan-Turanian one. Most have focused on the rise of an exclusive Turkish nationalism underlying or in the service of Pan-Turanian and/or Pan-Islamic dreams.[14] This nationalism was tied to Anatolia, the "birthplace" of Turkism, the last bastion after the loss of the European realms of the Ottoman Empire. In some cases, as if to moderate the burden of the crime, some have argued that the Genocide was the violent manifestation of an otherwise predictable and historically natural clash of two nationalisms in conflict, Armenian against Turkish; this explanation allows for the equation of the motivations of the two groups, with a difference only in the means used by each to achieve their goal.[15]

Evolving Turkish nationalism was, in fact, the major factor, which determined the course of Ottoman history during the first two decades of this century. Whatever subjective satisfaction Pan-Islamic and Pan-Turanian dreams gave to its adherents, whether under Sultan Abdul Hamid II or the Young Turks who replaced him, these ideologies remained vehicles by which energies outside Turkish nationalism could be harnessed to its service. The Young Turk-CUP elite cared not under what ideology it continued its domination. Religion worked for a while, in some places. It was particularly potent in moving the ignorant masses, in ensuring the support of the *mollahs* (Muslim clergy) and the *softas* (students of religion) for the Holy

War. The idea of unification of Turkish groups across Asia had some success as well; but Pan-Turanism too remained an abstraction for most of the people it was supposed to inspire.

By the time the CUP triumvirate decided to sign an alliance with Germany, its members had determined that whatever ideology emerged and regardless of who won the war, drastic measures were needed if the Turkish elite were to continue to rule over the remains of the empire. Long before the war, the CUP was already pursuing a policy of Turkification, which went beyond Pan-Islamism.[16] Arabs and Albanians were to speak Turkish; it was not sufficient that they were largely Muslim. The problem with the CUP was that they had not as yet given up on the idea of an empire, which required an ideology and a basis of legitimation wider than Turkish nationalism or dynastic allegiance.

Conditions were ripe for genocide to occur during a period of transition from the concept of an empire based on dynastic allegiance to that of a nation-state. Pan-Turanian and Pan-Islamic ideologies were stages that helped the Ottomans accept the break from a tradition of conquest. One of the vehicles for the building of Turkish nationalism was the identification of "enemies" of the yet-to-be-born nation; a second vehicle was its resistance to the loss of territory and dignity to Western imperialism. The self-definition in relation to the Armenian enemy was convenient, since Armenians were neither Turks nor Muslims; and the long history of the Armenian Question as an integral part of the Eastern Question made identification with outside enemies, in this case France, Great Britain, and Russia, easy.[17]

The Ottoman government had used wholesale massacres before against "enemies" of the state. Wartime conditions provided justification for extraordinary measures. Western governments, traditionally the only ones interested in and capable of intervention, were already at war, on the wrong side, as far as the Ottoman Empire was concerned. Germany, the Ottoman Empire's major ally, was capable of making a difference but opted not to.[18] Armenians, based on their history of past victimization, could easily be perceived as enemies of society or the state, given the paranoia of CUP leaders.[19]

It is possible to paraphrase Helen Fein, then, and reconstruct a Turkish "design for a new order." This would be based, on the one hand, on the assertion of sovereignty vis-à-vis the West by reversing the series of losses of territories; on the other hand, this design would insist on the establishment of "order" within the country, an order which was threatened by elements for whom the symbols of Turkism, Islamism, or Turanism could not mean much and who were seeking an alternate framework for identification with the state. In addition, these elements, i.e., Armenians, could be charged with collusion with the traditional enemy, Russia.

The basic explanation provided by Fein, however, does not preclude the further elaboration of the vision of the criminal state in its specific and more complex historical context. Many scholars have contributed to the understanding of genocide and to the identification of factors leading to it. Leo Kuper and Irving L. Horowitz have developed new perspectives on genocide as a political weapon in the twentieth century and argued for its study as a new category in social research. Vahakn Dadrian, a sociologist whose research focuses on the Armenian Genocide, has concentrated on the victimization theory and has pointed out sociological factors involved in the process of dehumanization leading to genocide resulting from the search for power.[20]

The Kurdish historian Siyamend Othman, in his doctoral dissertation and a subsequent article, attempted to explain the reasons why Kurds played such a prominent role in the deportations and massacres. His argument is that for Kurds within a feudal structure, the tribe provided group identity and therefore allegiance was to the chief, who was manipulated by the Ottoman government. Othman also points out that the common Kurd may have been harboring some resentment toward Armenians, who tended to be the usurers and capitalists in the marketplace.[21]

In a paper, Ronald Suny attempted an analysis of the sociological makeup of both Turks and Armenians and suggested that the existence of an Armenian upper class in control of many critical sectors of the economy might in fact have accentuated antagonisms.[22]

Of major importance is the analysis provided by Robert Melson. Melson has argued that one must go beyond victimization theories that generally point to victims of genocide as scapegoats or as provocateurs. He found instead that groups that have social mobility and adaptability to modernization, and thus tend to disturb the traditional orders, may tend to become victims in times of crisis. Melson has called for a somewhat more complex model within which the paranoia of the victimizer is as important in understanding—and foreseeing—genocide as the "success" of the victim.[23]

These points of view can be seen as suggestive and important efforts that provide specificity to the case of the Armenian Genocide and help shed light on the "formula" operative in the minds of the Turkish leaders that made possible the dehumanization and, eventually, the extermination of Armenians.

A Populist Agenda and the Alienation of the State

To the extent that the Ittihad decision to exterminate Armenians in the Ottoman Empire can be explained by the history of relations between the two, the period from 1908 to 1914 is obviously the most important. Armenian political parties, the SDHP (Social Democratic Hnchakian Party) and ARF (Armenian Revolutionary Federation), had opposed the Sultan's government until 1908, as had the various Turkish groups known as the Young Turks, of which the CUP became the most important. When the Young Turks took over the government in 1908 and restored the Constitution that had been promulgated in 1876 and prorogued in 1878, Armenian revolutionaries ended their armed struggle and pledged allegiance to the new regime and kept their pledge until the beginning of the Genocide.

Thus, the first point to be made regarding the pre-Genocide period is that Armenian political parties functioned as legitimate Ottoman institutions, whose goals and bylaws were recognized by the Ottoman government. While they differed in their assessment of the chances for successful reforms under the CUP government, there was and there could have been nothing in their programs or actions that could have been considered illegitimate or detrimental to the Constitution.

The second important fact with regard to these relations is that, along with a change in the ruling elite of the Ottoman Empire, the 1908 Constitution also produced a change in the representation of the Armenians. To negotiate Armenian demands for reforms, the Ottoman Turkish government had to deal with Armenian leaders of the revolutionary and guerrilla movement. The new spokesmen for the Armenians had won the right to represent Armenians by waging an armed struggle on behalf of economic and political rights.

A third important characteristic of the pre-Genocide Armeno-Turkish relations is that they evolved between 1908 and 1914. The major factor, which determined this change, was the retreat by the Young Turks, especially the CUP, from the liberal program, which some

Young Turks had advocated prior to, and immediately after, the 1908 takeover. As a whole, the Young Turks had linked the imperative of preserving the territorial integrity of the empire with the need to introduce general reforms. This willingness to recognize the importance of domestic social, economic, and political policies affecting the larger population had satisfied Armenians in their struggle to improve their situation, particularly the lot of the peasant and rural populations. Generally speaking, the Ittihad government discarded its liberal democratic ideals; it moved toward despotism and began relying, as its predecessor had done, on the reactionary classes and repressive measures to secure its position in power.

Based on documents being studied for the first time, it is possible to argue that the critical period when the fundamental change occurred was between 1909 and 1911.[24] By 1909, the excitement of the first days was over. Elections for the first Parliament were completed. The CUP had run on a platform with the ARF, and won. Furthermore, following the massacre of Adana, the government promised to take concrete steps to introduce long promised reforms, consolidate the constitutional regime, and resolve domestic issues that caused hardship to Armenians.

An agreement signed between the CUP and the Turkish Section of the Western Bureau (highest executive body of the ARF) seemed a secure path toward the realization of reforms throughout the empire. By 1911, in its Sixth World Congress, the ARF reached the conclusion that the party could no longer hope that the CUP would realize the reforms and consequently it could no longer remain in an alliance with the CUP.[25]

According to this agreement, the two parties were to develop a joint committee, above and beyond formal contacts and parliamentary negotiations. This committee would be composed of high-level officials whose task it was to find ways to strengthen the Constitution, educate the public on political issues and against the reaction, educate the Turkish masses on anti-Armenian prejudices, and increase political rights for all. In addition to the main committee in Constantinople, regional and district joint committees were also to be organized. The agreement was reached at a meeting between representatives of the Turkish Section of the ARF Bureau and the Central Committee of the CUP held in Salonika in August 1909, four months after the massacres of Adana. These negotiations may have been the price paid by the CUP in return for the willingness of the

ARF to ascribe the massacres to the reactionary forces, when in fact at least local CUP members were implicated.

The institutionalization of contacts at all levels seemed a good way to avoid future misunderstandings, to decrease tensions, and to open the way to important reforms. However, from the beginning, the ARF had difficulties in ensuring the functioning of the agreement. The first and most important committee, to be established in the capital, did not get its Turkish appointees until early 1910. In addition, the CUP avoided regular meetings from March to June 1910, and none of the important issues, foreign or domestic, were placed on the agenda by the CUP.

The ARF had its own agenda, which constituted basically its minimum and practical program. The party demanded:

1.   The end of feudal structures, laws, and practices in Anatolia.

2.   A change in the government's policy of total indifference toward social and economic development and the concomitant crises affecting all segments of society; economic development was necessary to provide opportunities for the improvement in the standard of living.

3.   The solution of the most critical issue, the agrarian crisis, which resulted both from inherent inequities and the feudal system as well as from the conscious policies of officials to expel Armenians from their farms, expropriate their lands, and give them to *muhajirs* or Muslim immigrants. The latter, often coming from the formerly Ottoman Balkan districts and the Russian Empire, were systematically directed into Armenian districts for resettlement, which would then take place at the expense of Armenian farmers.

4.   The end of regressive, extralegal, and illegal taxes, which particularly affected Christians, but generally had a negative impact on all subjects.

5.   The end of insecurity of life, honor, and property, particularly for Armenians, whose communal existence was threatened by continuing pillaging, lawlessness, and renewed open aggression and discrimination.[26]

These issues, and especially the agrarian crisis and the tax laws, were pointed to as threatening the economic foundation of the Armenian community.[27]

The ARF placed these and other, more specific, items on the agenda on many occasions. None of the issues, however, received satisfactory solutions. A second trip was needed to Salonika to determine why there was no action. In March 1911 two party plenipotentiaries went to meet again with the CUP Central Committee. The result was renewed promises for reform, once a new study was completed by two CUP leaders who were sent on a tour of the provinces. The CUP leaders seem to have agreed with the ARF representatives that the problem was not between Armenians and Turks or Kurds but between the poor and the rich, and that Turkish and Kurdish peasants often suffered as much as Armenians. Despite the agreement in principle and the promise to seriously confront the problem, the tour by the two dignitaries produced no changes in government policies. Reporting from Van, a member of the ARF's local Central Committee echoed the observation of many Armenians when he wrote: "[The two representatives] are here now and, frankly, we cannot understand what they are doing. They have shied away from all contacts with the popular masses and the rural folk; they are constantly surrounded by the local notables and government officials."[28]

Following two years of intense efforts and accommodation to a CUP agenda which seemed to Armenians to be lacking focus, the ARF came to the conclusion that it no longer could expect basic changes to come from the CUP. A memorandum accompanying the Report to the Congress listed a number of reasons for the inability of the CUP to respond:

1.   Feudalism was still not such an abhorrence to the CUP: at any rate, its leaders did not wish to alienate the Kurdish chieftains and local landlords, whose support they ultimately considered more important, and safer—since they demanded nothing in return—than that of the Armenians.

2.   The CUP allowed reactionary elements, such as great landowners and mollahs, to become members of the local CUP clubs, changing the liberal character of the organization: it was gradually taken over by those forces that constituted the backbone of the previous regime and had opposed constitutional change and parliamentary government.

3.   The fear ascribed by CUP leaders to Kurds but in fact shared by some Turks that should Armenians have an equal chance in the system they would overwhelm others by their numbers and achievements.

4.   The CUP did not wish to see the ARF or any other Armenian party strengthened.

5.   The ARF's unqualified support of the CUP allowed them to take that support for granted: the CUP did not need to return any favors for the support.

6.   The CUP did not wish to see an element in Asia Minor strengthened that might be favored by the Russians, particularly when the more important friend, Germany, had other plans for the region.

7.   The disagreement between two ARF members of the Ottoman Parliament on the best methods to develop the proposed railroad in Eastern Anatolia.

8.   Instability in the cabinet and its inability to make decisions.

In addition to the absence of reforms and the CUP's disregard for its own pledges, the authors of the memorandum listed the following governmental actions to support their conclusions:

1.   The CUP government had stopped prosecuting Kurdish chieftains accused of crimes against Armenians; one prominent criminal, Huseyin Pasha, had in fact been invited back into the country with a pardon.

2.   The CUP had favored the Baghdad railway line, which, in the view of the ARF, would only enrich foreign capitalists; the party had recommended instead the Anatolian railway, which would help the economic development of this poor region.

3.   No concrete steps were taken to return to Armenian peasants and farmers their lands, their principal means of livelihood. Such a distribution would hardly have affected the Kurdish or Turkish peasant, but it would have hurt the large landowners and muhajirs. The ARF's proposal to achieve such a return through administrative decisions was frustrated by the CUP's recommendation that the regular courts be used for that purpose; pleas that the courts had not yet been reformed since the revolution and peasants did not even have money to go to court or to bribe the corrupt officials were hardly heeded.

4.   Where joint committees had been formed, the CUP representatives had on occasion made unreasonable and suspicious demands, such as assimilation of the ARF into the CUP or turning over the lists of party members to the Committee of Union and Progress.[29]

Having determined that the party could no longer be in alliance with the CUP, the Sixth World Congress of the ARF resolved that it would continue its efforts as a party in friendly opposition in Parliament.

Thus, during the period of intense relations following the revolution, when the two groups were able to know each other and act on this knowledge, Armenian leaders discussed security of life, land reform, economic development, and political equality rather than autonomy or independence. Their disagreements and ultimate break were over bread and butter issues rather than over boundaries. Simon Zavarian, one of the founders of the party and a member of the Bureau's Turkish Section, argued in 1912 that of all the elements in the Ottoman Empire, Armenians had been the most supportive of the Constitution:

> This sympathy was not the consequence of [the Armenians'] high morals, [their] pro-Turkish inclination, or [their] political maturity. Rather, it is a question of geo-political realities and the current situation. Dispersed all over Asia Minor and mixed with Turks and other nationalities over the centuries, Armenians could not seek their future in a territorial autonomy, to lead an even more isolated political life. Armenians have tried to create [favorable] conditions for all Ottomans by supporting reform for the Ottoman state, [and to change] for the better the status of Armenians and Armenia.[30]

He observed, however, that Ottoman subjects had very little to show for the four years they had lived under a Constitution: "End of the internal identification cards, a few students to Europe, and some road projects... But what do peasants and craftsmen have to show?... One also cannot hope much from the new Parliament, since most new deputies have titles such as *beys, zades, pashas* and *mufties*."[31] The alienation of the Armenians from the state was most dramatically illustrated in the final defense statement of the SDHP leader Paramaz in 1915, who, after having been accused of plotting against the government, was hanged along with twenty other SDHP leaders. "I am not a separatist," said Paramaz. "It is this state which is separating itself from me, unable to come to terms with the ideas which inspire me."[32]

It seems, then, that long before the beginning of World War I the CUP, as well as the Armenian parties, had concluded that the Young Turk revolution had failed. Jemal Pasha, one of the ruling triumvirate, argued in his memoirs that the CUP failed to take root.[33] In 1912 Zavarian had been more explicit in his explanation of the failure of that party:

> Instead of waging a struggle, of establishing a popular militia, of creating a democratic party, a party with [political] principles, [the Ittihadists] went the way of their predecessors: they chose "the easy path." They kissed and allied with all the dignitaries and created a "union" of coreligionists.[34]

Armenian political parties wavered between clear signs that the liberal era had ended and the hope that they were mistaken. Meeting in Constanza in September 1913 for its Seventh World Conference, the SDHP had perceived the dangers inherent in CUP mentality. A new party policy was based, among other arguments, on the fact that the "fundamental principles [of the CUP] call for the preservation of a Turkish bureaucracy and that they do not allow for the emergence of a new state, and that it is the obvious goal [of that party] not only to assimilate but also to eliminate, and if need be exterminate, constituent nationalities."[35]

The SDHP concluded that Armenians should at least be ready for self-defense. Nonetheless, the SDHP, along with others, was determined to pursue the search for peaceful solutions. The ARF continued to advocate reform, whatever the source. In 1914 the ARF was still insisting on the need for reforms reduced to their minimum and resulted in a June 1912 editorial published in the party organ, *Droshak*. That editorial had listed six critical issues, in addition to land reform:

1. Better administration throughout the empire;
2. Decrease in taxes on the poor and implementation of progressive taxation;
3. Abolition of all feudal taxes;
4. Balanced budget by decreasing the number of officials and building up an economic infrastructure;
5. End to acts and policiesthat create fear of Turkification and Islamization of minorities;
6. Safeguarding of freedoms.[36]

After 1912, Armenians welcomed the renewed Western, and especially Russian, interest in pressuring the Ottoman government for reforms in the Armenian provinces of the empire, reforms which would be realized under the supervision of European governors.[37] This, however, did not change the fundamental relationship between the leaderships of the CUP government and Armenians and the political program each represented for the other.

Limitations of the Nationalist Perspective

While the issues raised by Armenians were in the area of social and economic development and political equality, general interpretation of the Genocide that followed this period remains mired in the limited and limiting perspective of Turkish and Armenian nationalisms.

The nationalist perspective creates many obstacles to an understanding of the full and real picture of Armeno-Turkish relations and mutual perceptions during the period preceding the Genocide. It is true that the nature of the crime and its inhumanity are such that it is difficult to imagine that the Armenians and Turks were able to have a relationship other than that of victim and victimizer—it seems that it was always in the nature of the relations of these two peoples to massacre and to be massacred; that it was in the spirit of the times for both peoples to develop traditions of modern nationalism; that these two nationalisms were bound to clash as they did; and that it was natural for the Turks to be the killers and for the Armenians to be the victims. Moreover, the current domination of the theme of genocide in Armenian life, the bitterness and resentment in the absence of international recognition, and the increasing intensity of the Turkish denial of the Genocide strengthen the misleading impression that all events preceding the Genocide led to the Genocide, and all events succeeding the Genocide have been caused by it.[38]

In other words, students of the period have difficulty imagining that Armenians were an integral part of Ottoman society for many centuries. This integrality was based on more than the physical occupation of lands under Ottoman dominion. It involved parallel developments in folk cultures, integration through a single economy, and mutual adjustments of social mores and values between Armenian and Turkish as well as Kurdish societies.[39] Thus Armenians constituted an integral part of the political life of the Ottoman Empire, whether defined as a millet or as an ethnic group with parliamentary representation under the Young Turks.[40]

Yet terms such as nationalism and independence have created a picture that places Armenians outside Ottoman history, just as the Genocide placed Armenians outside Ottoman society; and analysis revolving around conflicts over irreducible categories such as race and religion turn history into a field where, instead of human beings interacting, abstract concepts do battle. It is as if hordes of individuals think and act as prescribed by ideologies of nationalism, religion, or race. Terminology then comes to reconfirm the view imposed by the Genocide that, ultimately, one need not account for real Armenians leading real lives whose disappearance from their homes and from history must be accounted for; one is comforted by the thought that Armenians can be reduced to a corollary of a concept. The politician dehumanizes a nation in order to get rid of it; the historian does so to explain it away. Genocide becomes its own explanation; ultimately, it becomes its own justification.

The Young Turks, including the CUP, evolved in opposition to the despotic, reactionary, and corrupt rule of Sultan Abdul Hamid II as well as in reaction to his ineptness in protecting the territorial integrity of the Ottoman Empire against separatist tendencies and Western imperialistic encroachments. The latter were often justified in the name of persecuted minorities in the empire. Therefore there evolved a linkage between domestic reforms, particularly those that might affect non-Muslims and non-Turks, and the defense of the territorial integrity of the empire.

While all Young Turks agreed that the sultan must go and that the Constitution of 1876 must be reestablished, it was obvious from the start that not everyone agreed on the best possible solution to the problem of territorial loses. One group, led by Prince Sabaheddine, promoted the idea of a multinational empire, with not only equal rights to the non-dominant groups, such as Armenians, but also a decentralized government that recognized a degree of regional autonomy to these groups.[41] Ahmed Riza, on the other hand, whose views became the more dominant after the revolution, believed in an Ottomanism that minimized differences, in a centralized state which, while recognizing the equality of all under the law, would promote the evolution of a homogeneous, corporate body politic. According to one historian:

> [Ahmed Riza] used the word "Ottoman" freely in connection with individual inhabitants of the Empire, Muslim and Christian, as did Sabaheddine, but in Riza's vocabulary the word did not connote so much an individual with supra-national citizenship as a person who, if he was not already a Turk, must be hammered into a reasonable likeness to one.[42]

In 1908 the Young Turks took over the government and restored the 1876 Constitution. An era of brotherhood and renovation was thought to have begun; there was popular support for the move, and all problems were expected to be resolved soon with a new parliament.[43] Parliamentary elections were held twice during this period, in 1909 and 1912. These parliaments included representatives of various religious and ethnic groups, including Armenians, although there seems to have been constant haggling over the number of deputies each group was allotted, the Turks always retaining a comfortable majority.

But the CUP government, already weak in its commitment to democratization, was frustrated in its attempts to implement significant reforms. Between 1908 and 1914 the Ottoman Empire had to fight two wars against Balkan states during which it lost most of what it still retained of its European holdings; the Ottomans also lost Libya to Italy. Thus, their revolution had not guaranteed the territorial integrity of the empire. The Young Turks were particularly irritated by France and England, the two bastions of liberalism and the principal external sources pressuring for internal reform, who stood by while more and more Ottoman lands were taken away. The Young Turks were also naive in their belief that a parliament in and by itself constituted reform and could change a society. Impatient about criticism and unwilling to undertake reforms they thought would weaken the authority of the state, the CUP itself moved toward despotism, just as Abdul Hamid II had done over three decades earlier. The CUP leadership gradually eliminated not only opposition parties but also elements within the CUP who still linked the salvation of Ottoman society to domestic reforms and a vigorous constitutional life.[44] The coup d'état in 1913 led by Enver, Talat, and Jemal Pashas came as the logical conclusion of the evolution of the CUP toward a dictatorship. The three continued to believe that they embodied all the wisdom necessary to lead the empire toward salvation; and the salvation of the empire was couched in terms of molding the character and thoughts of its citizens in the image of some ideal Ottoman.

From the promise of reform and equality and political rejuvenation springing from the dedication to the ideal of a state that provided equality under the law, the CUP had moved to the position of a corporate state within which not only non-Turks would be designated "enemies" by definition, but also all liberals who insisted on a different vision than the one articulated by the CUP, however vague and shifting that may have been. Liberalism, which sought to reject the use of ethnic, religious, or national identity as the basis for legitimation of power, was seen as a weakness, as the lot of the forces of particularism and dissent, as a source of chaos and further disintegration, unworthy of the various visions of greatness that were motivating the CUP—the "true" successor of the once powerful sultans.[45]

The CUP distaste for liberalism is critical for the understanding of their policies before and during the war. In the Ottoman Empire liberalism and ethnic issues had been intertwined since the nineteenth century. Western pressures for reform always focused on the status of Christians. The Turkish and Kurdish masses in the empire had been denied a systematic exposure to the need for reform from their own revolutionaries.[46] They consequently viewed the Ottoman Constitution as a privilege only for Christians.[47] Moreover, the Turkish people felt a false sense of power through identification with the ruling dynasty and ruling elite. Ramsaur, who tends to see all minorities as budding nationalists, nonetheless recognizes that

> the Muslim minorities, such as those Albanians who professed Islam, were beginning to feel the sweep of nationalism as well, but they were somewhat weakened in their aspirations by the fact that they enjoyed better treatment than did the Christian minorities and because they had a religious bond with the dynasty that the latter did not possess.[48]

Naturally, non-Turks found it easier to understand and appreciate reforms. Being more affected by the corrupt and decrepit taxation and legal systems than others, Armenians had long developed a tradition of political thought of their own in reaction to Ottoman misgovernment, Turkish superiority, and despotic rule.

Nonetheless, these non-Turkish parties constitute as much a part of Ottoman history as those founded by Turks. The Armenian focus of these parties, for example, is a reflection of the religious/ethnic structure created by the Ottoman government, not a natural result of Armenian nationalism.[49]

By 1914, Armenians were the only significant non-Muslim people left in the empire, the only non-Turkish political element in Anatolia capable of measuring the actions of the government beyond the rhetoric of Pan-Turkism and Pan-Islamism, a rhetoric that certainly could not inspire Armenians. Armenians were also the only segment of the electorate still supporting the parliamentary system and the Constitution. While the promise of Russian-sponsored reforms may have diminished the need to see political reform for the majority in the Armenian vilayets (administrative divisions) of the empire, Armenians in central Anatolia, Cilicia, and the western provinces had no other hope. Armenians were certainly the only segment of the Ottoman population that placed agrarian reforms at the top of their agenda.

A Contractual Agreement

The Armenian liberal agenda was the legacy of the revolutionary movement, which developed following the failure of the signatories of the Congress of Berlin in 1878 to deliver on their promise of reforms for Ottoman Armenia. Armenians developed a liberation movement, which, while having been partially inspired by the Balkan movements, grew in reaction to Ottoman policies and to Armenian realities and needs and had at its basis a class-conscious worldview. Armenian groups were motivated much more by the socioeconomic disintegration of their society than by dreams of a renewed Armenian dynasty. Even the SDHP, the first revolutionary party and the only one to advocate independence when founded in 1887, did so because it argued that since there were no positive results to be seen decades after the promise of internal reforms and almost a decade after the Congress of Berlin, Armenians could no longer hope to see reforms general enough to bring a change in their status.[50] The ARF, founded in 1890, which in 1892 advocated a degree of autonomy and the opportunity to create "political and economic freedom," made clear that its purpose was not the replacement of a Turkish sultan with an Armenian one.[51] It was not surprising, therefore, that neither the Church nor the wealthy classes in Armenian society supported the revolutionaries; both remained very much part of the millet mentality fostered by the Ottoman government and, ultimately, were manipulated by it.

The liberation movement among Armenians, which turned into an armed struggle in the 1890s, acquired depth and an inter-ethnic scope in the 1900s. This included prodding Young and liberal Turkish groups into action against despotism and cooperation among the anti-sultan forces. One of the issues raised by the Armenian political parties during these early years was the need for Turkish liberalism to acquire a popular basis by addressing social and economic issues and by being ready to engage in an armed struggle to achieve the goal of a democratic and parliamentary regime. They also urged Turks to provide for a popular defense mechanism against any possible reaction following a revolution. In other words, the Young Turks were urged to make a revolution rather than a coup d'état. These positions were articulated clearly over a decade of relations between Armenian revolutionaries and Turkish liberals in Europe and in the Ottoman Empire.[52] The last time the ARF had insisted on the need for an Ottoman revolution was in 1907, during the second congress of Ottoman opposition forces, which had been convened on its initiative. Armenians did not have much faith in revolutions from above.

Although in 1908 it was the Ottoman army and not the people that toppled the sultan, the move was radical enough to invite the support of many segments of Ottoman society, and particularly Armenians for whom liberalism and reform had become political solutions as well as ideological tenets. The Young Turk revolution of 1908 produced important changes in the Armenian political scene. The SDHP had met in 1909 for their Sixth General Convention and decided to discard the party's demand for political independence for Armenia and voted to realize their ultimate goal, socialism, within the Ottoman context. Nonetheless, the SDHP registered its distrust of CUP nationalism and absence of commitment to reforms.[53] The ARF put into place a mechanism for realizing the federal structure it had envisioned in its Fourth World Congress in 1907, in collaboration with the Young Turks.[54] Finally, the Armenian bourgeoisie and well-to-do, who had never felt comfortable with the armed struggle and socialistic rhetoric of the two existing parties, created a third party, the *Ramkavar-Sahmanadrakan* or Democratic-Constitutional Party, which rejected violence and adopted capitalism as the proper form of economic development for the Ottoman Empire and the appropriate way to solve Armenian socioeconomic problems.[55]

All three parties worked within the bounds of the Constitution to achieve gains and to realize their goals. The coalition of the ARF and the CUP produced parliamentary victories for both. The SDHP formed an alliance with the Ittilaf Party of Prince Sabaheddine. More important, all three Armenian political parties shared a vision of the society they wanted to see evolve in the Ottoman Empire. This vision was based primarily on the need to address the problems facing a disintegrating Armenian rural society and a frustrated middle class. Equality, reform, and progress were slogans that everyone used and no one found to be against the interests of the state in 1908.[56] They were inspired by what educated Armenians considered the universal values of the Enlightenment. Armenians believed in progress and change at the expense of the traditional because, to paraphrase what has been said of German Jews, these attitudes facilitated emancipation from the political and social disabilities that had oppressed them for centuries; the Enlightenment gave them optimism and faith in themselves and humanity. It was this general belief that led the Armenians, but especially the SDHP and ARF, not only to participate vigorously in the first Russian revolutionary movement in 1905 but also to play a role in the Persian Constitutional movement before World War I. This role was critical enough for one of the leaders of the ARF, Yeprem, who had led his guerrilla fighters into many battles, to end up with the responsibility for the security of Tehran until his death in 1912.[57]

Among the Turks, enlightenment and progress were adopted by Prince Sabaheddine and the Liberal Party. However, they were small in number and lacked a popular base. Even the nascent Turkish bourgeoisie supported the CUP policies of economic nationalism and placed their hopes on a strong central government that might find it easier to make room for the growth of Turkish capital, as opposed to the traditional Ottoman capital that had been accumulated in trade by Armenians, Greeks, and Jews. The masses were more easily swayed by the rhetoric of glory, whether of the imperial or religious variety. When faced with the Western challenge, the Turkish reformers, whose liberalism was "ill digested," were more likely to be impressed by the technological and military advances—advances which, when borrowed, could have resolved the Ottoman problem as seen by Turks: military weakness against European powers and humiliation at the hands of former subjects.[58] Some also internationalized Social Darwinism, which made it possible for them to rationalize their insistence on the primacy of Turks in the empire, their internal imperialism.[59]

Even in 1908, therefore, there were two visions of society at work, both in opposition to the sultan, both favoring the Constitution, both based on the dual principles of internal reforms and territorial integrity of the empire. It was the first time since the articulation of Armenian political demands that so much common ground existed and that there was an opportunity for the solution of both problems. Yet for those in the CUP who had believed in some degree of equality and justice, the promise of reforms may have been the price to be paid in return for territorial integrity, and possibly aggrandizement. With the continued loss of territories in the Balkans and the threatened loss of the Arab provinces, the CUP lost even its weak interest in limited reforms and sought its aggrandizement elsewhere.

Armenian political parties, meanwhile, had been willing to make all the necessary adjustments to strengthen the Constitution; it was a welcome alternative to an otherwise difficult position. Armenians, particularly the SDHP and ARF, made serious compromises on the degree of socioeconomic reform needed in order to provide the best possible support to the liberal elements in Turkish politics. And while among the Young Turks they had always associated with Sabaheddine, the ARF agreed to run joint election campaigns with the CUP, which, as the party in power, the ARF thought needed the largest dose of liberal presence.

The Armenian parties made it clear, however, that their commitment to the Ottoman fatherland, their willingness to defend its territorial integrity and the search for Armenian reforms in the context of the empire-wide changes, were contingent upon one condition: the Ottoman Empire had to be a "democratic and parliamentary state."[60] This feeling was shared by the larger Armenian population as well. A letter to the editor of the *Droshak* stated it clearly:

> For citizens states are not goals. They are means to develop, to progress, to become strong. If a means to reach a goal is inappropriate, inadequate or weak, it becomes necessary to exchange it for a better and more appropriate form... The issue is not separation or inclusion in the Ottoman state, since these are fundamentally related to the larger purpose—our welfare. We, Turks, Armenians, Greeks, Bulgars, Kurds and other citizens like to remain and live and even, yes, sacrifice and be sacrificed, in a state where our welfare is [considered]. We shall shed our blood only for the flag which knows how to keep our heads up. Flags, which are miserable, shameful, often defeated, subject to derision and mockery do not deserve our blood.[61]

The SDHP in 1913 reaffirmed its intention not to seek a separate homeland; but it also made it clear that it did not intend to accept a regime where any group dominated the others.[62] In October 1913 all Armenian parties functioning in the Ottoman Empire signed a joint statement, which in addition to promising an end to internal conflicts, also reasserted their dedication to the Ottoman Parliament and Constitution.[63]

In other words, for Armenians allegiance was to basic forms of political association or organization rather than to a dynasty, a nationalism, a religion, or a race. They were ready to support a political system that allowed for the equitable and just solution to ethnic and religious as well as social and economic problems.[64] This was a "social contract," which was reminiscent of what Sabaheddine had come to learn and respect from contemporary readings.[65] With their concern for social, economic, and agrarian reforms and a democratic system of government, Armenians were thus part of the Ottoman political spectrum. But they occupied the left wing of that spectrum.

Two other issues were problematic for the CUP government. First, Armenian parties had strong popular bases due both to their long struggle and sacrifices and to their populist platforms. Second, given the socialistic nature of their programs, they had also made serious efforts, beginning in 1900, but especially after 1908, to spread the liberal creed among Turks, and even Kurds in Anatolia.[66] While they had had very limited success, there always was a danger that Armenian revolutionary parties with socialistic tendencies could create politically viable coalitions of peasants and rural craftsmen, supported by a liberal bourgeoisie, a coalition of forces that would be considered an obstacle to the vision of an autocratic and conservative state managed by the CUP.

War and the Transformation of the State

It was no accident that the Ottoman Empire entered World War I and did so on the side of Germany. A crisis situation, martial law, and war conditions in general would change the rules of politics and the need for accountability for failures, while creating the possibility of territorial expansion. Siding with Germany was in character with an elite in power increasingly hostile toward any element that reminded them of their promises and failures. Fighting the war on the side of Germany could free the CUP from its commitment to reform just as the Russo-Turkish war of 1877-1878 had freed Abdul Hamid from the pledge he made in 1876 to create a constitutional government.[67] A war that was to be fought against France and England, the liberal states of Europe, allowed the linkage between external threats and internal reform to be articulated in the measures taken against Armenians, now seen as the main threat, the enemy; the Turkish elite considered Armenians ideological allies of the French and British or as a population sympathizing with the traditional enemy, Russia, which in 1912 had resumed its role as the sponsor of Armenian reforms. The war provided an opportunity for the CUP to create a coherent world: an opportunity to prove Turkish military prowess by fighting on the side of a strongly militaristic non-liberal empire such as Germany, and against the bastions of liberalism, France and England.

But the war also made it possible to eliminate the particularities and dissent in the political arena by eliminating Armenians, who could never be part of the new vision since they were not Turks or Muslims, and who, by their political consciousness, were bound to become a permanent source of dissent and discontent, a particularity in a society that was expected to find solace in the Pan-Turanian, Pan-Islamic creeds or in Turkish nationalism rather than in the search for equality, justice, and a dignified human existence. Jemal Pasha, one of the CUP triumvirate and minister of the navy, conceded a fundamental relationship between the decision to enter the war, domestic policy, and the Armenian "problem":

> Of course, it was our hope to free ourselves through the World War from all conventions, which meant so many attacks on our independence... Just as it was our chief aim to annul the capitulations and the Lebanon Statute, so in the matter of Armenian reforms we desired to release ourselves from the agreement which Russian pressure had imposed upon.[68]

Jemal certainly did not imply that reforms were not needed, since in these memoirs he confesses having promised Armenians reforms as soon as the war was over, if Armenians functioned as a fifth column in Russian Armenia against Russia.[69] In a strange but intriguingly vague style, Jemal stated that "it was an active domestic and foreign policy" that drove the CUP to war. The most important domestic problem was the question of the minorities, Jemal asserted, and, among the minorities, the Armenians were the most critical.[70] Subsequent justifications of the deportations and massacres clarify the meaning of "active" policy. It seems to have been nothing less than the domestic equivalent of war on enemy states.

The desire to proceed with state building unfettered by any external or internal accounting was, according to Jemal, one of the reasons for the CUP's decision to enter the war. Of course, as soon as the war started, the two European governors who had just arrived in the country to supervise reforms in Armenian provinces were sent back. But the war allowed the Ittihad to do more. The purpose of the deportations and massacres, wrote the German missionary and eyewitness Johannes Lepsius, "seems to be to drive the idea of reforms out of the Armenians' minds once and for all."[71] Perhaps this will explain why the murder of the intellectuals took on such a gruesome character. It is said by eyewitnesses that on more than one occasion their skulls were crushed with stones and the brains were thrown to the ground with an invitation to the victim to dare to "think again."

When the news of the deportations and massacres reached Europe, many Turks dissociated themselves from the policies of the CUP. Attempting to do so publicly, Mehmet Sherif Pasha, the son of the first grand vizier of the constitutional regime in 1908, described the Armenians as industrious and peaceful people. Attempting to explain the carnage taking place in his homeland, Mehmet Sherif added that "the Armenians' agitation against despotisms in Turkey and Persia [is a quality] one suspects has not endeared them to the autocratic 'reformers' of the Young Turk regime."[72]

Genocide: A Radical Form of Political Repression?

The relationship between genocide and domestic change is a theme that precedes the Young Turks in Ottoman history. Evaluating the meaning of the Constitution first introduced by Midhat Pasha under the young Sultan Abdul Hamid II in 1876, Harry Luke wrote that, "[Midhat Pasha] was sufficiently shrewd and realistic a statesman to know that only by drastic internal reform, self administered, could the rapidly dissolving Empire stave off the coup de grace which Russia was impatient to administer."[73] Soon after he felt secure, the sultan exiled Midhat Pasha and replaced the Constitution with an administration repressive enough to invite a revolution from his most resilient subjects, the Turks. In the introduction to an unsigned study published in 1913, "Turkey: The Situation of Armenians in Turkey Introduced with Documents, 1908-1912," a commentator discussed the repression of the massacres of 1894-1896 in the following way:

> The top officials of the old regime were convinced that repression is essential to despotism and reforms are deadly weapons. Seeing the determination of Armenians to obtain reforms and to make their Turkish compatriots companions in their aspirations, they preferred to massacre the Armenians as the ones responsible for the situation, instead of undertaking general reforms which could have brought the end of despotism and their rule.[74]

Given this strong sense of the relationship between repression and wholesale massacre felt by Armenian leaders and nurtured by events, it is not surprising that both major Armenian parties as well as conservative leaders could see by 1913 that the Young Turks might be moving in the same direction as the sultan. "Turkey is promising reforms for European consumption," argued a *Droshak* editorial in June 1913, "but is actually aiming at the destruction of the Armenian element in Anatolia." Only the method would be different from the Hamidian massacres, argued the editorialist.[75] The SDHP thought that the scope would be different too.[76]

They were both correct, although it seems that none wanted to believe that the worst actually could happen. The parties did caution Armenians not to give any reason for provocations. During the initial stages of the roundups of leaders, the drafting of young men into the army, the inspections for caches of arms, and other preliminaries to the actual deportations and massacres, Armenians tended to accede to demands, avoided any actions that might have been construed as opposing the state, and hoped that the whole episode would ultimately be forgotten and that the community would survive with minimum damage. Local measures such as the murder of a few hundred intellectuals or a few thousand enlistees were nothing compared to what had been predicted. In most communities where any self-defense was possible the realization that the small incidents were part of the larger event came too late to be of any use. Where communities acted early, such as in Van, Shabin Garahisar, Musa Dagh, and Urfa, the self-defense became part of the justification for the Genocide while the Genocide was progressing.[77]

To complete the preliminary stages of the Genocide—the emasculation of the nation without risking much resistance—the planners had, in fact, counted on the infinite belief of Armenian leaders in the possibility of political solutions to their problems. Armenians were, after all, students of the Enlightenment and devotees of political discourse once discourse had been made possible by the elevation of the "revolutionary" Young Turks to power. To believe that their colleagues from the days of exile in Europe and from the Ottoman Parliament could in fact use the methods of the sultan and improve on them was to undermine the basic motivation for their adoption of the best that the West had to offer: belief not only in progress by man but also progress *in* man, in his perfectibility, in his ability to reason and to do what is reasonable.

When the Young Turks determined to exterminate the Armenians, they were not just ridding themselves of another ethnic group; they were also eliminating the social basis for a substantial change in the regime. They were not guaranteeing just a Turkified Turkey, but also a Turkey that was closer to the model of the empire in its heyday: virile and run by elites who were inspired by ideas beyond the reach of common men and women, particularly those of a lower race and religion, by ideas beyond the reach of discourse, abstracted from reality and, ultimately, from humanity.

The Genocide of the Armenian people may be a paradigm for "political" genocides, where the elite's vision was predicated upon the political and sociological dimensions of the society they wanted to rule over. The return to a traditional order where hierarchies are in place and unchallenged may be one such vision. Genocides, especially the Indonesian, the Cambodian, and the Ibo, have been more brazenly political in nature, confirming the worst fears that knowledge of evil does not necessarily result in abhorrence of evil; that human reasoning can always find ways to characterize evil as being something else and to conclude that some societies must be destroyed or must destroy parts of themselves to be saved.

Notes

1. The relationship between genocide and modernization has been discussed by, among others, George L. Mosse, *German Jews Beyond Judaism* (Bloomington: Indiana University Press/Hebrew Union College Press, 1985), with regard to the Jewish Holocaust, and by Robert Melson in a paper entitled "Neither Scapegoats nor Provocateurs: A Preface to a Study of Genocide with Special Reference to the Armenian Genocide of 1915 and the Holocaust," presented at the Conference on Genocide at Harvard University, April 13, 1985.
2. The best reference work for non-Armenian sources on the Armenian Genocide is Richard G. Hovannisian, *The Armenian Holocaust: A Bibliography Relating to the Deportations, Massacres, and Dispersion of the Armenian People, 1915-1923* (Cambridge, Mass.: National Association for Armenian Studies and Research, 1978 and 1980). Other sources include Aram Andonian, *The Memoirs of Naim Bey: Turkish Official Documents Relating to the Deportations and Massacres of Armenians* (London: Hodder and Stoughton, 1920; repr. Armenian Historical Research Association, 1964 and 1965); Dikran H. Boyajian, *Armenia: The Case for a Forgotten Genocide* (Westwood, N.J.: Educational Book Grafters, 1972); Gerard Chaliand and Yves Ternon, *The Armenians: From Genocide to Resistance* (London: Zed Press, 1983); Irving Louis Horowitz, *Taking Lives: Genocide and State Power* (New Brunswick, N.J.: Transaction Publishers, 1980); Leo Kuper, *Genocide: Its Political Use in the Twentieth Century* (New Haven: Yale University Press, 1981); Henry Morgenthau, *Ambassador Morgenthau's Story* (Garden City. N.Y.: Doubleday, Page, and Co., 1926; French ed., Paris: Payot et cie., 1919); Martin Niepage, *The Horrors of Aleppo: Seen by a German Eye-witness* (London and New York: Fisher Unwin, 1917 and George H. Doran Co., 1918: repr. New Age Publishers, 1975); Gerard J. Libaridian, ed., *A Crime of Silence: The Genocide of the Armenians. The Permanent People's Tribunal* (London: Zed Press. 1985); Jack Nusan Porter. *Genocide and Human Rights* (Washington, D.C.: University Press of America, 1982); Yves Ternon, *The Armenians: History of a Genocide* (Delmar, N.Y.: Caravan Books, 1981); Arnold Toynbee, *Armenian Atrocities: The Murder of a Nation* (London: Hodder and Stoughton, 1915; reissued New York: Prelacy of the Armenian Apostolic Church of America. 1975); Arnold J. Toynbee, *The Treatment of the Armenians in the Ottoman Empire: Documents Presented to Viscount Grey of Faltoden* (London: J. Causton and Sons, 1916).
3. For the early history of the movement, see Ernest E. Ramsaur, *The Young Turks: Prelude to the Revolution of 1908* (Princeton: Princeton University Press, 1957); for the prewar years see Feroz Ahmad, *The Young Turks: The Committee of Union and Progress in Turkish Politics, 1908-1914* (Oxford: Clarendon Press, 1969).
4. Historic Armenia was divided between the Ottoman and Safavid Persian empires, once in the sixteenth century and finally in the seventeenth century. The eastern, and smaller, part was occupied by Persia until the Russo-Persian war of 1827-1828, when it became part of the Russian Empire.

5.   Because of the presence of the diplomatic corps and an international community, Armenians in the capital were spared deportations, although their leadership there was rounded up and murdered. The regions of Izmir and Adrianople were spared because the chief of the German Military Mission during the war in the Ottoman Empire, General Liman von Sanders, threatened to use force against the Turkish soldiers and gendarmes should they implement the deportation orders. He told his story in Otto Liman von Sanders, *Fünf Jahre in der Türkei* (Berlin: A. Scheri, 1920), and repeated it during his testimony at the trial of Talaat Pasha's self-confessed executor, Soghomon Tehlirian, in Berlin in 1921. See *The Case of Soghomon Tehlirian* (Los Angeles: ARF Varantian Gomideh, 1985), pp. 83-85.

6.   The cities and districts that resisted included Van, Musa Dagh, Urfa, Shabin Karahisar, and Hajin. Only the first two were able to survive long enough to receive assistance from the outside and save their people: Armenians in Van were saved by the Armenian volunteers with the Russian army; those in Musa Dagh were rescued by a French ship off the coast of the Mediterranean. Resistance in most cases was not undertaken with the hope of ultimate salvation but rather to have a choice in the manner of death.

7.   Information on the role of this organization is fragmentary, often from oral history sources. The only substantial research on the subject, done as a doctoral dissertation by Philip Hendrick Stoddard, is silent on the organization's role in Anatolia and the Armenian provinces where the deportations occurred; see Philip Hendrick Stoddard, "The Ottoman Government and the Arabs, 1911-1918: A Preliminary Study of the Teshkilat-i Mahsusa" (Ph.D. diss., Princeton University, 1963).

8.   Over 4,000 interviews have been taped on cassettes with eyewitnesses and survivors of the Armenian Genocide. Significant numbers of interviews have been conducted by Professor V. L. Parseghian (Rensselaer Institute), Professor Richard G. Hovannisian (University of California at Los Angeles), and their associates, as well as by organizations such as the Armenian Library and Museum of America (Belmont, Mass.) and the Armenian Assembly of America (Washington, D.C.). The Armenian Film Foundation of Los Angeles has a collection of filmed interviews with survivors, while the Zoryan Institute for Contemporary Armenian Research and Documentation (Cambridge, Mass.) has over 300 videotaped interviews. Some press accounts of the deportations and massacres have been re-published in *The Armenian Genocide, as Reported in the Australian Press* (Sydney: Armenian National Committee, 1983), *The Canadian Press and the Armenian Genocide* (Montreal: Armenian National Committee, 1985), and Richard Kloian, ed., *The Armenian Genocide: News Accounts from the American Press* (Berkeley, Calif.: Anto Printing, 1985).

9.   Cipher telegram, Mahmud Kiamil, Commander of the Third Army to Governors General, July 10, 1915; cited in Gerard J. Libaridian, "The Ideology of the Young Turk Movement," in *A Crime of Silence*, ed. Gerard J. Libaridian (London: Zed Books, 1985), p. 49.

10.   See, for example, Yves Ternon, "Report on the Genocide," in *A Crime of Silence*, p. 116.

11.   The 1894-1896 massacres claimed over 200,000 Armenian victims throughout the Ottoman Empire; for an analysis of the events, see Robert Melson, "A Theoretical Inquiry into the Armenian Massacres of 1894-1896," in *Comparative Studies in Society and History* 24, No. 3 (July 1982), pp. 481-509. The 1909 occurrence, known as the massacre of Adana, was in fact a series of massacres in many Cilician cities. It claimed over 20,000 Armenian lives. Coming less than a year after the revolution, the outbreak was embarrassing to the Young Turks trying to project a

new image in Europe. The government sent Enver Pasha to participate in joint ceremonies condemning the massacres; see Msgr. Mouchegh, *Les Vépres Ciliciénnes* (Alexandria: Delia Rocca, 1909), and the report of an Armenian deputy of the Ottoman Parliament, a member of the Ittihad, Hagop Babigian, *Teghekagir* [Report] (Paris: N.p., 1919).

12.　There are no exact numbers or reliable census figures with regard to the various peoples of the Ottoman Empire. Figures proposed by the Armenian Patriarchate or the Turkish census have been challenged on various grounds. Figures used here are on the conservative side. See Hovannisian, Armenia, pp. 34-37; Turkish census figures have been used by Justin McCarthy, *Muslims and Minorities* (New York: New York University Press, 1983).

13.　Helen Fein, *Accounting for Genocide* (New York: The Free Press, 1979), pp. 29-30.

14.　This has been the dominant view among Armenian writers for decades. The most widely known works in this category are Haygazn Ghazarian, *Tseghasban turke* [The Turk, Author of Genocide] (Beirut, 1968), and Zarevant, *Miatsyal ev angakh turania gam inch ge dsrakren turkere* [United and independent Turanian or what the Turks are planning] (N.p. 1926).

15.　The most prominent scholar to advance this view is Bernard Lewis, *The Emergence of Modern Turkey* (Oxford: Oxford University Press, 1961), p. 356. As Robert Melson has pointed out in his paper "Neither Scapegoats nor Provocateurs" (see note 1), the equation between the nationalism of a Turkish elite with access to resources such as an empire and that of a relatively small and altogether unarmed subject people as the Armenians is not a valid one.

16.　Bernard Lewis, *The Emergence of Modern Turkey*, 2nd ed. (Oxford: Oxford University Press. 1968), pp. 218-19.

17.　The Armenian Question, i.e., the interest the Great Powers had regarding the Armenians of the Ottoman Empire as part of their imperialistic designs or occasional humanitarian concern, should not be equated with the Armenian revolutionary movement, however the two were connected for tactical or strategic considerations. See chapters 4, 5, and 6.

18.　Tessa Hofmann, "German Eyewitness Reports of the Genocide of the Armenians, 1915-1916," in Libaridian, *A Crime of Silence*, pp. 61-92; Susan K. Blair, "Excuses for Inhumanity: The Official German Response to the 1915 Armenian Genocide," *Armenian Review* 4 (1984), pp. 14-30; Ulrich Trumpener, *Germany and the Ottoman Empire, 1914-1918* (Princeton: Princeton University Press, 1968).

19.　Melson, "Neither Scapegoats nor Provocateurs."

20.　Vahakn N. Dadrian, "A Theoretical Model of Genocide, with Particular Reference to the Armenian Case," *Armenian Review* 2 (1979); idem, "The Structural-Functional Components of Genocide: A Victimology Approach to the Armenian Case," in *Victimology*, vol. 3, and "The Common Features of the Armenian and Jewish Cases of Genocide: A Comparative Victimological Perspective," in *Victimology*, vol. 4, ed. Israel Drapkin and Emilio Viano (Lexington, Mass.: D. C. Heath and Co.. 1974 and 1975); idem, "A Typology of Genocide," *International Review of Sociology* 2 (1975); Vahakn N. Dadrian. *The History of the Armenian Genocide: Ethnic Conflict from the Balkans to Anatolia to the Caucasus* (Providence, RI: Berghahn Books, 1995).

21.　Siyamend Othman, "La participation des kurdes dans les massacres des Arméniens, 1915," *Critique Socialiste* 13 (1982), pp. 31-48. See chapter 9.

22.　Ronald Suny, "Background to Genocide: New Perspectives on the Armenian Massacres and Deportations of 1915," paper presented at the Conference on Genocide, Harvard University, April 13, 1985.

23. See note 1.
24. Studies of the 1908-1918 period are rare. Existing works also have made rare use of Armenian sources: historians have functioned under the assumption that Armenians could not have been that important in the minds of the Turkish leaders, even when the issue was the state's attitude toward the Armenians. See, for example, Tarik Z. Tunaya, *Turkiyede siyasi partiler, 1859-1952* [Political parties in Turkey, 1859-1952] (Istanbul: N.p., 1952). For brief discussions of this period sec Hovannisian, *Armenia*, pp. 28-34, and Mikayel Varantian, *H. H. Dashnaktsutian batmutiun* [History of the Armenian Revolutionary Federation], vol. 2 (Cairo: N.p.. 1950), pp. 183-235.
25. This agreement has been referred to briefly by Varantian, ibid., pp. 203-4. Members of the Turkish Section of the Dashnaktsutiune's Bureau were asked by the Sixth World Congress of the Dashnaktsutiune in 1911 to prepare a comprehensive report on the relations between the party and the Ittihad. The resulting study consists of two documents. The first is a diary-like notebook of about forty-six pages with entries on meetings between ARF and CUP leaders between 1909 and 1911 (Archives of the Dashnaktsutiune, File 78/a-1). The second is entitled a "Memorandum" on the same issue: the document has forty-six pages (File Number 78/a-2). These archives contain extensive files on the period under study and are certain to yield much critical information once studied.
26. Archives of the Dashnaktsutiune. File 78/a-1.
27. Simon Zavarian, "Asdijanagan vochnchatsum" [Gradual extermination], *Azadamard*, August 9 and 26, 1911. The article provides statistical evidence of the dramatic decrease in the number of Armenians and Armenian-owned houses, farms, and farm utensils in a number of districts over a period of thirty years.
28. Shamil, to Western and Eastern Bureaus of the Dashnaktsutiune, August 10, 1911. Archives of the Dashnaktsutiune, File 671, Doc. 46.
29. Archives of the Dashnaktsutiune, File 78/a-2. For the last point, see also Jemal Pasha, *The Memoirs of a Statesman* (New York: Dial, 1919), p. 254. Jemal states that the CUP asked the ARF to come under the umbrella of the Ittihad as should all other parties. The argument was that there was no need for divisions when everyone was now an Ottoman.
30. Simon Zavarian, "Barekamutian ardunke" [Result of friendship], *Azatamart*, April 19, 1912.
31. Simon Zavarian, "Himnakan vdange" [The fundamental danger], *Azatamart*, May 17, 1912. The titles indicate large landownership, other great wealth, or positions of traditional authority.
32. Arsen Kitur, *Patmutiun S. T. Hnchakian Kusaktsutian* [History of the Social Democratic Hnchakian Party], vol. I (Beirut: N.p., 1962), p. 389.
33. Jemal Pasha, *Memoirs*, p. 256.
34. "Azadagrutian janaparhe" [The path to liberation], unsigned editorial, *Azatamart*. May 18,1912.
35. Kitur, *Patmutiun S. T. Hnchakian*, p. 365.
36. Unsigned lead article, *Droshak*, June 1912.
37. Hovannisian, *Armenia*, pp. 38-39.
38. The denial/justification pattern was set during the Genocide itself and consecrated by none other than Talaat Pasha, the minister of interior of the CUP most responsible for the Genocide, in "Posthumous Memoirs of Talaat Pasha," *Current History* (November 1921), pp. 287-95.
39. To prove his humanitarian concerns, Jemal Pasha remembers having argued against deporting and killing all Armenians since these actions would have disastrous ef-

fects on the economy, especially the agriculture of Anatolia (Memoirs, p. 278). Zavarian had characterized the role of the Armenians in the empire as "the milking cow" (*Azadamard*, August 5, 1911). It should be noted that Armenians were involved in the reform movement, although in a different way, in the first constitutional period too, under Midhat Pasha. Krikor Odian, a Paris-trained lawyer who had played a major role in the development of the Armenian "National Constitution" for the millet in 1860-1863, was an advisor of Midhat Pasha, and is thought to have been instrumental in the writing of the 1876 Ottoman constitution. The integration was particularity strong in folk culture, where language and other barriers break down; comparative studies in folk music and dance should be revealing.

40.   Benjamin Braude and Bernard Lewis, eds., *Christians and Jews in the Ottoman Empire, Volume I, The Central Lands* (New York: Holmes and Meier, 1981).

41.   Prince Sabaheddine, who was related to the sultan and whose family went into exile, became one of the leading figures of the Young Turk movement. He became the founder of the Hurriyet ve Ittilaf Firicasi (Freedom and Private Initiative Party), which included Greeks, Turks, Armenians, Arabs, and Bulgarians. See Ahmad, *Young Turks*, p. 99, and Ramsaur, *Young Turks*, pp. 82-83.

42.   Ramsaur, *Young Turks*, p. 92.

43.   Ibid.. p. 44.

44.   Ahmad, *Young Turks*, p. 163.

45.   Ibid., p. 158.

46.   Ramsaur points out that one of the reasons why the Young Turk Damad Mahmud's critique of the sultan's regime was effective with Turks was that "he was a Turk and a Muslim himself, as well as a member of the royal family," p. 59.

47.   Droshak (Geneva), October-November 1909; Garo Sasuni, *Kurd azkayin sharjhume ev hay-krdagan haraperutiunnere* [The Kurdish national movement and Armeno-Kurdish relations] (Beirut: Hamazkaine Press, 1969), pp. 155-57.

48.   Kitur, *Batmutiun*, p. 319; Ramsaur, *Young Turks*, p. 73.

49.   It seems to this writer that had the political, economic, and social reforms supported by Armenian political parties been part of the program of Turkish parties, Turkish historians would have found them relevant for understanding Ottoman history; some of them also might have found echoes in the concerns of more contemporary perspectives.

50.   "Dsrakir" (Program), Hnchak (London), October-November 1888; also in Kitur, pp. 32-37.

51.   Unsigned editorials, "Heghapokhutian ayb ben gime" [The ABC of the revolution], *Droshak*, November 1893 and January 1984.

52.   "Gordsi brobakant" [Propaganda for action], *Droshak*. October 1907 and *passim*.

53.   Kitur, *Batmutiun*, p. 323.

54.   "Chorrord endhanur jhoghovi voroshumner" [Resolutions of the Fourth World Congress] (Vienna, 1907); unsigned proclamation on the occasion of the Young Turk revolution, *Droshak*, September 1908.

55.   The SDHP and the ARF continue to function to this day; the Ramgavar-Sahmanatragan Party joined with two smaller groups in 1921 to form what has since become the Armenian Democratic Liberal Party.

56.   Mosse, *German Jews Beyond Judaism*.

57.   H. Elmasian, Yeprem (Tehran: N.p., 1964), and Andre Amourian, *Heghapokhakan Yepremi votisakane* [The odyssey of Yeprem the Revolutionary] (Tehran: Alik, 1972).

58.   Ramsaur, *Young Turks*, p. 147.

59.   Ramsaur recognizes the role of the resentment of European interference in the internal affairs of the Ottoman Empire in the beginnings of Turkish nationalism, but

he adds, "In their attitude toward the Armenians and other subject peoples, the Young Turks are basically imperialistic" (p. 44).

60. *Droshak*, September 1980.

61. *Droshak*, February-March 1914.

62. Kitur, *Batmutiun*, p. 328.

63. *"Kaghakagan hay gusagtsutiunneru hamerashkhutiune: Haydararakir"* [The harmonious cooperation of Armenian political parties. Proclamation], October 1913, Constantinople, Archives of the Dashnaktsutiune, File 53-179. The document was signed by the Hnchakian Party, the Reformed Hnchakian Party, the Ramgavar-Sahmanatragan Party, and the Dashnaktsutiune.

64. *Droshak*, January 1913.

65. Sabaheddine seems to have been impressed by Edmond Demolins, *Anglo-Saxon Superiority: To What it is Due* (New York: R. F. Fenno & Co., 1889), in which the author argues that patriotism works when it is "founded on the independence of private life" in which the individual will defend his fatherland to protect his own freedom, when the state exists to facilitate the individual's own independence, and when the fatherland is made for man and not the other way around. See Ramsaur, *Young Turks*, p. 82-83.

66. Ramsaur, *Young Turks*, p. 70; see also chapter 2.

67. Ramsaur, *Young Turks*, p. 8.

68. Jemal Pasha, *Memoirs*, pp. 97, 276.

69. Ibid., p. 276.

70. Ibid., p. 97.

71. Johannes Lepsius, *Der Todesgang des armenisches Volkes. Bericht liber das Schicksal des armenisches Volkes in der Tiinkei rahrend des Weltkrieges* [The death march of the Armenian people. Report on the fate of the Armenian people in Turkey during the World War] (Heidelberg: N.p., 1980), p. 227.

72. *Daily Telegraph*. October 9, 1915.

73. Ramsaur, *Young Turks*, p. 7.

74. *Droshak*, February-March 1913.

75. *Droshak*, June 1913, p. 97.

76. Unsigned editorial, *Hnchak*, November 1913.

77. *Aspirations et agissements révolutionnaires des comités Arméniens avant et aprés la proclamation de la Constitution Ottomane* (Constantinople: N.p., 1916 and 1917).

9

Ideology and History: Problems in the Study of Armeno-Kurdish Relations

For many centuries Kurds and Armenians have shared a territory both consider part of their fatherland. During the last five centuries they were both subjects of the Ottoman Empire, which shaped the larger outline of their histories. The two peoples also shared dimensions in culture, which survived the westernizing tendencies among both peoples. During this long period of history, similarly, social and economic contacts between Armenians and Kurds have been intense.

Politically, these relations have covered the whole spectrum of possibilities, from massacres to strategic alliances. They have played a crucial role in the question of the political and physical survival of both peoples. During the nineteenth and early twentieth centuries, the power of Kurdish chiefs was manipulated against Armenians. Given the importance that Anatolia and Armenia/Kurdistan acquired for Turkish nationalism toward the end of the nineteenth century, Armeno-Kurdish relations constitute an important problem also for the understanding of modern Turkish history and the moral foundation of the republic that replaced the empire. The transition in Turkish political thought and practice from an imperial tradition to the nation-state model became, of course, a key element in Near East history: it was pivotal for the genocidal policies of the Young Turk government toward the Armenian people,[1] the massacre of over 700,000 Kurds and the dislocation of many more,[2] and the resulting death through starvation and disease of at least an equal amount of Turks in the same areas.[3]

Kurds and Armenians are two of the three peoples in the Near East that were denied self determination after the First World War; their relations, therefore, have relevance also for the current political geography of the Near East and on Turkish policies toward Kurds and Armenians.

Yet, with rare exceptions, the question of Armeno-Kurdish relations has failed to attract the attention of scholars. The existing literature tends to treat the two elements separately, if at all. The purpose of this article is to review briefly some works that have attempted to fill the gap, to speculate on the possible reasons underlying this failure in historiography, and to propose some steps that may help overcome the difficulty.

It is possible to ascribe the absence of interest in such momentous changes as described above to problems in the field of Near Eastern studies itself, which has already assumed an autonomous development. One can also be charitable and argue that the complexity of the problem had earlier scared rather than challenged researchers.

A more fundamental explanation must be sought, however, in the subjective nature of research itself. It is often necessary to articulate in words what is a basic but ignored truth: historians and scientists are not abstract entities who develop interests and conclusions in a vacuum. They usually begin with perspectives that predetermine the subjects to study as well as the questions to be raised with regard to that subject. While the procedure followed to reach a particular conclusion may be grounded in objective rules, the ideology within which the analysis occurs constitutes the ultimate test for a scholar in determining the concerns of that yet-to-be-written history and the values it will consider inherently legitimate or defensible.

Historians for Statism

For most Western and Turkish historians of Turkey the nation-state constitutes the test of legitimacy of a people. Thus, as a general rule, studies of the Ottoman Empire and of modern Turkey will tend to reinforce the claim of the Turkish state that a Kurdish people does not exist and thus discard the legitimacy of Kurdish concerns and claims. Similarly, the Armenian issue is treated as that of a small minority, often troublesome, that could not have a life of its own but came to the arena of history to be massacred. In other words, historians tend to reproduce the distortions and values of the politicians they are supposed to explain and evaluate.

This statist approach to history extols then the survival of the state in a given form and at all cost not only as the political concern of a ruling group but also as a morally defensible and absolute value.[4]

The problem is even more acute for historians of the Ottoman Empire and Turkey who, for the most part, follow the official line. Most of their writings on the non-Turkish dimension of Ottoman-Turkish history betray a conscious or unconscious participation in the ideology, if not mythology, of modern nation building in which most states but particularly new ones are engaged. This process implies more than rewriting history: here history turns into a story, and the historical category of nation is transformed into an absolute category; history then is a predictable chain of inevitable, almost divinely ordained events leading to the establishment of the nation-state. Most histories of nineteenth century Near East have begun to assume that pre-1923 Ottoman history was merely a prelude to the founding of a Turkish republic. The implication is that non-Turkish elements such as Armenians and Kurds were outside of history by definition, regardless of their numbers, of their socioeconomic or political position, or of any rights, including the right of self determination, they might have had. The Genocide of the Armenians and the massacres and deportations of the Kurds, then, become at least understandable, even justifiable, steps in the process of realizing a manifest destiny, the establishment of a Turkish nation-state.

The rest were mere details. When otherwise respectable scholars insist upon denying the Genocide of the Armenians in face of overwhelming evidence, they are in fact insisting upon the irrelevance of the Armenians within their worldview, and their understanding of the policy that aimed at making Armenians irrelevant, the Genocide.[5] The refusal to make the current Kurdish situation a subject of serious research is the manifestation of a larger bias than what a given scholar may think of a particular Kurdish claim or organization. Turkish state ideology denies the issue of class and the right of non-Turkish groups to exist; its apologists reject the possibility that class and, by extension, socioeconomic issues that engender state-minority relations, have any relevance for either the development or the understanding of history.

The Burden of Liberalism and Leftism

The problem is not limited, though, to reactionary or conservative Turkish scholars, although they are the ones promoted and rewarded by the Turkish government. It is important to point out that most liberal and leftist historians too seem to appreciate the opportunity to analyze a Turkish society unburdened of its heterogeneity. Yet rigid and simplistic "Marxist" formulas on economic stratification are difficult to apply to the mosaic of the Middle East; here ethnic, religious, and class differentiations must be sorted out with greater insight and less certainty. Nonetheless, many scholars who dare deviate from official state ideology by incorporating into their worldview socioeconomic dimensions and motivations commit the same kind of error as the statists. What changes is the rational for dismissing non-Turks.[6]

While it is possible to argue that as a conceptual framework class is more relevant then ethnic/cultural identity, it is doubtful that any category is more relevant than existence. The problem of Armenians and Kurds happens to incorporate a more complex category that was articulated early by Armenian revolutionaries: a people with a distinct ethnic-cultural identity treated as an oppressed class, and the justification of oppression and exploitation of the group on the basis of the group's distinctive character, leading eventually to its repression or physical elimination.[7] Mass slayings and genocides are a greater calamity—and the worst imaginable form of denial of the humanity and human rights of a group—than the oppression of a class. Yet, notwithstanding the popular fascination with horror, genocides have an inherent dimension of finality and fail to attract the attention class struggles do except for the attention of governments seeking radical or "final" solutions to political problems.

Some Hopeful Signs

Some recent publications outside of Turkey may be indicating subtle changes within the Turkish intelligentsia toward the recognition of the Kurdish and, to a lesser extent, Armenian problem.[8] But these are far from coming to terms with what constitutes a critical dimension of Turkish history: the non-Turkish peoples within the Ottoman Empire. Research in this area has been done largely through the prism of the millets. Yet, the millet approach to the "minorities" of the Ottoman Empire leaves out, by definition, the Kurdish people, who were ostensibly part of the Muslim or main community.

Also, historians studying problems of Ottoman peasantry and agriculture showed neither the inclination nor developed the tools to consult extensive Armenian sources, when Armenians constituted a significant and integral part of that sector of the Ottoman economy as they did in commerce. As non-governmental sources closer to the actual life of the people, these archives would tend to portray aspects of peasant life and agricultural policies not reflected in official documents or statistics; under circumstances less impregnated with ideology, such collections would have been regarded as treasures for the reconstruction of the past. But there has been a "natural" tendency to disregard any fact or document that defies state ideology or historians' prejudices.

Failing to deal directly with elements so much part of Ottoman society, social scientists have had to deal with its consequences. At least one Turkish economic historian has discovered that war-related disruptions alone cannot explain the drastic decrease in agricultural output obvious during postwar years; it became necessary to recognize the destructive policies of the Ottoman government against Kurds and Turks, but especially against Armenians, in order to give history a semblance of reality.[9]

Serious inquiries into Armenian-Kurdish relations—an inquiry free not only of racial prejudices but also of political/philosophical biases—may help students of Turkey understand some of the more intricate aspects of state policies not only toward Armenians and Kurds and how one was used against the other, but more generally, how religion and race were effectively used by the state to alienate the Turkish population from the others, to defend them from modes of thought which lead to demands for political freedom and equality—demands that were more easily adopted or internalized by oppressed socio/ethnic groups such as the Armenians, Arabs, Greeks, and to some extent, Kurds.

The Weight of Defeat

Armenian and Kurdish historians and intellectuals have done only slightly more to compensate for the dearth of studies on the relations of their peoples. A cursory, though not a comprehensive, search reveals some works of an impressionistic nature, written before the First World War.[10] One would expect that the postwar period would have produced more studies.

The fact is that there are only two studies of interest. The first is entitled *Kurt azgayin sharzhume ev hay-krtakan haraberutiunnere* (The Kurdish national movement and Armeno-Kurdish relations). The study was first published in serialized form in the *Hairenik*

Amsagir, a Boston-based Armenian language monthly journal during 1929-1931, and more recently as a single volume in Beirut in 1969. The author of the study, Garo Sasuni, was a well-known Armenian writer born in the mountains of Sasun in Western Armenia. Sasuni had been a guerrilla fighter during the later phases of the Armenian revolutionary movement; survivor from the Genocide; and provincial governor during the independent period of the Republic of Armenia. Having been born and grown up in an area of the Ottoman Empire where Kurds and Armenians lived together, Sasuni was one of the strongest supporters among Armenians of an Armenian-Kurdish cooperation. His study was written, in fact, toward the end of the Kurdish revolt of 1929 in which he had been active on behalf of the ARF. The study provides a historical and political overview of Armeno-Kurdish relations and covers the institutional and to some extent economic factors that may explain the changing character of the relations between two peoples whose histories were intertwined. Unlike many of his contemporaries, Sasuni was able to see the Kurds as a heterogeneous people whose varied actions must be understood within the context of the social and political stratification of its institutions. On the whole, the work remains an argument in favor of closer ties and cooperation.

The second and most recent study is by the Kurdish scholar Siyamend Othman, an Iraqi Kurd. Othman's "Participation des Kurdes dans le massacre des Arméniens-1915" was published in the *Critique Socialiste* (1982) and was based on his thesis, "Le Kurde et le Sang Versé des Arméniens" presented in 1981 at the Ecole des Hautes Etudes en Sciences Sociales. The article remains a singularly brave and focused piece. Dealing directly with the thorniest and most painful issue between Kurds and Armenians, Othman discards religious differences between Armenians and Kurds as a cause of the Kurdish participation in the Genocide of Armenians in 1915; he points out that a feudal-tribal structure was manipulated toward creating the conditions for such a participation, the tribal chieftains/feudal lords having been co-opted within Ottoman policy. He also argues that the economic preponderance of an Armenian bourgeoisie in the marketplace might have predisposed Kurds against Armenians.

The author argues against all forms of racism that blind individuals and groups and increase the impact of tragedies that peoples have already suffered. The study was written at a time when the Kurdish struggle was becoming more critical and when secretly organized Armenian groups had, through political violence, brought back to the attention of the world the Armenian case itself. While some of the points raised by Othman require further investigation,[11] there is no doubt that the article's appeal to reason and objectivity makes great strides toward overcoming the ideological, social, and historical prejudices that have plagued this field.

Neighborly Alienation

It may be that despite the importance of the issues discussed here, there is yet another dimension in the problem of Kurdish-Armenian relations that has defied the historical categories used thus far; for the reality is that despite commonalties and parallels in their history and geography, Armenians and Kurds continue to exist and articulate their cultural and historical problems as if they are unaware of the existence of the other. Even in those cases where political or strategic cooperation is advocated, the conclusion is reached following a conceptualized reasoning ("two oppressed peoples") or based on an argument in favor of a tactical need to face a common enemy ("Kurdish arms and Armenian brains").[12] However self-evident these arguments may seem, they are not derived from the natural course of history or the cohabitation of the two peoples for so long or from a sense of a common destiny. This near total alienation between Kurds and Armenians does not even exist between Armenians and Turks or between Turks and Kurds.

To what extent did this alienation exist before the radical policies imposed by the Young Turks between the two peoples? Or, is it a problem of the cultural reconstruction that followed the massacres and deportations of the two peoples? It is possible to argue, for example, that the Armenian peasantry, the element closest to the Kurd in culture as well as in adversity, was completely wiped out by the Genocide; moreover, post-Genocide perceptions of the Genocide were defined largely by surviving urban elements who had little contact with Kurds, except as marauders and occasionally saviors during the massacres and deportations, but nonetheless as external forces. Conceivably both factors have played a role in defining this paradox.

Popular perceptions of Kurds during the pre-Genocide period cover the spectrum of attitudes beginning with genuine feelings of kinship in some areas, including the belief that many of the Kurdish tribes were converted Armenian feudal families, and extending to outright hatred due to the pillage and destruction caused by tribal practices. It is not uncommon to discern both attitudes held simultaneously.

It is important to note that Armenian spokesmen and commentators whose vision of Armenia has been based on populist thought were aware of both attitudes and have advocated a path that would lead to the coexistence of all elements. Khrimian Hayrik, who was born in Van and was elevated to the highest positions of the Armenian Church during a long career spanning the second half of the nineteenth century, identified the duality in the Kurdish position and preached both self defense against Kurds but at the same time sought to reach out to them by understanding their socio-political structure and advocating agrarian settlements.[13] He advocated the idea that the Kurds be encouraged to adopt a settled agricultural lifestyle.

The early political activists, and particularly Mkrtich Terlemezian or Avetisian, the real leader of the Armenakans of the 1880s, could not leave out the Kurds from his worldview. In a series of leading articles in Armenia, he advocated the translation of objective realities into a common political program. Most notably, though, it was the political parties, the SDHP and ARF that articulated clearly the political program by advocating a radical solution to the problem of the empire through a coalition of opposition groups, including Kurds who would support reforms. Following futile attempts in that direction, the ARF reached a series of tactical agreements with Kurdish tribal chiefs, thus attempting to at least neutralize, if not co-opt, the Kurdish feudal opposition to the Armenian guerrilla movement between 1896 and 1908.

While the Kurdish problem intrigued the more progressive thinkers, generally speaking it was concluded that real cooperation was difficult to obtain given fundamental differences in the socioeconomic structures of the nomadic Kurdish and settled Armenian societies.

It is also important to note that in pre-Genocide as well as post-Genocide periods the ability to see some objective realities has been hampered by an obsession among both peoples with their internal divisions. While Kurds were divided into tribes and by international boundaries, Armenians had a longer list of conflicts.

This fact is important not only because it tends to direct the sharpest insights, the area where complexities are acceptable, inward, but also because it delineates the arena within which both groups sought the articulation of their problems. Armenian society gradually looked at Western culture to provide the terminology to describe its problems, to define the principles why the status quo was unacceptable; it was also in the West that Armenians sought their most congenial political alliances. The nature of Armenian society and its economic concerns—agricultural, local, and international trade—required security, continuity, and protection. Western nationalism, even when adapted to Armenians needs, retained its cultural underpinnings inherited from the French Revolution. In fact, it was the cultural dimension that provided the motivation to regard one's status as no longer acceptable to dare dream of a better future; in the nineteenth century to dare dream of change and improvement one had no model but that provided by the western "advanced" nations, who regarded their advancement as a sign of the liveliness of their culture.

To look to the West, to its dynamic culture, to its articulation of the possibilities of change, and inevitably to the strategies for change it offered—the diametrically opposed routes of revolution and imperialisms—was more congenial to Armenians. Armenians seeking allies for their political progress gravitated toward the West; Kurds moved toward acceptance and alliance with the Ottoman state. The Kurdish leadership, generally speaking, sought the retention of the status quo as the best guarantee for the continued domination of a feudal structure. The result was further alienation from their neighbors, and especially from the Kurds.

Thus, even though on a day-to-day basis the standard of living of a large number of Armenians in the agricultural sector and settled Kurds were more often than not the same, each group's cultural world provided it with a different, if not conflicting, set of social and political values when looking at the future. This alienation before the First World War transcended then the impact of daily complaint forwarded by Armenians against Kurdish marauders and of any exploitation of Kurds by Armenian merchants. It required more than a leap in political imagination to overcome such differences—a leap, incidentally, that the Armenian revolutionary attempted by adopting the socialist-Marxistic view of the world.

Since that war, Diaspora Armenians know of Kurds only as incidents in their individual lives and a bane in their collective past. They are a grandfather's killer or savior during the Genocide. For many Kurds, who hardly have any reason to remember in detail the events of 1915 and who like others grow up to think that the world is as it seems it is now, Armenians are a vague memory, at best a historical mistake.

The appearance of a new resistance among both peoples against Turkish hegemony have had both peoples perplexed. The recognition of common needs thus required a logical argument. While conflicting territorial demands made them cautious, there has been a sense of mutual curiosity, like old neighbors long separated. It required the near extermination and total exile of the Armenians and the threat of a similar fate for the Kurds to overcome unwelcome memories and deep-rooted prejudices.

Nonetheless, historians and social scientists grew up with those memories and prejudices. This estrangement of culture dominated as Western Armenia became the new dispersion and as Kurdistan joined Armenia as a banned word in Turkey until the 1980s.

Overcoming Biases

The purpose of the following remarks is to contribute to a process started by scholars such as Siyamend Othman and intellectuals such as Yilmaz Guney,[14] a process that integrates a conscious effort to come to terms with the problems underlying historiographic issues as a means of overcoming one's own biases, ideological and otherwise. It is my hope that these remarks will contribute to a healthy dialogue between social scientists and intelligentsia of the various peoples of the region.

1)   Social scientists with interdisciplinary interests should be encouraged to devote some time to study interethnic relations between various classes within different peoples rather than limiting studies to formal acts and to relations between the elites within each.

2)   Conceptual categories developed in the social sciences relating to non-state social categories, such as tribes and peoples, should be applied toward the understanding of Near Eastern societies.

3)   Before generalizations reduce history to platitudes, it may be worth undertaking studies of the complex range of interethnic relations within small regions and districts as case studies.

4)   The notion that history consists of the discovery and pursuit of the idea of nation-state should be discarded; the idea that decisions taken by leaders responsible for governments and countries can be evaluated and justified solely by the degree to which they bring closer the

realization or the defense of the nation-state should be challenged, at least for historical periods when the "nation" was not the foundation of a state and for regions where the multi-ethnic character of the "nation" makes an abstraction of the notion of "nation-state," and a dangerous one at that. Specifically, one must discard the notion that Armenians, Kurds, and Turks have always felt, thought, or acted as they did once the generation that witnessed the events of the First World War disappeared.

It seems obvious at this point that, given the cultural differentiations and class antagonisms within the Ottoman Empire, the challenges of the West and other factors forcing changes in the Ottoman Empire did not produce a perception or a set of problems common to all subjects. Nor did these peoples adopt an abstract nationalism as their ideology. One should at least recognize that even when the terminology was borrowed from the West, and to the extent that systematic articulations were made, different peoples understood nationalism to mean different things. As a general rule, despite its meanderings in liberal-democratic directions, Turkish political thought tended to be concerned with the survival of the state and the maintenance of a dominant role of the Turkish element within it. Whether as a justification or as a consequence of this, the question of political and economic justice for all subjects, classes, and ethnic groups seems easily discarded as a priority.

5)   One must discard the notion that Turks, Kurds, Armenians, and others can be discussed as single categories, as if they were cohesive entities.

6)   A serious analysis must be made of the impact of the Western economic penetration in the Near East since the eighteenth century, of the taxation systems, and their impact on the various elements of the Ottoman and Turkish population. The concentration on the diplomatic and political history at the exclusion of social and economic factors tends to promote the nationalistic and otherwise distorted view of the past.

These comments also suggest the need for social scientists from different ethnic and religious groups to develop concrete and joint studies. Such an undertaking could solve one of the more difficult issues in historiography, the knowledge of many languages, particularly the language of minorities. Such projects may also end up defining areas of study that provide the possibility for maximum denationalization of these histories. Finally, in addition to producing better histories, this may also be a means by which social scientists, whether European, Turkish, Kurdish, Armenian, or American, can learn to deal with the prejudices apparent in many—a prelude to the phase where it becomes possible to debate intelligently the thornier, subjectively loaded, and politically sensitive historical and human issues.

Notes

1. See chapter 8.
2. N. Kendal, "Le Kurdistan de Turquie," *Les Kurdes et le Kurdistan* (Paris, 1978).
3. Justin McCarthy, *Muslims and Minorities* (New York, 1983), p. 134.
4. The most important representative work in this category is Stanford and Ezel Kural Shaw, *The History of the Ottoman Empire*, vol. I. (London, 1978); see Rifaat Abu-el-Hajj's review of this work in the *American Historical Review* 197.
5. The most representative historian in this group is Kemal Karpat.
6. See Pierre Vidal-Naquet's Preface to *Le Crime de Silence*, Gerard Chaliand, ed. (Paris, 1984). (English text in *The Crime of Silence* [London, 1985].)
7. The equation of an ethnic group with a class, an important dimension of twentieth-century national liberation struggles, may have been seen for the first time in the case of the Armenians in the Ottoman Empire. See chapter 5.
8. In the journal *Khamsin* (London, no. 11, 1983) devoted to Turkey, A. Ender has presented the Kurdish problem in a substantial way; the July-August 1984 special issue of *Les Temps Modernes* (Paris) devoted to Turkey includes two important rejoinders, one by Anaide Ter-Minassian on the Armenian issue (pp. 419-446), and a second by Joyce Blau on the Kurdish problem (pp. 447-461). Unlike many Western and Turkish publications, the chronology included in the latter journal too integrates the Genocide of the Armenians as an important event in Ottoman Turkish history. Such a recognition may be due to the increased consciousness among many social scientists in Turkey and abroad since the 1980 military coup as to what the state is capable of doing as a substitute to solving basic social issues; renewed Kurdish fighting and Armenian political violence may also have helped in sensitizing writers to the plight of these two peoples.
9. The point was made explicitly by a Turkish economic historian during a seminar at Harvard University in 1983. The historian, at the time of his presentation, asked that his name be withheld when discussing some of his views to avoid reprisals by the military government of Turkey.
10. Hagop Shahbazian, *Krda-hay patmutiune* [Kurdsih Armenian History] (Constantinople, 1911); S. Ximenez, *Kurds and Armenians* (London, 1895). There are also a number of articles and booklets by Armenian social scientists or observers discussing Kurdish society that appeared between 1900 and 1914. One such work is M. T. Shvod's *Krtere tajkahayastanum. azgagrakan niuter* [The Kurds in Turkish-Armenia. Ethnographic studies] (St. Petersburg, 1905).
11. A major area that must be investigated further is the relationship between genocide and the nascent Turkish bourgeoisie at the beginning of the twentieth century. This bourgeoisie, along with the military, provided a major social basis for developing Turkish nationalism. The elimination of the Armenian element would have created the vacuum necessary for that class to occupy the preeminent position in the economy. It is also true that an important percentage of the provincial usurers were Armenian; they preyed on Kurds and Turks as much as on Armenians. Yet, it is becoming evident to students of the Genocide that, although antagonisms inspired from the marketplace was a factor in the participation of the common people in the massacres and deportations, wealthy Armenians still had the best chance to escape the massacres; the survival rate among the higher classes seems to be higher than those who had no means to bribe or purchase goods to continue their existence. This is one of the points made, for example, by J. Lepsius during the trial of Soghomon Tehlirian, who had been charged with the assassination of Talat Pasha in Berlin in 1921.
12. *The Economist*, London, June 18, 1983, p. 54.

13. See the complete works of Khrimian Hayrik, *Amboghjakan gordser* (New York, 1952).
14. See the late film director's statement to the Permanent Peoples' Tribunal session on the Armenian Genocide held in Paris, April 13-16 1984, published in *Le Crime de Silence* (Paris, 1984), among other places.

10

Re-Imagining the Past, Rethinking the Present: The Future of Turkish-Armenian Relations

The problem of Turkish-Armenian relations has the dubious distinction of being emotionally wrenching, politically explosive, and intellectually challenging. The topic has something to do with the collective memory, identity, and destiny of two peoples that have grown up damning each other, but are condemned to live together, whether in their homelands or as Diaspora communities sharing citizenship in new countries in Europe and the Americas.

The topic also relates to the foundations as well as to the present and future relations of two states that, though neighbors, grew further apart with time.

The reasons for these paradoxes are many. They relate not only to what happened before and during 1915, but are made up of what happened, the role assigned to those events, the politics of the two peoples, and the way these peoples relate to the rest of the world.

Much valuable work has been done on this problem, yet the historiography is not adequate to address the delicate issues mentioned above. While some intelligent and intelligible discourse has begun to emerge during the last decade or so, some of what has been written has tended to obscure rather than illuminate, to create a web of beliefs and political positions rather than disentangle and enlighten.

This chapter raises sets of questions the existing literature has not probed directly and sufficiently: What is the problem we are dealing with? Whose problem is it? What has been done with the problem, or why is it that in some cases the problem has been internalized in a manner that almost ensures that it will never be resolved?

What is the Problem?

In the first place, it is necessary to identify the areas of disagreement between "Turks" and "Armenians," admittedly a very vague terminology, but one that foretells the character and depth of the problem as it best represents the generally held perceptions of the issue.

Is the problem one of accounting history—the nature of the policies and the actions of the Ottoman government and/or of the Armenian leadership? Are the numbers of those killed the issue? Is internationality the problem? Is it a matter of characterizing what happened or the name that is given to it? Would archival, historical, or logical evidence make a difference in what one calls these events? What would it take to agree on or change labels, such as "unfortunate events," "civil war," "deportations and massacres," "tragedy," or "genocide?" What does one do, for example, with the argument made privately by a high official of the Turkish government, that since the Armenians of Istanbul were not subjected to the same massacres as those in the rest of Turkey, the events of 1915 could not be characterized as genocide? Would a cogent legal and logical argument—that to be recognized as genocide, not all the members of a group have to be victimized—be sufficient to change the position? And would a change in his thinking make a difference on official Turkish policy regarding the denial of genocide? Finally, had the principle of coming to terms with the policies of the Ottoman government during the First World War reached its logical conclusion and had Turkey been compelled to recognize the Genocide, as was the case with post-World War Two Germany, would these questions remain subject to debate today?

Had there been agreement on the genocidal character of Ottoman policies, would it matter if we found a good reason for these policies? And if such policies were justified, would such justification make it less of a genocide?

In other words, are we facing a problem of scholarship or of terminology that could be resolved through a sustained and possibly joint scholarly and intellectual effort? Or are we dealing with other factors, such as vested political interests vital enough or fears deep enough to override all other considerations?

The discourse on the subject has been mutually unintelligible to those engaged in writing on the subject, because the problem is not a conflict between opposing views of a history. The discourse has consisted of two histories, as if separate and unrelated. The two histories are written as if two peoples that coexisted for centuries did not interact except when they crossed each others paths during massacres, each performing the predetermined and inescapable role their characters mandated: one, that of the victim; the other, that of the victimizer. A debate on the victim-victimizer paradigm is, at best, a debate on morality—necessary in and by itself—but it is not a historical debate. Even as a debate on morality this one is distorted, as it tends to justify some otherwise questionable actions on both sides during the last century in the name of an absolute value or end.

The dominant paradigm of two nationalisms in collision takes too much for granted and reinforces the "two history" approach. It seems that the common past—for it is a common past, whatever the differences—has been hijacked and our inescapably interwoven history—however heroic, criminal, or tragic—has been held hostage by those who have accepted the nation-state model and nationalism as absolute values. At a time when the notion of sovereign state itself is in question, there are some who still insist on the nation-state concept both as the purpose and end result of the inexorable march of history.

Is it possible to understand history under those circumstances? Would it be, in fact, history or some sort of factionalized narrative, when our understanding of the past is based on our perception of our own realities, created after—and to some extent as a result of—the events of the First World War? On occasion historians seem to act like failed gods: they recreate the past in their own image, once they realize they cannot do so with the future. It seems to me that one should begin by questioning the ideological underpinnings of history as it is written today. The problem begins here.

Whose Problem is It?

Since there is a problem with the reading and writing of history, then the next question would be, whose problem is it? The dominant perspectives assume that a description of the events constitutes, in and by itself, the explanation of these events. The more detailed the description of cruelties, some Armenian authors believe, the more convincing the case for the label "genocide" and as to why it must have happened. For accountants of history, the implication is that Turks killed because it is their nature to do so, and it is the manifestation of that evil nature that must be highlighted. Turkish writers in this category have a more difficult task: they cannot describe a non-event. However, they can hope to dissipate serious transgressions, especially in the last decades of the Ottoman Empire, in idealized descriptions of the Ottoman administrative genius and spirit of tolerance and in repetitions of a listing of vile Armenian intentions and fifth column activities. Such stories would make the Ottoman Empire the first in history to have been established and maintained strictly through humanitarian policies.

Anti-Armenian accounts can, furthermore, talk about the wealth and important positions some Armenians had in the Ottoman Empire, which would deny the possibility of any anti-Armenian policy while simultaneously implying a justification for whatever "atrocities" were committed.

There seems to be less disagreement on the consequences of what happened. For Armenians, it was the end of their collective existence on land that was their home from time immemorial. For Turkey, the problem caused by Armenians, however defined, was resolved. One way to avoid the abstractions that nationalist perspectives must inevitably make of real people is to look at whole patterns of relations between people, leaders, and decision-makers. That is, instead of treating individuals who made decisions as the mere executors of the sacrosanct, abstracted ideas of nation and nationalism, one might want to have a second look and ask, why did it happen and how did it come to happen? For, between the narratives, the diatribes, and the mourning, one is missing the discourse on the cause or causes of a very historical event.

The difference between history, on the one hand, and collective memory or narrative, on the other, is in the ability of the first to make sense of events evidenced by observable changes, to explain as many disparate facts as possible, to understand as many decisions as discernible in human terms. History requires such a standard, even if facts and events relate to decisions that might otherwise be considered inhuman; so inhuman, in fact, that one may not want to resist the temptation to discard the casual dimension, if for no other reason than to reconfirm or show one's own humanity. Yet we know that such events have taken place and are taking place often enough that genocides can no longer be cast outside the realm of history.

A past event then becomes part of history when it is given a credible explanation, an explanation that also can account for more than itself, when it can survive the challenge, which seemingly contrary facts and phenomena preceding it and accompanying it would pose. One could not claim to write the history of that period without accounting for the whole range of relations and problems confronting those who made decisions for the Ottoman state and for its Armenian subjects. That, in turn, is possible only when one rethinks the past, in fact when re-imagines it, hopefully jointly, without the constraints that ideological thinking and the politics of genocide recognition have imposed on the understanding of that past.

Is it possible for Turkish and Armenian historians, for example, to imagine the history of the prewar period by suspending knowledge of subsequent events? Is it possible to think of relations between Turks and Armenians without taking the Genocide as that event to which all history was leading to and which determined all subsequent relations? Was genocide inevitable, could it have been avoided? Is it possible to think of the establishment and history of the Republic of Turkey while making the Genocide part of its inheritance from the Ottoman Empire? Is it possible for Turkish historians to think of Ottoman history while avoiding looking at the Turkish Republic as a pre-ordained outcome? Is it possible for Armenian historians to imagine the history of Armenian decision-making and policies as part of what happened before and during 1915? Can we imagine the thinking process of those who made decisions before they made the decisions? Was it possible, for example, that the behavior of Armenian leaders did little to account for the logic that sustained the CUP (Committee of Union and Progress) thinking? Is it possible that a more resolute and systematic policy of resistance would have reduced, at least, the scope of the calamity? What did Young Turk leaders see when they were talking to Armenian representatives, and vice versa?

To begin to unravel this complete set of issues, it is possible to begin with some observations. First, Turkish-Armenian relations are not merely a problem of relations between Turks and Armenians. Rather, they are Turkish-Armenian-Great Power relations. There are, in fact, three sets of players, not two, whether one is trying to understand history and politics or wishing to assign responsibility. The role of the Great Powers, i.e., imperialist powers, individually and collectively, is integral to the processes we are trying to understand.

Second, each set of players represents a different kind of entity. One player, the Ottoman Empire, is a state hijacked by a political elite fully motivated by a peculiar kind of nationalism. That elite has at its disposal all that a state can provide, including subjects who can kill and deport and be killed and be deported upon the orders of the state as represented by the political elite. The second player, the Armenians, are a people, one of the subject groups in that state, with different centers of power claiming to speak and/or act on its behalf. The third player, the so-called Great Powers, constitute a group of states—for that period, super-states—that are in competition, but collectively determine the rules of the game, a game in which others that are engaged wittingly or unwittingly can only try to cope with. Naturally, the study of the functioning and role of such different entities cannot be uniform in approach, beginning with the character and location of extant archival materials.

Third, each of the three players has a dual identity or role in the larger scheme of things.

On the one hand, the Ottoman state was an empire, ruling over peoples, territories, and former kingdoms, regressive and repressive, especially at the end of its existence. On the other hand, the Ottoman Empire was also a target of Western imperialism, of states that are bent on carving it away and dominating as much of its territory as possible and exacting a high price for allowing the Ottoman state to play the game and survive. The Ottoman state is both victimizer and victim, if one is to use the accepted terminology.

The Great Powers, in one sense, were states whose domestic, political, and intellectual culture constituted the source of inspiration for the political aspirations of others, for individual and collective rights. They produced, after all, the enlightenment, democracy, socialism, and the scientific revolution. They also represented models of state building. Yet, these were states with superior military technology that they used to the detriment of smaller nations and aged empires, including the Ottoman.

The Armenians were predominantly peasants, farmers, craftsmen, and traders, impoverished by over-taxation and extra-judicial exactions, paying the cost of the Ottoman debt, with an ever-weakening economic base of family and community existence, losing markets for home industries to Western industrial products. These were the Armenians of eastern provinces and central Anatolia, whose interests more often than not clashed with those of the privileged ones, largely in Istanbul. The grievances of these same Armenians are articulated increasingly by a liberal and then radical intelligentsia, largely European educated Ottoman Armenians and later still more radical Russian Armenians. Armenians project themselves as the vanguards of Western enlightenment, bringing to bear ideas of individual freedoms and formulating populist aims. But, however, the tactical purpose of popular agitation followed by guerilla warfare adopted by Armenians was to secure the intervention of the Great Powers—enlightened and imperialist—which the Turkish political elite considered to be the mechanism that victimized the Ottoman state in the name of reforms.

We thus come full circle. The problem for the Turkish elite was how to deal with the challenge of the Great Powers, how to ensure the survival of a strong state (if not Ottoman, then at least Turkish). The question was whether to do it through reforms or repression. Reforms did not result in neutralizing Western and, this time, Balkan policies regarding some Ottoman territories. The problem for Armenians was how to achieve reforms: a change in state structure through rebellion, Great Power intervention, or both? For the Turkish elite, that placed the Armenians on the side of the victimizers, the enemy. While the military capabilities of this enemy served as a role model for the leaders of the Ottoman Empire, it gave Armenians nothing but false hopes.

The history Armenians write is the story of their own victimization. The history written by Turks is that of Turkish liberation from Great Power imperialism. Both histories are based on victimization and liberation. The difference is that the first ended tragically, the second more successfully. The history Armenians write ignores the role they played in the hands of the Great Powers to weaken the Ottoman state, at least in the minds of those obsessed with the survival of a strong empire or a strong state. The history written by Turks ignores the social, economical, and political problem Armenians had. For the CUP, Armenians were the problem. One history is written to come to terms with defeat and find something redeeming in being a victim, the other to justify success by celebrating the state. In the end, what the Armenians consider reforms the Turkish elite considers an attempt to weaken Turkey. But that is not all.

What did the Turkish elite consider a "strong" state? Where did Armenians fit in that scheme, or did they fit at all? The Armenian reform movement or revolution was, in fact, a rebellion of peasants, artisans, and intellectuals, articulated in the terminology of contemporary European liberal and socialistic thinking. The Young Turk coup d'état of 1909 had put an end to the experiment of democracy and power sharing. Europe appeared as a hypocrite whose designs had little to do with the kind of treatment Christians had. Democracy was seen as the Trojan horse that would destroy Turkey. Yet the Armenian parties constituted the only popularly-based political force that still believed in and insisted on a parliament and a liberal political agenda (see chapter 8).

The problem of the Genocide is not just a matter of human rights and wrongs, but also one that has affected the development of Turkish politics and the Turkish state.

As the ultimate form of repression, it is not just an Armenia problem; it is as much a problem of and in Turkish history. Of course, it is and should be a problem of the Great Powers then and their successors and equivalents today. If one were to substitute "reforms" with "human rights," "nation-state formation" with "territorial integrity," one may appreciate an important dimension of repeat performances of genocide.

The Politics of Genocide Recognition

A generation or two after the events, surviving Armenians had recovered sufficiently to look at what had been done from a wider perspective than the individual, family, and communal losses and tragedy. The terms "massacres" and "deportations" reflected what individuals had witnessed and lived, what they knew happened to the people in their own communities, villages, and towns. While they knew the Ottoman actions were widespread even before the war had ended, the anger felt by survivors was largely interjected. They were too busy coming to terms with their own fates and creating new lives, new families, and new communities, if such is possible after death.

The collective memory of what had happened and how it had happened remained very much part of the lives of the new generations. However, it was not until the beginning of the 1950s that Armenians, now fully conscious of the impact of the amplitude and historic significance of these massacres and deportation, were able and willing to give this memory a political articulation. The Genocide then became an important, if not the most important, dimension of the collective and political identity of most Armenians.

Political parties articulated the need for the recognition of the Genocide in their program in the 1960s, with the full support of church, compatriotic, educational, and other community organizations in the Diaspora. The failure of "politicization" to secure recognition was followed by the emergence of groups that used assassinations and bombings against Turkish targets from 1975 to 1983.

The response of the Turkish state from the start was denial. The more Armenians coordinated their actions, for the most part peacefully, the more systematic became the Turkish denial. Given state control over the media and academic institutions, there were, for a long time, no dissenters in Turkey or in the Turkish Diaspora from the official position. Young Turks in Europe or in the United States had internalized the government's position and were as adamant about denial as young Armenians were about the factuality of the Genocide and the necessity of recognition—followed, for many, by reparations. There was no forum for discussion. At the same time, continuing non-recognition of the Genocide by Turkey constituted a rejection of the identity of the new generation.

The Non-dialogue

On the Armenian side, the discourse was coarse and indiscriminate. It accused all Turks, past and present, of being party to the criminal action. It was, or appeared to be, a battle of all Armenians against all Turks. Given the state-induced ignorance of these events, the only way a Turk could counter the accusation for a crime he or she knew little or nothing about was to deny the crime itself. Recognition by a Turk would be tantamount to betrayal of Turkish identity and treason toward the Turkish nation. The Armenian discourse seemed to find more gratification in anti-Turkish feelings than in any serious attempt to reach out and understand the roots of denial. It also made it almost impossible for Armenians to look at the past critically. The discourse legitimized a kind of orthodoxy regarding the past and present that discourages critical thinking.

Secondly, the discourse quickly turned into a rejection of the Turkish state itself. Anti-Turkey and anti-Turkish activities in the Diaspora became natural extensions of the Genocide-recognition campaign. The policy of denial of the Genocide was seen as the mere manifestation of the evil nature of Turkey and of Turks. Very soon the Genocide occupied a central dimension of Diaspora identity and was transformed into an organizing principle. This, in turn, justified in the eyes of the Turkish state the anti-Armenian character of Genocide denial. The Turkish state thought duty bound to interpret the principles espoused by Mustafa Kemal Atatürk for the establishment of the new Turkish state as mandating the rewriting of history, ultimately in a manner that questioned the very existence of an Armenian nation or an Armenian state. Official Turkish treatment of events related to Armenians and others in Turkey since the independence of Armenia in 1991 was no better. It precluded a dignified and intelligent dialogue.

Thirdly, Armenian political parties considered a Turkish recognition of the Genocide as the first step and the legal basis for territorial demands from Turkey. Even if there were no other reasons, this linkage would have been sufficient for the Turkish state to deny the Genocide at any cost.

Fourthly, the actions of armed Armenian groups against Turkish diplomats and institutions were seen by the Turkish state as real and direct threats to the security of the state. Turkey could not even consider recognition of the Genocide under such circumstances. In fact, Turkey hardened its position, placing these actions, along with most of the international community, in the context of international terrorism. Many senior officials of the Turkish government were friends and colleagues of those who were killed or wounded as a result of Armenian actions and they considered themselves targets. For them, any recognition of the Genocide today would be tantamount to a betrayal of the memory of those who were killed and a reward for actions against the state.

Fifthly, the Armenian campaign for the recognition of the Genocide sought the support of Western countries as a form of pressure on the Turkish state rather than as a form of accepting their own responsibility in the affair. For Turkish leaders overly sensitized to the role of the Great Powers in the dismantling of the Ottoman Empire and the use of reforms in the Armenian provinces to extract concessions and weaken the state, such a campaign seemed like a repetition of a part of history they knew and accepted. For example, European states often used the Armenian Genocide and the Kurdish issue as excuses to couch the religious/ethnic bias underlying their objection to Turkey's joining the European Union. The "Sévres Syndrome," the embedded fear that their country will be carved up by major powers and minorities, became part of the security concept of the Turkish Republic. A former minister of foreign affairs labeled it "a healthy obsession." Any recognition of the Genocide would require a critical revision of official history, which may also imply debunking the fear of new partitions of the Turkish homeland. Just as for the Armenians the campaign for recognition, directed through Europe and the United States, has become an organizing principle in the Diaspora, for Turkish governments the Sévres syndrome is an organizing principle that provides some direction, or the appearance of coherence, to Turkey's difficult relations with many of its neighbors, or even a cover for the continuing maintenance of a "national security"-based environment in domestic affairs. The denial of the Genocide to avoid Armenian territorial demands—a particular manifestation of the larger syndrome—seems to have become an essential ingredient for the realization of the deeper fear, whether rational or not.

Regardless of the style, form, or content of the Armenian campaign, the ideology of the Turkish state and the official history of state formation would have made it very difficult to place an event such as the Genocide at the time and place of its genesis. Even with the distaste and ambivalence Republican Turkey felt toward the Young Turks, it is significant that those Young Turks most responsible for the Genocide—Talat and Enver Pasha—have been the first to be rehabilitated by having boulevards named after them in Turkish cities and their remains repatriated for official re-interment in Turkey.

It does appear that some, on both sides, value the problem more than a solution and the extremes need and sustain each other.

Turkish-Armenian Relations: Old or New?

With the independence of Armenia, for the first time in living memory "Armenians" and "Turks" have started talking of the Genocide issue in the context of Turkey-Armenia state relations, rather than of Turkish-Armenian relations in the context of the Genocide and its recognition.

Independence and the centrality of the Genocide issue to the Armenian discourse—largely in the Diaspora but also for some forces in Armenia—collided at the genesis of independent Armenia. One consequence of the shift from anti-communism to anti-Turkism was that an important segment of the Diaspora lived through moments of anxiety and some were even antagonistic to the decision of the citizens of Soviet Armenia to secede from the Soviet Union and make Armenia an independent state. Armenia could not defend itself, it was argued, against an unreformed Turkey that would certainly attack an independent Armenia and kill the rest of the Armenians. Similarly, anti-independence, i.e., pro-Moscow, forces attempted to derail the independence movement by raising the specter of new genocide and Pan-Turkism.

Meanwhile, the leadership of the ANM (Armenian National Movement) supporting independence had reached the conclusion that an independent Armenia could exist, relations with Turkey could and should be normalized, and that neither the Genocide nor its recognition would constitute the basis for Armenia's foreign policy and relations with Turkey. Armenia voted overwhelmingly for independence in a general referendum in September 1991. The collapse of the USSR accelerated the recognition by the international community of the independence of all former Soviet republics, including Armenia. An Armenian and Turkish dialogue that began in 1992 continues without reaching an agreement on the establishment of diplomatic relations (see chapter 12).

With the rise of strategic interests and designs in the region, Turkey-Armenia relations acquired a new significance. Some geostrategists in the region regarded the establishment of diplomatic relations between Turkey and Armenia and the opening of the border—including land and rail connections—as a threat to their own interests. Genocide recognition was a card some tried to play in ensuring that Turkey-Armenia relations did not normalize.

While Armenia's policy, at least until the end of 1997, was free of these restraints and looked forward to larger and common strategic interests, Turkey remained hostage to its allegiance to the Azerbaijani negotiating strategy of choking Armenia economically and diplomatically. Whatever the reasoning and its underlying motivations, Turkish policy failed to seize a historic opportunity to decrease tensions in the region, thus tending to strengthen the position of those who wanted to impose the traditional view of Turkey and Turks.

Genocide and the Nagorno Karabakh

Ostensibly, the obstacle to the establishment of diplomatic relations between Turkey and Armenia is the Nagorno Karabakh conflict. Nagorno Karabakh and the Genocide have their own points of intersection (see chapters 11 and 12).

It should be noted that the pattern on non-debate on the events in Baku in January 1990 has every resemblance to that of the Ottoman state in 1915. Armenians remember the pogroms against their own that resulted in the expulsion of 200,000; Azerbaijanis remember that invasion by Soviet troops, using the anti-Armenian pogroms as an excuse, to quell the Azerbaijani independence movement.

Turkey is the only country to side completely with Azerbaijan by refusing to establish diplomatic relations and open its borders with Armenia and by providing unquestioned diplomatic support for the Azerbaijani position. It has not been difficult for Armenians to consider Turkey as part of the problem and a party to the conflict rather than as part of the solution, which the Ter-Petrossian administration wanted to do by accepting Turkey as a full partner in the Organization for Security and Co-operation in Europe (OSCE) and having more confidential negotiations on the conflict.

Just as in the case of the Genocide, the official Turkish discourse ignored the impact of the Azerbaijani policy early on to seek a military solution to the conflict and its inability to deal with the problem. Instead it focuses on the generally accepted right of the state—especially a powerful one—to do whatever it deems necessary to solve a "secessionist" problem. Additionally, the Azerbaijani government refuses to see any problems that Armenians in Nagorno Karabakh may have had while under Azerbaijani jurisdiction and ascribes all grievances to Russian manipulation, just as the Turkish official line refused to consider any problems that Armenians might have had and ascribed difficulties to the role of outsiders.

Also, a number of prominent Azerbaijani personalities, beginning with a former minister of foreign affairs, became the first in line to take upon themselves the Turkish battle of denial and made public declarations that there had been no Genocide in 1915, thus linking the two battles in a manner that could not but help equate Azerbaijanis and Turks and represent both as unreconstructed killer groups on the other side.

Another intersection of the two issues occurred with the change of administration in Yerevan and the assumption of the presidency by Robert Kocharian in early 1998. While continuing the policy of seeking a normalization of relations with Turkey without preconditions, President Kocharian—for reasons not fully articulated—decided to bring the question of the recognition of the Genocide to the table of negotiations with Turkey and make it part of Armenia's foreign policy discourse, though not a precondition to diplomatic relations.

It seems that in the battle for and against recognition, both sides appear to be repeating the logic of the past in order to justify it. The tail ends of the two rejectionist positions—comprehensive rejection of the other—seem to be feeding off each other. The vicious circle—from the Turkish Sévres syndrome to Armenians' reliance on intermediaries who are expected to deliver them Turkish territory or Turkish recognition of the Genocide, who in turn use Armenians to settle their own accounts with Turkey—is not yet fully broken.

Part V

11

From People to State, Once More:
An Overview from 1980 to 2003

In the 1980s, few individuals, in government or academia, imagined that within a few years the Union of Soviet Socialist Republics, one of the two superpowers in the world, would collapse under its own weight. Power and permanence were measured by the number of nuclear warheads and the projection of that power. One exception might have been the security services of the Soviet Union itself. After all, they were specialists in detecting weaknesses, among other capabilities. Another, the French scholar Hélène Carrère D'Encausse, predicted the demise of the superpower, but she thought the end would come as a result of demographic tensions between the east of the empire, Muslim populated and endowed with natural resources, and the western part, Christian and industrialized. In fact, the Soviet Union collapsed under its own weight, economically bankrupt, unable to face the challenge presented by constituent republics like Armenia to its political legitimacy and leadership.

Outside of those mentioned above and possibly others who did not advertise their views, the rest of the world had settled to a relatively comfortable modus vivendi. Relations between the West—the United States and Western Europe—and the Soviet Union, the two superpowers, were improving with treaties controlling nuclear and conventional weapons. While in strategic outlook the two still managed to see each other as the main potential threat, neither could find a reason not to accommodate the other as far as the major issues confronting them were concerned. Gone were the days of the Cold War when the United States encouraged "captive nations" to maintain their ideological struggle against communism and Russian imperialism or when the first secretary of the Communist Party of the

Soviet Union (CPSU), Nikita Khrushchev, threatened to bury the
West and its system.

Accommodations

The modus vivendi seemed to justify itself when, in 1985, Mikhail
Gorbachev was elected as first secretary of the CPSU. Succeeding a
series of tired septuagenarian party leaders whose short reigns were
characterized by stagnation, Gorbachev recognized dangerous weaknesses in the system. He did not believe these were irreparable problems. He introduced *glasnost* and *perestroika*, in essence liberaliz-
ing public discourse and the economic system, respectively, as a
means to rejuvenate the decaying political and economic structures
and find new legitimacy for the ruling party.

The West regarded these changes, guaranteed by the personality
of the new leader, as further justification for the thawing of relations
and evidence for future qualitative improvements in the behavior of
the Soviet Union, internally and in the international arena.

The accommodation of the Soviet Union by the West was paralleled by the adjustment the Armenian Diaspora made in its view of
the Soviet Empire and Soviet Armenia. Some segments within the
dispersed communities had reasoned that despite their reservations
toward the system, the USSR had been a guarantor of the security of
the Armenian people and its nascent statehood since the Genocide
in the Ottoman Empire and the Sovietization of the First Republic of
Armenia in 1920.

The Diaspora, still moving from the Middle East toward the West
and in constant turmoil, needed a level of psychological comfort
with its identity and a stability that would reflect its economic up-
ward mobility. Some found it in an affirmation of Diasporan identity
disengaged from Soviet Armenia. Most of the organized community
needed to see a continuity and constancy rather than conflict. It became easier, therefore, for the Diasporans to regard the Soviet Armenian state as an Armenian entity, to disregard ideological differences, and to ignore the repressive nature of the regime. The process of accepting the Soviet state was assisted also by the political
impact of Armenian terrorist groups that targeted Turkish diplomats
in many parts of the world (1975-1983) in the name of justice, revenge, or demands for recognition of the Genocide and reparations
by Turkey. The Dashnaktsutiune (Armenian Revolutionary Federa-

tion, ARF), once the most ardent supporter of independence of Soviet Armenia, relegated the idea of an independent Armenia to the
category of a far distant dream and shifted its priority to the question
of Genocide recognition and territorial reparations. The deep fis-
sures within the community turned into organizational rather than
political or ideological conflicts. In the context of the thawing of the
Cold War and the improving image of the USSR in the West, all
these factors led the Diaspora to think that everything was now in
order. Soviet intelligence too had worked toward changing the anti-
Communist and anti-Soviet attitudes within major organizations in
the Armenian Diaspora, with some apparent success.

Thus, by the end of the 1980s Armenian political parties, the
Church, and other organizations had reached a point of agreement
on the major agenda of the Armenian Diaspora: the battle for international and Turkish recognition of the Armenian Genocide of 1915-
1917 in national and international forums. Many in the Diaspora
considered the sense of unity, at least unity of purpose that resulted
from this shift, as one of the important achievements of the Diaspora
as well as a vehicle for the preservation of national identity.

An Important Exception to Accommodations

The problem was that Armenians in Soviet Armenia and in other
parts of the Soviet Union, just as other nationalities and segments
within the USSR, looked upon the changes in the Soviet Union and
the West's accommodation from very different angles. Generally,
the Gorbachev reforms were considered too little and too late to
revive the empire. Nonetheless, the changes did provide an opportunity for the peoples and especially the politicized elements to articulate long repressed concerns, values, and goals. Above all, Soviet Armenians were ready to have a second look at history and ask,
can and should Armenia be an independent state? Can Armenia
achieve strategic, political, and economic viability as a sovereign
state capable of defining and pursuing its own vital national interests or does Armenia's survival condemn the country to being a vas-
sal state to an imperial power in return for protection?

Of course, interdependence does not deny governments and states
the right to define national interests and a national agenda or to determine the cost they are willing to pay to achieve an agenda item.
But when Armenians asked that question, they did so in a specific

historical and geographic context. The smallest of the Soviet republics, without natural resources, and in a questionable neighborhood, Armenia also had a history and a perception of that history that claimed to provide lessons for the future.

For too long the fear of neighbors had been the most dominant factor in determining the answer to the question of independence. Engendered by a series of massacres and a genocide in the twentieth century, strengthened by the imagery of the brutal Turk, nurtured by the surviving specter of Pan-Turkism, internalized as the psychology of the victim and the colonized, manipulated by Armenia's self-appointed protectors, that fear has, in fact, distorted the perception of national interests, and has been confused with strategic thinking. Armenians, it seemed, were not allowed to think beyond the context of physical survival.

The Genocide, its exploitation, and its denial by Turkey have paralyzed the collective psyche of the Armenian people. A nation of victims—first of the violence and then of the denial—is incapable of sustaining rational discourse or acting on it. A nation could not imagine a future of its own making if the only thing the future would bring was further victimization. The denial of the future justifies the denial of the present and mandates an obsessive treatment of an overburdened past. Under the circumstances, the function of history is to chronicle the causes of the fear and thus legitimize it.

This fear, both justified and imagined, had been exploited and manipulated to rationalize—even welcome—the absence of independence of and democracy in Soviet Armenia, both in Armenian ruling circles, in its historiography, and in many segments of the Diaspora. A sort of permanent state of war or siege had justified the suspension of rights, the incorporation of Armenia in the Soviet Union, and its governance by the Communist Party. Seeming powerlessness had its advantages, of course. One did not have to make serious decisions; and one did not have to take responsibility for one's thoughts and words, since they could not possibly have any impact on events. After all, this fear made the lack of independence and democracy seem to be in the national interest of Armenia and Armenians; it was indeed in the interest of those who governed Armenia and whose power was legitimized by the center of the empire and who considered independence and democracy luxuries at best. Organized Armenian political leadership in the Diaspora too, for the most part, shared that view. Political and strategic discourse was intended for domestic and community audiences, not to achieve actual change in the status of Armenia.

Beginning in 1988, the national democratic movement in Armenia, initially known as the Karabakh Committee and institutionalized as the Armenian National Movement (ANM), criticized the validity of the paradigm based on fear, questioned the imminence of a Pan-Turkic danger, reestablished the right of Armenians to determine a national agenda, and introduced rational discourse as the means to answer questions. In speeches, articles, interviews, and informal debates, the Karabakh Committee members and their supporters argued that membership in the Soviet Union had meant the discarding of a national agenda or its subordination to a logic that had little to do with the interests of the people of the Republic either as citizens or as Armenians. The Soviet Union had particularly failed, they concluded, in the one area that had been accepted as the ultimate wisdom: lack of independence and democracy had to be accepted as the price to be paid for the physical protection of Armenians from imminent or potential threat from neighbors and Pan-Turkism. Yet pogroms in Azerbaijan, beginning in Sumgait in 1988 and continuing through 1990, had proven that wisdom to be faulty. Such a critique of the present was supported by a new historiography that questioned the common perceptions of the past as well. Pan-Turkism, concluded the ANM, is the scarecrow that distorts the nation's view of its past, obscures other, real issues facing the nation, and denies Armenian the right to imagine the future, thus serving the interests of Russian imperialism. The ANM made a distinction between the historical fact of the Genocide and the strategic assumptions underlying future relations with Turkey just as it distinguished between legitimate Russian interests in the region and Russian imperialism.

In addition to larger considerations, the ANM also considered that the scenario of 1918, where multiple wars with three of the fours neighbors weakened the state to a degree that it lost half of the territory it controlled as well as its sovereignty, may be repeated. The USSR may collapse under its own weight, just as the Romanov Empire did, with unforeseeable consequences and Armenia could not afford not to be ready.

Armenian political thought had for the first time reached out to the ideals of independence and democracy on pragmatic grounds in such a crystallized manner. Now necessities, the two ideals were also interrelated. A clear view of the past, present, and the future, as well as rational discourse on options, require a democratic society. Democracy cannot be achieved without independence. Independence is needed to develop a better basis for security relations; independence must also have the support of the people. A change in thinking and behavior of Armenia could not, of course, guarantee a change of behavior in the neighbors. But the assumption was that Armenia and Armenians would become active participants in the making of their present and future and take responsibility for their words and actions that could ultimately make a difference in the perception of the neighbors. Armenia should address, according to the ANM, those issues that it could resolve. The question of Nagorno Karabakh was a matter of human rights and self-determination for the majority Armenian population still living in that region and that made it different from other territories historic Armenia had lost. Territorial "demands" from neighbors, ostensibly to be fulfilled on the basis of international law or Russian arms, were regarded as dangerous to the state and having little to do with the tenets of the world community of which Armenia wanted to be a full-fledged member. If Russia was interested in a greater Armenia, argued the ANM, it had the opportunity in 1920-1923 and later to make that happen.

Underlying the strategic and political considerations were the changes that were necessary in the self-perception of Armenians and their perception of others. Once national sovereignty was obtained, Armenians would have to think and act as citizens of a state—rather than as representatives of empires, ideologies, or a religion—that had its rights and responsibilities in the international arena.

The strength of the Karabakh Committee and the ANM was based on three factors. First, the ability of its leaders to present a coherent critique of the existing order without being ideological, negative, or vindictive; second, their ability to create credibility, to replenish the moral basis of political authority after seventy years of degradation of politics; third, their ability to appeal to the masses' readiness to think and judge rather than to their emotions. The ANM shared with the people the process of argumentation, the logic underlying their positions, and not just their conclusions or beliefs. Armenians supported the ANM because, for once, they were looking at the future, a future in the making in which they were participating.

The answer to the question regarding independence was obvious.

Yet that answer raised other questions. New thinking and new strategies are often as problematic as the old ones. Would the new leaders of Armenia be able to translate them into programs? Would Armenia's neighbors reassess their own past behavior and respond positively to a new opportunity to achieve real peace and security in the region? Can the redefined nation-state succeed where the ideological empire failed in creating a sense of normalcy?

The paradox of the ANM as a movement that sought to change engrained political thinking and psychology was that it became a force and assumed leadership on the question of Nagorno Karabakh and it achieved its success through military victory in that conflict with Azerbaijan. The attempt, on the one hand, to achieve sovereignty, to establish democracy and state institutions, to create a new economy on the rubble of an ideologized Soviet central command system and, on the other, pursue the Nagorno Karabakh conflict that had its own logic and command on the sense of national identity proved to be inimical at the end. The attempts of the ANM government to take the Karabakh problem out of its nationalist context following the independence of Armenia and Azerbaijan ultimately failed when that conflict became a convenient tool for the manipulation of Armenian politics for nationalists and traditionalists within Armenia and forces outside. That failure has also placed limits in the other spheres where the ANM had successes.

The Politics of Change

In Armenia, as elsewhere in the USSR through 1989, the only political party functioning legally was the Communist Party. There were a variety of non-recognized groups and groupings; only Paruyr Hayrikian's National Self-Determination Union came close to constituting an opposition political party in Armenia, and he was exiled by Gorbachev.

Changes began in an otherwise quiet Soviet Armenia in the fall of 1987, when a nascent environmental movement organized street demonstrations to protest an unsafe chemical industry polluting the city and the equally hazardous nuclear power plant of Medzamor near Yerevan, the capital. About five thousand citizens participated.

But it was a decision taken on February 20, 1988 by the governing body of the Armenian-populated Nagorno Karabakh, Autonomous Region within Azerbaijan that galvanized Armenians throughout. On that date, the City Council of Stepanakert, capital of Nagorno Karabakh, adopted a resolution requesting that Moscow adjust the borders between Armenia and Azerbaijan to make Karabakh part of Armenia. This was a minor procedure within a state, the likes of which had been performed about a dozen times during Soviet rule. Both republics, Armenia and Azerbaijan, were part of a single state, the USSR, and the procedure would have constituted an internal administrative change with no international ramifications. The leaders of Karabakh also believed, or they were led to believe, that Moscow was sympathetic to such a request, if the request was submitted formally and nudged by public display of Armenian popular support. Armenians believed such a rectification of borders would constitute the third dimension of liberalization—de-Stalinization of nationalities policy—following glasnost and perestroika.

Karabakh's request was supported by massive rallies and demonstrations in Yerevan. Unusual in their character and sheer volume, these demonstrations received worldwide attention. They were, in fact, the first such movement by a people in what was then the Soviet bloc.

The reaction in Azerbaijan was strong and violent. For three days in late February and early March, Armenians living in the Azerbaijani industrial town of Sumgait were subjected to pogroms. The pogroms polarized public opinion in the two republics; in Armenia it evoked memories of the Genocide and undermined the Soviet government's role as guarantor of Armenian security. The inability of Soviet authorities to deal with and resolve the problem early increased the number of demonstrations. On occasion, the number of demonstrators reached the one million mark, close to one third of the Republic's population. Yet the crowds were always well-behaved and never violent. An initial "Karabakh Committee," made up largely of well-known Soviet Armenian intellectuals friendly to Moscow, was unable to diffuse or resolve the crisis. By May of 1988 the original group was replaced by a more permanent Karabakh Committee, consisting of unknowns: Levon Ter-Petrossian, a philologist and historian; Vazgen Manukian and Babken Ararktsian, professors of mathematics at Yerevan State University; Hambartzum Galstian, an ethnologist; Rafael Ghazarian, a physicist; Ashot Manucharian, a Communist Party Youth activist; Vano Siradeghian, a writer; as well as Davit Vardanian, Samvel Gevorkian, Samson Ghazarian, and Aleksan Hakobian. It was this group that assumed the political and organizational leadership of what came to be known as the Karabakh Movement.

Unable to resolve the growing political unrest and ethnic antagonism that now appeared in the two republics, Moscow arranged for what amounted to an exchange of populations between Armenia and Azerbaijan, though not involving Nagorno Karabakh. About 170,000 ethnic Azeris were compelled to leave Armenia and were moved to Azerbaijan, while a still larger number of Armenians in Azerbaijan, close to 300,000, suffered the same fate and became refugees in Armenia, Russia, and some of the Central Asian Republics. Yet neither this move, nor others taken by Moscow, resolved the problem of Karabakh. In fact, with every new step the conflict became bloodier and more complex.

The movement in Armenia, while remaining non-violent, acquired more and more the character of a drive toward democracy and independence.

In early December 1988 an earthquake devastated the north of Armenia and claimed over twenty-five thousand lives. As the world focused on the tragedy Soviet authorities in Moscow and Yerevan took the members of the Karabakh Committee into custody. They were imprisoned in Moscow. A second tier leadership continued leading the Movement's activities, until the Committee members were released as a result of domestic and international pressure in June 1989. Soon after that the Committee concluded that they must take charge of the Armenian state. The Karabakh Committee institutionalized its activities as the Armenian National Movement (ANM).

The ANM became the umbrella organization for a coalition of forces that compelled the Communist Party of Armenia to allow non-Communists to participate in the legislative elections and contest seats in the otherwise rubber stamp Soviet Armenian Supreme Soviet. In May and July, the elections produced a near majority for the ANM-led coalition. The ANM became the Government of Soviet Armenia in August 1990. Ter-Petrossian was elected president of the Presidium of the Supreme Soviet and promptly designated Vazgen Manukian as prime minister. Other members of the Karabakh Committee as well as second tier leaders of the movement gradually took over the important positions in the Supreme Soviet and the Council of Ministers.

Within a few months, the Supreme Soviet passed fundamental laws changing the character of the Republic: a multi-party system, a free market economy, distribution of land to the peasants, freedom of religion and conscience, separation of Church and State, and others. By the end of 1990, Armenia was functioning as a sovereign state in domestic and economic matters, independent of Moscow, although it had yet to declare its independence. The ANM government also negotiated with Moscow the right of conscripts from Armenia to serve in units stationed in the territory of Armenia, a policy that facilitated the formation of a regular army.

In April 1991 Soviet army units, assisted by Azerbaijani Interior ministry forces, began the ethnic cleansing of Armenian populated villages in the north of Nagorno Karabakh, possibly as a punishment for Armenia's moves toward democracy and as a reward to Azerbaijan where the Communist Party continued to rule. The conflict was now militarized. Local resistance was minimal; villagers could not fight the army or armed forces with hunting guns. The population of twenty-four villages was deported, compelling Karabakh and Armenian authorities to organize groups of fighters that eventually constituted the core of the army of Karabakh.

The militarization of the conflict strained the ability of an ad hoc system of government to function adequately. While the Supreme Soviet retained legislative power, executive power was shared by the prime minister and his cabinet and the Presidium of the Supreme Soviet. In the summer of 1991 the Supreme Soviet passed legislation authorizing a referendum on independence and creating the office of an executive president, with a clear separation of executive and legislative powers. In September 1991 an overwhelming majority of voters approved the referendum on independence and Armenia declared independence.

While Vazgen Manukian thought he would be the one to assume the presidency, Levon Ter-Petrossian's popularity compelled Manukian to withdraw his candidacy. Ter-Petrossian won the 1991 presidential elections with 83 percent of the popular vote. Paruyr Hayrikian, the dissident independent who had served seventeen years in Soviet prisons, came in second, with 7 percent of the vote. Other opposition candidates, including communists, the Armenian Revolutionary Federation (Dashnaktsutiune, ARF), newly re-implanted from the Diaspora, and independents, shared the balance. By the end of 1991 the USSR collapsed and the international community recognized the independence of the constituent republics of the USSR.

A Peaceful but Incomplete Revolution:
The Ter-Petrossian Administration

Independence

The political agenda facing Armenia in 1990 consisted of items that would shape the country's character: Should Armenia remain part of the USSR or become an independent country? Should Armenia have a single party or multi-party system? Should Armenia have a centrally-planned economy based largely on state-owned means of production or should it adopt a free market economy?

The first major issue to confront the new government was independence.

While some members may have had independence in mind all along, the Karabakh Committee had not started with such a goal. The goal of independence followed the logic of the internal situation, some said the logic of history—Armenian and world history—and at the end independence was inevitable.

Hambartsum Galstian, the youngest member of the committee and the future mayor of Yerevan, was one who believed very early—in fact, by May 1988—that the whole story would end up with independence. Eventually, events left no alternative. Once it made the choice, the ANM went all the way for independence, but did so peacefully, and according to the USSR Law on Secession enacted by Gorbachev.

The last chance to stop the march toward independence was the election of the president of the Presidium of the Supreme Soviet of the Armenian SSR following the spring 1990 general elections to that Soviet-style legislature. There were, in essence, two parties represented at the time in the Supreme Soviet: the official Communist Party (CP) and the ANM-led coalition, the opposition. It was not an easy election. The result of the election of the Supreme Soviet president would indicate the direction in which the country was headed on major issues. Neither side was assured of a clear majority. Communists voted for Vladimir Movsisian, the first secretary and that party's candidate. The ARF, still a Diasporan institution, sent its two most prominent members to Yerevan and lobbied parliament to vote for Movsisian. At the end, most newcomers and a few Communists, including the pivotal decision of Vigen Khachatrian, secretary of the CP Gugark Regional organization, voted for Levon Ter-Petrossian, the ANM candidate. Movsisian lost but did not hold a grudge against Ter-Petrossian, nor did Ter-Petrossian against Movsisian. The latter subsequently served as head of the State Agency for Refugees, minister of agriculture and provincial governor under Ter-Petrossian. Other Communists too joined the new administration. Gagik Harutiunian, head of the CP Central Committee's Economic Affairs Department, for example, was elected a vice-chairman of the Supreme Soviet, then vice president of the Republic (1991-1995) on the Ter-Petrossian ticket, and was appointed president of the Constitutional Court following the creation of that body in 1995.

Armenia, along with a few other republics, refused to participate in the March 1991 USSR-wide general referendum on the desirability of maintaining a reformed USSR. The Armenian government argued that it was up to the people of Armenia alone to decide their political future and promptly decided to hold its own referendum on independence in the same year.

As the September 21 referendum drew closer, the CP knew it was too weak to resist the inexorable march toward a declaration of independence. It knew independence would mean loss of power. Some among the party had genuine concerns about the ability of Armenia to stand on its own feet. They were also concerned with what Moscow would say and do regarding Armenia. The question of "loyalty" and the consequences of rejecting Russia and the USSR weighed heavily on the minds of many. Nonetheless, the CP knew they could not do much to slow that march. For the most part, the last leaders of Soviet Armenia acted honorably and in a manner that spared the nation and the republic new traumas. The ARF too, however reluctantly, found it impossible to oppose independence, although it had been the founder of the First Republic in 1918 and bearer of the torch of independence since then. The other two Diasporan parties supported independence, although historically they were the ones with reservations on that subject.

None of the parties that were founded following the adoption by the Supreme Soviet of the multi-party system in Armenia opposed independence. Most supported it enthusiastically. The referendum for independence adopted independence with a crushing majority. Although no major challenge has been mounted against independence since, beginning in 1997 the new Communist Party of Armenia (CPA) and a few activists have on occasion agitated in favor of

Armenia joining the yet to be consummated Russia-Belarus Union.

The transition from a Soviet to an independent republic had been peaceful and orderly. The country avoided internal clashes or worse during a transition that created havoc in the neighboring two republics, Georgia and Azerbaijan. Despite a few attempts to introduce violence, stability prevailed. This remains an important fact and major achievement. For that, credit must go first to the people of Armenia, but also to the Karabakh Committee-ANM, Armenia's Communist Party, and to Armenia's first president.

There were also no witch hunts, no zeal to avenge the abuses of the past or punish former leaders for the state of affairs at the time the ANM took over the government from the Communists in 1990. On the contrary, former leaders willing to contribute to the new state were given positions in the new administration, and in industry and academia.

But there was also no critique of the former regime, no evaluation of the impact of Soviet rule on the economy, political culture, morals, and intellectual health of society. The "intellectual" class failed to examine the values by which intellectuals, writers, and artists were promoted and the impact of the values they represented on the spiritual and cultural well-being of society. By and large industry managers did not address the financial bankruptcy, management failure, infrastructural decay, and obsolete machinery that would make economic recovery difficult. Physicians failed to expose the antiquated and disastrous health system and medical practices, from Stalin's rules on childbirth to the treatment of the mentally ill. Educators failed to challenge an educational system that was antiquated and colonial in mentality, Stalinist in pedagogy, and rotten to the core.

Instead, segments of once privileged elites now tried to protect their positions by covering up the failures of the past, including their own. They opposed every effort to change and chimed in the rhetoric of "intellectuals," who denounced the new administration and its problems, as if Armenia had just been created and all had been the fault of the ANM. They wanted everyone else to believe that independence and the new administration were responsible for everything from blockades to the barter economy, from poverty to prostitution, from corruption to crime.

To become a normal, healthy society, Armenia needed radical change not only in the political and economic systems but also in the educational, judicial, health care, and social security systems.

Resistance to change on the part of institutions, bureaucracies, professional groups, and privileged elites has been part of the cause for Armenia's inability to create a new and dignified society. To secure constituencies, political parties transformed resistance to change into respectable political agendas; "national ideology" provided a convenient cover for regressive politics.

An independent Armenia also needed a sound foreign policy and security system. Ter-Petrossian's government and the ANM-led Supreme Soviet opted for a policy of normalization of relations with all neighbors, integration in regional and international organizations and markets with the clear goal of creating normal conditions for social and economic development.

This policy had the support of most people and political forces in the country, who appreciated its balanced, pragmatic approach and circumspection, to the chagrin of Communists and the ARF.

Democratization

During the period from 1990 to 1998 Armenia—as an internationally recognized independent state from early 1992—was governed by Ter-Petrossian, the ANM-led coalition, and technocrats, on the basis laws passed in the second half of 1990. These laws altered the fundamental structures of governance and Soviet-era legislation that waited to be superceded by new laws and, ultimately, a Constitution. Ter-Petrossian, first elected president of the Republic in October 1991, was reelected in 1996 and resigned in February 1998, less than two years into his second term.

It was a time of state building. Political reforms needed to be entrenched and the separation of powers clarified; new institutions, such as a foreign ministry and an army created; old institutions, such the parliament and various ministries overhauled; economic reforms widened and deepened, including the creation of currency, banking, taxations, and customs systems; judicial reforms initiated; education, health, and social security reforms conceived and implemented; and the 1988 earthquake zone rebuilt.

These challenges, serious enough for any state, were exacerbated by the Azerbaijani blockade supported by Turkey, paralyzing shortages of energy, near complete collapse of the Soviet-era economy, dangerously high unemployment, a fully militarized conflict in Nagorno Karabakh, and some vociferous segments of the opposition that thought they should have power by divine or natural law and thus turned their opposition into disruptive practices, to say the least. These difficulties were somewhat mitigated by the sense of unity and purpose that characterized the Ter-Petrossian administration until 1995 and the support of the Diaspora. Many of the reforms were successful, others not.

The president was assisted by a vice president, elected on the same ticket as the president during a general election, until the adoption of the Constitution in 1995, which abolished the position of vice president. The vice president from 1991-1995, the only one Armenia has had, was Gagik Harutiunian, an economist by training. Harutiunian was appointed president of the newly created Constitutional Court in 1995 and serves in that position to this day.

Executive authority was shared with a prime minister, who ran the government on a day-to-day basis. The president had a more direct authority over policy in the ministries of Foreign Affairs, Defense, Interior, and Security. These ministers nonetheless reported to the prime minister in administrative and budgetary matters, while the prime minister had direct responsibility in the economic, financial, and social spheres. Cabinets were formed on the basis of recommendations of the prime minister, approved by the president and confirmed by the parliament. Most ministers tended to be technocrats with no political allegiances, while the many running the four ministries reporting to the president on policy matters tended to be individuals with strong political credentials.

Ter-Petrossian refused demands by some opposition groups to appoint their designees to ministerial positions in return for their support, mainly because he knew their policies to be contrary to the ones adopted but also because his clear majority in the parliament did not require a coalition government with fractured policies. (He did value personal qualities, however. In 1991 he asked two members of the ARF—a medical doctor and an economist, both Diasporans—to assume the positions of ministers of health and economy, respectively, in their individual capacities, not as party appointees. Both declined. In 1993 he appointed his former comrade and prime minister and now one of his main opponents, Vazgen Manukian, to the position of defense minister.) In return, Ter-Petrossian offered opposition parties seats in the Security Council, where the most important decisions and policies were discussed. The opposition preferred to stay out. Ter-Petrossian thought a government needed an opposition that advocated policies different from what he espoused and welcomed the public debate on issues such an opposition would entail. He hoped that the Armenian polity would coalesce around two main parties. The ANM or its inheritor would constitute the center right of the political spectrum, while others would engender a center left party, both sharing a belief in the fundamentals of the Constitution and staying away from adventurous policies that would endanger the sovereignty of the state and security of its people. Elections would constitute choices between the two and would bring one or the other party to power to correct each other's excesses, while parties at either end of the political spectrum would remain marginalized. He did not think Armenia could afford violent behavior and instability in the country, the consequences of which were evident in neighboring Georgia and Azerbaijan.

Four prime ministers served under Ter-Petrossian from 1990 to 1996, two from the time of his reelection in 1996 until his resignation in 1998. In addition to Vazgen Manukian, who held the position for a year, Gagik Harutiunian and Khosrov Harutiunian (not related), a former regional secretary of the Communist Party, held the position for a combined one year. Harutiunian's appointment was understood to be temporary, more like a place holder, since he was also serving as vice president. Both prime ministers were, nonetheless, very tentative in their commitment to economic transformation.

Hrand Bagratian, an economist affiliated with the ANM, assumed the office in 1993, and held it the longest, until the presidential elections in late 1996. It was during this time that most of the economic, fiscal, banking, currency, taxation, and privatization reforms were introduced, at first in a rush to legislation but eventually as an organized program. The Medzamor Nuclear Plant, shut down since the 1988 earthquake, was reopened, easing the energy crisis. Relations were established with the World Bank and the International Monetary Fund. The thankless but essential position of prime minister consumed the very young Bagratian. To succeed him, Ter-Petrossian invited Armen Sarkissian, at that time ambassador of Armenia to the UK, to assume the office. A politically savvy and non-affiliated diplomat who commanded respect, Sarkissian proved to be an admired but short lived prime minister. Due to serious and recurring illness, he had to resign from the premiership in February 1997.

Once more Ter-Petrossian reached outside the immediate political and partisan circles of Yerevan, in some cases with vested interests that could result in conflicts of interest, to find a prime minister. This time he asked Robert Kocharian, the president of Nagorno Karabakh, to become prime minister of Armenia. In addition to Kocharian's administrative capabilities, this appointment, controversial in many ways, was probably due to Ter-Petrossian's hope that the Karabakh leadership would see the problem of Karabakh in the full context of Armenia's problems and thus recognize the need for a solution based on mutual compromises.

Kocharian accepted the challenge and worked hard to make government more efficient. But at the end of 1997 he balked at a resolution of the Karabakh conflict. Kocharian engineered the opposition in the Cabinet—especially of the defense and security ministers—and a sufficient number of deputies to deny Ter-Petrossian a majority support in the parliament for his decision to accept a proposal by the OSCE as the basis of negotiations. The president was compelled to resign in early February 1998, the differences being too essential for him to continue in his position. Babken Ararktsian, the very capable president of the National Assembly and close ally of the president, along with some other close allies in the government, resigned as well, immediately before or after Ter-Petrossian did.

Beyond the immediate reason for the president's resignation, Ter-Petrossian also faced other problems. The war had been all consuming. The 1994 cease-fire allowed some concentration on state and institution building. But the general decline in the social-economic standards of the population had eroded the overwhelming support he had enjoyed earlier. His too honest warnings that it would require time to produce the recovery did not sit well with a populace that wanted a quicker solution to their problems, a solution others promised readily, while his search for a solution to the Karabakh problem as a key to bring along that recovery was blocked by those who believed progress could be achieved without compromises to the other side.

Equally important, the political consensus that had been the strength of the Karabakh Committee and later the ANM administration disappeared as soon as some major items on the agenda (independence, basic laws on political and economic reforms, and a cease-fire) were resolved. Between 1991 and 1993 some members of the Karabakh Committee had left the ANM to organize their own parties and join the ranks of the opposition: Vazgen Manukian (the first prime minister) and Davit Vardanian (head of the Supreme Soviet's Permanent Committee on Foreign Relations) founded the National Democratic Union (NDU); Ashot Manucharian (senior national security adviser to Ter-Petrossian until 1993) and Rafael Ghazarian (chairman of the Supreme Soviet's Permanent Committee on Education and Science) later formed the Civic Union of Scientists and Industrialists (CUSCI); by the time he left his position as mayor of Yerevan to become a businessman, Hambartzum Galstian had also drifted away from the ANM. Samson Ghazarian, a member of the Supreme Soviet, joined the ARF then returned to the ANM fold.

Over time, second tier leaders too started distancing themselves from the ANM and Ter-Petrossian. Hrand Bagratian, the longest serving prime minister (1993-1996), founded his own party when replaced following the 1996 presidential elections; Edward Yegorian, chairman of the National Assembly's Permanent Committee on State Building, and the day-to-day manager of the Constitutional Commission, created his own "*Hayrenik*" or Fatherland faction in parliament; and Davit Shahnazarian, an adviser and special negotiator to and, subsequently, minister of security under Ter-Petrossian, resigned his posts and became critical of the administration without joining any opposition party, at least at first.

Ten years in positions of power and leadership had taken their toll on the leaders in different ways. The ANM had lost its top leadership to the legislative and executive branches. Particularly following the 1995 legislative elections, the governing party had become complacent, arrogant, self-confident, and careless, while the opposition had turned impatient. In addition, three years of the cease-fire had given an opportunity for new issues to surface and old ones to be redefined and re-strategized. Parties had proliferated since 1991 and three Diasporan parties had established branches in Armenia as well.

Opposition parties had already disagreed with the government on many issues but focused their attention on the negotiations to resolve the Karabakh conflict and on corruption. Ter-Petrossian sought a resolution based on compromises, which others characterized as defeatist and anti-national, if not treasonous. At the end, the leadership of Karabakh, too, began to assert its own, more intransigent position on the resolution of the conflict. By the end of 1997, a weakened presidency and governing party could not withstand the pressures of those within the government who disagreed with Ter-Petrossian's attempt to find a solution to the Karabakh problem.

The Parliament

The moribund Supreme Soviet of Soviet Armenia was vitalized in 1990 with the election of ANM-supported members and eventually of Levon Ter-Petrossian as its chairman. Until the adoption of the Law on the Office of the President of the Republic in the summer of 1999, it was governed by the Presidium of the Supreme Soviet, whose functions included executive decision-making as well as responsibility for outlining economic reforms and matters of foreign and security policy. The new leadership, which also included Gagik Harutiunian, Babken Ararktsian, Ara Sahakian, and others, gradually adapted the rules of the parliament to accommodate the multiplicity of parties within that body.

When Ter-Petrossian and Harutiunian were elected president and vice president of the republic, Ararktsian became president of the Supreme Soviet. Ararktsian and his colleagues were responsible for the tedious task of making that institution function as an independent branch of government. The fact that the parliament leadership and majority were of the same party did not mean that that body acted as a rubber stamp to the president's wishes. On the one hand an atmosphere of collegial consultations and Security Council meetings, of which the president of Parliament was a member, deliberated on most major issues and policies in earnest. On the other hand, as parliament developed its own internal mechanisms and interests, differences arose between the president and parliament that were resolved through compromises and vigorous debate between opposing parties represented in parliament.

The 1995 Constitution changed the name of the parliament to the National Assembly and reduced the number of deputies to a more manageable 131. The Constitution also semi-professionalized the legislature by paying salaries to chairmen and members of standing committees, now reduced from sixteen to six. The National Assembly also became more exigent in expecting accountability from the prime minister and his government, who had to appear personally on a weekly basis to answer questions from deputies. These sessions were hardly ever love fests, even if the general policies of the two bodies were not, as a general rule, in conflict. President Ter-

Petrossian made occasional personal appearances to explain major policy decisions to the parliament.

The 1995 legislative elections returned an ANM-led coalition to power. Ararktsian was reelected as president of the National Assembly. A number of other parties, new and old, also returned to parliament. Some of the opposition groups, such as the NDU, the ARF, and the Communists did not fare as well as they expected, a situation they ascribed to government manipulation and interference in the results. Many boycotted the Assembly sessions. Parliament continued to produce legislation on reforms and restructuring, reviewing and adjusting international treaties, and performing its prerogative of accepting or rejecting members of cabinets at a steady pace and with increasing professionalism as well as with institutional vagaries.

The resignation of Ararktsian soon after Ter-Petrossian's, following the desertion from the coalition of factions that had supported the ANM, left the leadership of that body to leaders acceptable to the Kocharian-Sargsian tandem.

The Constitution

While it was generally agreed that Armenia needed a constitution, there were two views on how to proceed. Ter-Petrossian and the ANM believed that if the Constitution were to have any degree of respectability, it would have to reflect the country's specific needs and endure the test of time. Such a document could not be drafted without some testing and deliberation. Paruyr Hayrikian of the NSDU and others insisted that a constitution should be adopted immediately. The ANM prevailed.

A Constitutional Commission was formed in 1992. It included scholars and judges as well leaders of parties represented in parliament. As opposition parties hardened their position against the administration, over the next three years some parties ended their participation in the process. The Commission completed its draft in 1995 and the Constitution was adopted by a general referendum in July 1995.

By and large the Armenian Constitution of 1995 provided for a liberal democracy akin to Western models and incorporated, sometimes with changes, many of the basic laws that had been adopted since 1990, including the separation of powers. By and large, human, civil, and political rights were based on international conventions Armenia had adhered to and Council of Europe standards.

Some issues, such as the death penalty and Church-state relations, turned into thorny ones. Ter-Petrossian advocated the abolition of the death penalty, while some, including within the ANM circle, thought it should be preserved for special circumstances. A compromise was reached: the death penalty would not be abolished outright, but it would only require a vote of parliament to do so, rather than as a constitutional amendment that would require a general referendum. Its application would also be limited to exceptional cases. Ter-Petrossian vowed, nonetheless to continue the moratorium on the death penalty that he had observed since assuming the presidency. There was also much pressure to ensure through the Constitution, special privileges and assistance to the Armenian Apostolic Church, which had trouble keeping up with the Armenian Catholic and Protestant denominations and Western sects that had become active with external support. Here too a compromise was reached. The Constitution recognized the special role the Apostolic Church had played in Armenian history but secured the freedom of conscience and worship.

The thorniest problem was the balance of power between the executive and legislative. Was Armenia to be a parliamentary or a presidential democracy?

In the early days of the ANM-led administration, the Supreme Soviet had full legislative and a degree of executive authority. The first prime minister, Vazgen Manukian, who was still in the ANM in 1990, did not feel he had enough independence and power to effectively run the executive branch. After a few months in office, he asked the Supreme Soviet for special powers for six months in order to effectively implement the changes in the government and to run the economy. These powers were given to him.

When the six months expired, he returned to parliament in the spring of 1991 with a request to extend and expand those special powers. Parliament refused, saying that such broad powers were equivalent to a dictatorship. Manukian then argued that what the country needed was a clear separation of the two branches of government and a strong executive president, elected directly by the people, with a clear mandate to lead the country. The Supreme Soviet agreed and passed the Law on the Presidency in July 1991.

Ter-Petrossian's election in September 1991 marked only the beginning of the battle of the powers of the presidency. A number of unsuccessful candidates, who had earlier advocated a strong presidency and voted for the law defining the future president's powers, began arguing that what the country needed was a parliamentary democracy. Paruyr Hayrikian, one of the most ardent advocates of a strong presidency, became one of its most insistent critics.

The 1995 Constitution provided for a mixed system. The beliefs of some uninformed analysts notwithstanding, the president of Armenia is powerful if he or she has the support of the majority in parliament. In case the opposition controls parliament, the president is reduced largely to a figurehead. A parliamentary majority in opposition to the president could compel the president either to accept the majority's candidate for prime minister, resign, or dismiss parliament. But the Constitution did not allow dismissal during the first year after a parliamentary election, during the president's last six months in office, or if parliament had initiated impeachment proceedings against the president. Meanwhile, a prime minister from the opposition means control over most appointments since the president can only choose from nominees offered by the prime minister. In this important respect, Armenia's system is similar to the French Constitution, which has already had two instances of "cohabitation."

The Law on the Presidency adopted in 1991 provided that an override of a presidential veto required a two-thirds vote of the legislature. The 1995 Constitution changed that to a simple majority, that is, a president could suggest changes to the National Assembly in a law that it had already passed; the president could object, argue, and cajole. But only a simple majority is still needed for an override of the veto, and the National Assembly need not consider the president's objections as anything more than suggestions. The National Assembly could pass the same law and the president would have no choice but to sign it.

Thus, with regard to appointments and vetoing, there was not much the president could do if the opposition controlled parliament. In fact, technically speaking and from the constitutional point of view, that was exactly what happened in February 1998. The prime minister and the president's appointee, together with two ministers, refused to accept a foreign policy decision of the president. There was a stalemate within the executive, with authority remaining with the president, who could have dismissed those in the Cabinet opposing his policy. But the president's authority dissipated as soon as a group of supporters that usually voted with the ANM and provided the president his majority in the National Assembly changed their position and became part of the opposition. The moment the president lost the majority in the parliament, he could no longer fight the battle on policy. Nonetheless, most opposition leaders ascribed Ter-Petrossian's authority until then to the Constitution and many sought to change the system.

The battle over the powers of the presidency continued after Ter-Petrossian's resignation. Most candidates in the 1998 presidential elections (the ANM did not present a candidate), including Kocharian, still supported a change in the Constitution so as to take power from the presidency and give it to the parliament; some called for an outright parliamentary system. Once elected, though, Kocharian realized that the president's powers were really not that great. No candidate in the field, once elected, would have reached a different conclusion.

The problem is not so much the system provided for by the Constitution, which should not be amended by temporary circumstances, even if the last few years have highlighted some faults and contradictions. Rather, the problem is its full application in the areas of separation of powers, the institutional development of the Constitutional Court, and, in general, the judicial system and its independence. During the Ter-Petrossian presidency the Constitutional Court did develop as an institution and its president, Gagik Harutiunian, tried to articulate a role for the Court as the guardian of the Constitution and the rule of law. On at least one occasion, the Court rejected an international agreement that the administration had signed and submitted this decision for approval as required by the Constitution in the name of the law of the land. Nonetheless, the Constitutional Court, and in courts in general, were perceived as part of the administration rather than as an independent branch of government.

Parties

Political parties are still considered essential to democracies. But even in advanced democracies, maybe especially in advanced democracies, political parties no longer have the same power and significance they used to enjoy in the nineteenth century or earlier in the twentieth century. Particularly in free market economies, much is decided outside the party structures and campaigns: Central banks, mega-business, multinational corporations, and citizens' initiatives decide issues through processes that are outside party politics. And with changes in world economic structures and relations, the traditional distinctions between the left and the right have become more blurred.

Parties in Armenia display even less of an ability to reflect the concerns of voters in a manner credible to them. Nevertheless, until 1998 parties still occupied the political landscape in Armenia and remained the vehicles through which candidates and options were offered to the citizens.

Furthermore, the citizens of Armenia have a basic, almost instinctive, distrust of political parties, all parties. The great majority of citizens are not members of or do not associate with any of them. This distrust began with their Communist Party experience during the Soviet period. The new parties did not give Armenians much reason to change their opinion, partly because of unrealistic expectations and partly as a result of the citizens' distaste for the behavior of the new parties and their leaders.

Preferences for candidates in elections reflected the sense of the candidates' demeanor as well as discourse, and cannot necessarily be interpreted as support for the candidate's party. As one observer noted, Armenians are also immune to propaganda. The Soviet abuse of language has led them to mistrust leaders who talk too much, claim too much, and promise too much.

Nonetheless, the rise and functioning of a variety of political parties was to be one of the most important mechanisms for the democratization of society.

When the ANM-led coalition won control of the Supreme Soviet in the summer of 1990, there was general agreement that Armenia should become a multi-party, liberal democracy. New parties were established and some members of the Supreme Soviet joined parties that had not existed in Armenia before. By mid 1991, the parliament had ratified the Law on Political and Public Organizations, the Law on the Freedom of the Press, and the Law on Freedom of Religion and Conscience (which also separated Church and State).

In addition to the ANM, the most important parties during this period were the NDU, the NSDU, the CP, and the ARF, followed by smaller ones like "*Sahmanatrakan Iravunk*" (Constitutional Law) and the Republican Party. The ANM had both leadership recognition and a nationwide organization, though it never managed to garner financial resources. The NDU and NSDU had the name recognition of the founders, Vazgen Manukian and Paruyr Hayrikian respectively, as well as reasonably strong organizations. The CP and ARF had less known leaders but benefited from their traditional strengths, party organization, and external support. *Sahmanatrakan Iravunk* and the Republican Party were founded by two Soviet era dissidents, Hrand Khachatrian and Ashot Navasardian respectively, and tended to reflect the views of their founders and a few close associates.

Political parties in Armenia underwent a process of mutation. Splits appeared among those who had fought battles together. As mentioned above, a number of parties currently functioning in Armenia are shoots of the ANM, including the NDU itself. To those mentioned one might add the *Yerkrapahs* (Homeland Defenders), the group in parliament responsible for Ter-Petrossian's loss of parliamentary support, which was formed by Vazgen Sargsian, defense minister and a second generation ANM leader; and Shamiram, a women's organization founded by Vano Siradeghian, a member of the Karabakh Committee and leader of the ANM.

Two parties, the Communist Party of Armenia (CPA) led by Sergey Badalian and the Democratic Party of Armenia (DPA) led by Aram Sargsian were offshoots of the Armenian Communist Party of the Soviet period that dissolved itself in 1991. Three parties, the ARF, the Armenian Democratic Liberal Party of Armenia or Ramkavar Party (ADLA), and the SDHP (Social Democratic Hnchakian Party) were imported from the Diaspora following the adoption of the multiparty system in 1991. The ADL, originally implanted in Armenia under the leadership of Vigen Khachatrian, split twice during this period. While mutations and changes in party fortunes are quite normal and should not be considered, in and by themselves, a problem, the dominant role of personalities could be. That is one of the reasons why few parties could claim significant increases in their membership during the period that followed their initial appearance.

Another problem in a small republic such as Armenia is the financial support some parties receive from sources outside the country. External financing is illegal in Armenia, as in other countries. Whether for specific activities or as general support, contributions from abroad distort public perception of the relative strength of parties, give unfair advantage to some over others, and could be a way for foreign governments to influence issues, agendas, policies, and personalities in the country. Given the cost of publishing, the most immediate and obvious impact of foreign financing of local parties is manifest in their ability to have publications that secure their presence on the political scene, propagate their views, and project a strength that their numbers do not justify. Besides, foreign ties project an exaggerated view of their significance in Armenia to the outside world.

Most of the seventy-four political parties registered in Armenia by the end of 1998 had not been and may never be heard from. They were too small and too insignificant. They did not have field organizations, significant numbers of members, or well-known political figures at their head.

Economic Transformation

The question of Armenia's future economic system appeared on the national agenda even before independence. Most shared the sense that, whatever the original intent and promise of the Soviet model, something had gone terribly wrong. Few were ready to defend it. Adopting a free market economy was as much a political statement as a choice of economic system. The attraction was toward the liberal world, politically and economically. In the mind of many new leaders deeply disillusioned by the Soviet model democracy and market economy went together. That interdependence was also encouraged by the West, especially the United States. It was natural, therefore, that the Armenian SSR Supreme Soviet under ANM leadership voted overwhelmingly in favor of a free market economy. Neither the ANM nor its offshoots that ended up in opposition have significantly strayed from that path.

Since independence, "economic reform" has been a problem challenging the Karabakh conflict, more difficult than developing institutions of statehood, more defying than winning a war, more challenging than writing a working Constitution, more intricate than creating a civil society, and more misunderstood than the pervasive corruption. Yet it was a problem related to and possibly underpinning all others. For the citizen, this translates into the right to work, the right to make a decent living, in dignity, by one's labor, and includes other rights and opportunities that ensue from it.

The problem begins with the term "reform" itself. Calling what needed to be done "reform" of the economy was to misdiagnose the problem and, eventually, delay the real cure. Even "transformation" does not come close to recognizing the depth of what needed to be done.

Economic reform signaled a change of the system from centralized planning to a market economy. The state had to relinquish control of an economy dictated by a political ideology. That much was clear. But the center of planning had not been Yerevan; it had been Moscow. What passed for an economy in Armenia had little economic logic and did not make sense outside the parameters of the Soviet bloc and some client states. It was one thing to change the centrally planned economy of an independent state, where the problem was the ownership of the means of production, so to speak. It was another thing to begin with the leftovers of an economy which had produced the tires of a car in Yerevan, the body in Estonia, the engine in Kazakhstan, all to be finally assembled as a car in Ukraine. The logic of the economy was not only ideological but also imperial.

The industrial base of the economy faced other problems as well. Most of the machinery in factories was painfully outdated and, with few exceptions, the quality of goods produced could no longer compete in the world market. For two decades, when the world economy had been revolutionized, the Soviet planners had made no serious investments in the infrastructure of the country, including roads and communications. Moreover few, if any, in the country had any concept of marketing and still fewer knew the actual markets where the products were sold or bartered by the central planners. The country needed a new economy and not just a reform of the old one. It would have been easier to begin from scratch than to build on what Armenia started out with.

A market economy required much that was lacking: a new commercial code and lawyers and judges who understood it; an independent judiciary; customs and tax codes and services. It required a legal infrastructure and the institutions to go with it. Most of all, it required capital investments. Changing the laws on ownership was hardly sufficient to change the system and the mentality that rationalized it.

Neither the state nor the citizenry had the capital to invest in change. The uncertainties compelled the holders of what capital there was to invest in short-term trade rather than long-term industrial production that had little chance to find its way to world markets. Armenia itself was also too small and too poor to constitute a viable market for foreign investments that could replace or complement domestic capital.

Armenia's economic crisis was exacerbated also by the blockades imposed by Azerbaijan in early 1991, long before the conflict was militarized, as a form of political pressure on Armenia to give up its support for Karabakh. Russian natural gas reached Armenia through Azerbaijan, which also provided the country one of the two rail links with Russia. The second rail link, through Georgia, stopped functioning when in 1992 the Abkhaz conflict erupted in Georgia. The immediate result was a disruption of communications and transport and a paralyzing energy crisis. With the increasing successes of the Armenian forces, Turkey too supported the Azerbaijani strategy of strangling Armenia's economy. The blockades also made the import of raw materials and the export of finished products extremely expensive if not impossible. Meanwhile the war claimed priority on existing scarce resources and made impossible the creation of a larger, regional market for goods that could be produced in Armenia.

Each of these factors would have presented a challenge to any government. Their confluence tested the intellect, imagination, patience, and endurance of any official who tried to deal with them. Whatever the degree of progress made in this direction, there is no doubt that at the end, the economic dimension is the one affecting immediately and on a daily basis almost every aspect of the lives of Armenians—as individuals, as families, as a society. Independence and democracy, national visions and international aspirations, spiritual yearnings and cultural achievements, traditional ties and moral choices could flounder when up against the rock of one reality: the poverty in which the majority of citizens had sunk with the collapse of a bankrupt economy. As elsewhere, for the citizen to link independence and poverty and to ask "What, after all, is the advantage of independent statehood?" could be a temptation difficult to resist.

The other problem with the transformation of the economic system was that not many knew much about a market economy. What they knew were bits and pieces of models of other countries. Even fewer—in Armenia, in the former USSR republics, or the rest of the world—knew how to transform such a system, international experts notwithstanding. There was no firsthand knowledge or accumulated experience of mechanisms for the transformation of a centrally planned economy to a free market one in a republic where the economy was anything but national.

Unable to receive raw materials, energy, and state subsidies from an economically stranded government or to export manufactured goods, many factories were shut down; exports lost their markets and transport routes and could not compete with cheaper and higher quality products on the international markets; inflation and unemployment raged, while Russia changed its currency compelling the Armenian government to expedite the introduction of the national currency. In the meantime, the middle class in Armenia had all but disappeared, poverty and emigration became endemic, and reconstruction of the disaster zone was practically halted.

Successive prime ministers, supported by the president and parliament, struggled to struggled to make the economy function, and do so on a new basis. In 1991, before it had even declared independence, Armenia passed legislation that allowed the privatization of the agricultural sector. Ninety percent of local communities voted to do so; arable land in these communities was distributed free to the peasants who were working on it as members of collective or state farms. As radical and welcome as the policy was, the agrarian revolution remained incomplete without adequate provisions for the use of machinery, credits, storage, and transportation to markets. Yet the action, which remained unparalleled in its scope in other republics for some time, did give the peasant families the sense of ownership and opportunity that translated into political capital in favor of independence and economic transformation.

Large-scale privatization of shops, medium size enterprises and major industrial plants followed slowly. Each phase and method was accompanied by complaints and charges—sometimes legitimate and often absurd—in which systemic failures played as much a role as favoritism, nepotism, and corruption.

The full meaning of a market economy and its implications emerged slowly over time. So did the significance of the blockades and the Russian decision to leave Armenia and others out of the ruble zone, and the war, which constantly challenged projections. It was not until the end of 1993, after two years of experimentation and groping, that with the involvement of the International Monetary Fund and the World Bank the enthusiastic yet haphazard reforms were organized around macroeconomics goals and strategies. The energy problem was resolved, at least temporarily, with the re-

opening of the Medzamor Nuclear Power Plant, closed under popular pressure following the 1988 earthquake. The economic slide was
stopped and some gains started appearing. Taxation and customs
services had been created, a central bank established, national currency introduced. But for the majority of citizens life remained a
daily struggle.

During these first years of the new Republic, except for the views
of the CP and minor groups, debate on economic issues focused on
mistakes in the planning and execution of the dismantling of a centrally planned economy and on the pace and methods of privatization,
not on whether to achieve these; divergences covered the manner in
which the new system was being erected, not whether or not to erect
a new system.

During his presidential campaign of 1996 Vazgen Manukian focused on this aspect and linked three arguments: The administration
was mishandling economic reforms; the administration was unable to
bring in foreign investments; and government officials were corrupt,
clannish, and "Mafia" bosses. The result, he argued, was the poverty to
which the former middle class, most of the citizenry, had sunk.

Regarding the first argument, Manukian and his NDU, as well as
the other parties that eventually supported his candidacy in 1996,
explained that government officials were incompetent and uninter-
ested in the welfare of the people, indifferent to the future of the
country, and absorbed in securing personal gain. They argued that
the NDU and other opposition parties had a higher degree of dedication and would be more efficient in implementing economic reforms and attracting foreign investments.

For the opposition, the solution was to bring them to power. The
new administration would be efficient, clean, and dedicated to national ideals and values. The opposition would make Armenia a great
nation. Science and industry would be restored, along with morality.
As a practical step, Manukian promised to increase the salaries of
the state sector employees, still the majority of wage earners, ten-
fold, without providing a clue as to where such resources would
come from.

The counter-argument, not always so clearly articulated, was that
there was no magic solution to the problem of poverty, no quick
fixes to the economic crisis. Significant changes required steady legal and institutional reforms as well as improvement in the security
environment in the region to ensure foreign investments. It was not

possible to provide substantial increases in the salaries of civil servants, argued the administration, without an increase in productivity and real growth in the economy. The only other way to increase salaries was the printing of money, which would increase inflation and erode the buying power of the citizen as well as his trust in the currency.

Furthermore, "making the factories work" was a good electoral slogan, but it was not made clear how this would be done, with what capital and machinery, to produce what goods, and how to transport and which markets to sell in.

The opposition discussed corruption in moral terms. They exploited a popular definition of the word "Mafia"—in the former Soviet Union it applied to anyone who made money quickly, whether legally or illegally. They also lumped together corruption on high levels of government and the petty corruption of traffic policemen, and bureaucrats. Corruption, more rampant under the Soviets but also illegal to reveal and discuss at the time, was for the most part an economic and not a moral problem. Legal measures and disciplinary actions would fail at the end to uproot corruption as long as the judge, prosecutor, bureaucrat, and policeman did not earn enough to make a decent living. For that part of the electorate which had turned skepticism into an art form if not an analytical tool, it was better to keep "those who had already filled their pockets" in power, rather than bring a new cast of players who would have to start all over.

The CPA, under Badalian, had not joined the group of opposition parties supporting Manukian's candidacy. Still, the guardians of the old faith too had reservations in the area of economic policies, but did not express them forcefully in the early stages. Their confidence had been shaken and they lacked credibility. Even if they had a good argument in favor of a moderate or gradual change that took into consideration the social impact of these radical changes, the Communists would not have been taken seriously.

Gradually, however, as the economy hit bottom and the middle class disappeared in Armenia, the communist parties became bolder and criticized the government not just on methods but also on substance. But they were not able to articulate an alternative that made sense to the voter.

A more radical critique of the economic reforms, at least on the conceptual level, was introduced in 1996 by the CUSCI, which selected Ashot Manucharian, the former senior adviser to Ter-Petrossian, as its presidential candidate. The CUSCI too maintained its independent candidacy in 1996. An ingenious though not always a productive thinker, Manucharian recognized that the Soviet model had not worked, but neither would the capitalist model, he argued. Manucharian displayed a genuine Marxian, even if not Marxist, concern for the working and unemployed classes. He proposed a "third way." Unfortunately he failed to provide any details. He did insist, nonetheless, that this third way was not relevant just to Armenia: it had universal significance, and not only in the realm of economic choices but also in terms of human and civilizational values. The voters failed to appreciate him; in the 1996 presidential elections he received less than one percent of the vote.

By 1995 economic indicators had started showing signs of recovery due to the end of the conflict in 1994 and the cumulative impact of the reforms. But that did not mean that the life of the average citizens had improved. Citizens continued to leave the country to find jobs abroad. Although statistically recovery continued, by 1997 it was clear that improvement would come in small increments and economic indicators could not continue to improve with the same pace. The economy had sunk so low in 1993 that any progress would produce a phenomenal change in economic indicators. Yet it would be difficult, if not impossible, to maintain the pace of progress without a qualitative change in the overall environment within which the economy was functioning: investments, employment, production, communications, and markets. The state needed to increase its tax base to sustain the reforms that had been implemented and to undertake new ones. The cease-fire had provided some relief in terms of the state distribution of available resources but the "no peace no war" situation continued to place heavy pressures on the budget to maintain battle readiness; for foreign capital the lack of a peace agreement made investment not worth the risk; the blockades would continue to limit the country's production and, hence, its capability to create jobs in the private sector.

While much had been accomplished, the state was unable to care properly for those affected by the economic crisis and the effects of transition to a market economy. At the end, many projects also remained on the books: Education, health and welfare reforms were discussed and planned but the state had to delay them in the absence of resources. Environmental concerns that produced the first street demonstrations in Yerevan in the fall of 1987 had to be set aside. Much depended on turning the cease-fire into a peace agreement.

Nagorno Karabakh and the Karabakh Movement

The Nagorno Karabakh issue that sparked the fire of the popular movement and came to symbolize the aspirations of the nation evolved over a decade in more than one way. A political conflict turned violent. An administrative issue within one state, the USSR, was transformed into war between two independent states, with serious implications for regional and international security. Simultaneously, the significance of the conflict in domestic politics changed, as did its role in the national discourse, national economy, and in the programs of parties.

Thus a distinction should be made between the problem of Nagorno Karabakh and the Karabakh Movement in Armenia. In Karabakh, the Movement was and remained a single-issue campaign: the future of status of the region. In Armenia, the Karabakh issue sparked the Movement but could not limit its agenda and evolution. If speeches made during February and March 1988 were limited to Karabakh, by May 1988 the leaders of the movement were addressing questions of democracy, value systems, corruption, the non-national character of the state (Russification and the birthrate of the ethnic Azeri population), and, in the case of some, independence.

This evolution was due to three factors.

First, when the regional government of Stepanakert, capital of the then Autonomous Region of Nagorno Karabakh, raised the issue of unification with Armenia on February 20, 1988, the expectations, both in Karabakh and in Armenia, were that it would be resolved quickly in favor of Karabakh's request. Adjustments to the internal administrative boundaries within the USSR had occurred over a dozen times in the history of the USSR. Furthermore, individual activists who had had conversations with "Moscow" had concluded that, "the center would respond favorably to a popular request for such a readjustment." It was, after all, the period of glasnost, perestroika, and de-Stalinization. If corrections were being made in the political and economic system imposed by Stalinism, there was reason to believe that the third pillar of the Soviet order, the internal boundary system unfair to many ethnic groups, could also be changed.

Moscow's failure to respond positively and anti-Armenian pogroms in Azerbaijan that started in Sumgait in late February and early March led Armenians to question the system itself: After all, being part of the Soviet Union was supposed to have guaranteed the security of Armenians.

The change was not too different from the evolution of Armenian political thinking in late nineteenth and early twentieth centuries. Internal Ottoman reforms, including the democratization of the extraterritorially defined National Assembly of Armenians, had produced no results. Inviting Western Powers to pressure the Ottoman government to introduce reforms had a similar fate. As a result, moderate forces gave way to revolutionaries, who eventually pursued a dual policy of guerrilla warfare and external intervention; the state responded with massacres. Revolutionaries then started asking why Western countries were not systematic in their support for reforms. The answer was simple: the imperialistic interests of capitalist Europeans and the non-democratic character of Russia. This answer led some of the revolutionaries to seek the solution of the "Armenian Question" in the radical overhaul of the world system. Some joined the anti-imperialistic camp and Russian movement and adopted Marxist and marxistic, not just socialistic, political ideologies.

A second important reason why the Karabakh demonstrations evolved into a movement of national renaissance was the significance of street demonstrations for the common citizen. As important as the issue of Karabakh was (or became) for most, what mattered was the symbolism of effectively articulating opposition to the state for the first time. The system was politically and morally bankrupt; people were dissatisfied; and now they had a chance to join up with the rest of the nation to make a personal statement about that system. Their disgust was not related solely to the status of Karabakh, a dormant issue for most. Rather, it was related to the system that ruled every aspect of their lives. Karabakh became the trigger and the symbol of the protest movement against the system, but could not limit its agenda. This also explains the change of leadership of the movement from the single-issue nationalist-communist intellectuals such as Zori Balayan, Sylva Kaputikian, and Igor Muratian, to the newer, largely unknown faces of Vazgen Manukian, Levon Ter-Petrossian, Babken Ararktsian, and the others.

The third factor was the difference between the legal status of Karabakh and of Armenia. Karabakh was an Autonomous Region within Azerbaijan, with limited access to and interaction with Soviet-wide institutions and no international standing, while Armenia was a constituent republic of the USSR. As the struggle took shape, Armenia's interaction with Moscow, Azerbaijan, and the rest of the world compelled it to define issues in the context of all other dimensions of its relations with Soviet authorities and the international community.

As the Karabakh Committee relentlessly pursued the goal of obtaining a change in administrative boundaries that would reunite Karabakh with Armenia, Armenia's only legal and ruling party, the Armenian SSR Communist Party, responded with a timid attempt to control the Movement. While some officials sympathized with the Movement's primary goal, most were concerned with its direction and implications. When the mass movement became compelling and the slogans began to transcend the boundaries of the original issue, the Communist Party and government bodies began to co-opt the Movement in a futile attempt to prevent its radicalization. Radicalization would challenge communist rule and the status of Armenia within the USSR, and the issues of democracy and independence would rise to the surface.

The imprisonment of the movement leaders by Soviet Armenian authorities following the December 1988 earthquake turned out to be a major mistake. Yet allowing them to organize popular support for the relief efforts would also have been a mistake: The movement would have de facto replaced a government that could no longer inspire or organize. By the time popular frustration with a bureaucratic and corrupt government compelled Moscow to release the prisoners in June 1989, the landscape had changed substantially and the Karabakh Committee, soon to become the ANM, adopted a wide-ranging political agenda: It demanded nothing less than the revamping of Armenian political and economic structures, in addition to the resolution of the problem of Karabakh by uniting it with Armenia. The ANM offered a program of national regeneration.

Despite their differences, the ANM and the Soviet Armenian government had a civil relationship for the most part. The elections to the Supreme Soviet of Armenia in the spring of 1990 brought the ANM-led coalition into power. The Communists fought hard but lost the presidency of that body. The Supreme Soviet became a vehicle of change, a true legislative body, with direct control over the

Council of Ministers and executive powers. That was the beginning of institutional and political transformation.

With the assumption of power by the ANM and recognition of Armenia's independence by the international community, the character of the Karabakh problem changed drastically. Karabakh became, by definition, one of the items on the agenda of the new government and new sovereign state. While Karabakh too declared its independence unilaterally in 1992, Ter-Petrossian refrained from recognizing that declaration. Nonetheless, the relationship between Armenia and Karabakh remained cordial and sound.

In June 1992 efforts at mediation between Azerbaijan and the Armenian side by Russia and Iran were overshadowed by negotiations mediated by the Organization for Security and Cooperation in Europe (OSCE, CSCE at the time). Both Armenia and Azerbaijan had joined the organization as independent states soon after the recognition of their independence. Shortly after, in March 1992, the two new states in conflict agreed to the mediation by that organization. Although the original mandate of the OSCE was to find a solution to the problem of the status of Karabakh at an international conference to be held in Minsk, Belarus, intensification of the military confrontation on the ground compelled the mediators to seek a halt to the fighting as the dominant item on the agenda of what came to be known as the Minsk Group within the OSCE.

Participation in these negotiations became the next contentious issue. Karabakh, invited as "an interested party," first refused to participate. Karabakh was supported by opposition parties in Armenia that, in the summer of 1992, organized street demonstrations demanding that Armenia recognize Karabakh's independence. The parties pressing the issue included the two communist parties, Vazgen Manukian's NDU, Paruyr Hayrikian's National Self-Determination Union (NSDU), and the ARF which, having failed to achieve electoral success in Armenia, had sought to strengthen its position in Karabakh.

Ter-Petrossian refused to recognize Karabakh's unilateral declaration of independence. He argued that a permanent and durable solution would require reaching a solution through negotiations based necessarily on compromises on both sides and that such a step would foreclose all negotiations and the problem would remain unresolved. Under pressure from Yerevan, Karabakh eventually agreed to participate in the OSCE-led negotiations.

The conflict intensified in 1992 with the Azerbaijani blockade of Karabakh and the use of air force, artillery, and tanks to subdue the region. In May 1992 Karabakh forces were able to take Shushi, a largely Azeri-populated town overlooking the capital Stepanakert and used by the Azerbaijani military to bombard the city; the Armenian side was also able to break through the blockade of Karabakh by establishing a land connection with Armenia through the Lachin district. Following some reversals, Armenian forces ended up occupying an additional six districts of Azerbaijan surrounding Karabakh. The war came to a halt with the May 1994 ceasefire mediated by Russia and turned permanent through direct negotiations in July and August of the same year. Since 1988 the conflict had also produced new refugees and internally displaced people on both sides: close to 350,000 Armenians from Azerbaijan and Karabakh, and almost 700,000 Azeris from Armenia, Karabakh, and surrounding Azerbaijani districts.

The Minsk Group focused its mediation on the achievement of a cease-fire by developing a number of "timetables" for actions by the parties to the conflict, which would end hostilities and open the Minsk Conference to solve the problem of the status, its main mandate. Russia continued separate initiatives until 1994, when it became a co-chairman of the Minsk Group. Others too attempted their own luck with the parties to the conflict. But the OSCE mediation remained the main venue and served as an umbrella for most negotiations. Secret negotiations in Geneva from late 1992 to April 1993 with the participation of Russia, Turkey, the United States, Armenia, and Azerbaijan too eventually involved the Minsk Group, at that time under Italian chairmanship. Even the confidential negotiations held from December 1995 to October 1996 between the special representatives of the presidents of Azerbaijan and Armenia, the first substantial negotiations on the status problem, foresaw the eventual involvement of the Minsk Group co-chairmen.

Until the end of 1996 the Minsk Group negotiations did not tackle the status problem. Attempts to do so in the first half of 1997 failed, but they did crystallize two distinct approaches. One was a comprehensive solution to the problem, known as the "package deal," that would cover the question of occupied territories (by the Armenian side outside of Karabakh and by Azerbaijan inside Karabakh), the blockades of Karabakh and Armenia, the refugee and IDP problem, security guarantees, and the future status of Karabakh. The second came to be known as the "step by step" approach. The latter would leave out the problem of status and security links with Armenia for a subsequent phase of negotiations but would still constitute a peace treaty. Yerevan did not reject the first approach but found the latter more accessible. The Karabakh leaders and Azerbaijan by and large favored the first, although both at times flirted with the latter, making negotiations methodologically difficult.

At the end of the day the argument in Armenia on the question of negotiations and Karabakh revolved around one question within the administration itself. Having agreed that Armenia's economy and related problems required a major infusion of investments and open communications, could these goals be achieved without resolving the Karabakh conflict? Ter-Petrossian and a segment within his administration, including the ANM, argued that Armenia had done much to improve the economy under the circumstances but that its resources were limited to function in a world economy without a resolution of the conflict, even if it did not include a solution to the problem of the status; that the diversion of resources to defense in a no war/no peace situation was inhibiting the growth of the tax base, without which social, health, and educational reforms—necessary to complete the transition—would be impossible; and that a resolution of the conflict, inevitably based on mutual compromises but guaranteeing the vital interests of Karabakh and its population was necessary to move to the next stage of economic recovery. The absence of a resolution of the conflict would inevitably end in another war, argued Ter-Petrossian, with unforeseen consequences since the advantages Armenia had in 1992-1994 would become less relevant in a few years, while Armenia's economy would deteriorate in real terms without communications with neighboring countries and regional cooperation.

Any attempt to identify differences in approaches to the solution to the Karabakh problem within the Armenian polity raises a number of difficulties. First, the word "compromise" was politicized before it was clarified. Second, the issue became easily manipulated for political purposes and parties have been sending conflicting signals. Third, many of the opposition parties preferred to speak in slogans and extol "national ideals" and nationalist ideology rather than confront complex realities. Opposition political parties and leaders rarely presented clearly articulated views on the solution of the Karabakh problem or a strategy on how to achieve it, before or after

Ter-Petrossian's resignation. Many opposition parties, such as the communist groups and the ARF, reacted strongly against any mention of compromise, but offered no constructive plan for the solution of the conflict. With time, the occupation of Azerbaijani districts outside of Karabakh was invested with new and old historical significance by some, and the reluctance to return them increased. Others spoke of compromise but did not clarify what they were ready to compromise. At the other end of the spectrum *Nor Ughi* (New Path), an offshoot of the ANM led by Ktrich Sardarian and Ashot Bleyan, offered the simplest, though the least popular, solution: to secure guarantees for the human and political rights of Karabakh Armenians and leave Karabakh within Azerbaijan. Nor Ughi leaders argued that Karabakh would be the albatross that would choke Armenia, cause the loss of its ability to function independently, and the mechanism by which traditional thinking would reenter Armenian foreign policy.

The opposition within the administration, led by Robert Kocharian, argued that Ter-Petrossian was exaggerating the impact of the blockades; that the main reasons why the economy was not moving to the next phase were administrative inefficiency, corruption, Ter-Petrossian's style of government, as well as his relations with the Diaspora. The Diaspora could replace international investment, argued that side, if only Armenia's government made Diasporans feel at home in Armenia. Ter-Petrossian, argued Kocharian, had alienated the potential investors in the Diaspora by refusing to adopt Genocide recognition as part of its agenda with Turkey and the international community and by banning the ARF, the most organized party in the Diaspora.

In May and July of 1997 the OSCE Minsk group failed to bring all three parties to the negotiating table with "package deal" proposals, Stepanakert and Baku being the least ready to accept them. The Minsk Group presented, in September 1997, a new proposal based on the "step by step" approach. This last proposal was accepted by Azerbaijan and Armenia as a basis of renewed negotiations, but was rejected by Karabakh leaders, Kocharian, now prime minister of Armenia, and Vazgen Sargsian, minister of defense and otherwise close ally of the president. This led to the resignation of Ter-Petrossian and the election of Robert Kocharian as president of Armenia.

Tests of Democracy

The democratization process was marred by three developments during the Ter-Petrossian administration. The first occurred in the summer of 1990, soon after the ANM had won control of the Supreme Soviet. A paramilitary group occupied a building in Yerevan and challenged the new government. The Presidium of the Supreme Soviet sent Vita Ayvazian, a young economist and a member of parliament, to discuss matters. Ayvazian and his aid were shot and killed as they were approaching the building. Ter-Petrossian presented an ultimatum and obtained the surrender of the group, sparing Armenia the fate of neighboring Georgia and Azerbaijan.

The second development was the order signed in late December 1994 by the president banning the ARF. Ter-Petrossian had received evidence that the party was responsible for criminal acts and was engaged in illegal activities. Within forty-eight hours of this order, the attorney general asked the Supreme Court to decree the same on two grounds: terrorist activities and violation of the Law on Political and Public Organizations, which included the provision that no political organization can be governed by a leadership from abroad and by non-citizens. The Supreme Court rejected the first argument, stating that responsibility for crimes must be proven in court before punishment is meted. The Court upheld the president's ban on the second ground, instructing the party to provide evidence that it had complied with the law before the ban could be lifted.

The law on political parties that banned foreign control of parties had been passed in 1991 with the support of the ARF members of the legislature. The reasoning was that no state can permit non-citizens—of whatever ethnic origin—residing in foreign countries to constitute the leadership of a political party functioning in that state. If other countries do not have such a ban articulated clearly as law, it is because they do not face the same problem, not because such provisions are alien to functioning democracies. There are also a number of functioning democracies whose Constitution allows the banning of political parties (or otherwise groups prone to violence but passing as political parties or religious groups) under specific circumstances.

When it decided to register in Armenia as a political organization in 1991, the Armenian Democratic Liberal party of Armenia (ADLA), also a Diaspora transplant, was established as an organizationally

independent unit from the Diaspora ADL and had a leadership composed of citizens of Armenia. The same year, the ARF insisted on
registering the party in Armenia as an integral part of the worldwide
organization with a leadership made up foreign citizens and residing abroad. Although this was against the law, with the support of
the prime minister the Ministry of Justice registered the party in the
spirit of inclusiveness, as a gesture toward the Diaspora. But it did
so with the understanding that the ARF would adjust its structures to
Armenian law. But the ARF did not comply with the law, despite
warnings by the Ministry of Justice in 1993 and 1994 that its status
was in question. What was tolerated before December 1994 was not
now deemed acceptable when that tolerance, in the view of the Ministry of Security and the president, was abused by a party otherwise
known for its activities outside of legally defined parameters and for
its secretive deliberations.

Part of the legal case presented against the ARF by the prosecu-
tion was that it had instituted a secretive "security council" within its
own structure, a body not envisioned by the by-laws of the organization, a council that seemed to be accountable to no one and was
clearly involved in illicit and illegal activities. A number of young
men continue to serve prison terms until now for such crimes, even
if their superiors were released subsequently for political reasons.

Some Western governments and many Diasporan leaders criticized the ban, even when the law permitted it and when there were
no restrictions on individual members of the party to run for office
and propagate their views. Kocharian lifted the ban when he became president, an act that further strengthened the support of that
organization in and outside of Armenia.

The other area where democratization was thought to have been
set back were the contested results of the 1995 referendum on the
Constitution and parliamentary elections and the presidential elections of 1996. Procedural irregularities and violations of the law—
sometimes on the part of opposition groups but mostly by administration supporters—occurred on each of these occasions. Technical
problems were somewhat improved between 1995 and 1996. In the
case of the first two votes, the international observers presented mild
criticism. The noisy exaggerations of some opposition parties notwithstanding, the results were hardly in question: an ANM-led parliament and the adoption of the Constitution. A few members elected
to the National Assembly from the opposition boycotted the ses-

sions of the parliament in protest against an "illegitimate" Constitution. Yet, once Ter-Petrossian had resigned, Vazgen Manukian's NDU, Paruyr Hayrikian's NSDU, the ARF, and Aram Sargsian's DPA returned to the same National Assembly, their leaders became advisors to President Kocharian, and all worked on the basis of the legitimacy granted to Kocharian by the same Constitution they had rejected.

Ter-Petrossian ran again for the office of president in 1996. He won by a thin majority of 51.7 percent, but the election process was seen as faulty by OSCE observers, though less so by the CIS observer team. The Ter-Petrossian administration pledged to review election procedures to ensure that in the future these complied with the standards of the Council of Europe and OSCE and violations were eliminated. Meanwhile, the opposition, largely rallied around the candidacy of Vazgen Manukian, declared their candidate the winner and challenged the results in the Constitutional Court and in the streets. The Constitutional Court, having effectuated a recount of ballot boxes in question, eventually rejected the legal challenge, arguing that the proven violations were not sufficient to declare the results non-valid.

It was the challenge outside the courtroom that produced a dangerous situation. At a demonstration where some ten to fifteen thousand people had gathered in support of the victory of the opposition, Manukian invited the "people to take matters in its own hands" and, along with others, led a mass of protestors to the grounds of the National Assembly. Demonstrators broke into the compound. They kidnapped and beat up the president of the National Assembly, Babken Ararktsian, and physically abused its two vice presidents. Ter-Petrossian ordered the army troops into the compound to support the riot police. The attempt to take over the Presidential building as well failed. The rioters were dispersed when the soldiers were permitted to fire into the air. Ararktsian was recovered. A few of the leaders of the opposition directly involved were placed under custody for incitement to violence and released in a short time.

The degree of violations and their impact on the results of these votes may be difficult to determine in an atmosphere that remains politically charged. It is to be noted that the problem consisted of violations of the laws that protect the fairness and openness of elections. Until 1998 no one in the administration suggested eliminating the laws or the system.

The use of violence to obtain power, even if rightfully denied an electoral victory, and the use of army troops to end such violence constitute another problem. Obviously such scenarios are not likely to happen in mature democracies, where political culture has evolved over a period of time and every participant in the process respects certain rules. The Democrats in the United States did not riot and kidnap the speaker of the House when Al Gore was declared the loser, even though Gore, Joseph Lieberman, and a majority of Democrats believed and still believe they were the winners.

One of the differences is that the opposition in Armenia was led by two parties that did not accept any rules. In different ways, each believed they and they alone were entitled to lead, and that they could decide which laws they should obey.

As early as in 1991, Manukian had argued in a newspaper article that while Armenia should be a democracy, Armenia's democracy need not necessarily follow the Western model. Subsequently, and especially before and after the 1996 elections, Manukian often evoked the preamble of the U.S. Declaration of Independence, which, in his view, validated his inclination to use violence to overthrow a government he considered unacceptable. The ARF considered itself above the law and on more than one occasion asserted its right to function outside the law and use "revolutionary" means to achieve power in the name of higher values and visions, consistent with their belief that the state of Armenia was just one vehicle to achieve the "national ideal" of which the party was the main, if not only, mechanism.

In fact, the program of the opposition parties, including the ARF, that joined efforts behind Manukian's candidacy in 1996 called for the suspension of the Constitution and the dissolution of the parliament. Another point apparently agreed upon on the eve of the release of the program and communicated by Hayrikian but not included in the printed text, was the formation of a "security council" to govern the country until such time as a new constitution could be drafted and adopted.

The third problem that has had a destabilizing effect has been the assassinations, political or otherwise, of prominent public figures. A first wave, which stopped in 1994, ended the lives of Hambartzum Galstian, member of the Karabakh Committee, mayor of Yerevan, and later businessman; a Soviet-era head of the KGB, Martiros Yuzbashian; and a former minister of railroads. Hypotheses regarding motives and culprits abounded but these crimes remain unresolved. Their non-resolution may have had as much of a destabilizing effect on society as the acts themselves, especially when a second, more ominous series of assassinations returned to the Armenian political scene after 1998.

Foreign Affairs and Security

The principles and goals of Armenia's foreign and security policies during the Ter-Petrossian administration have been discussed earlier. Its diplomacy during this period served those policies within the limits of possibilities. Armenia established diplomatic relations with most members of the international community and opened embassies in many of them, often with the assistance of local Armenian communities. Armenia became a member of international organizations such as the UN and its various agencies, for example UNESCO, the IMF and the World Bank; and of the CIS, the OSCE, and the Black Sea Cooperation organization. It signed bilateral agreements and treaties with many of them that regulated and encouraged economic, cultural, political, and other forms of cooperation and exchange.

Relations with Georgia, the neighbor to the north, presented few problems, but also few opportunities. Both were poor countries, with little to offer each other. Georgia was and still is Armenia's rail and sea link to the rest of the world. Given the blockades of Armenia, the latter has little to offer in that respect to Georgia. The governments of Georgia and Armenia cooperate to ensure that the various grievances of the majority Armenian population in the Akhalkalak/ Javakheti region of southern Georgia and bordering Armenia are dealt with appropriately and do not translate into a major political conflict for the parties involved, especially considering the presence of a Russian military base in the district.

After the assumption of power of Edward Shevardnadze in 1993, Georgia too adopted a non-ideological and non-nationalistic approach to foreign policy and security issues. But plagued with internal instability and secessionist conflicts, Georgia considered Russia to constitute the main threat to its security and stability. Hoping to bank on Shevardnadze's high standing in the West as well, Georgia gradually tilted more towards a pro-American policy, which, in turn, irritated Russia, especially those who have not as yet forgiven Shevardnadze for his role in the last few years of the USSR. Armenia considered Russia a strategic ally in regional security matters. Both countries cooperate with NATO's Partnership for Peace Program. Georgia is part of GUUAM (the Georgia-Ukraine-Uzbekstan-Azerbaijan-Moldova semi-formal anti-Russian and pro-Western entente) from which Armenia stayed aloof. Given its own problems, Georgia has also sympathized with Azerbaijan on the question of Nagorno Karabakh. During the Ter-Petrossian administration the two countries treated their differences in their policies cautiously and with mutual understanding, avoiding public, harmful quarrels.

Armenia's relations with Iran have historically been positive and precede Armenia's Christianization in the fourth and Iran's Islamization in the seventh centuries. Iran is also home for a sizable and vibrant Armenian community, the largest non-Muslim minority in the country, whose presence precedes the Genocide. Diplomatic relations between the two countries were established early in 1992. Iran even took the initiative to mediate the Karabakh conflict in the first half of the year, Tehran still in the euphoric belief, akin to Turkey's, that it could fill the vacuum it though the USSR had left. The administration of President Ali Akbar Rafsanjani was critical of Armenian military operations during the Karabakh war, as it was concerned that the war could spill over if Iranians of Azeri origin in the north of the country became involved in support of Azerbaijan. Iran opposed any change of borders in the region and supported Azerbaijan's territorial integrity but also resisted demands from Azerbaijan and expectations from Turkey that Iran too should close its border with Armenia. Iran also provided humanitarian assistance to the Azerbaijani war refugees as well to the Nakhichevan enclave.

Trade with Iran was critical for the availability of foodstuffs and consumer goods and for the stabilization of prices in Armenia during the worst years of the economic collapse and energy crisis. Economic and cultural ties developed gradually during this period. In 1995, agreements were signed to connect the electrical grids of the two countries and to build a natural gas pipeline to export Iranian gas to Armenia and possibly elsewhere. The grid connection project was completed and functions to the benefit of both countries. The gas pipeline has lagged ostensibly for lack of financing on the Armenian part. Armenia did not succumb to American pressures to fall in line with the latter's policy of isolating Iran; in fact, in addition to bilateral relations, Yerevan participated with Iran in two separate trilateral groupings involving Greece, in the case of one, and Turkmenistan, in the other. But at the same time Armenia was not involved in any effort to produce a so-called North-South axis (Russia-Armenia-Iran) to counteract the evolving) U.S.-supported East-West axis (Turkey-Georgia-Azerbaijan).

Armenia had a "special" relationship with Russia, primarily due to the absence of a security framework in the region and the particular character of its relations with Turkey, which explains the unique position of the Russian military base near Gyumri, abutting Turkey. Although not contiguous to Russia, Armenia also depended on that country for the sustenance of its energy sources—natural gas and the nuclear plant—and on the remittances of a very large number of Armenian citizens working in that country to their families. Ter-Petrossian and President Yeltsin developed a close relationship as did Vazgen Sargsian, the Armenian defense minister, with his counterparts in Moscow. Moreover, Russia constituted the main market for a number of goods still being produced in Armenia.

Finally, Russia was the supplier of arms both to Armenia and Azerbaijan and a determining presence in the area of mediation, within and outside the OSCE Minsk Group context. Russia clearly and consistently supported the principle of territorial integrity in the Karabakh conflict, the wishful thinking of some on the Armenian side notwithstanding. Moscow maintained direct contacts with the leadership of Nagorno Karabakh, as did Iran, at times making consultations between Yerevan and Stepanakert more difficult.

Russia and Armenia signed a number of bilateral agreements culminating in the 1997 Treaty of Friendship and Cooperation. Armenia also supported the CIS, led by Russia, as a vehicle that ensured the soft landing of an exploding USSR and possible form of regional cooperation through devolution of centrally planned economic ties. But Yerevan opposed any attempt by the CIS to revive the logic of an imperial economy. In 1995, for example, Armenia voted against a Russian proposal to create a common customs zone: Russia was an energy exporting country, while Armenia was an importer and the interests of the two did not coincide. In many other cases, in the CIS, in bilateral relations, or in the context of Russia's role as mediator, differences were explained and respected in quiet diplomacy. Russian-Armenian relations, with a long and mixed history, needed to be nurtured, but the two sides also needed to learn to develop relations on the basis of mutual respect. But already by the end of

the Ter-Petrossian era Armenia's economic difficulties were opening the way for Russian companies to make inroads into the country's
infrastructure, in a way that might compromise the country's ability
to maintain an independent decision-making.

Diplomatic relations with Azerbaijan were, of course, non-exis-
tent, due to the Karabakh conflict. It was also obvious it would have
been ridiculous to attempt discussions on the subject until such time
as a peace treaty was signed between the two countries. Outside of
Karabakh-related negotiations, contact existed in the context of the
CIS meetings, the Black Sea Cooperation organization, the OSCE,
and occasionally between diplomatic missions in third countries. For
the most part a civil atmosphere dominated such contacts. Beyond
that, Presidents Levon Ter-Petrossian and Haydar Aliyev met privately a number of times using such venues. Azerbaijan rejected
cooperation even in non-military, non-political spheres in the context of future regional development. While some trade between
Azerbaijani and Armenian merchants transpired in the Georgian town
of Sadakhlo that bordered the three republics, for all practical purposes economic relations had ceased between Armenia and
Azerbaijan.

The Karabakh conflict had an equally nefarious impact on diplomatic relations with Turkey. Turkey recognized Armenia's independence, and although there was some delay, did start negotiations
with Armenia. But by the spring of 1993 Turkey linked the establishment of diplomatic relations and opening of the border and communications with Armenia to the resolution of that conflict—or at
least to significant progress in negotiations—and leaned towards
support of Azerbaijan (see chapter 12).

Armenia considered the European Community (later the European Union, or EU) and European countries, especially France, Germany, and the United Kingdom, important spheres of diplomatic
and political activity, in view of the immediate economic and developmental assistance that these sources could provide, as well as the
long-term prospect of association, even membership, in the EU. Armenia fought hard in the early days of independence, successfully,
to convince European structures that the south Caucasus should be
seen as part of Europe on a variety of grounds. For Yerevan, the
integration of Armenia and its neighbors into European structures
constituted another dimension of its future economic and strategic
security. Furthermore, the OSCE, an essentially European structure,

was the mediating institution in the Karabakh conflict and included the United States and Russia, making the Minsk Group an effective and balanced mechanism for that purpose. Finally, Armenia could benefit from historical, political, and cultural ties with Europe that were made more relevant with the Armenian Diasporan presence there, especially in France.

By and large the EU and European countries responded positively to Armenia, as they did to Georgia and Azerbaijan, by developing bilateral and institutional ties. Yet the EU looked at the three republics as a unit for the purposes of long-term assistance and insisted on regional cooperation before it would undertake large-scale developmental aid. Also, European countries and the EU considered territorial integrity an essential element of the framework for the European security architecture and the resolution of conflicts.

For a number of reasons, some obvious, relations with the United States acquired a special and multi-layered character. The only superpower after the dissolution of the Soviet Union, the United States had an aggressive, well thought out, even if sometimes wrong, strategic view of the region that encompassed not only the question of Russian and Iran influence but also energy, military cooperation through NATO's Partnership Program, academic scholarships and institutional exchanges, and financial and diplomatic mechanisms to support such concerns turned into programs. Washington weighed in at the IMF and World Bank, the OSCE and the Minsk Group, the UN Security Council, and with direct foreign aid.

After an initial policy of trying to impact the newly independent republics by attempting to change radically Russian behavior, Washington opted for policies directed at specific regions and countries of the former USSR and country politics. The United States supported Armenian independence, institutional development, and was flexible enough to turn its foreign aid into humanitarian assistance in the form of provision of fuel and wheat to avoid a humanitarian disaster in Armenia. Eventually, as conditions began to stabilize, Yerevan asked that humanitarian assistance be replaced gradually by technical and investment assistance.

At the UN and within the OSCE Minsk Group the United States supported the principle of the territorial integrity of Azerbaijan, as did other countries, albeit it did so in a manner that mollified the American Armenian community. The fierce opposition to the Ter-Petrossian administration of the well-connected ARF helped divert the attention of the community from the basic support U.S. policy provided to the Azerbaijani position. That support acquired a larger significance once Azerbaijan agreed to American and Western exploitation of its hydrocarbon resources.

Washington political culture allowed lobbies to influence specific action in foreign policy and the sizeable American Armenian community had turned that into a relatively formidable weapon, not always in line with the policies of the Ter-Petrossian administration. In fact, at the worst moment of Armenia's economic collapse, energy crisis, and military hostilities with Azerbaijan, one of the two main lobbying groups, the Armenian National Committee supported by the ARF, campaigned against foreign aid to Armenia. The Clinton administration was susceptible to lobbying by the ARF for domestic political reasons. The other group, the Armenian Assembly of America, supported the government in Yerevan as a general policy. In 1992, when the U.S. Congress adopted the Freedom Support Act that provided assistance to the former Soviet republics, the Armenian lobby in Washington was able insert sanctions against Azerbaijan for its blockade of Karabakh and Armenia, in what came to be known as Section 907. The Clinton administration opposed the provision and gradually chipped away at the sanctions until they were suspended by the Bush administration after the September 11, 2001 attacks on New York and Washington. But for some within the Diaspora and the American Armenian community, being anti-Azerbaijan—and anti-Turkish—was more important than being pro-Armenia. At the same time, remittances from immigrants from Armenia and assistance from the established Armenian community continued to provide significant direct support to families in Armenia.

American diplomacy had advantages. It constituted a fresh injection, a balancing influence, and American diplomats pursued policies energetically and in an organized manner in all forums. Washington was adamant about democratization and human rights; its demarches, along with those from European institutions and countries, prodded Armenia in the right direction. Yet, unlike the Europeans, American diplomats sometimes liked to tell Yerevan what to do in every case, their actions amounting to direct interference in the domestic affairs of the country. Especially in the early years, though, Washington could not compete with the intimate knowledge that Russia and Russian diplomats had of Armenia and the region, and with their ability to impact events.

Armenia signed a number of bilateral agreements with the United States that facilitated investments. Yet, given the political risks and uncertainties in the region, investment levels never reached their potential. Given the resources of the United States, American-Armenian relations are defined to a large extent by Washington's strategic concerns in the region, and it is difficult to argue that Armenia is a significant player (see chapter 13).

Policy towards the Arab Middle East presented a special challenge to Armenian diplomacy. Syria and Lebanon have large and established Armenian communities, while Egypt, Jordan, Iraq, and others have smaller ones. Armenia and Armenians appreciate the willingness of these countries and the Arab people in the aftermath of the Genocide to accept the survivors and help them restart life. Large numbers of the citizens of the Republic are post-World War II immigrants and are from these countries, including Ter-Petrossian, who was born in Aleppo, Syria, and was one year old when his family arrived in Yerevan. (Many others are also children and grandchildren of Genocide survivors who found refuge in what had been then Russian Armenia and later the First Republic of Armenia.) These citizens continue to have relatives in the Arab countries. Considering geographic proximity, travel to and from those countries is much easier. Arab countries also constituted an important market for Soviet and Armenian goods. Armenia's policy toward the Arab countries reflected those considerations, which created problems in view of the Palestinian-Israeli conflict and American support for Israel. Israel, meanwhile, has developed strong ties with Turkey and Azerbaijan, while the Israeli lobby in Washington has by and large positioned itself against causes espoused by the Armenian lobby, including the recognition of the Genocide.

Following a cautious policy, Armenia established diplomatic relations with the Arab countries and signed bilateral agreements that encouraged cultural and economic cooperation. Yerevan has also established diplomatic relations with Israel. However, neither country has a resident ambassador in the other. Israel is represented in Yerevan by its ambassador in Georgia, and Armenia in Israel by its ambassador in Egypt.

Three comments may serve as a summary of Armenian foreign and security policy under the Ter-Petrossian/ANM administration. The view that Armenia acted as Russia's *platzdarm* (enforcer, in a sense) in the region is more than exaggerated. Armenia acted as its interests dictated. Second, Armenia did not follow the dictum that "my friend's friends were my friends" or the opposite, nor did it subscribe to the belief that "whatever is bad for my enemy is good for me." Armenian diplomacy during the Ter-Petrossian administration did not function on the basis of "friend" or "enemies," defined traditionally or in the new context. Despite the vociferous opposition from some quarters and disappointment in others, for example, Armenia did not oppose Turkey's entry in the European Union and on more than one occasion supported the lifting of U.S. sanctions against Azerbaijan. The Ter-Petrossian administration considered Turkey's integration in European institutions a positive step for Armenia's long-term security and economic vitality. Similarly, it viewed a developed and democratic Azerbaijan with whom Armenia would eventually establish normal relations as a major asset for regional stability and economic development. Third, Armenia recognized the limits of its resources and capabilities and acted pragmatically with the idea that independence must, first and foremost, serve its citizens. The Ter-Petrossian administration sought to create options in foreign and security policy that would reconcile the interests of the state as the guarantor of the security of its people, and to forge a path for the social and economic development of its citizens, as well as for Armenians in Karabakh and Javakheti.

Ter-Petrossian's resignation in February 1998 on a matter of policy he considered critical raised more questions than it answered. Above all it belied charges that he was a dictator in love with power. Ter-Petrossian withdrew to a quiet life as did the ANM, at least for a period of time.

That resignation also brought to an end an era that was marked not only by the recovered independence but also by a bold attempt by the ANM to reshape the way Armenians thought of themselves, of their nation and their state, and of their place in the region and the world. That peaceful revolution has a significance beyond the confines of the Third Republic and for the sweep of Armenia's long history. But the battle for the soul of the Republic between pragmatic strategists and believers in visionary politics (detailed elsewhere) was lost, at least for the time being.

Much had been achieved during this period, but much was also taken away. Certainly not all opportunities were taken advantage of. Possibly the most important achievement was that the much-reviled Constitution of 1995 had worked in ensuring a peaceful transition of power at a time when fundamental differences arose within the governing elite. It would also work during a second crisis the Republic faced in 1999. The most important failure was probably the absence of a consensus within the body politic on the fundamentals of statehood and governance: agreement on peaceful mechanisms to resolve differences. Some had learned from history; others had learned how to use it.

The Kocharian Administration

Immediately following Ter-Petrossian's resignation, Babken Ararktsian, the constitutionally mandated successor as president of the National Assembly, resigned as well. The prime minister, the third in the line of succession, assumed the office of president. Kocharian also decided to run for the office of president.

This decision presented a problem. The Constitution requires that to be eligible for the presidency one would have to have been a citizen and permanent resident of Armenia for at least ten years. Kocharian was not technically a citizen of Armenia and had been a resident of Karabakh during that period. The Constitution of Armenia did not recognize Karabakh as part of Armenia, the de facto situation notwithstanding. Despite protests from a variety of groups and with the eloquent silence of the U.S. State Department that otherwise objected to any action it considered illegal or ill-advised, the Central Election Commission registered Kocharian as a candidate. The Constitutional Court rejected a legal challenge in a short decision that found no grounds to review the case, and Kocharian won the March-April 1998 presidential elections.

The Politics of Convenience

His main opponent was Karen Demirjian, the former first secretary of the CP of Soviet Armenia, who had been forced out by Gorbachev and by street events in 1988. Demirjian had withdrawn from the political scene during the tenure of Ter-Petrossian. Until 1998 he was content to be the director of the large state-owned factory he had to leave to become the first figure of Soviet Armenia in the 1970s. Demirjian's hastily organized People's Party of Armenia (PPA) quickly became a force to reckon with. International observers found evidence of irregularities in the presidential elections, but were not too sanguine about them; many local observers believed

Demirjian had won the elections, as did Demirjian himself, whose candidacy was quietly supported by Moscow. Demirjian accepted the verdict, did not take to the streets, and bid his time.

Upon assuming the presidency, Kocharian appointed a number of party leaders as his personal advisors, but not to positions of power. Davit Vardanian of the NDU, Paruyr Hayrikian of the NSDU, Vahan Hovannisian of the ARF, and Aram Sargsian of the DPA were co-opted, at least temporarily, into the administrative structure, thus making it difficult for these parties to oppose the new president, and eventually causing the weakening of the parties themselves when time came to disagree with him.

Kocharian appointed Armen Darbinian as prime minister. Darbinian, an economist, had served as deputy minister of economy under Ter-Petrossian and as minister of economy when Kocharian was prime minister. The new administration continued the economic policies of liberalization. Darbinian's tenure as prime minister came to end with the parliamentary elections in 1999.

Meanwhile, relations of the defense minister and erstwhile ally of Kocharian, Vazgen Sargsian, had soured very quickly. Vazgen Sargsian reorganized the Yerkrapahs by integrating them in the small Republican Party of Armenia (founded by Soviet-era dissident Ashot Navasardian, RPA), which then joined hands with Karen Demirjian's PPA to present a united front against Kocharian for the parliamentary elections. Kocharian believed that with the support of the ARF, some smaller parties, and state institutional mechanisms he could consolidate his position and govern without Sargsian.

The combination of Sargsian and Demirjian proved irresistible to the voters of Armenia—already suspicious of Kocharian's tactics, personality, and ultimate concerns. In the parliamentary elections of mid 1999 the Sargsian-Demirjian coalition won a comfortable majority and became the opposition to President Kocharian. Demirjian was elected president of the National Assembly and, reluctantly, Kocharian had to appoint Vazgen Sargsian prime minister. Kocharian's powers were severely curtailed, for the second time tipping the balance of power in favor of the parliament. While formally cordial, relations between president and National Assembly and between Kocharian and Sargsian deteriorated.

The new prime minister, who as defense minister had often clashed with prime ministers, for the first time had assumed the responsibility of reconciling the exigencies of a "no-war no-peace" situation with social-economic progress. He declared war against corruption and inefficiency, tightened the tax collection system, confessed love for the Diaspora, and tried to facilitate investments. Known for his close contacts with Russia, he even paid an official visit to Washington, hoping to dispel his image as a point-man for Moscow. More immediately, he thought a visit to the United States would result in the wealthy community there delivering on their potential for investments. After all, the whole idea of removing Ter-Petrossian was based on the critique of his policies regarding the Diaspora. Prior to his visit, the administration had just concluded the first Diaspora-Armenia conference in Yerevan, a love affair designed to show Diasporans that the new leadership cared for it and its political agenda. While the official part of the visit had been useful, Sargsian returned from America deeply disappointed, at least in terms of the level of investments he could expect from the Diaspora and doubted his own earlier assertion that the economy of the country could improve without a solution to the Karabakh problem.

On October 27, 1999, when the Cabinet was in parliament for its mandated weekly appearance to answer questions, five gunmen entered the National Assembly hall and fired automatic weapons, killing President of the National Assembly Karen Demirjian, his two vice presidents, Prime Minister Vazgen Sargsian, a minister, and four others in attendance. The tragedy of the carnage was paralleled only by the trauma of the country following the event from which it has yet to recover. Parliament had been assaulted once more, half the top leadership of the country had been decimated, leaving major gaps in the constitutional succession order in case anything was to happen to the president. The president's personal involvement in direct and personal negotiations with the assassins, the uncertainty, especially in the initial hours regarding the motives of the assassins and followup action by possible associates outside the parliament, created confusion and anger. The minister of defense, General Mikayel Harutiunian, brought out the army and secured the roads leading to the capital. He was later sacked by the president. A large number of officers and opposition leaders gathered within the Defense Ministry, trying to make sense of the situation and trying to find ways to express their anger, most suspecting that the president was involved. For the military, Vazgen Sargsian was the founder of a victorious army and the inspiration of the armed forces. The breakdown of the constitutional order was averted in no small measure through the efforts of the president of the Constitutional Court. Harutiunian shuttled between what had become two parties, the Presidents and the anti-Presidents, and instructed them on how to pursue their grievances through constitutional means.

The five killers were apprehended and an investigation undertaken, hinting at the possibility of a conspiracy involving individuals and groups behind the five. After an aggressive start, the prosecutor brought charges against the five in a manner that placed full responsibility of the killings on them, reducing the possibility that the investigators would continue their work. Months later the trial of the five started but it was interrupted prior to the 2003 presidential elections. The course of the judicial proceedings have left most Armenians with the impression that there has been a cover up, further eroding their confidence in the executive and judiciary authorities.

The crisis following the assassinations had been resolved constitutionally but in the political arena two facts became prominent. Demirjian and Sargsian did not only hold two of the highest offices in the Republic but they also were the leaders of two parties that opposed the president, parties that had become strong by the sheer strength of the personalities of their leaders. Second, Kocharian faced a parliament now determined to oppose him. Some members of the National Assembly initiated impeachment proceedings against the president. The National Assembly, led by the RPA and PPA, compelled Kocharian to designate Vazgen Sargsian's younger brother, Aram, as prime minister. Aram Sargsian, a young and astute director of Armenia's main cement factory, had not been a political figure, nor much interested in politics. The well-intentioned but inexperienced new prime minister was unable to maintain the reins of government long. Kocharian chipped away at the unity of the opposition through appointments and other tactical steps. By 2000, he was able to dismiss Aram Sargsian without any serious reaction and appointed a relatively little known leader from the RPA and former Soviet official, Andranik Margarian, as prime minister.

The National Assembly, too, became more docile under the presidency of Armen Khachatrian, a compromise candidate whose qualities of leadership were not very obvious. Parliament was weakened already after the 1999 elections, when many experienced legislators did not participate or were not elected and were replaced often with deputies with business and political credentials but often lacking the appetite for the tedious task of legislation. These weaknesses became more evident after the assassinations. Debate became less frequent and the legislative initiative passed to the president and a few advisors and active ministers.

Political parties were essentially eviscerated. Vazgen Manukian's NDU split into three segments. The Yerkrapahs, and the RPA itself, developed a split, some supporting Kocharian, others engaged actively in campaigns against him. The leader of the DPA, Aram Sargsian, first accepted the position of adviser to the president and then resigned and turned into opposition. Paruyr Hayrikian, another adviser, at times acted as if he was in opposition, but was essentially co-opted by the president's circle. Other parties, too small and weak to make a difference, were either unable to have electoral successes or did not even try.

The only two parties that made apparent progress—although without any electoral successes—were from the Diaspora: the ARF, the main organized group supporting Kocharian, and the ADLA, which had reduced its support of Ter-Petrossian by 1997 and actively courted Kocharian afterwards.

The ANM had not participated in the parliamentary elections and remained withdrawn. It went through two leadership changes, but was unable to recover from its loss of power in 1998, although many of its leaders remained active in small groups. Although some signs of regrouping and activation became evident prior to the 2003 presidential elections when the possibility of a Ter-Petrossian candidacy arose, the former president's decision not to run dampened the newly found enthusiasm. Nonetheless, the party still has a sizable membership and experienced leaders, some of whom believe their day will come again. At any rate, the ANM, now rejoined by Davit Shahnazarian, and one of its offshoots, the civic group "*Armat*" (Root), established by Babken Ararktsian, remain the only sources that critique the administration on matters of policy, strategy, and thinking beyond the question of Kocharian's legitimacy and style.

As for the PPA, associates of the assassinated Karen Demirjian were finally able to convince the latter's son, Stepan, to take over the party leadership and challenge Kocharian in the 2003 presidential elections. Grown up in a political family but without political experience himself, Stepan Demirjian had a shaky start in the campaign. But soon he commanded popular support that had rarely been seen since the early days of independence. The combination of mistrust of the president, the deeply felt need to have a full investigation of the assassination, a resurgent support that his father had enjoyed and now was transferred to the son, and the simple yearning for a fresh face turned Stepan Demirjian into a viable candidate. Other leaders opposed to Demirjian sensed for the first time that it was possible to defeat Kocharian and joined Demirjian's campaign. A number of candidates withdrew in his favor. A novice in politics with no credentials had galvanized popular discontent.

The February 2003 presidential elections turned into a contest between personalities: experience versus inexperience, stability and continuity versus uncertainty and, just below the surface, of a Karabakh leader and his "clan" versus a "Yerevan boy." The first round of elections did not produce a clear winner, according to official results. The Demirjian camp, certain that their candidate had won, and other groups, documented massive fraud; OSCE observers wrote a scathing criticism of the way the election had been handled; the candidate who came third challenged the results in the Constitutional Court. A CIS delegation declared the elections fair. (Kocharian had the full and expressed support of Russia this time.) Demonstrations multiplied, some rhetoricians called for action by the people, but Stepan Demirjian asked everyone to remain within the limits of the law, and they did. Regardless, the administration rounded up a few hundred opposition activists on various charges. The opposition argued that the detainees were election workers important to the campaign. A runoff election between Kocharian and Demirjian followed in March. Kocharian was declared the winner by a two to one unlikely margin.

The scenario repeated itself more or less without any change on the situation on the ground. On the one hand some officials recognized irregularities but argued that these would not have changed the outcome of the elections. Others, faced with serious warnings from the Council of Europe and trying to explain the difference between CIS and OSCE assessments of the election processes, argued that Westerners do not understand Armenia, while CIS observers do; Armenia, therefore, could forego Western blessings for its style of democracy.

The only surprise came when the election process was completed and there was no doubt that Kocharian would continue to occupy the office of president. The Constitutional Court ruled on the legal challenges. The Court recognized irregularities and illegal actions, mainly on the part of the Kocharian campaign, but argued that these would not have changed the outcome of the balloting and confirmed the results pronounced by the Central Election Commission: Kocharian had been reelected president of the Republic. However, the Court also took the unusual step of recognizing the deep chasm dividing the reelected president and the opposition and the dangers it represented for the country. Almost casting doubt on its own legal ruling, the Court advised the president and the parliament to organize a consultative referendum on the president in one year. The president of the Court recognized that the Constitution did not foresee such a referendum. But Gagik Harutiunian, president of the Court, in essence argued that not all problems were constitutional and the political nature of the division in society should be addressed through the proposed extraordinary step. Both sides were shocked by the Court's extra-legal opinion. Kocharian and his supporters argued that the Court had exceeded its authority. The opposition, not yet knowing what to do with the proposal, objected to the basic ruling. However, the unusual and risky statement of the Constitutional accomplished three important goals: it absorbed some of the tension that had been built up in the opposing camps, even if that meant diverting the ire of the sides against the Court; it made the Court relevant and worth listening and appealing to; and it paved the way for a possible, more radically independent, opinion regarding future challenges.

Both sides geared for the parliamentary elections of May 2003. Yet parliamentary elections are fueled by different dynamics than presidential elections, where the citizen is asked to vote between two candidates and the race can be reduced to a preference of personalities. In the absence of clearly articulated policy differences and in circumstances where voters in different electoral districts are asked to vote for a variety of candidates and parties, the opposition acts divided and opposing parties must fight to secure their individual share of representation in parliament to prove their strength and relevance. The impact of the personality who brought the opposition together in the presidential election is reduced, while the significance of level of party organization and administrative leverage is multiplied. Furthermore, while Stepan Demirjian's style of brief messages and circumspect behavior served him well in the presidential race, if his candidacy were to be translated into parliamentary power, he would have to project a more proactive image and knowledge of local issues and candidates than he was able to display.

The results of the parliamentary contest were predictable, even if by the estimation of some observers these elections were the most brazenly and openly fraudulent. According to Central Election Commission figures, six parties obtained a minimum of 5 percent of the popular vote to claim a share of seats in the category of proportional representation. The RPA, led by the Prime Minister Margarian and Defense Minister Sargsian, received the largest number of seats, forty, when combined with those directly elected; Orinats Yerkir (OY), an otherwise small party led by Arthur Baghtasarian and enjoying the support of Kocharian and Sargsian, ended up with twenty-two seats. Stepan Demirjian's coalition of opposition parties, Ardarutyun or Justice Bloc, was able to secure seventeen seats. The ARF was awarded eleven seats, while Geghamian's National Unity Party was allotted nine seats. An unknown group, United Labor Party (ULP) chaired by Gurgen Arsenian, managed somehow to obtain six seats. The balance of the 131 seats, a total of twenty-six, was won by independents, both organized and on an individual basis. By and large the new parliament will distinguish itself by the presence of an even larger number of businessmen of all sorts compared to the last one.

The new government was formed on the basis of a formal coalition between the RPA, OY, and the ARF. Margarian will retain the premiership of a reconstituted cabinet within which ten of the sixteen ministers are appointees by the three coalition parties. Baghtasarian was elected president of the National Assembly; the RPA and ARF were also awarded a vice presidency of the parliament. The RPA and OY were allotted the chairmanship of two standing committees each, the ARF and ULP one each.

The opposition led by Demirjian also failed to turn a referendum on proposed amendments to the Constitution into an issue. Held at the same time as the parliamentary elections, the referendum attracted little attention, although the proposed amendments touched two-thirds of the articles of the basic law and would have introduced subtle yet substantial changes in basic rights and distribution of powers. Some of the changes in the definition of human, civil, and political rights would have brought the Armenian Constitution closer to European standards; yet certain amendments would have made these vaguer and more subject to legislative fiat. One amendment would have extended the right to appeal to the Constitutional Court to individual citizens. Another proposed to lift the existing ban on dual citizenship. The death penalty would have been removed. The proposed Constitution would also extend the right to tax to local governments.

Other amendments detailed the functions and powers of officials such as ministers and of state agencies such as the Central Bank. A National Security Council would be enshrined in the Constitution, instead of being permitted under the "advisory bodies" that the president had the right to create. Parliament would be reduced from 131 to 101 and would have the added responsibility of developing a "national security concept." The amendments also proposed to adjust the balance of power, in some respects giving the prime minister and parliament more specific powers. Yet it was the powers of the president that would have been most affected by the proposed amendments. The president would have exclusive authority to appoint the prosecutor-general, instead of sharing that power with the prime minister; the president's emergency powers would increase in some critical areas: the president would be able to declare war almost single-handedly and suspend presidential elections in time of war. In addition, impeachment proceedings would be less dependent on the legislative branch. Finally, the circumstances under which a president would be able to dismiss parliament would be less stringent.

In presenting the constitutional amendments to a referendum, the government failed to follow the required schedule of presentation and distribution of the issues subject to the referendum. Consumed by the politics of elections, political leaders also failed to debate the proposed amendments. Only "Armat," the civic group chaired by Ararktsian, produced a comparative study of the proposed changes and made an attempt to initiate a public education program, considering the impact the amendments would have, if approved, to be the equivalent of a treacherous act against the Republic and people of Armenia.

The proposed amendments did not get the approval of the voters. Although according to official results some 46 percent of those casting ballots (552,000) did vote yes, that number did not constitute a majority of those voting and at least one-third of all eligible voters, as required by the Constitution.

Economy

The Kocharian administration has, in broad terms, continued the economic policies of its predecessor. Successive governments have pushed through parliament legislation to complete the liberalization process, in some cases adjusting existing laws. There has been some effort to improve the investment climate and simplify the tax code. The currency, the dram, has generally been stable and inflation remains low.

The administration has painted a rosy picture of the economy and claimed major progress. Statistics on GDP growth and other economic indicators have been positive. Some foreign investment continues, especially in canning, diamond cutting, software development, and service industries. The largest single infusion has come from the American Armenian Kirk Kirkorian, who made a one time, $100 million donation for the improvement of streets in central Yerevan and other infrastructure projects. In absolute terms, remittances to families and social assistance from the Diaspora constitute the largest infusion into the Armenian economy, making possible for a large segment of the population to achieve minimal survival. A very small segment of the population may now be classified as middle class, their income achieved through the private sector of the economy.

Yet, statistics can be deceiving as well as deceitful. There has been no change in the investment pattern since the first administration—the kind that has serious implications for the unemployment problem, which remains high, and the tax base of the state, which remains low. An aggressive campaign of privatization of major industries has provided only temporary relief to the state budget. International investors and multi-national corporations are reluctant to invest in Armenia and the country still lacks the capital to fuel an economic recovery. Almost half of the population has a below poverty level income and emigration has continued, even if it is somewhat stabilized now. Although a number of Diaspora organizations continue their humanitarian and technical assistance, donations through the All-Armenia Fund, the major organization that brings the leaders of the Republic and the Diaspora together, can no longer match earlier levels. Instead of decreasing over time, there is also a general perception that corruption has become endemic within the Kocharian administration.

The most important economic indicator may be the consumption of energy and the ability of the Armenian economy to pay for it. There is evidence that consumption has decreased; the country's ability to pay for it certainly has. The debt to imported Russian natural gas accumulated and, instead of cash, Armenia paid Russia by turning over ownership of major factories and the nuclear power plant to Russia.

The economic platforms of candidates in major elections during this period have all addressed the crisis. There has been no serious challenge to the basic policy of transforming the economy but many have argued for the need to ensure the "social dimension" during transition. If there was a difference between Kocharian and his two opponents during the 1998 and 2003 elections, it consisted of the more cautious attitude that the Demirjians displayed toward the privatization of major factories compared to Kocharian. Except for the ANM, parties and candidates have avoided looking at the root cause of the economic crisis (see chapter 12).

The Stalemate on Nagorno Karabakh

Kocharian's assumption of the presidency was conditioned by his disagreement with Ter-Petrossian on the question of settlement of the Karabakh conflict. Azerbaijan, Turkey, and other countries were wary of the consequences of the change in administration in Yerevan. But the United States all but welcomed it. The thinking in Washington was that as the former "strong man" of Karabakh, Kocharian would be best placed to achieve a resolution of the conflict and make it acceptable to Armenia and Karabakh.

It is important to note that as the chairman of the Defense Council of Karabakh, Kocharian had, in 1992, encouraged opposition parties in Armenia to press for the recognition of Nagorno Karabakh's unilateral declaration of independence. When he became president of Armenia in 1998, Kocharian's advisers included Vahan Hovannisian, leader of the ARF of Armenia; Paruyr Hayrikian, of the NSDU; and Aram Sargsian, leader of the DPA. Davit Vardanian, Vazgen Manukian's deputy in the NDU, had become director of an important department in the president's office. All represented parties that had joined in such a demand. Neither Kocharian nor any of his advisors or their parties have raised that question then or since.

The OSCE Minsk Group, which had taken a pause during the fierce debate in Yerevan on the 1997 September proposal that ended with the change of administration, reactivated its mediation in the summer of 1998. In the fall the Minsk Group presented a new proposal, known as the "common state" proposal, another version of the package deal approach that included a solution to the status problem. The proposed solution was to keep Nagorno Karabakh as part of Azerbaijan but to do so on the basis of "horizontal" relations between Stepanakert and Baku. The proposal is best described as a marriage of convenience agreed upon contractually by hypothetically equal partners. In that respect the proposal was not different from what Russia had earlier proposed for Trans-Dniester and Moldova. Although it established the perimeters of the relationship between Karabakh and Azerbaijan—a very complex set of arrangements—the proposal left a number of major issues regarding the content of those relations unresolved. From a technical point of view, it would have been extremely difficult to negotiate its details and what had not been specified.

Armenia and Karabakh accepted the proposal as a basis of negotiations—they considered it a vindication of their opposition to the September 1997 proposal—but noted that they had serious reservations regarding a large number of provisions that would have to be negotiated. Azerbaijan, after a tentative positive reaction, rejected the proposal. Publicly, at least, the term "common state" was the main culprit. But it was obvious that the problem was more than terminology, as Armenia was willing to consider dropping the term. The Minsk again evaluated the situation.

The next phase of the negotiations consisted of a long series of direct meetings between Presidents Aliyev and Kocharian, beginning with their encounter in Washington in April of 1999 on the occasion of the fiftieth anniversary of the founding of NATO. Aliyev had twice met Kocharian much earlier in Moscow when the latter was the leader of Karabakh, at the urging of Ter-Petrossian and Russian diplomats. He had left the meeting with an impression that Kocharian was not a hopeful partner to establish peace. But urged by a number of sources, he agreed to the dialogue. At no point during these meetings, close to twenty by 2003, did President Arkady Ghukasian of Karabakh, or a representative of his, participate in the deliberations.

The first meetings between Aliyev and Kocharian were consumed by reviews of existing proposals for a resolution of the conflict. By the summer of 1999 the two agreed that there were fundamental differences that made previous documents useless. The two then agreed, in principle, on a new formula: a land swap between

Azerbaijan and Armenia. Azerbaijan would concede Nagorno Karabakh, which would become an integral part of the Republic and Armenia would relinquish the Meghri district in the south of Armenia. Armenia would have the best possible solution to the status problem but would lose its border with Iran, while Azerbaijan would establish a land connection with Nakhichevan as well as allow direct access for its oil pipeline to Turkey. The deal, agreed to "in principle," created an immediate negative reaction within the small circle of presidential advisers in both countries who learned about it. The formula, which received the energetic support of Washington and Ankara, underwent a number of changes, mainly in the exact amount of Meghri territory involved and the degree to which Armenia would relinquish sovereignty over said territory. As the simple idea evolved into a complex formula, Azerbaijan liked it less and less. Moscow took the official position that it would accept whatever solution the two presidents agreed on, but for most officials in Moscow the formula was unacceptable. Iran was concerned with the repercussions of such a solution and made its objections clear to Yerevan. Discussion of the formula had ended by the summer of 2002. The mediators and presidents blamed the peoples for not being ready for peace—in fact, they blamed them for their own failures. The formula had no chance of success, considering the geopolitical importance of the Meghri district; and, as before, the peoples were never really consulted.

During 2002, two meetings of deputy foreign ministers of the Aliyev and Kocharian administrations met in Europe to see if progress could be made. The representative of Armenia insisted on discussing the land swap formula. The Azerbaijani representative refused to engage in that discussion, arguing that the formula in question was the domain of the presidents. On his part, the Azerbaijani diplomat proposed that a partial solution be considered, as a first step toward a solution of the problem: the withdrawal of Armenian forces from four of the seven occupied Azerbaijani districts, the ones bordering Iran, in return for the opening of the railroad that ran through it and crossed Meghri, reached Nakhichevan, and from there connected to Iran in the south and Yerevan in the north. In addition, the Azerbaijani representative promised that Azerbaijan would not object to the opening of the rail line between Armenia and Turkey. Armenia rejected the proposal.

Since then negotiations have halted and mediation efforts have stalled. Mediators and major powers have been overwhelmed by other concerns, from Afghanistan to Iraq. They also have not seen any reason to make new efforts in this arena. For Azerbaijan, the status quo has become politically more intolerable, producing a consensus on the eventual need to resort to war; some in Armenia and Karabakh consider the problem resolved. Karabakh has its own government, even if it depends on Armenia for its security and budget, and Armenian forces occupy the surrounding districts. If Karabakh is a problem, as have posited supporters of Kocharian such as the ARF, it is a problem for Azerbaijan, not for Armenia or Karabakh.

Foreign Policy

In its basic approach, the Kocharian administration did not deviate from the outline delineated by its predecessor on matters of foreign policy. Yet the tactical changes it has introduced, the radically opposing attitudes of its supporting organizations, the changes in the international world, and, above all, its unwillingness to find a compromise solution to the Karabakh problem have made foreign policy principles hallow, irrelevant, and unproductive.

Armenia is still not at peace with Azerbaijan. It has also been unable to normalize relations with Turkey, a goal retained by the Kocharian administration. The informal dialogue between the two countries was only complicated by the decision of the administration to place Genocide recognition on the foreign policy agenda. Public charges that Georgian-Turkish relations constitute a threat to Armenia and provocative statements by ARF leaders close to Kocharian on the Javakheti issue in Georgia have made Tbilisi nervous and more concerned. Negotiations with Azerbaijan on the basis of a land swap have produced questions regarding Yerevan's projection of the future for the region and relations with Iran. The Armenia-Iran natural gas pipeline, the first gas export agreement signed by Iran in 1995, remains a contentious issue between the two countries.

The change of administration in Moscow too has altered the context in which Russian-Armenian relations are seen. President Vladimir Putin's goal of integrating the foreign and security policies of Moscow with those of European and even of the United States has transformed much of what made Armenia special secondary to larger concerns.

In the absence of progress in Karabakh negotiations, relations with Europe and the United States have stagnated. Armenia has joined the Council of Europe and the World Trade Organization (WTO). Yet the Council of Europe has become weary of the progress of democracy in Armenia, and the benefits of WTO membership remain limited, to say the least, given the economic situation in the Republic. The United States, preoccupied with far more important countries and issues, places more significance on Azerbaijan as a source of energy, a transit country for Caspian resources, and as a gateway to Central Asia. Without a settlement of the Karabakh conflict and a regional approach to development, relations with the United States will remain limited.

Robert Kocharian assumed the presidency as a pragmatist and projected a "strong" personality who could resolve problems. In time autocratic tendencies evident when he was the leader of Karabakh manifested themselves through his impatience with party and parliamentary politics.

The incremental changes Kocharian introduced in the political culture and foreign policy amounted to a qualitative disfigurement of both. Whatever his ostensible successes in the economic sphere, the state and the people remain poor and the process of Diasporization continues. Meanwhile, political and historical discourse is being renationalized. Given developments in the country, the region, and the world, the question as to the validity of his argument that Armenia can develop its economy without resolving the Karabakh conflict has become almost moot.

There have been attempts to impose a certain orthodoxy of thought that would determine, above all, the national agenda and limit the parameters of debate by ideologically oriented forces that have no solutions to the country's real problems. Even if yet unsuccessful, an atmosphere of fear characteristic of the Soviet era is prevalent among those who would otherwise challenge the premises and limits of the nationalist discourse.

12

The Re-Imagined Future: Turkey-Armenia and Turkish-Armenian Relations since Independence

No subject dominates the Armenian mind more than Turkish-Armenian relations and its core event, the Genocide organized by the Young Turk government of the Ottoman Empire during the First World War. No subject has aroused as much passion as the policy of modern Turkey to deny it. Explicitly or otherwise, Armenian collective memory and, since the 1960s, public discourse focused on that event. This state of mind is particularly true for the Armenian Diaspora and less so for Armenia.

Soviet Armenia did not have a policy towards Turkey since foreign and security policies were within the jurisdiction of Moscow, and Moscow had normal relations with the Republic of Turkey. In successive treaties the USSR reaffirmed the borders between the two countries and Genocide recognition did not figure on the Soviet agenda. Soviet Armenian historians, on the other hand, had started exploring the issue in books and articles, and a monument had been erected in the capital to the memory of the Genocide victims.

For successive Turkish governments the problem was the Diaspora, especially communities in Europe, the Americas, and the Near East. Having adopted and honed a state policy of total denial and justification, these governments viewed Turkish-Armenian relations from the prism of their perception of the Diaspora.

In the Diaspora historians researched the facts of the tragedy and political organizations, supported by community organizations, lobbied governments and international organizations for its recognition. The battle moved beyond academia and lobbying when, beginning in 1975, two Armenian groups unleashed a series of attacks on Turkish diplomats and embassies in many parts of the world. For the Justice Commandos of the Armenian Genocide these attacks constituted another method to bring the matter to the attention of the world and, ostensibly, compel the Turkish government to recognize the events that changed Armenian history. The Armenian Secret Army for the Liberation of Armenia (ASALA) saw its actions as part of a wider, "third world liberation" type struggle, akin to Kurdish and Palestinian ones. Along with traditional parties in the Diaspora, these two groups considered the recognition of the Genocide as a first step toward reparations, including, for some, territorial reparations. The Armenian terrorism that claimed the lives of over thirty Turkish diplomats and a number of bystanders ended in 1983. But it left a deep impression on the Turkish state and defined its view of Armenians, especially in the mind of the foreign policy establishment, and the military, obsessed with state sacrifice.

The Genesis of a Paradox

When the Karabakh issue erupted in February 1988, the Turkish state tended to explain events mostly from the prism of its view of the Diaspora. Even when the Karabakh movement evolved toward independence, the Turkish state had difficulties imagining relations with an independent Armenia outside that context.

Nonetheless, an important debate had already taken place in Armenia, a debate that considered the relationship between the two most important and consequential events for Armenians in the twentieth century: the Genocide and the experience of the First Republic of Armenia, 1918-1920. Obviously, one had to draw lessons from history. The problem was, what were these lessons?

The debate revolved around specific questions. What was the place of the Genocide and Genocide recognition in the foreign and security policy of an independent Armenia and in the shaping of a sovereign nation? Could Armenia become independent again without facing the threat of another genocide? This debate was as much about foreign policy options as it was about national identity and the nature of Turkey.

The debate had been public as well as official. In addition to articles and speeches, the Supreme Soviet in July 1990 devoted long sessions to the subject when framing the Declaration on Independence, a document that proclaimed the right and intention to independence and preceded the Declaration of Independence by fifteen months. Even Diasporans were invited to make their views known.

The debate was also predicated upon two major reversals that had taken place since the 1960s. The division within the Diasporan political groups, pro- and anti-Soviet, had ended, when, beginning in the 1970s, the ARF (Armenian Revolutionary Federation, Dashnaktsutiune) shifted its priority from pursuing independence for Soviet Armenia to aiming at the unification of Turkish Armenian lands. This meant focusing on the Genocide as the more important issue and the basis for territorial claims, seeing Turkey rather than Europe as the bad guy in Armenian history, as well as seeing Russia as a protector of Armenia and Armenians. This change was, at best, discussed within the higher circles of the ARF and did not have a public airing. Nonetheless, in doing so, the ARF joined the others in adopting the traditional view in Armenian political thought of the last 200 years or so: that the cost of security for the Armenian nation is the nation's independence.

Thus Armenians in Armenia were moving toward the idea of independence just as the Diaspora was feeling comfortable with the USSR.

The second reversal was that thinking in Armenia itself had evolved. The ANM had reached the conclusion that independence could happen, that it was possible and necessary to normalize relations with all neighbors, including Turkey; that damage to vital national interests had been caused by maximalist visions in the hands of those who claimed monopoly over patriotism; that looking at the Genocide as a political rather than historical event was bound to limit independent Armenia's options and might lead to a repetition of historical mistakes.

The fierce debate in the Supreme Soviet ended up with a compromise between those who wanted to make the Genocide and related matters the centerpiece of the Declaration on Independence and those who wanted the document to focus on the question of independence alone. The compromise consisted of a reference to events in history and historic rights in its preamble. Although both subsequent relevant documents, the Declaration of Independence and the Constitution, refer to the July 1990 document, neither includes it.

Nonetheless, when the ANM won the contest of leadership in the Armenian SSR Supreme Soviet and the USSR collapsed, it had a clear policy towards Turkey: establishment of diplomatic relations and normalization of relations at the earliest possible date, without any preconditions. Historical claims were not the basis of relations between the two neighbors. Obviously this policy was not due to a lack of knowledge of history within the ANM. Levon Ter-Petrossian was a historian, as were some of his close collaborators and advisers. The difference with the position of other historians was not the absence of an appreciation of the significance of the Genocide; rather it was how to interpret that event, how to analyze the policies and strategies of the First Republic, how to view the current state of world and regional affairs, and, above all, how to imagine the future.

Following the collapse of the USSR, Turkey, along with the international community, recognized Armenia's independence. Turkish-Armenian relations moved into a new, state-to-state arena. But recognition of independence was still not the same as the establishment of diplomatic relations. During initial, informal contacts, it became obvious that this would not be a simple matter.

When Turkey-Armenia relations first became a subject of public discussion, prior to August 1992, Turkish diplomats insisted, in unofficial statements, that the establishment of diplomatic relations with Armenia would have to be preceded by a promise by Armenia that the Armenian state would not raise the issue of the Genocide and Genocide recognition and would take it upon itself to convince the Diaspora to also desist from doing so. Actually, Turkish diplomats, none of them historians, played the role of historians, and wanted Armenia's leaders to do the same, by abolishing history. The Armenian government made it clear that it was not willing to make such commitments, that it was unreasonable for Turkey to make such demands, and Turkey should emulate Armenia in eliminating preconditions.

Turkey soon reversed its position and dropped those demands. The change might be explained by a number of considerations: a realization that the initial position was unreasonable; a tactical step to test the new government in Armenia; or a reflection of its larger ambitions to fill the supposed power vacuum in the Caucasus and Central Asia created by the collapse of the USSR. Armenia's decision not to object to Turkey's presence on what would become the CSCE/OSCE Minsk Group might also have helped the situation. Yerevan thought that Turkey would become part of the problem if it were not part of the solution. Regardless, Turkey and Armenia agreed that an official delegation from Turkey would visit Yerevan to undertake initial discussions.

First Phase

The Turkish delegation arrived for bilateral talks in Yerevan in August 1992. During two days of talks, hosted by the presidency, neither Turkey nor Armenia placed preconditions for the establishment of diplomatic relations. The stage was open for the second act. The parties agreed to start negotiations on the Protocol for the establishment of diplomatic relations between the two countries. Negotiations on the draft of a Protocol that fall and during the winter of 1993 progressed normally. With the increasing realization by Turkish officials that Armenia's position was not opportunistic or based on isolated thinking, goodwill prevailed on from both sides.

The positive atmosphere survived a number of serious hurdles. The main one was the militarization of the Nagorno Karabakh conflict. In the spring of 1992 the Azerbaijani side lost the town of Shushi and the Lachin corridor; and throughout the Conference on Security and Cooperation in Europe (CSCE, later the OSCE, as "Conference" was replaced with "Organization")-mediated negotiations the Armenian side refused to return them to Azerbaijan, a precondition set by Azerbaijan for the opening of the Minsk Conference on the future status of Karabakh.

A second, minor hurdle were statements made by the minister of foreign affairs of Armenia, Raffi Hovannisian, which deviated from the policy of the administration. The minister was asked by the president to resign, for this and other reasons.

During this period, Turkey permitted the use of its railway connection with Armenia at Leninakan/Gyumri for a transfer of a planned 100,000 tons of European Community-subsidized wheat to Armenia: the war in Abkhazia had ended the last operating railroad Armenia had with the outside world, once Azerbaijan had imposed its energy and transport blockade of Armenia in January 1991. During the Soviet period the rail connection with Turkey had been open to one passenger train a week. That service was stopped with the collapse of the USSR in the absence of diplomatic relations and in solidarity with the Azerbaijani blockade of Armenia. Life would have been seriously disrupted had Turkey not allowed that gradual transfer, sometimes even advancing wheat from its own storages.

The Protocol for the establishment of diplomatic relations was negotiated and almost completed, except for one issue: the formulation on the recognition of existing borders. The Turkish side was considering an Armenian proposal when discussions were overtaken by events. In April 1993 the Armenian side in the Karabakh war occupied Kelbajar, another Azerbaijani district situated between Karabakh and Armenia and used by the Azerbaijani side to shell both. Turkey interrupted the negotiations. In addition, it halted the transit shipment of wheat to Armenia. Soon after Turkey set withdrawal of Armenian troops from Azerbaijan as a precondition for the establishment of diplomatic relations and the opening of its border with Armenia. This condition remains to the present time, although the specific demands changed over time.

The change in Ankara's negotiating position might have been the result of an increasing sense of identification with Azerbaijan as a consequence of Azerbaijani losses being seen as Turkey's. Azerbaijanis closely identified themselves ethnically and culturally with Turkey, especially under nationalist President Abulfaz Elchibey, and Turks responded in kind. Or, Azerbaijanis might have become more effective in their lobbying in Turkey to end the negotiations in order to come closer to their policy of forcing a change in Armenia's Karabakh policy through economic strangulation. It is also possible that for many in the Turkish establishment Armenia's actions constituted a further example of an irredentism that might later turn against Turkey itself.

Whatever the actual reason or reasons for the change, President Turgut Ozal of Turkey made some threatening remarks toward Armenia following the fall of Kelbajar; Russian Defense officials responded in kind and Armenia found itself in a situation it was trying to avoid: an object of international relations, rather than a determinant of its policies. When President Ozal died a few days later, Armenia used the occasion to lower tensions by being present at the funeral with a high level delegation led by President Ter-Petrossian. Tensions subsided as Turkey saw an opportunity in this visit to advance its role as a mediator. A short meeting between Presidents Elchibey and Ter-Petrossian, while failing to achieve concrete results, did reaffirm Armenia's desire to end the conflict.

The war in Karabakh and Turkey's decision to link the negotiations on the establishing of normal relations with Armenia to the conflict brought to an end this first, most promising phase of diplomacy between the two countries.

But the negotiations had created a new reality. Regular contact was established between Yerevan and Ankara that provided for consultations on a variety of issues and kept tensions down. Armenia formulated and articulated its own policies toward Turkey. Second, Armenia made a rational choice regarding the foundations of its foreign and security policy. Normal relations with all neighbors was the principal foundation of Armenia's long-term security and prosperity; and the fact that Turkey was a neighbor could not be changed. All other issues could and should be resolved in that context. Armenia now spoke for itself.

Second Phase

The second phase in the relations between the two countries stretched from April 1993 to February 1998 or the end of the Ter-Petrossian presidency. It was defined by Turkey's insistence on a linkage between the Karabakh conflict and the establishment of diplomatic relations but also by continuing contacts and progress in some areas.

The war continued and by August 1993 the Armenian side occupied five more districts of Azerbaijan around Karabakh, which also produced almost 300,000 new Azerbaijani Internally Displaced Persons (IDPs).

It is true that for some Turkish officials the absence of relations with Armenia made its larger designs less palatable and threatened its strategic interests. After a while the blockade of Armenia was seen as harmful to Armenia's prospects for economic development but hardly effective in bringing about a change in Armenia's negotiating position. Besides, Turkish antagonism towards Armenia was pushing Armenia closer to Russia than it needed to be.

For other Turkish leaders who thought the worst of Armenians, the changes in the fortunes of war were more evidence of the expansionist designs Armenians had for the region, and of their untrustworthiness. Similarly, in Armenia and the Diaspora some critics of the Armenian government's policy toward Turkey argued that the Turkish refusal to normalize relations was an expression of Turkish hatred of Armenians, and that Karabakh was just an excuse to cover up the evil intentions of an unrepentant Turkey.

But for all practical purposes Turkey was reacting to the events unfolding in the war. The plight of Azeri IDPs and ethnic affinity created the emotional backdrop to the Turkish position of unconditional support for the Azerbaijani cause. The Turkish refusal to normalize relations with Armenia and open the border between the two countries was the most important factor in making the blockade of Armenia effective. Changing that policy would have been considered undermining the position of an Azerbaijan that was already losing on the battlefield.

Turkey was also dealing with a new factor: the projected Baku-Ceyhan oil pipeline that would make Turkey a major player in the energy sector as a transit country for Caspian oil, a position that depended on Azerbaijan's consent. Gradually Turkish policy toward Armenia turned hostage to the underlying assumptions of Azerbaijan's negotiating position on the conflict.

Moreover, Turkey had to deal with sanctions the U.S. Congress had imposed on direct American aid to Azerbaijan in the Freedom Support Act of 1992. Section 907 of that Act was adopted as a result of American Armenian lobbying organizations at a time when Azerbaijan had imposed blockades of Armenia and Karabakh even before the conflict was fully militarized. For Azerbaijan as well as for Turkey the removal of these sanctions acquired practical as well as symbolic significance, especially when the tide of war turned and Azerbaijan was seen as the victim, and when the Armenian government was able to overcome the worst effects of the blockades. The Turkish government was unwilling or unable to accept a tradeoff between the removal of Section 907 and normalization of relations with Armenia. Additionally, when on two occasions the government of Armenia did conclude that such a removal might help negotiations with Azerbaijan, it was unable to convince even one well-disposed organization to support the removal of Section 907. For Diasporan organizations too these sanctions had acquired strategic and symbolic value.

Another important factor during this period was the position of the United States, which supported the normalization of relations between the two countries and spent considerable energy in that direction, mainly in Ankara. Washington considered normalization of relations between the two countries critical to its interests in the region. However, it too was unable to convince Turkey to change its policy. At one point American officials presented the Baku-Ceyhan pipeline, in the version that would cross Armenia to reach Turkey, as the "peace pipeline," to induce the Armenian side to make sufficient concessions on the Karabakh issue to make the pipeline route acceptable to Azerbaijan and Turkey. Armenia was not ready to make concessions that might endanger Karabakh's security for the sake of the pipelines.

Nonetheless, over time, Turkey did change the details of its precondition to normalize relations with Armenia. At first Turkey expected the Armenian side to return the occupied territories and recognize Azerbaijani sovereignty over Karabakh before it would normalize relations with Armenia. Gradually, the position mellowed and Turkey stated that the signing of a document leading to the resolution of the conflict, even if not to an actual solution, would suffice. At some point, even that was softened further, and Turkey asked for a symbolic gesture: the return of an occupied district or part of a district. Such a gesture would show Armenian goodwill and prove that the Armenian side did not intend to occupy these territories forever. While there was some support in the Armenian government for such a gesture, the focus in the Karabakh negotiations remained Azerbaijan. There were serious concerns that the impact of any unilateral action on the Armenian side might harden the Azerbaijani position and harm the negotiations in the long run.

It was still during this period that Armenia and Turkey agreed to establish an air link. Armenian Airlines was allowed to operate two flights a week to Istanbul and facilitated visas for citizens of Armenia. Also, with the encouragement of the two governments, businessmen in the two countries started a Turkish-Armenian Business Council. The Council initiated exchanges, lobbied in the two capitals for normalization of relations, and began planning such an eventuality. Local officials on two sides of the border, mainly Gyumri and Kars, established contact and visited each other. So did journalists.

In 1995 a State Commission chaired by the president of Armenia organized a number of activities, including the convening of an international conference and the founding of a museum, to commemorate the eightieth anniversary of the Genocide. Taner Akcam, a Turkish sociologist, attended the conference in Yerevan and labeled the events of the First World War as genocide. The Turkish government did not react.

Despite efforts from many directions, Turkey was unable to transcend the limitations inherent in its perspective of things Armenian. The Karabakh conflict was certainly a major factor. But Turkey was also unable to remove the stranglehold Baku held on what many Turkish officials had come to believe was the next panacea to Turkey's economic and strategic problems, the Baku-Ceyhan pipeline. Furthermore, Turkish officials may have become victims of the same public opinion that they created, making normalization of relations with Armenia more difficult for politicians. Turkish diplomats and leaders arguing in favor of normalization for the sake of larger regional considerations had little chance to impose their view. Armenia, in turn, was not in a position to make yet another leap in diplomatic imagination to give Turkey what it wanted to normalize relations, if that meant endangering the process of negotiations or Karabakh's security, although Armenian officials were ready to defend and did stand behind their policy toward Turkey despite the fierce criticism of some opposition groups in Armenia and the Diaspora and the emotions the subject aroused.

The absence of normalized relations with Turkey was probably one of the reasons that made the Russian-Armenian Friendship and Cooperation Treaty of 1997 the substantive document it became.

Although no movement forward had been marked between April 1993 and February 1998, there was also no repudiation of the basic premise on both sides that normalization of relations and cooperation on regional issues would remain the goals of the policies in the two countries. Despite the upheavals brought about by war until the 1994 cease-fire and the difficulties of negotiations throughout this period, contacts and consultations continued bilaterally and in multilateral forums. Incidents were not allowed to degenerate into tensions and crises. The new precepts survived the difficulties of the second period.

Third Phase

The third phase in Turkish-Armenian state-to-state relations began when Robert Kocharian, prime minister of Armenia and former president of Karabakh, assumed the presidency of Armenia in April 1998.

Relations with Turkey were one of the first issues Kocharian addressed as president. The new president believed normalization of relations was in Armenia's best interests. In substance, he reconfirmed the policy of the Ter-Petrossian administration: Armenia wanted to establish diplomatic relations and normalize relations with Turkey without preconditions. Nevertheless, Kocharian, whose interest in history was minimal as opposed to his predecessor, who was a historian, argued that Armenia would raise the problem of

Genocide recognition with Turkey and would make international recognition of the Genocide part of its foreign policy agenda.

Kocharian's reasons for this change were rather tactical. He thought that by raising the question, a thorny one for Turkey, he would counter Turkey's insistence on the resolution of the Karabakh conflict before normalization proceeds. The corollary was that for Armenia not to raise the Genocide question, Turkey would withdraw its own precondition which, in turn, would weaken the Azerbaijani negotiating position and strengthen Armenia's economy and standing. In addition, lacking an organizational base in Armenia, Kocharian further secured the support of the ARF and other parties in Armenia, for whom Genocide recognition and related matters were the main stated goal. Finally, Kocharian believed that his tactical step would be welcomed in the Armenian Diaspora as result of which the Diaspora would multiply its investments in the country, thus solving Armenia's economic woes. The Diaspora, Kocharian argued, was alienated from the Ter-Petrossian administration because of the latter's refusal to make Genocide recognition the basis of its foreign policy toward Turkey and part of its foreign policy agenda.

Yet the Kocharian administration still insisted that recognition of the Genocide by Turkey was not a precondition for normalization of relations between the two countries. While the change in policy sealed the support of some parties in Armenia and elated the Diaspora, it failed to produce the leap in investments Kocharian had hoped for. Equally important for many in Turkey, Kocharian's new formulation of policy signaled the domination of Yerevan policies by the Diasporan agenda; and the Diaspora agenda was essentially anti-Turkish and culminated in territorial demands. Kocharian had miscalculated. He had not understood the role the Genocide issue played in Turkey's security mentality supported by the Sévres Syndrome: the fear of being dismembered. For a while, at least, Yerevan's new position strengthened the position of those officials in Turkey who had opposed normalization to begin with, arguing that Armenians were all the same, hopeless irredentists. Not having received the concession he expected by raising the Genocide issue and realizing the depth of the reaction in Turkey, Kocharian took the desperate step of reassuring Ankara that Armenia had no legal basis for territorial demands from it, to the dismay of segments of the Diaspora and political parties that were now more interested in being part of the power structure in Armenia.

Nonetheless, Turkish officials tolerated Kocharian because they believed Kocharian was working hard in 1999 and 2000 toward a resolution of the Nagorno Karabakh problem by engaging in direct negotiations with President Heydar Aliyev of Azerbaijan on the basis of a new formula of strategic value to Turkey and Azerbaijan. Following a few, fruitless meetings, Aliyev and Kocharian agreed in principle to resolve the Karabakh conflict on the basis of a territorial exchange between Azerbaijan and Armenia. Azerbaijan would relinquish Karabakh to Armenia and Armenia, in turn, would cede the Meghri district in southern Armenia that separates Nakhichevan from the rest of Azerbaijan and borders Iran and Turkey (see previous chapter).

With the failure of the exchange formula and the end of Karabakh-related negotiations for all practical purposes, attempts at normalization of relations seem to have become less urgent. The changes in the regional and international situations following the September 11, 2001 terrorist attacks on New York and Washington, the war in Afghanistan, and subsequently in Iraq in 2003 has made it difficult to focus on difficulties in bilateral relations of less important countries. Nonetheless, considering American strategic considerations in the Caucasus, a new government in Turkey, and United States-Iran tensions, Washington did make a new effort to push the two countries toward an accommodation in 2002 and in the spring of 2003. The question remains whether the new Turkish government, certainly less beholden to past policies and commitments, would be willing to spend its political capital to make compromises on the issue of its relations with Armenia. Similarly, with the increase of the power of the ARF in the new Armenian parliament and cabinet, it is questionable whether the Kocharian administration will now even be in a position to continue what it had been proposing during the past five years. The chairman of the parliament's foreign relations committee, a member of the ARF, has stated publicly and unequivocally that relations with Turkey could not be discussed without the latter's recognition of the Armenian Genocide.

The Business of Business is Politics

As indicated earlier, beginning in 1993 the two governments encouraged businessmen in both countries to explore areas of cooperation of trade. In the early days following independence and in view of the policy of the first administration, the most imaginative proposal came from Itzhak Alathon, a Turkish industrialist and entrepreneur, and Hrair Hovnanian, an American Armenian real estate magnate and philanthropist, to rebuild the Turkish port of Trabzon as a gateway to Armenia. The proposal died due to the lack of a positive conclusion in the negotiations between the two countries to establish diplomatic relations as well the noisy objections made by some quarters in both countries. Contacts were established between the local governments of Kars and Gyumri on the two sides of the border, with the support of the local populations, who realized the mutual benefits of open borders and trade. Here too the efforts were stalled due to the absence of normalization of relations. Despite these failures, contacts between businessmen have continued, so far producing only small trade, mainly through Georgia. Furthermore, journalists and public interests groups continue to visit each other, however sporadically, and attempt to create new levels of understanding and mutual perception.

Equally important for Turkish-Armenian relations beyond state-to-state discussions are two projects that have changed the atmosphere: the Turkish Armenian Reconciliation Commission (TARC) and the Turkish-Armenian Historians' Workshop.

TARC was established in the year 2001 as an independent group but with the approval, if not engagement, of the two governments to deal with the whole range of issues of common interest, including differences in perceptions of history. The idea of a commission was originally discussed in 1992, during the early days of negotiations, when Armenia proposed that the question of the Genocide and the Turkish-Armenian past be taken up by a mixed group of historians. The Turkish side was non-committal and the idea was dropped as negotiations stalled. TARC's mandate was wider—it aimed at reconciliation on the basis of current mutual interests—and less focused.

TARC has five Turkish members, four of them former diplomats with strong ties to the state, led by Ozdem Sanberk; the fifth is an academic. The four Armenian members of the group included a former minister of foreign affairs, Alexander Arzumanian, an adviser to the current minister of foreign affairs with academic credentials, a Russian-Armenian political scientist, and an American Armenian lawyer active in community affairs. The project had the support of the U.S. Department of State but its formation invited the wrath of various groups in both countries and in the Diaspora. None-theless, the Commission met a number of times and agreed that normalization of relations between the two countries was in the interest of both, that cultural, economic, and other ties should be encouraged. On the thorniest problem of the Genocide in 2002, the members of TARC agreed to ask the New York-based International Center for Transitional Justice to conduct an independent study and answer some questions: Did the events of 1915-1917 constitute genocide under the UN Convention on the Prevention of Genocide and other international instruments? Do the provisions of such instruments apply to the case of the Armenians? The answer to the first was positive; it was negative as far as the second question was concerned. Some Turkish members of the Commission distanced themselves from the conclusions by arguing that the study had exceeded its mandate, even denying that there had been a formal decision to submit the questions for an opinion. The Armenian side was vindicated on the main question. The work of TARC has slowed down since then. This was due not only to the reaction of some of the Turkish members of the Commission, but to the withdrawal of the tacit support of the government of Armenia following earlier objections of parties that otherwise supported President Kocharian, as well as to the tensions between the senior member of the Armenian group and the administration.

Despite these difficulties and imbalances, many members of TARC on both sides seem to be determined to continue their efforts, even if the results do not produce the results that were anticipated when the commission was created.

Academic Underpinnings

The second project, the Turkish-Armenian Workshop, was initiated in 2000 and aims at establishing an intellectual and scholarly framework within which the Genocide can be looked at as a historical phenomenon and dealt with as objectively as possible. The Workshop is organized by a small group of Turkish and Armenian scholars led by Professor Ronald Suny of the University of Chicago, a historian and political scientist, and Professor Muge Gocek, a sociologist at the University of Michigan, Ann Arbor. The project is independent of any government and its gatherings are supported by academic institutions.

The Workshop has met three times since its inception. The first meeting was held at the University of Chicago, the second at the University of Michigan in 2002, and the third at the University of Minnesota in 2003. The fourth is planned tentatively for 2004 in an academic institution in Europe. Involving at first a dozen or so Turkish, Armenian, and Western scholars from Turkey, Europe, and the United States, the number of participants has grown to about forty in 2003, including a historian from Armenia. The total number of those engaged in the process exceeds sixty and includes many on both sides who at first objected or were reluctant to participate. There were also some elements among Turks and Armenians who found cause to oppose the project, arguing that their respective positions "could not be negotiated."

The Workshop consists of formal papers on specific themes related to Ottoman-Armenian relations preceding, during, and following the First World War and on comparative studies as well as discussions in a depoliticized environment. From its tense beginnings, the Workshop project has now matured to a healthy interchange that inspires new research and focuses on the causes of genocide and the processes that define it. Much has changed since the days when Taner Akcam was the lone Turkish scholar, who confounded the neat division among scholars by using the term "genocide" to describe the events of 1915, when Armenian scholars who tried to explain the Genocide in historical terms were considered renegades at best, when scholars felt bound by official positions, and when debate could not move beyond the question of the use of the term "genocide." The impact of the Workshop on the understanding and interpretation of the history of Turkish-Armenian relations and eventually on public perceptions of the past in Turkey, Armenia, and the Turkish and Armenian Diasporas will be slow but it will be significant.

Thus, progress has been made in Turkish-Armenian relations, both in the state and public spheres, since the early days of independence in 1991, without the establishment of diplomatic relations between the two states or bringing about reconciliation between the two peoples.

Turkey failed to use opportunities to normalize relations with Armenia due to its inability to overcome its sense of ethnic solidarity with Azerbaijan. Many Turkish diplomats, including some who could have made a difference then, now think that it was a mistake for Turkey to impose preconditions on the negotiations. The process has also become more difficult with the decision of the new administration in Yerevan to inject history into the relations and its lack of readiness to pursue actively a resolution to the Karabakh problem.

The goal of establishing normal relations with Turkey has become the norm in Armenia without ever becoming a major issue in any of the presidential or parliamentary elections. The belief of some journalists and academics notwithstanding, Ter-Petrossian was not weakened domestically because of the position he took on this question. Kocharian's continuation of the basic policy regarding Turkey is the best testimony in that regard. Except for the vociferous minority parties—largely implants from the Diaspora and Communists or nationalist-communists—normalization of relations with Turkey without preconditions was accepted, even if apprehensively by some, as a rational foreign policy. As long as national security did not yet depend on it, the policy was accepted. No party that advocated the contrary ever reached 10 percent of the vote in any election. While every Armenian would like to see the Genocide recognized, especially by Turkey, large segments of the Armenian public also recognize, at least for the present, the need to distinguish between general aims and the requirements of independent statehood. The battle for the soul of the new republic (is it to be defined by the Genocide and anti-Turkism or become a normal state in peace with its neighbors and in pursuit of the welfare and security of its citizens?) is not over yet. As in other foreign policy decisions, President Kocharian may have unwittingly opened the door to nationalists and nationalist-communists to turn his tactical step regarding the Genocide issue into a strategic weapon. A shaky hold on power will also contribute to his inability to resist the temptation to look strong and desist from undertaking new, imaginative steps toward Turkey and the resolution of the Karabakh conflict.

In Turkey, similarly, the basic policy of successive governments to seek normalization with Armenia has not featured as a matter of debate in any election and it has not caused the fall or rise of any government. Much has changed in Turkey in the last two decades. The parameters of public discourse are wider now and civil society has started to assert itself against the monolithic structure and to use its right to disagree with state policy. In this context, efforts to seek a more nuanced and truthful understanding of the past can be seen among scholars, intellectuals, students, and journalists. Yet both the Turkish state itself and public opinion still feel the need to shield themselves against the potential consequences, especially in terms of Armenian territorial demands, should Turkey recognize the Genocide.

13

Armenia's Strategic Significance

To the extent that Armenian political thought ties the security, economic development, and the future of Armenia to the country's strategic significance, a discussion on the subject should begin with the simple question, is Armenia a strategically important country today? To answer this question, it is necessary to make three general remarks.

First, strategic significance for a country is very different from the significance of a country. Armenia means and signifies something to all Armenians, to one degree or another. That significance may be personal, historic, emotional, economic, political, etc. Strategic significance is always significance for some other country or countries.

Second, there should be a distinction made between strategic significance and strategic options. More often than not, it is not up to a country to decide whether it has strategic significance or not. A country may have strategic significance for others because of its geographic location, natural resources, or other factors; in this case that country cannot decide on its own, as a foreign policy option, whether it has strategic significance or not. In fact, unless you are a major power or a superpower, there are always other countries—major powers and superpowers—that will assign less powerful states strategic functions as defined by their worldview and interests.

Third, the foreign policy of a state must deal with what is inevitable in its strategic significance in a manner that minimizes damage and maximizes benefits as far as its national interests are concerned. Also, it must create options that may redefine and redirect perceptions underlying the first function.

Does Armenia have Strategic Significance?

Traditionally, Armenians have thought of Armenia as having an important place in history due, above all, to its geographic location:

between East and West, North and South; between the Black and
Caspian Seas; part of the larger Near East, while being independent
of larger empires; on the Silk Road; and on the fault line of regions
and religions, cultures and civilizations, of passing empires and enduring states. All of this is true. The fact remains that it is the "others" who play the leading role in the perception of Armenia's significance in regional or world history and in its strategic value.

But a close look at this common perception raises some questions.

First, it is not only Armenians who have that perception of their
homeland in the region. Georgians, Azerbaijanis, Turks, and Iranians think of their homelands as playing or having played a similar
role in the region. That means, at the least, that neither the geographic space nor the function is uniquely Armenian.

Second, from the perspective of public perception in neighboring
countries, today's Armenia does not seem to be strategically a very
important place. The media in those countries pay little attention to
what many consider the most important place on Earth. The exception is Azerbaijan, which has a difficult time forgetting its military
confrontation with Armenians and its losses during the war; but even
here, the discourse is on what to do about Armenians and Armenia
rather than the latter's strategic value. This observation is even more
so in Europe, the United States, and even, to a large extent, Russia.
Admittedly impressionistic, the observation is also symptomatic.

Searching beyond impressions, the question is, what strategic value
does Armenia have in regional and world affairs in 2003, twelve
years after independence?

One way of looking at Armenia's strategic significance is to see
where Armenia is with regard to the three processes that determine
the limits and possibilities of strategic significance: integration/dis-
integration of political units, globalization, and American manage-
ment/domination of world affairs.

Armenian and the Three Major Processes

Integration/Disintegration

The first to be considered is the simultaneous process of integration and disintegration of political units. On the one hand, Europe
unites and regional organizations sprout as a result of those political
boundaries that become less relevant and aspects of sovereignty are
ceded by groups of countries to various types of regional organiza-

tions. On the other hand, the USSR and Yugoslavia disintegrated and there are peoples and territories within and without Europe that are trying to secede and create new borders. While ten countries in Central and Eastern Europe are about to join the European Union, some Corsicans want to leave France, Basques want to leave Spain, the Northern League considered separating from southern Italy. The Balkan states still face the problems of Kosovo and Montenegro, among others. Elsewhere, Quebec has not altogether abandoned the idea of separation from Canada; China, Indonesia, Sri Lanka, the Philippines, and others face armed separatist movements in Asia; and Northern Ireland continues to have problems with the United Kingdom.

Regionalization, while keeping political boundaries intact, is minimizing their economic significance through the reduction or elimination of tariffs and bringing economic systems closer, all for the purpose of increasing trade, spurring production, creating jobs, and improving economies. Though regionalization and integration may mean having to adjust laws and even ceding elements of sovereignty, when achieved voluntarily and through negotiations such processes increase the perimeters of the area where one's voice and vote count, in addition to bringing obvious economic benefits and opportunities. Integrative processes are seen by the international community as constructive, while policies that might produce disintegration are seen as disruptive to world stability and security.

Armenia is not involved in any serious integrative process that would make a real difference to others or to itself in the near future. Armenia is a member of the Commonwealth of Independent States (CIS), but the CIS has yet to prove it is of any relevance today. It is too poor to mean anything, and even its leading member, Russia, is determining its policies having Europe, China, and the United States in mind, not the CIS. Armenia is a member of the Black Sea Cooperation Organization (BSEC). Yet BSEC membership means little if Armenia has no diplomatic and economic relations with Turkey, the major member of that organization closest to its borders, and if Armenia cannot benefit even from the little that BSEC has to offer. Armenia is a member of the Council of Europe, the benefits of which are, however essential, very long term, possibly too far in the future to make a difference in the self-perception of Armenians and of Armenia. European structures are too far—in concept and in physical distance—to consider Armenia's participation a significant factor.

After the contested 2003 presidential elections in Armenia severely criticized by observers from the Council of Europe, among others, some members of the Kocharian administration argued that Armenia's democracy does not have to look like Western ones, indicating that suspension of Armenia's membership in that body or the threat of expulsion were of little value.

In terms of a more realistic outlook, a regional process involving the three South Caucasus republics might have made more sense. Yet there is no movement in that direction. All three republics are attracted toward far off centers of power and money: Washington, Brussels, or Moscow. One reason for this lack of focus on regional cooperation is that all three republics are poor and poor countries make poor partners. Another reason is that each of the republics has opted for a different approach towards its security guarantees. Yet such cooperation remains the potentially the most effective. To be the distant relative of far away families is not an alternative to developing a trusting relationship with immediate neighbors.

The most obvious reason for Armenia's irrelevance to this process is, of course, the fact that Armenia has no diplomatic relations with Azerbaijan. In fact, Azerbaijan considers itself technically at war with Armenia. The Nagorno Karabakh conflict makes any cooperation that involves Armenia—economic, political, or on regional security—unacceptable for Azerbaijan.

More importantly, the Nagorno Karabakh conflict places Armenia in the category of countries that support disintegration, from the point of view of the international community. At the time of the collapse of the USSR and Yugoslavia, the international community, including Russia and Armenia's four neighbors, had determined that the world would recognize the independence of the constituent republics of the USSR and Yugoslavia only (fifteen in the first and six in the second) and would insist on the territorial integrity of those recognized. This meant that territories and peoples wishing to separate from these new republics would be refused recognition as independent entities, all other principles and reasons notwithstanding. There could be no recognition of Karabakh's independence or union with Armenia therefore, unless Azerbaijan did so, which was an unlikely solution.

Moreover, as a consequence of the absence of a solution to the conflict, Armenia has been unable to open its borders with another neighbor: Turkey. The fact that Turkey has allowed Armenia to be a member of the Black Sea Economic Cooperation organization does not mean that it will change its policy regarding diplomatic relations or border openings with Armenia.

Whatever it may mean to Armenians, from the point of view of the international community the Karabakh conflict is at best a nuisance, at worst a conflict that can be manipulated by other states to achieve goals unrelated to the conflict. At any rate, it places Armenia on the wrong side of the integration/disintegration process. Not only is Armenia not part of any integration process, regional or otherwise, but it also does not fulfill the minimum standard of international relations: normal relations with its neighbors.

Globalization

The second process is usually referred to as globalization. Globalization has a number of definitions. But all definitions recognize the importance of communications, economic interaction, interdependence in the fields of energy, and movement of capital investments. The World trade Organization (WTO) best embodies that process. One may disagree with the premises of globalization, be dismayed by the way it functions, or critique its consequences. But it would be difficult not to recognize the fact that globalization is occurring and that it constitutes the driving force of economic transformation at this juncture of history.

It is true that Armenia became a member of the World Trade Organization and has made some advances in the high technology field. Yet the republic is far behind in the attraction of foreign investment, and local capital is not sufficient to perform the task of capitalization. Armenia is not in a position to take serious advantage of its membership in WTO and many other regional and international organizations, since for multinational corporations Armenia's risk factor—a country still technically at war with Azerbaijan—would not justify any major investment. Armenia does not have the kind and speed of return that Azerbaijani hydrocarbon resources provide, even if that country too is not, technically, at peace. The Kocharian administration's expectation that Diasporan Armenians' capital would compensate for the absence of international investment, by and large, has not materialized. After all, Armenians in the Diaspora did not become wealthy because they made patriotic investments in their countries of adoption.

Furthermore, in essential aspects of regional trade and globalization, Armenia has forfeited many opportunities to become a regional player, at the least. Armenia has no access to any sea. But it has the infrastructure to be the hub of rail communications for all of its four neighbors. Yet the rail lines are idle with three of four neighbors: Turkey, Azerbaijan, and Iran. Armenia cannot use its links to the first two because of the conflict with Azerbaijan, and to Iran because its connection to that country passes through the Azerbaijani territory of Nakhichevan. In 2002 Armenia turned down a new Azerbaijani proposal to open these rail lines if the Armenian side would return some of the occupied territories. Armenia's rail communication with Georgia, the only one functioning today, is one of the slowest ever. While Armenia's rail links to the other three neighbors are sitting idle, Armenia's four neighbors have or are planning to have connections among themselves, bypassing Armenia and making Armenia's rails irrelevant in the future. Georgia and Turkey are planning a new line; Georgia and Azerbaijan and Turkey and Iran have functioning connections; and Azerbaijan and Iran are planning a direct line.

Furthermore, with its roads to Turkey and Azerbaijan closed, for surface communications Armenia must rely on its less than adequate connection to Georgia and its route to Iran, which passes through the hazardous Zangezur Mountains and becomes treacherous in the winter. The state has no funds to upgrade these roads, the European-supported TRACECA Project that would have helped has faltered, and the Diaspora-supported All-Armenia Fund can hardly manage to keep alive road projects with and within Karabakh.

Armenia has no air communication with Azerbaijan, but there are flights to Istanbul and Tehran, as well as a number of flights to European, Russian, and Middle Eastern cities. A new connection has been established with Tbilisi. A few foreign airlines fly into and out of Yerevan. But even here, willful misconduct or mismanagement of Armenian Airlines has bankrupted the state-owned company, and most of its operations have been taken over by a Russian company. International commerce and transport, at any rate, are not achieved primarily by air transport, even though air transport is essential to commerce.

Finally, Armenia is not part of any of the energy transport systems that are being built or contemplated in the region. Hydrocarbon resources in Azerbaijan, Iran, and the Caspian Sea are one of the main reasons why this region has strategic significance. But with the blockade that Azerbaijan has imposed since 1991, the old connections hardly work and Armenia is not part of the new ones. Until 1990 Armenia received its natural gas from Russia through a pipeline that reached Armenia through Azerbaijan. When Azerbaijan imposed its blockade of Karabakh and Armenia in January 1991, a bypass was constructed that brought gas through Georgia.

Since then Iran has constructed a pipeline directly to Turkey, while the plan to build one to Armenia, the agreement for which was signed in 1995 before the Turkish-Iranian agreement, remains to be built. Had that been achieved, the Iran-Turkey pipeline may have been less viable, especially if the Armenian grid was also connected to the Turkish system. Russia could have supplied Turkey with natural gas through Georgia and Armenia. Instead, Russia built a gas pipeline under the Black sea directly to Turkey, known as the Blue Stream. With major discoveries of offshore natural gas in Azerbaijan, there are plans now to construct a gas pipeline from Azerbaijan to Turkey, going through Georgia, alongside the Main Export Pipeline (MEP) for Azerbaijani and Caspian oil.

In the mid 1990s an old oil pipeline from Baku to the Black Sea passing through Georgia was fundamentally repaired. Azerbaijani oil flows again and now reaches the Georgian town of Supsa. The MEP, known also as BTC—Baku-Tbilisi-Ceyhan—will be the main export system for Azerbaijani and some Caspian oil. The MEP could have crossed. Even though transit through Armenia would have been financially and technologically more feasible, Armenia was bypassed because of Azerbaijan's refusal to fuel the Armenian economy and have any dependence on it while the Karabakh conflict is not resolved.

Capital investment, a major challenge for all countries, is another major problem for Armenia. The Republic does not have the natural resources that might produce that capital domestically. In the absence of a peace treaty with Azerbaijan, Armenia and the region would be considered unsafe for major investments related to normal economic activity, rosy statistics and wishful thinking on Diasporan capital notwithstanding. Economic activity and growth are often better assessed by the consumption of energy and the ability to pay for it. Armenia's economy was unable to pay for the natural gas it was importing from Russia or for the nuclear energy Armenia itself was producing at the Medzamor plant. As a form of payment Russia demanded and received ownership of some of the most important industrial plants in Armenia at the end of 2002 as well as the Medzamor nuclear plant in early 2003, hardly the behavior of a country that considers Armenia a strategic ally. With some creative accounting on the part of the administration in Yerevan, the minister of trade announced that the amount Armenia owed Russia and paid back by turning over these plants to Russia would be counted as foreign investment, thus assuring that the figures for that important indicator would be inflated by at least 25 percent for 2002 and 2003.

Traditional Armenian strategic thinking seems to have returned with the Kocharian administration. According to that thinking, Armenia is the center of the region, and its future lies with Russia and is insured by historical antagonisms between Iran and Turkey, Turkey and Russia, Russia and Azerbaijan, Azerbaijan and Iran. The flow of capital and energy and communications projects of strategic significance—already completed, underway, or planned—belie such thinking. None of these countries have been able to resist the logic of economic survival and development, whether that logic is defined as globalization or not and whether development is accomplished the capitalist, Chinese, or a third way, as vaguely projected by some demagogues in Yerevan. Even with its current problems with Georgia, Russia remains engaged and continues to provide gas to Georgia in order to maintain its leverage and impact developments in that country. Whether they "like" Turkey and Azerbaijan or not, Russia and Iran have developed links with these countries with long-term implications for strategic interests, in addition to the immediate economic benefits such projects provide.

Under the circumstances, it is difficult to argue that Armenia is part of the globalization process in any way that gives it strategic significance for its neighbors or anyone else. Intended or not, the impact of Armenia's policy not to resolve the Karabakh conflict has been disengagement from the processes that are defining the future of the region and of relations between its neighbors near and far.

American Management/Domination of World Affairs

The evolving role of the United States in the world constitutes the third major trend in international relations. Since the collapse of the Soviet Union and its assumption of the mantle of the only superpower by far, the United States has sometimes acted as a leader of the community of nations and, increasingly, as the new imperial power.

During the last decade, between the two wars on Iraq and especially after the September 11, 2001 attacks on New York and Washington, the United States has moved from acting on behalf and through the international community toward acting alone and striking directly. The new administration in Washington, led by President George W. Bush after his victory of 2000, not only slighted the United Nations, but even when a country like Turkey—for so long a staunch ally on whom Washington has relied to defend and pursue its strategic interests—refused to facilitate military operations against Iraq in 2003, it was able to execute the war on Iraq once it made a decision to change the status quo in Baghdad and topple the regime. The 2003 war on Iraq indicates, furthermore, that in the context of new warfare capabilities, geographic proximity is not as important as it used to be.

No empire has survived history, of course. Yet American use of the window opportunity it has during the next decade or so to reshape the geopolitical map of regions where it has strategic interests must be taken into account by any state, more so by small states like Armenia for whom every year at this juncture is critical.

One dimension within this evolution important to Armenia is the uncertain but evolving U.S.-Russia relations. Neither Washington nor Moscow have yet decided on a single assessment of the other, thus both capitals pursue multiple policies. It is clear, nonetheless, that Russia was unable and/or unwilling to stop American troops from being stationed in a number of former Soviet republics, including Georgia and some Central Asian ones. Russia sees limits to its ability to play the game by the old rules.

Russia, even in its less than superpower status, still remains important to Armenia. Until such time as a new security system emerges, Armenia will continue to rely on Russia for its overall security. Armenia's security guarantees are enshrined in the 1997 basic treaty between the two countries.

But conventional wisdom regarding Russian-Armenian relations conveys an ideologically-based reliance on that state. Conventional wisdom places Armenia on the side of Russia not only because Armenia needs Russia, but because Armenians want to believe that Russia needs Armenia and loves Armenians. The Russian treatment of Armenia's debt is symptomatic of the radically diminished value Armenia has for Russian concerns.

For Russia, the South Caucasus is of vital interest because the region constitutes Russia's southern flank, a flank made unstable because of Chechnya. Russia would like to see friendly governments in its south. Should its fortunes improve and should it emerge as an economically more viable state and reform its armed forces, Russia may increase the level of its ambitions. But at this point it is functioning with limited goals and within its limits. That makes it possible to cooperate with the United States on major issues and still keep a competitive edge on secondary issues. Within the same limits set by a pragmatic policy, Russia has also been cooperating with Azerbaijan regarding Caspian resources. In addition to agreeing with Azerbaijan on the division of the Caspian, Russia has resolved with Azerbaijan the problem of visas for Azerbaijani workers in Russia, and it has become less active in the area of the Baku-Tbilisi-Ceyhan pipeline. Russia's increasing volume of trade with Turkey and Turkey's importance as a market for Russia's hydrocarbon resources changed perceptibly the relations of these two countries.

With Russian control of Armenia's energy sector, major industrial concerns, and supply of arms, Russia can now take Armenia for granted. This factor may be more important in any future solution to the problem of Karabakh than all the love that can be exchanged between some Russian and Armenian intellectuals and political pundits. Thus for Russia, too, taken individually, Azerbaijan is more important than Armenia, and certainly Turkey is more significant. At this point, one can also argue that Georgia is more important to Russia than Armenia. Once Armenia is taken for granted, it is Georgia that will hold the key, as far as Russia is concerned, to the future of the region, since Azerbaijan depends on Georgia to make its resources count.

The South Caucasus is strategically important for the United States because it borders Turkey, Iran, Russia, and the Caspian Sea. But this is an interest in the region, not necessarily in Armenia, and the United States can and possibly has resolved its problems through Georgia and Azerbaijan. Of the countries in the region taken individually, Azerbaijan is important because of its reserves of and proximity to hydrocarbon resources. From the point of view of the transport of these resources, Iran would have made more sense than any other route but the United States has blocked that route. The rest are a series of tactical decisions; moving those resources through Armenia would have been less expensive, but that is not essential. Georgia too can move Caspian oil and gas to Turkey.

Finally, the war against terrorism and the campaign against the proliferation of weapons of mass destruction may be considered important items on the contemporary American foreign policy agenda by which Washington assesses the significance other countries have for it. While they do not constitute principles of world organization, they do determine aspects of today's international relations. Very quickly after September 11, 2001, that war became part of the American drive to manage, if not reshape, the world security architecture, among other goals. Given its size and homogeneous population, Armenia has virtually no significance with respect to the fight against international terrorism.

As for the issue of proliferation of weapons of mass destruction, Armenia faces two problems. The first is the nuclear power plant and nuclear technology know-how. Armenia has a policy of full transparency and the Medzamor Plant is under the regular observation of the International Agency for Atomic Energy. While there have been some concerns regarding transfer to Iran of scientific knowledge that might assist that country in the area of biological and chemical weapons development, these concerns have been addressed. Nonetheless, in such a context, Armenia is a subject of observation rather than a significant contributor in the active battle against them.

From the point of view of the United States, it would be better if Armenia followed the Georgian and Azerbaijani drive towards NATO and the American orbit. Given the mounting tensions between the Unites States and Iran in the post Iraq war context, Washington would like to see Armenia minimize its relations with and decrease its dependence on Iran. To achieve this goal, the Bush administration has renewed its pressure on Ankara to settle its problems and establish normal relations with Armenia. Expressed good wishes on all parts notwithstanding, it is doubtful that such a breakthrough can be achieved, considering the multitude of obstacles in the two countries. The United States will probably be satisfied with a decent level of cooperation by Armenia and non-disruption of American designs in Azerbaijan and the region, whether out of its own ambitions or as a substitute for force for Russia. In return for not creating problems, Washington would be willing to tolerate the inadequate state of affairs as far as democracy and human rights are concerned.

The United States and Russia are still exploring the limits and potential of their cooperation, including in the South Caucasus. While the South Caucasus is one of the last regions where a new Cold War is playing a determining role, nonetheless the differences in the security and foreign policy outlooks between the three South Caucasus republics do not seem to be the kind that have given Armenia, at least, any advantages. The maneuvering room that Armenia has may be the result of its insignificance rather than any strength it has for either. The two million-strong Armenian community in Russia was unable—apparently even unwilling—to stop the factories- and Medzamor-for-debt debacle; just as the one million-strong Armenian community in the United States, endowed with a formidable lobbying capability, was not able to stop the Bush administration from lifting whatever had remained of the Freedom Support Act, Section 907 sanctions against Azerbaijan. Should the U.S.-Russian competition in the region turn into a serious antagonism, Armenia will play an important role in the strengthening of the north-south axis involving Russia and Iran that would counter the U.S.-driven west-east axis that involves Turkey, Georgia, Azerbaijan, and Central Asia. However, at this point Russia is positioning itself more in line with U.S. concerns. Even in Iran there are voices that do not see relations with the United States in ideological terms. One should not assume that even in the case of worsening relations between the United States and Russia that any increase in Armenia's strategic significance will be beneficial to Armenia.

The most important strategic value assigned to Armenia has been its role as the buffer between Turkey and the rest of the Turkic world: Azerbaijan and Central Asia, which means Armenia's 42 km border with Iran, the Meghri district in the south of Armenia. The more one fears Pan-Turkism, the more strategic significance this border assumes. In the early 1990s, immediately following the dissolution of the Soviet Union, Turkey labored to fill the vacuum left by Russia by relying on its linguistic and ethnic affinities with Azerbaijan and Central Asian republics. The United States encouraged Turkey in this endeavor as a proxy for its own designs, promoting Turkey as a model of a Muslim society with a secular regime and Western orientation. Thus it became a matter of American interest to see continuity and homogenization of policy in the region; and if a sense of ethnic solidarity among Turkic states could contribute to the acceptance by states in the region of foreign and security policies defined by American strategic interests, then the United States was willing to foster such a sense. Turkey developed ambitious plans to provide economic support and to export nation-building mechanisms. But that still did not constitute Pan-Turkism as traditionally conceived. Turkey was unable to deliver on its promises and the newly independent Muslim-populated republics, including Azerbaijan, were not ready to replace Russian domination with a new big brother. Traditional-style Pan-Turkism did raise its head too, but only within particular political groups in Turkey without becoming state policy.

Nonetheless, Turkey supported Azerbaijan diplomatically, politically, technically, and, in a limited manner, militarily in the Karabakh conflict. Armenians perceived the refusal of Turkey to establish relations with Armenia in support of Azerbaijan as a remnant of Pan-Turkism—for some groups that was a harbinger of things to come.

Thus, in the context of American and Turkish interests in the region, Armenia by its geography did appear again as a spoiler of a connection between Turkey and Azerbaijan. That may explain the American and Turkish enthusiasm for a land swap-based solution to the Karabakh problem discussed by the presidents of Armenia and Azerbaijan between 1999 and 2002, involving the Meghri district or parts of it, in some form or another. Under the circumstances, the formula had no chance of success. Few in Armenia were ready to lose any part of the republic, especially the country's common border with Iran, and give Turkey a land connection to Azerbaijan, even in return for Karabakh. Some Karabakh leaders too had doubts about the wisdom of such a solution. Iran opposed it vehemently. And Russia's formal position regarding such a solution, that it would respect any agreement reached by the two presidents, could not be taken seriously.

But concerns about pan-Turkism in any of its manifestations are not the driving force behind the day-to-day policies of countries around Armenia. These concerns do not seem to stop Russia or Iran from having normal relations with Turkey and Azerbaijan and compete for their business and favors. In addition, American ability to project its power directly and the possibility of a change in Iranian-American relations may make Meghri less of a geostrategic factor in the future. Besides, Turkey can and is bypassing Armenia's small territory to link up with Azerbaijan through Georgia and to some extent through Iran.

In the spring of 2003 the United States stepped up efforts to activate the loose group known as GUUAM (Georgia, Ukraine, Uzbekistan, Azerbaijan, and Moldova), initially described as an economic cooperation effort but increasingly assigned defense and strategic significance. Assurances to the contrary notwithstanding, GUUAM is seen by Washington and the member states as a factor against Russian influence in the region. Given tensions between Washington and Ankara following the 2003 war in Iraq, GUUAM may even end up performing some of the functions that in earlier times might have been assigned to Turkey. Even if Azerbaijan had no objections, it is difficult to imagine Armenia being part of the group, given its close association with Russia. American strategists will have to decide if whether for their designs in the region to succeed, local antagonisms—Armenia and Azerbaijan, Armenia and Turkey—must be resolved or just mitigated.

Armenia's current foreign policy reflects two conflicting strains. The first is based on the assertion that the country has strategic significance, that it is part of important world processes, that it is engaged in active diplomacy on many fronts, and that it has been successful in achieving political and economic reforms commensurate with its international commitments. At some point, during Kocharian's administration, Armenia has even offered its services to mediate in regional conflicts and antagonisms, as proof of its international standing. The second strain, now gaining strength, is that Armenia is self-contained and is best left alone, except for what the world and its neighbors owe it due to history.

Each of these directions is based on different assumptions with regard to mutual obligations between Armenia, its neighbors, international organizations, and the world community at large. In addition to the fact that these two strains are in conflict, the non-resolution of the Karabakh problem undermines both of them. In the case of the first, lofty principles and bold assertions will remain hollow-sounding without normalization of relations with Azerbaijan and Turkey, the actual participation in integrative processes, and qualitatively significant economic and political development. In the case of the isolationist trend, reliance on one or two states will become the norm, and Armenia will still have to come to terms with what its neighbors and the international community think Armenia owes them, i.e., a resolution of the conflict.

It is obvious that to count on U.S.-Russian or traditional regional antagonisms to achieve any strategic significance is, at best, a very risky business. The character of international relations has changed and new rules are being made up as Washington determines the form and degree of the projection of its power. To play by the old rules only means making oneself irrelevant at best, vulnerable to external manipulation, at worst. More than ever, foreign policy in a country like Armenia requires a clear and real definition of national interests to guide one through uncharted territory.

The United States will look at the region and find the friends it needs, and it has; and Russia will have to come to terms with the other two republics in the region. Additionally, to count on historic enmities between Armenia's neighbors to create room for maneuvering is much more than dangerous. It is outright irresponsible. In the context of the three major worldwide trends outlined above, one can see Georgian-Turkish relations expanding everyday, Georgian-Azerbaijani relations deepening with every project, Azerbaijani-Iranian relations improving with every official visit, and Iranian-Turkish relations displaying signs of maturity difficult to reverse. The only problem in the region is between Russia and Georgia. Even there, one can see a very cautious approach on both sides.

For some Russian thinkers Armenia's significance lies in its ability to create problems for Azerbaijan and Georgia, to make sure that they do not go too far in the wrong direction. According to this logic, Azerbaijan can be kept weak by the non-resolution of the Karabakh conflict, while Georgia can be checked through Armenia, which is in a position to exploit the tensions in Javakhk or Javakheti, the Armenian populated region in southern Georgia bordering Armenia. The assumption is that it is in Armenia's interest to have both neighbors remain weak, unstable, and unsettled. This is not the first time that opinion leaders functioned in the twilight zone of permanent and blissful confusion between ideological tenets and strategic interests. Whether this is actual Russian policy or not—it is not all that clear that many Russian officials would agree with this assessment—it is obvious that assuming strategic significance as the spoiler would be at the cost of Armenia itself remaining economically weak and politically unstable, less resourceful in the settlement of the Karabakh conflict, a pariah in the world community, and a troublemaker for its neighbors, the same neighbors with whom Russia itself will end up with very good relations, as it has always done in the past.

The Armenian Diaspora has often been presented as a strategic asset for Armenia. As the past decade has shown, Diasporan investment in Armenia, while significant, has failed to compensate for the absence of major international investment in the country. All nationalistic rhetoric and love of homeland aside, the Diasporan mentality is such that its support—whether humanitarian or in the form of investments—increases when Armenia's standing is high in the international community, especially in the host countries. And, as events have shown, the Armenian Diaspora too has been unable to play a significant role in defining or redefining issues in a manner that gives Armenia new strategic value. The largest and wealthiest communities reside in Russia, France, and the United States. These three countries also happen to co-chair the OSCE Minsk group mediating the Karabakh conflict. Yet this has made little difference in the way these three perceive the resolution of that conflict. The fact that Armenia may benefit from the presence of Diasporan communities in these countries does not give Armenia strategic significance; at best, it gives Armenians domestic significance in the host countries. Such presence or lobbying may facilitate some assistance to Armenia or compel policymakers in the host countries to speak softly regarding Armenia and have its diplomats spend time with the community in order to explain their policies or even neutralize community opposition to such policies. But Armenian lobbying hardly alters the strategic interests or visions of host countries. Furthermore, whatever meaning it may have in other arenas, the Diaspora's Genocide recognition agenda and the adoption of that issue by the second Armenian administration of independent Armenia as part of its foreign policy agenda in 1998 constitutes a mere nuisance to many of the host countries, at best, and limits Armenia's agenda options and makes Armenia and Armenians vulnerable to external manipulation, at worst.

Is It Good to Have Strategic Significance?

Whether due to one's geographic position or one's resources—natural or otherwise—a country's strategic significance derives from the assessment and needs others have. Whether a state is trying to manage its significance, increase it or reduce it, it has to have a foreign policy that serves the adopted goal, a policy that creates options, while avoiding dramatic consequences. Clearly one cannot live in isolation and antagonism, in contrast to larger trends, and expect to have or create options.

Where is Armenia and where are Armenians today compared to two thousand and five hundred or more years ago, having once been strategically important for so many empires, powers, and superpowers? How has Armenia managed its significance and status in the past? These questions are not inspired by nostalgia for a glorified or idealized past. On the contrary, they constitute an invitation to an objective inquiry into how those in positions of decision-making for Armenia have managed the country's resources and advantages. The past cannot be brought in only to justify what some want to believe and say today; and policies today cannot be based on a mere reiteration of ancient formulas, tired moralistic judgments, or on what makes people feel good and rightful.

Even at the risk of oversimplification, one would have to admit that Armenia's record on the subject is not encouraging. Armenia is now a tenth of the Armenia some time ago, 29,000 square kilometers today versus the historic 300,000; a population of one million in the tenth century, the same as England at the time, and still only two or three million in Armenia today, while the process of diasporization that started in the eighth century continues. It appears that historically, when others decided that Armenia was important to them, they managed to solve their problem at considerable expense to Armenia.

Of course, history is not that simple. Sometimes those in a position to make decisions could only try to minimize the impending damage; sometimes they were overwhelmed. Yet in many cases it was a question of correctly assessing or creating options; sometimes those claiming the right to lead the land and the people confused dynastic, feudal, commercial, and, in modern times, partisan or ideologized perspectives with the larger interests. The fact that many of these processes were caused or enhanced by events beyond Armenia's control may only reinforce the judgment that it might not have been such a propitious thing to have been at the crossroads of anything. It is also true that many of these events had similar impacts on other societies. But neither of these arguments absolve those who spoke and made decisions in the name of Armenia and Armenians—whether emperor, king, prince, cleric, merchant, or political party leader—from the responsibility they bear in the history of Armenia and Armenians. These changes could not have happened only as a result of external forces. After all, Armenians have to decide that either they are part of history—that they often had options and made decisions and must, therefore, assume responsibility for the consequences of these decisions—or that they have only been victims of larger forces and therefore what they thought and decided is irrelevant. Unfortunately, many are those who prefer to believe that Armenia's misfortunes were caused by two kinds of powers: those that wished ill for Armenia and those that promised to do good but then reneged on their promises. These are the leaders and opinion-makers today who are likely to think that hating the first group and convincing the second not to repeat their moral sin constitutes the only strategy for Armenia, a strategy they think is vindicated by history. It is possible, of course, to draw lessons from history that avoid the mistakes of the past rather than legitimize them by repeating them.

At this point Armenia does not seem to have more than a minor role at best in any of the major trends in world affairs. Armenia has been unable to benefit from any advantages its geographic position at the crossroads of continents and seas offer, advantages shared by others; and it has managed to maximize the disadvantages of being a landlocked country. Current Armenian foreign and security policy has failed to create options that strengthen its ability to make sovereign decisions vital to its national interest; instead, Armenia is again becoming a mere dependency of one country, which increasingly and once again, is taking Armenia for granted. Once more, then, it will resolve its problems at Armenia's expense.

This last point is lost to those who look at this situation and find reason to rejoice. Let the world occupy itself with other things, they maintain, and maybe it will forget and leave Armenia alone, especially when Armenians now control Nagorno Karabakh and seven Azerbaijani districts; maybe the world will forget it all, they argue, and Armenia will come out of this current situation keeping everything. The absence of relations with two of four neighbors and the lack of participation in any regional or international integration is not a high price to pay, they would argue, to keep the status quo with regard to the Nagorno Karabakh conflict. For them isolation is a tactical weapon.

In fact, there are even those who perceive regional or international cooperation or integration as a form of loss of sovereignty, character, and power. For such groups isolation seems to be a strategic weapon. And still for others the absence of relations with Azerbaijan and Turkey is a positive fact; after all, the argument goes, these two could overwhelm Armenia economically and Armenia would be in danger, as if some day by some magic Turkey and Azerbaijan will cease to be neighbors of Armenia. Such groups have adopted isolation as an ideology.

To expect the world and neighbors to forget the Karabakh conflict and its consequences is to seek refuge in wishful thinking. Peoples have not and do not forget their losses and neither does the international community. Both Russia and the United States, along with the rest of the international community, reject the maximalist position that Armenia and Karabakh have taken regarding the solution to the conflict. Both countries have insisted on the principle of the territorial integrity for Azerbaijan. At best, Armenia is maintaining what it had at the time of the cease-fire in 1994; for some that means having the upper hand. In fact, though, maintenance is not sufficient if the other side is gaining. In time the Karabakh conflict will become a nuisance even to supporters and, in the absence of a negotiated solution based on compromise, a solution will be imposed on a weakened and less sovereign Armenia, again at Armenia's expense.

Regardless, wittingly or unwittingly, Armenia's foreign policy has resulted in a form of self-imposed isolation, an isolation that is leading to economic, political, and strategic strangulation. Armenia's neighbors, meanwhile, are intensifying their relations in every respect and in all possible directions. Armenia's "enemies" are gaining advantages it may not be able to overcome. The same Turkey that some consider an eternal enemy and a hopeless despotism is working hard to become a member of the European Union, a membership that means ceding some of its sovereignty and accepting compromises on otherwise important issues for Turkey, such as the way it governs itself and the Cyprus question.

Cooperation and integration do provide new opportunities; while they may subtract something from the conventional definitions of borders and sovereignty, they do add to a country's field of action and influence, as well as opportunities to expand the area where its policies and views count.

Armenia and Armenians must decide whether Armenia is part of this region, with its history and its realities, or is a country misplaced by some dark and evil force and must, therefore, shield itself from its neighbors near and far, but especially those near. The instincts of preservation and the siege mentality are deeply rooted in the Armenian collective psychology, for understandable reasons. In fact, the current policies of some neighbors have only encouraged those instincts. But reactions to integration or regional cooperation, in their old and new versions, are making it difficult to separate the social-psychological dimension from the political-strategic one.

Armenia seems to be deeply and dangerously alienated from the region in which it is condemned or blessed to be and from the processes that are driving the policies and motivations of its neighbors. The price of preserving the status quo may be repeating the historical cycle. Although it is not the only reason, Armenia is seen as the main reason for the lack of cooperation among the three South Caucasus republics: Georgia, Azerbaijan, and Armenia. At the end of the day, that cooperation is the best guarantee for the independence, sovereignty, and genuine economic progress of the peoples of the region.

Strategic significance is not an end in and by itself; it is not a matter of glory and self-importance. The purpose of strategy and of strategic significance is to ensure long-term security and to use and benefit from regional and international conjunctions to improve the social, economic, and political health of the citizens, individually and collectively. Armenia still has a vibrant population and a remarkably brilliant new generation. But they need more than charity and sympathy or wholesale condemnation; they need to make progress individually and collectively: human, economic, social, and political. Blaming the people for the mistakes of their elected or self-appointed leaders or accusing them of unwillingness to compromise is misplacing responsibility. Progress and real, long-term security are not possible without peace with one's neighbors as well as progress and stability in neighboring countries, especially given Armenia's geography. That is the political and historic responsibility of today's leaders.

Glossary of Terms

Abdul Hamid II: The Ottoman Sultan (1876-1909) considered responsible for the Armenian massacres of 1894-96. In 1908 the Young Turk revolution forced him to reinstate the Ottoman Constitution of 1876. He was deposed in 1909 when he tried to plot a counterrevolution and was succeeded by his brother, Muhammad V.

ADL: See Armenian Democratic Liberal Party.

ADLA: See Armenian Democratic Liberal Party of Armenia.

Alishan, Ghevond: A scholar, historian, poet, and member of the Mekhitarist Armenian Catholic order (1820-1901). His pioneering works on history, ethnography, and geography, as well as his patriotic poetry, had a major influence on young Armenian students for generations.

Aliyev, Haydar: The president of Azerbaijan since 1993. Aliyev was the first secretary of the Central Committee of the Azerbaijan Communist Party (1969-1982) and a member of the Political Bureau of the Central Committee of the Communist Party of the Soviet Union.

Amira: A title for Armenians belonging to the upper social class in the Ottoman Empire composed largely of moneylenders, high-level bureaucrats, and a few other influential families prominent until the 1800s.

ANM: See Armenian National Movement.

Ararktsian, Babken: A member of the Karabakh Committee, later president of Armenia's National Assembly until 1998, and a close associate of President Levon Ter-Petrossian. In 1998 he founded the civic organization *Armat* (root).

ARF: See Armenian Revolutionary Federation.

Armenakan Party: One of the first Armenian political organizations in the Ottoman Empire, founded in 1885 in Van.

Armenian Democratic Liberal Party: The ADL was founded in Egypt in 1908 and reorganized in 1921. Based on upper- and middle-class elements, it was committed to the free enterprise system and its mission was to offer Armenians an alternative to the revolutionary, socialistic parties.

Armenian Democratic Liberal Party of Armenia: A sister organization of the Armenian Democratic Liberal Party operating in Armenia.

Armenian National Movement: A political party based on the Karabakh Committee and encompassing a variety of minor groups (1989); the governing party in Armenia from 1990-1998.

Armenian Revolutionary Federation (ARF, Dashnaktsutiune): A dominant Armenian political party founded in 1890 in Tbilisi. The party had a socialist agenda with a focus on the liberation of Western (Ottoman) Armenia, and was also active in Russian Armenia.

Armenian Secret Army for the Liberation of Armenia: A militant Armenian group formed in the early 1980s in Lebanon. The group called for armed struggle to force Turkey to recognize the Armenian Genocide and cede territory to Armenians. Some of its members were also active in the war in Karabakh.

Armeno-Tatar clashes: A series of ethnic clashes in 1905-07 between the Armenian and the Tatar (Turkish/Azeri) population of the Caucasus.

ASALA: See Armenian Secret Army for the Liberation of Armenia.

Badalian, Sergey: The first secretary of the CPA, one of the small communist parties in Armenia. Badalian was a candidate for the presidential elections in 1996 and 1998.

Bagratian, Hrand: A prime minister of Armenia (1993-1996), responsible for the radical economic reforms in the new Republic. He founded his own party, *Azatutyun* (freedom), when replaced following the 1996 presidential elections.

Balayan, Zori: A writer and an ecological activist. Born in Karabakh, he was one of the communist intellectuals who first raised the Karabakh unification issue in 1987 and remains active.

Baku-Tbilisi-Ceyhan pipeline: See Main Export Pipeline.

Black Sea Economic Cooperation Organization: An organization established in 1992 as a Turkish initiative, involving the countries around or neighboring the Black Sea, including Armenia.

Bleyan, Ashot: Once a member of the ANM, Bleyan founded his own party, *Nor Ughi* (New Path). Bleyan was the deputy mayor of Yerevan and minister of education during the Ter-Petrossian administration.

BSEC: See Black Sea Economic Cooperation Organization.

BTC: See Main Export Pipeline.

Buro: The highest executive body of the ARF. The Buro is elected by the party's World Congress and usually has a tenure of four years.

Catholicos: Supreme head of the Armenian Church elected for life. The Armenian Church has two catholicoses, the catholicos of All Armenians in Etchmiadzin and catholicos of the Great House of Cilicia, now seated in Antelias, Lebanon.

Catholicossate of Cilicia: One of the two main Sees of the Armenian Church. Originally established in the medieval Armenian kingdom of Cilicia, the See moved from the city of Sis (Cilicia) to Antelias (a suburb of Beirut) after the Genocide. During the Cold War, the House of Cilicia was dominated by ARF sympathizers and was used to balance the influence of the Soviet-dominated Catholicossate of Etchmiadzin.

Catholicossate of Etchmiadzin: The original and historic seat of the Armenian Apostolic Church. The catholicoses of Etchmiadzin have the title "Catholicos (patriarch) of All Armenians."

Cilicia: District of Southwestern Anatolia, on the northeastern corner of the Mediterranean coast. In the eleventh through fourteenth centuries, an Armenian state flourished there. Until the First World War it was a region with a strong Armenian presence.

CIS: See Commonwealth of Independent States.

Committee of Union and Progress: One of the most influential of the Young Turks groups. The CUP took control of the Ottoman Empire before the outbreak of World War I. The decision to enter the war on the German side proved costly and led to the downfall of the empire. The leadership of the CUP was responsible for the planning and execution of the Armenian Genocide.

Commonwealth of Independent States: A loose association comprising the former Soviet republics (except for the Baltic States).

Communist Party of Armenia: One of the successor parties of the Soviet-era Communist Party still active in Armenia.

CPA: See Communist Party of Armenia.

CUP: See Committee of Union and Progress.

Dashnaktsutiune: See Armenian Revolutionary Federation.

Demirjian, Karen: First secretary of the Communist Party of Armenia (1975-1988). Demirjian resigned in 1988 but returned to active politics in 1998 as a presidential candidate. Having formed his own People's Party of Armenia (PPA), he took part in the parliamentary elections, he was elected president of the National Assembly in 1999, and was assassinated, along with other leaders, in October of the same year.

Demirjian, Stepan: The son of Karen Demirjian, who took over the People's Party of Armenia after his father's assassination and opposed Robert Kocharian in the 2003 presidential elections.

Democratic Party of Armenia: An offshoot of the Armenian Communist Party of the Soviet period, founded by Aram Sargsian in 1991.

DPA: See Democratic Party of Armenia.

Droshak: The official publication of the ARF Buro, published, with some interruptions, since 1890.

Enver Pasha: A Turkish general, one of the leaders of the Committee of Union and Progress (Ittihad ve Terakke, CUP), and minister of war from 1914-1918.

Erzerum: Formerly Karin, present-day capital of Erzerum province in Turkey. The city was important for the history of Armenian culture and revolutionary activities.

First Armenian Republic: The short-lived Republic (1918-1920) that reinstated Armenian statehood in the Russian-dominated part of historic Armenia.

Galstian, Hambartzum: One of the founders of the Karabakh Committee, later mayor of Yerevan. He drifted away from the ANM and became a businessman. Galstian was assassinated in December 1994.

Gevorkian Seminary: The ecclesiastical seminary of the Cathedral of Etchmiadzin. Along with the Nersisian School, it became one of the centers that prepared numerous Armenian scholars, intellectuals, and clerics.

Gorbachev, Mikhail: A statesman, general secretary of the Communist Party Central Committee and president of the USSR (1985-1991), who carried out radical reforms before the collapse of the USSR.

Harutiunian, Gagik: The former head of the Armenian CP's Department of Social and Economic Affairs, under the ANM administration he served as deputy chairman of the Supreme Soviet, vice president of the Republic and, since 1995, president of the Constitutional Court.

Hay Heghapokhakan Dashnaktsutiune: See Armenian Revolutionary Federation.

Hayastani Ramkavar Azatakan Gusagtsutiune: See Armenian Liberal Democratic Party of Armenia.

Hayots Hamazgayin Sharzhum: See Armenian National Movement.

Hayrikian, Paruyr: A Soviet Armenian dissident who was exiled from the Soviet Union for his political activities by Gorbachev after serving seventeen years in prison. He was a presidential candidate in Armenia during the 1991 elections and later became the presidential advisor on human rights issues to President Robert Kocharian.

Hnchak: The official newspaper (1887-1915) of the Social Democratic Hnchakian Party (SDHP).

Hnchakian Party: See Social Democratic Hnchakian Party.

Hoja: A title used in the Ottoman Empire meaning master.

Ittihad ve Terakke: See Committee of Union and Progress.

Jemal Pasha: The minister of Navy of the Ottoman Empire, military leader and one of the leaders of the Committee of Union and Progress, who held a variety of civil and military positions. A member of the triumvirate held responsible for the Genocide, Jemal was assassinated by Armenians in Tbilisi in 1922.

Kaputikian, Sylva: A poet and a political activist. For a brief period, she was one of the Armenian representatives on the Karabakh issue during the early days of the movement in 1998.

Karabakh Committee: A group of Armenian intellectuals formed the Karabakh Committee in 1988 to lead the popular movement supporting the reunification of Nagorno Karabakh with Armenia. In the spring of 1989 they transformed the group into the Armenian National Movement (ANM), which became the dominant party in Armenia until 1998.

Kars and Ardahan: Two districts on the Turkish-Russian border that became part of the Russian Empire in 1878 and were relinquished to Turkey in 1921.

Kelbajar: An Azerbaijani district between Nagorno Karabakh and Armenia occupied by Armenian forces in 1993.

Khanjian, Aghassi: The popular first secretary of Armenia's Communist Party from 1930 to 1936. He was killed during the Stalinist purges in 1936.

Khrimian, Mkrtich: Affectionately known as *Hayrik* (Father), he championed the cause of the rural population and the poor in Western Armenia; Armenian patriarch of Constantinople (1869-1873), prelate of Van (1880-1885), and catholicos of all Armenians (1892-1907). A writer, newspaper editor, and political leader, he led the Armenian delegation to the Congress of Berlin (1878).

Kocharian, Robert: One of the leaders of Nagorno Karabakh, elected the first president of the Nagorno Karabakh Republic in 1994.

In 1997, he became prime minister of Armenia and succeeded Levon Ter-Petrossian as president in 1998.

Main Export Pipeline: A pipeline designed to transport Azerbaijani and Caspian oil through Georgia to the Turkish-Mediterranean port of Ceyhan.

Manucharian, Ashot: A member of the Karabakh Committee, later senior national security adviser to President Ter-Petrossian until 1993. Considered close to Russian interests, Manucharian became one of the founders of Civic Union of Scientists and Industrialists (CUSCI) and political secretary of Socialist Armenia Association and the leader of National Accord Front, opposed to Kocharian.

Manukian, Vazgen: A leader of the Karabakh Committee and ANM, Manukian became the first prime minister of independent Armenia (1990-91). Following his resignation, he founded the National Democratic Union (NDU) party and ran against Ter-Petrossian in the presidential elections of 1996 as the unity candidate of the opposition. He remains active in Armenia's politics.

Medzamor: The site of Armenia's Soviet-made nuclear power plant closed after the 1988 earthquake and reopened in 1994 because of the energy crisis.

Mekhitarists: A Congregation of Catholic Armenian scholar monks founded in 1717 by Abbot Mekhitar in Venice, on St. Lazarus Island. A dissenting group in the nineteenth century founded a separate monastery in Vienna. The Mekhitarists were instrumental in bringing about an Armenian cultural renaissance.

Meliks: The last remnants of Armenian nobility in Eastern Armenia, who tried to regain their independence in the early eighteenth century and retained their autonomy until the end of the eighteenth century.

MEP: See Main Export Pipeline.

Miasnikian, Alexander: One of the first Armenian communist leaders. He was sent to Armenia by Lenin to mollify anti-communist sentiments immediately following the Sovietization of the Republic.

Mikayelian, Kristapor: One of the founders and ideologues of the ARF. He was killed while planning the assassination of Sultan Abdul Hamid II.

Millet: The Ottoman system of extraterritorial self-management granted to non-Muslim minorities headed by their religious leaders.

Movsisian, Vladimir: The former first secretary of the Communist Party of Armenia. He subsequently served as head of the State Agency for Refugees, minister of agriculture, and provincial governor during the Ter-Petrossian administration.

Muratian, Igor: An intellectual and vocal supporter of Karabakh's reunification with Armenia in late 1980s; member of the first Karabakh Committee.

Mush: A city in southeastern Turkey that had a large Armenian population until 1915, intimately involved in the revolutionary movement.

Nagorno Karabakh (NK): Part of the Artsakh province of historic Armenia, during the Soviet period NK had the status of an autonomous region within Azerbaijan. That status was challenged by the Karabakh movement beginning in 1988, resulting in a military confrontation that ended in 1994 with NK achieving the facto independence from Azerbaijan. The conflict remains unresolved.

Nakhichevan: An Azerbaijani autonomous republic enclosed between Armenia, Iran, and Turkey. Nakhichevan was once part of historic Armenia and populated by Armenians, whose last remnants left in 1988.

National Democratic Union: A political party in Armenia founded in 1991 by Vazgen Manukian and Davit Vardanian, when they split from the ANM.

National Self-Determination Union: A political party founded by Paruyr Hayrikian in 1987.

Nazarbek, Avetis: Russian-Armenian activist who, along with his wife Maro Vardanian, helped found the Hnchakian Party, SDHP.

NDU: See National Democratic Union.

New Path (Nor Ughi): A political party founded by Ktrich Sardarian and Ashot Bleyan. It was an offshoot of the ANM and called for securing guarantees for the human and political rights of Karabakh Armenians and to leave Karabakh within Azerbaijan.

Nor Ughi: See New Path.

NKR: See Nagorno Karabakh.

NSDU: See National Self-Determination Union.

Organization for Security and Cooperation in Europe: An organization initiated in 1973 as the Conference on Security and Cooperation in Europe (CSCE) for the purpose of establishing a security dialogue between the Western and Soviet blocs. In 1992 the organization assumed responsibility for mediation in the Karabakh conflict through the Minsk Conference, later known as the Minsk Group process.

OSCE: See Organization for Security and Cooperation in Europe.

Ottoman Armenia: See Vilayets.

Pantukhts: A term used for migrant workers who left Western Armenia for Istanbul and other major cities to make a living working in the lowest menial labor positions.

Pashtpan Hayreniats (Defenders of the Fatherland): One of the earliest Armenian political organizations, founded in Erzerum in 1881.

Patriarchate of Istanbul: One of the four major centers of the Armenian Church (the others being the Armenian Patriarchate of Jerusalem and the Catholicossates of Etchmiadzin and Cilicia), established by the Ottoman government in the sixteenth century to accommodate the millet system. The patriarch of Istanbul was in charge of all the Armenians in the Ottoman Empire. The Patriarchate continues to function until today.

Portukalian, Mkrtich: Teacher, journalist and political thinker. Exiled by the Ottoman government in 1885, he founded the newspaper *Armenia* in Marseilles, France. In 1885, inspired from his political teaching, a group of his students founded the first Armenian political party, the Armenakan Party in Van.

Ramkavar Azatakan Kusaktsutiune: See Armenian Liberal Democratic Party.

Rayah: Literally meaning "flock," it was used to designate the non-Muslim population of the Ottoman Empire.

Sargsian, Aram: The founder and chairman of the Democratic Party of Armenia (DPA), which has a communist orientation. Sargsian ran for presidential elections several times without much success.

Sargsian Aram: Briefly prime minister of Armenia after the assassination of his brother, Vazgen Sargsian, in 1999; still active in politics.

Sargsian, Vazgen: Second tier ANM leader, founder of the armed forces of independent Armenia and the Yerkrapahs, minister of defense and later prime minister. He was assassinated in the Armenian parliament, along with other leaders of the Republic, in October 1999.

Sarraf: A title given to moneylenders in the Ottoman Empire. The sarrafs were mostly either from the Armenian or Jewish communities.

Sasun: An Armenian district situated in Southeastern Anatolia. Sasun rebelled several times against the Ottomans (the most prominent uprisings being the ones in 1894 and 1904) and had the reputation for being the home of courageous and proud people.

SDHP: See Social Democratic Hnchakian Party.

Shahnazarian, Davit: A second tier ANM leader, Shahnazarian became presidential adviser, special negotiator and minister of security under President Ter-Petrossian, until 1995. He later founded his own party, "21st Century," but rejoined the ANM in 2002.

Shevardnadze, Edward: Leader and president of Georgia since 1993. He was the foreign minister of the USSR under Gorbachev. Shevardnadze was a member of the Political Bureau of the Central Committee of the Communist Party of the Soviet Union.

Shushi: A historical Armenian urban center of Karabakh situated on a mountain plateau, 10 km from Stepanakert, populated largely by Azerbaijanis during the Soviet period and taken by Karabakh forces in May 1992.

Siradeghian, Vano: A member of the Karabakh Committee and later president of the ANM, minister of interior, and mayor of Yerevan under Ter-Petrossian.

Social Democratic Hnchakian Party: The first full-fledged Armenian political party, founded in 1887 in Geneva with a socialist agenda, the party was active in the Ottoman Armenia. Despite the various splits within the organization, the party continues to be active in the Diaspora and less so in Armenia.

Srvantstiants, Garegin: A clergyman, writer, ethnographer, and student of Khrimian.

Stepanakert: The capital city of the Nagorno Karabakh. The city is named Stepanakert in honor of Stephan Shahumian, one of the Bolshevik leaders in the Caucasus.

Sumgait: An industrial city in Azerbaijan, 25 km northwest of Baku. It became a gloomy symbol for Armenians since February 1988, when Azerbaijani mobs committed anti-Armenian pogroms. Many were killed and almost all of the remaining Armenian inhabitants fled.

Talat Pasha: The secretary general of the Committee of Union and Progress (CUP) in 1912, minister of interior and grand vizier in the Ottoman government. One of the triumvirate responsible for the Genocide, Talat was assassinated in 1921 by an Armenian.

Ter-Petrossian, Levon: An Armenian scholar and statesman, one of the leaders of the Karabakh Committee and one of the founders of the Armenian National Movement (ANM). In 1991, he became the first popularly elected president of Armenia and led the Republic until his resignation in 1998.

Turkish Armenia: See Vilayets.

Van: A city populated mostly by Armenians up until 1917, situated on the eastern shore of Lake Van in Southeastern Anatolia. Van became one of the centers of Armenian revolutionary activities. At the time of the Armenian Genocide of 1915, it also became a center of Armenian resistance.

Vilayets: Literally means administrative divisions within the Ottoman Empire. In an Armenian historical context, it refers to the six eastern vilayets of the Ottoman Empire: Erzerum, Van, Bitlis, Diarbakir, Harput (Mamuret-ul-Aziz), and Sivas, where most Armenians lived.

Western Armenia: See Vilayets.

Yerkrapahs (Homeland Defenders): An organization of veterans from the early confrontations with Azerbaijan, founded in 1995 by Defense Minister Vazgen Sargsian.

Zeytun: An Armenian district in the Taurus Mountains of Cilicia, where a degree of autonomy continued until the end of the nineteenth century, and known in Armenian history for its resistance to Ottoman centralization through arms.

Bibliography of Modern Armenian History

General History

Aghayan, Ds. P. et al., eds. 8 vols. *Hay zhoghovrdi patmutiune* [History of the Armenian People]. Yerevan, 1967-1981.

Bournoutian, George A. *A Concise History of the Armenian People*. Costa Mesa, CA: Mazda Publishers Inc., 2002.

Hovannisian, Richard G., ed. 2 vols. *The Armenian People: From Ancient to Modern Times*. New York: St. Martin's Press, 1997.

Walker, Christopher. *Armenia: The Survival of a Nation*. Palgrave, 1990.

Nineteenth and Twentieth Centuries

Aghayan, Ds. P. *Hayastane 1801-1870 tvakannerin* [Armenia during the years 1801-1870]. Yerevan, 1974.

———. *Hay Zhoghovrdi Azatagrakan paykari patmutiunits* [Of the History of the Liberation Struggle of the Armenian People]. Yerevan, 1976.

Ajemian, Hayk. *Hayots Hayrik*. Tiflis, 1929.

Allen, W.E.D. and Muratoff, P. *Caucasian Battlefields: A History of the Wars on the Turco-Caucasian Border, 1828-1921*. Cambridge UK: Cambridge University Press, 1953.

Ananun, D. *Rusahayeri hasarakakan zargatsume* [The social development of Russian Armenians] vol. 1 (1800-1870) and vol. 2 (1870-1900). Etchmiadzin, 1916, 1922.

Aramian, Dj. *Zeytuntsik ev lusavorchakan hayk* [The People of Zeytun and Apostolic Armenians]. Istanbul, 1867.

Artinian, V. *The Armenian Constitutional System in the Ottoman Empire, 1839-1863*. Istanbul, 1988.

Braude, Benjamin and Lewis, Bernard, eds. *Christians and Jews in the Ottoman Empire: The Functioning of a Plural Society*. New York: Holmes & Meier Publishers, 1982.

Davison, Roderic H. *Reform in the Ottoman Empire, 1856-1876*. Princeton, NJ: Princeton University Press, 1963.

Etmekjian, J. *The French Influence on the Western Armenian Renaissance, 1843-1915*. New York, 1964.

Etmekjian, Lilian. "The Reaction and Contributions of the Armenians to the Ottoman Reform Movement." M.A. thesis, University of Bridgeport, 1974.

———. "The Armenian National Assembly of Turkey and Reform." *Armenian Review* 1 (1976): 38-40.

315

Hamalian, A. "The Armenians: Intermediaries for the European Trading Companies." *University of Manitoba Anthropology Papers.* 14, 1976.

Inalcik, Halil, ed. *An Economic and Social History of the Ottoman Empire, 1300-1914.* Cambridge: Cambridge University Press, 1994.

Issawi, Charles, ed. *The Economic History of the Middle East, 1800-1914.* Chicago: University of Chicago Press 1967.

Langer, William. *The Diplomacy of Imperialism, 1890-1920.* New York: A. A. Knopf, 1935.

Lewis, Bernard. *The Emergence of Modern Turkey.* Oxford: Oxford University Press, 1961.

Megrian, L. "Tiflis during the Russian Revolution of 1905." Ph.D. dissertation, University of California at Berkeley, 1975.

Nassibian, Akaby. *Britain and the Armenian Question, 1915-1923.* New York: St. Martin's Press, 1984.

Nersisian, M.G. *Hay zhoghovrdi azatagrakan paikare trkakan brnatirutian dem, 1850-1870* [The liberation struggle of the Armenian people against Turkish tyranny]. Yerevan, 1955.

Ramsaur, Ernest E. *The Young Turks: Prelude to the Revolution of 1908.* Princeton: Princeton University Press, 1957.

Rshtuni, V. *Hay hasarakakan hosankneri patmutiunits* [Of the history of Armenian social trends].Yerevan, 1956.

Sachar, Howard M. *The Emergence of the Middle East: 1914-1924.* New York: Knopf, 1969.

Sarkissian, A. O. *History of the Armenian Question to 1885.* Urbana, 1938.

Sarukhan. *Haykakan khentirn ev azgayin sahmanadrutiune* [The Armenian Question and the National Constitution]. Tiflis, 1912.

Sasuni, Garo. *Kurd azgayin sharjhume ev hay-krdakan haraperutiunnere* [The Kurdish national movement and Armeno-Kurdish relations]. Beirut: Hamazkaine Press, 1969.

Shaw, Stanford J. and Shaw, E. K. *History of the Ottoman Empire and Modern Turkey.* Cambridge; New York: Cambridge University Press, 1977.

Suny, Ronald G. *Looking Toward Ararat: Armenia in Modern History.* Bloomington and Indianapolis: Indiana University Press, 1993.

————, ed. *Transcaucasia, Nationalism, and Social Change.* University of Michigan Press, 1996.

Ter Minassian, Anaide. "La Question Arménienne." *Esprit*, April 1967.

Tokhmakhian, Arsen. *Hayreniki pahandjnere ev hay gughatsin* [The needs of the fatherland and the Armenian peasant]. Tiflis, 1881.

Tunaya, Tarik Z. *Turkiyede siyasi partiler, 1859-1952* [Political parties in Turkey, 1859-1952]. Istanbul: N.p., 1952.

Vardanian, H. G. *Arevmtahayeri azadagrutian hartse* [The question of liberation of Western Armenians]. Yerevan, 1967.

Political Parties

Avetisian, V. A. *Hay hasarakakan mtki zargatsman Marks-Leninian puli skzbnavorume* [The beginnings of the Marxist-Leninist phase of the development of Armenian social thought]. Yeveran, 1976.

Darbinian, Artak. *Hay azatagrakan sharzhman oreren* [Of the Days of the Armenian Liberation Movement]. Paris, 1947.

Dasnabedian, H., ed. 3 vols. *Nuter H.H. Dashnaktsutian patmutian hamar* [Documents for the History of the Dashnaktsutiune]. Beirut, 1973-1977.

Elmasian, Eprem H. and Amurian, Andre. *Heghapokhakan Yepremi vodisakane* [The odyssey of Yeprem the Revolutionary]. Tehran: Alik, 1972.

Guzalian, Garnik. *Hay kaghakakan mtki zargatsume ev H.H. Dashnaktsutiune* [The development of Armenian political thought and the ARF]. Paris, 1927.

Hagopian, J. M. "Hyphenated Nationalism: The Spirit of the Revolutionary Movement in Asia Minor, 1896-1910." Ph.D. dissertation, Harvard University, 1943.

Hovannisian, M. *Dashnaktsutiune ev nra hakarakordnere* [The ARF and its Adversaries]. Tiflis, 1906-7.

Hovannisian, Rafik. *Arevmtahay azgayin-aztagrakan sharzhumnere ev Karini "Pashtpan Hayreniats" kazmakerputiune* [Western Armenian liberation movements and the "Defenders of the Fatherland" organization of Karin (Erzerum)]. Erevan, 1965.

Kitur, A., ed. 2 vols. *Patmutiune S.D. Hunchakian Kusaktsutian 1887-1962* [History of the S(ocial) D(emocratic) Hunchakian Party 1887-1962]. Beirut, 1962-1963.

Leo (Arakel Babakhanian). *Turkahay heghapokhutian gaghaparabanutiune* [The Ideology of the Turkish-Armenian Revolution]. Paris, 1934.

Nalbandian, Louise. "The Origins and Development of Socialism in Armenia: The Social Democratic Hnchakian Party 1887-1949." M.A. thesis, Stanford University, 1949.

———. *The Armenian Revolutionary Movement.* Berkeley: University of California Press, 1967.

Ter Minassian, Anaide. *Nationalism and Socialism in the Armenian Liberation Movement, 1887-1912.* Cambridge, Mass.: Zoryan Institute, 1984.

———. "Aux origines du marxisme arménien: les specifistes." *Cahiers du Monde russe et soviétique,* 1-2 (1978): 67-117.

Varandian, Mikayel. 2 vols. *Haykakan sharzhman nakhapatmutiune* [Prehistory of the Armenian movement]. Geneva, 1912, 1913.

———. 2 vols. *H.H Dashnaktsutian patmutiune* [History of the ARF]. Paris, 1932 and Cairo, 1950.

Vratsian, S., ed. *Divan H.H. Dashnaktsutian* [Archives of the ARF]. Boston, 1934.

Yervand, H. *Ramkavar Azatakan Kusaktsutiun. Ir aysore ev vaghe* [Democratic Liberal Party: Its Today and Tomorrow]. Boston, 1927.

The Armenian Question, Genocide, and World War I

Ahmad, Feroz. *The Young Turks: The Committee of Union and Progress in Turkish Politics, 1908-1914.* Oxford: Clarendon Press, 1969.

Anderson, M. S. *The Eastern Question, 1774-1923: A Study in International Relations.* New York: St. Martin's Press, 1966.

Berberian, Ruben. "Hay masonnere ev 'ser' otiake Polso mech" [Armenian masons and the "Love" Lodge in Istanbul]. *Hairenik Monthly* 5 (1937): 80-81.

Beylerian, A. "L'imperialisme et le mouvement national arménien." *Relations Internationales* 3, (1975): 19-54.

Chaliand, Gerard and Ternon, Yves. *The Armenians: From Genocide to Resistance*. London: Zed Press, 1983.

Cloud, G. H. "The Armenian Question from the Congress of Berlin to the Massacres, 1878-1894." M.A. thesis, Stanford University, 1923.

Dadrian, Vahakn, N. *The History of the Armenian Genocide: Ethnic Conflict from the Balkans to Anatolia to the Caucasus*. Providence, RI: Berghahn Books, 1995.

Fein, Helen. *Accounting for Genocide*. New York: The Free Press, 1979.

Hanioglu, M. Sukru. *The Young Turks in Opposition*. New York, 1995.

Hovannisian, Richard G. *The Armenian Holocaust: A Bibliography Relating to the Deportations, Massacres, and Dispersion of the Armenian People, 1915-1923*. Cambridge, Mass., 1978.

Lazian, G. *Hayastan ev Hay Date—vaveragrer* [Armenia and the Armenian Case Documents]. Cairo, 1946.

Libaridian, Gerard J. ed. *The Crime of Silence*. London: Zed Press, 1985.

———. "Objectivity and Historiography of the Armenian Genocide." *The Armenian Review* 31, no. 3 (Spring 1978): 86-93.

Marashlian, Levon. *Politics and Demography: Armenians, Turks, and Kurds in the Ottoman Empire*. Cambridge, Mass: Zoryan Institute, 1991.

McCarthy, Justin. *Muslims and Minorities*. New York: New York University Press, 1983.

Melson, Robert. *Revolution and Genocide: On the Origins of the Armenian Genocide and the Holocaust*. Chicago: University of Chicago Press, 1992.

Othman, Siyamend. "La participation des kurdes dans les massacres des Arméniens. 1915." *Critique Socialiste* 13 (1982): 31-48.

Stoddard, Philip Hendrick. "The Ottoman Government and the Arabs, 1911-1918: A Preliminary Study of the Teshkilat-i Mahsusa." Ph.D. dissertation, Princeton University, 1963.

Toriguian, Shavarsh. *The Armenian Question and International Law*. Beirut: Hamazkayin Publishing, 1973.

Trumpener, Ulrich. *Germany and the Ottoman Empire, 1914-1918*. Princeton, NJ: Princeton University Press, 1968.

The First and Second Armenian Republics, 1918-1991

Aspaturian, R. *The Union Republics in Soviet Diplomacy: A Study of Soviet Federalism in the Service of Soviet Foreign Policy*. Geneva: E. Droz, 1960.

Caprielian, A. "The Sovietization of Armenia: A Case History in Imperialism." *The Armenian Review* 20, no. 3 (Autumn, 1967): 22-42.

Gidney, J. B. *A Mandate for Armenia*. Kent, Ohio, 1967.

Goldhagen, E., ed. *Ethnic Minorities in the Soviet Union*. New York: Praeger, 1968.

Hovannisian, Richard G. *Armenia on the Road to Independence*. Berkeley: University of California Press, 1967.

———. 4 vols. *The Republic of Armenia*. Berkeley: University of California Press, 1971-1996.

———. "Armenia and the Caucasus in the Genesis of the Soviet-Turkish Entente." *The Armenian Review* 27 no. 1 (Spring 1974): 32-52.

Katz, Z., ed. *Handbook of Major Soviet Nationalities*. New York: Free Press, 1975.

Kazemzadeh, F. *The Struggle for Transcaucasia*. New York: Philosophical Library, 1951.

Khodjabekian, V. E. "HSSH bnakchutiune, erek, aysor ev vaghe" [The population of the A(rmenian) S(oviet) S(ocialist) R(epublic) yesterday, today and tomorrow]. *Lraber* (Yerevan) 12 (1972), p. 53.

Kirakosian, J. S. *Hayastane midjazgayin divanagitutian ev Sovetakan artakin kaghakakanutian pastateghterum* [Armenia in the documents of international diplomacy and Soviet Union foreign policy]. Yerevan, 1972.

Lipset, H. "The Status of National Minority Languages in Soviet Education." *Soviet Studies* 19, no. 2 (October 1967): 181-189.

Matossian, M. K. *The Impact of Soviet Policies in Armenia*. Leiden, 1962.

Mouradian, C. S. *De Staline à Gorbachev: Histoire d'une Republique Soviétique: L'Arménie*. Paris, 1990.

Pipes, Richard. *The Formation of the Soviet Union*. New York, 1968.

Reddaway, P., ed. *Uncensored Russia: The Human Rights Movement, in the Soviet Union*. London, 1972.

Sanders, G. *Samizdat, Voices of Soviet Opposition*. New York: Monad Press, 1974.

Silver, B. D. "Levels of Socioeconomic Development Among Soviet Nationalities." *American Political Science Review* 68 (1974): 1618-1637.

———. "The Status of National Minority Languages in Soviet Education: An Assessment of Recent Changes." *Soviet Studies* 26, no. I (January 1974): 28-40.

Simmonds, G., ed. *Nationalism in the USSR and Eastern Europe in the Era of Brezhnev and Kosygin*. Detroit: University of Detroit Press, 1977.

Torosian, S. "Soviet Policy in the Armenian Question." *The Armenian Review* II, no. 2 (Summer 1958): 27-39.

Vratsian, S. *Hayastani Hanrapetutiune* [Republic of Armenia]. Beirut, 1958.

Vucinich, W. S., ed. *Russia and Asia*. Stanford, 1972.

The Third Republic, 1991-2003

Bremmer, Ian and Taras, Ray, eds. *Nations and Politics in the Soviet Successor States*. Cambridge: Cambridge University Press, 1993.

Dawisha, Adid and Dawisha, Karen, eds. *The Making of Foreign Policy in Russia and the New States of Eurasia*. M.E.Sharpe, 1995.

Herzig, Edmund. *The New Caucasus: Armenia, Azerbaijan, and Georgia*. London: Chatham House, 1999.

Hunter, Shireen. *The Transcaucasus in Transition*. Washington: CSIS, 1994.

Libaridian, Gerard J. ed. *Armenia at the Crossroads: Democracy and Nationhood in the Post-Soviet Era.* Watertown: Blue Crane Books, 1991.

———. *The Challenge of Statehood: Armenian Political Thinking since Independence.* Watertown: Blue Crane Books, 1999.

Malkasian, Mark. *Gha-ra-bagh! The Emergence of the National Democratic Movement in Armenia.* Detroit, Mich.: Wayne State University Press, 1996.

Menon, Rajan; Fedorov, Yuri E.; and Nodia, Ghia, eds. *Russia, the Caucasus and Central Asia: The 21st Century Security Environment.* New York: M.E. Sharpe, 1999.

Parrot, Bruce, ed. *State Building and Military Power in Russia and the New States of Eurasia.* Armonk, NY: M.E. Sharpe, 1995.

Shahmuratian, S., ed. The *Sumgait Tragedy: Pogroms against the Armenians in Soviet Azerbaijan.* New Rochelle, NY, 1990.

Starr, Frederick S., ed. *The Legacy of History in Russia and the New States of Eurasia.* Armonk, NY: M.E. Sharpe, 1994.

Suny, Ronald Grigor. *The Revenge of the Past.* Stanford: Stanford University Press, 1993.

Verluise, Pierre. *Armenia in Crisis: The 1988 Earthquake.* Detroit: Wayne State University Press, 1995.

The Nagorno Karabakh Conflict

Arbatov, Alexei et al., eds. *Managing Conflict in the Former Soviet Union: Russian and American Perspectives.* Cambridge: JFK SG, 1997.

Chorbajian, Levon et al. *The Caucasian Knot: The History and Geopolitics of Nagorno-Karabagh.* London; Atlantic Highlands, NJ: Zed Books, 1994.

Chorbajian, Levon., ed. *The Making of Nagorno-Karabagh: From Secession to Republic.* Houndmills, Basingstoke, Hampshire; New York: Palgrave, 2001.

Cornell, Svante E. *Small Nations and Great Powers: A Study of Ethnopolitical Conflict in the Caucasus.* Surrey, UK: Curzon, 2001.

Croissant, Michael P. *The Armenia-Azerbaijan Conflict: Causes and Implications.* Westport, CT and London: Praeger, 1998.

Dawisha, Karen and Parrott, Bruce. *Conflict, Cleavage and Change in Central Asia and the Caucasus.* Cambridge: Cambridge University Press, 1997.

Duncan, Raymond W. and Holman, Paul G., eds. *Ethnic Nationalism and Regional Conflict.* San Francisco: Westview Press, 1994.

Luchterhandt, Otto. *Nagorno Karabakh's Right to State Independence According to International Law.* Boston: Armenian Rights Council, 1993.

Potier, Tim. *Conflict in Nagorno-Karabakh, Abkhazia and South Ossetia: A Legal Appraisal.* The Hague, London, Boston: Kluwer Law International, 2001.

Tutuncu, Mehmet, ed. *Caucasus: War and Peace.* Harlem: SOTA, 1998.

Vaux, Tony and Goodhand, Jonathan. *War and Peace in the Southern Caucasus: A Strategic Conflict Assessment of the Armenia-Azerbaijan Conflict.* Humanitarian Initiatives, 2002.

Walker, Christopher. *Armenia and Karabagh.* London, 1991.

The Diaspora

Alpoyajian, A. 3 vols. *Patmutiune hay gaghtakanutian* [History of Armenian Emigration]. Cairo, 1941-1961.

Atamian, Sarkis. *The Armenian Community*. New York, 1955.

Bakalian, Anny. *Armenian-Americans: From Being to Feeling Armenian*. New Brunswick, NJ: Transaction Publishers, 1993.

Caprielian, A. "The Armenian Revolutionary Federation: The Politics of a Party in Exile." Ph.D. dissertation, New York University, 1975.

Der-Karabetian, A. and Melikian, L. "Assimilation of Armenians in Lebanon." *The Armenian Review* 1 (Spring 1974): 65-72.

Donabedian, K. "Armenians Abroad." *The Armenian Review* 28 (Spring 1975): 85-99.

Khurshudian, L.A. *Spurkahay kusaktsutiunnere zhamanakakits edabum* [The Parties in the Armenian Diaspora in Their Contemporary Phase]. Yerevan, 1964.

Minassian, Gaidz, *Guerre et Terrorisme Arméniens*. Paris: Presses Universitaires de France, 2002.

Mirak, Robert. "Outside the Homeland: Writing the History of the Armenian Diaspora." *Recent Studies in Modern Armenian History*. Cambridge, Mass., 1972, pp. 119-125.

————. *Torn Between Two Lands: Armenians in America, 1890 to World War I*. Cambridge, Mass.: Harvard University Press, 1983.

Sanjian, Avedis K. *The Armenian Communities in Syria under Ottoman Dominion*. Cambridge, Mass.: Harvard University Press, 1965.

Index

Abdul Hamid II, 15, 66, 127, 141, 152, 153, 159, 161

ADL, *see* Armenian Democratic Liberal Party

ADLA, *see* Armenian Democratic Liberal Party of Armenia

Aliyev, Haydar, 245, 261, 262, 276

amira class, 52, 53, 55

ANM, *see* Armenian National Movement

Ararktsian, Babken, 206, 215, 217, 218, 232, 240, 250, 254, 258

ARF, *see* Armenian Revolutionary Federation

Armenakan Party, 104; and Kurds, 176

Armenia, Eastern, 8, 14, 15, 22, 24, 90, 93, 140, 160; economy of modern, 225-31, 236, 247, 259-60; First Republic of, 21, 22, 23, 200; parties in modern, 216, 222-23, 224, 238; Persian, 13; relations with Arab countries, 248; relations with Diaspora, 3, 237; relations with Iran, 243; relations with Turkey, 9, 193, 194, 245, 268-76, 279; Russian, *see* Eastern Armenia; Soviet, 3, 6, 8, 9, 22, 24-32, 38-40 *passim*, 194, 200-02 *passim* 207, 217, 233; strategic significance of, 282-301; Third (modern) Republic of, 192, 193-94, 199, 203-09, 210, 211, 214

Armenian Church, as keeper of the national character, 6, 53, 65; of Kirikhan, 35; properties, 20, 96; as a revisionist institution, 17, 94, 155; as a social organization, 36, 201; *see also* Catholicossate and Patriarchate

Armenian Democratic Liberal Party, 3, 167n55; founding of, 37, 38, 156; and Soviet Armenia, 39-40; and split in Armenia, 223

Armenian Democratic Liberal Party of Armenia 223, 238-39; and support to Kocharian, 254

Armenian Genocide, 4, 5, 36, 76, 137-42, 162, 171, 180n8, 265; in Armenia's foreign policy, 237, 263, 268, 275, 280, 297; in Armenian identity, 140, 190; denial by Turkey, 4, 151, 171, 184, 191-92, 196, 201-02, 275, 276, 280, 281; participation of Kurds in, 175; and Karabakh conflict, 194-95; in Turkish Armenian relations, 193-94, 203, 266, 277-78

Armenian National Movement, challenging Communism, 6, 209, 211, 233-34; governing Armenia, 9, 194, 203, 205, 207, 212, 215, 217, 218, 220, 224, 233, 238, 249, 267; leadership of, 216, 218, 223; strength of, 204; as successor of Karabakh Committee, 203, 207, withdrawal from politics, 254

Armenian Revolutionary Federation, and the 1892 program, 103-07; and the 1907 program, 107-11; and the 1991 presidential elections, 208; and the 1995 parliamentary elections, 218; and the 2003 parliamentary elections, 257; in Armenian image, 84; banned from Armenia, 237-39 *passim*; and the First Republic, 21-23 *passim*; and the issue of Genocide, 40-41, 200-01, 267, 276; and the Kurdish revolts, 174, 176; organizing in the Diaspora, 37; platform, 15, 16, 18, 95-98, 103, 113; relations with the Armenian bourgeoisie, 17, 108; relations with the Young Turks, 145-50, 156-58 *passim*, 166n25, 166n28; role of during Armeno-Tatar conflict, 17, 107;